YALE LAW LIBRARY SERIES IN
LEGAL HISTORY AND REFERENCE

MEMORY AND AUTHORITY

The Uses of History in Constitutional Interpretation

JACK M. BALKIN

Yale

UNIVERSITY PRESS

New Haven and London

Published with support from the
Lillian Goldman Law Library, Yale Law School.

Yale University Press books may be purchased in quantity for
educational, business, or promotional use. For information,
please e-mail sales.press@yale.edu (U.S. office) or sales@yaleup.co.uk
(U.K. office).

Set in Janson type by Integrated Publishing Solutions.
Printed in the United States of America.

Library of Congress Control Number: 2023938997
ISBN 978-0-300-27643-5 (hardcover)
ISBN 978-0-300-27222-2 (paper)

A catalogue record for this book is available from the British Library.

10 9 8 7 6 5 4 3 2 1

For Bernard Balkin, Bettye Balkin, and Jan Balkin
May their memories be a blessing

Contents

PART I

Making Historical Arguments

CHAPTER ONE

Arguing with History

THIS IS A BOOK about how people use history when they interpret the Constitution. History matters to constitutional interpretation because people believe that history bestows authority on their arguments or, conversely, that it undermines the authority of opposing arguments. History matters in constitutional interpretation because authority matters.

People employ history in constitutional law to make arguments for or against particular interpretations. Therefore, to study the uses of history in constitutional interpretation is to study the *forms of argument* that use history in constitutional interpretation.

These "uses of history" are plural, not singular. When people interpret the Constitution, they employ a collection of standard types of constitutional argument. So the "uses of history" in constitutional interpretation are the ways that people channel history through these standard forms of legal argument.

In 1982, Philip Bobbitt pointed out that constitutional arguments tend to fall into different rhetorical categories.[1] There were arguments based on the constitutional text, arguments about purpose, arguments about features of constitutional structure, arguments from previous judicial precedents, and so on. A few years later, Richard Fallon offered a slightly different list.[2] Bobbitt called these different forms of argument "modalities," and ever since then, constitutional theorists have used this term to describe the different forms of constitutional argument.[3]

When it came to history, however, Bobbitt and Fallon were heavily influenced by the debates over originalism that were just getting started. So both of them called arguments about the intentions of the framers "historical" arguments.[4] By speaking in this way, they encouraged people to think that there was only one kind of historical argument—originalist argument—and, more specifically, arguments about original intention.

This fostered an unnecessary confusion. Most constitutional law arguments that use history are not about the intentions of the framers; they may not even be about the history of the adoption of the Constitution or its amendments.

In this book, I revisit the study of constitutional arguments that Bobbitt began. I offer a more expansive list that is better designed to explain how people use history when they make constitutional arguments.

It turns out that there is no single modality of "historical argument." Rather, history is useful for making many different kinds of constitutional arguments, and the way that people use history is shaped by the kind of argument they are making. How people use history, what they look for in history, how they characterize history, and what they emphasize and de-emphasize in history depends on the modality of justification they are using. This is the interdependence of history and justification.

Most discussions of the uses of history in constitutional argument employ a fairly simple model:

(1a) People use history to support or authorize a proposed interpretation of the Constitution; or

(1b) People use history to undermine their opponents' proposed interpretation of the Constitution.

According to this model, the central question about "the uses of history" in constitutional law is whether people have gotten their history right. People might not get the history right because they are reading the history out of context, because the historical record is more complicated than they let on, because they are engaged in an anachronism, or because, as Alfred Kelly once put it, they "ask[] questions of the past that the past cannot answer."[5]

But this simple model does not describe what is actually going on when people use history to make constitutional arguments. Instead, the situation is something more like this:

(2a) People use a standard form of legal argument—for example, arguments from purpose, structure, consequences, tradition, precedent, and so on—that rests on a background or unspoken theory of legal justification, and they use history to help them make that kind of argument; or

(2b) People use history to show why their opponents' proposed interpretation is unjustified given a particular modality of argument.

How people use (or misuse) history—what they look for in history and how they characterize history—depends on the underlying modality of legal justification. And this modality may not be explicitly stated. Often it must be inferred.

Not only is there not a single kind of historical argument, but there is not even a single kind of *originalist* argument. There are different kinds that correspond to the different modalities. Whether people are arguing about adoption history or nonadoption history, they still channel their historical claims through the same modalities in the same way. Originalist argument is a special case of a more general phenomenon.

Moreover, not all arguments about the founding of the United States or about the adoption of the U.S. Constitution or its amendments are originalist arguments. Originalist arguments are what I will call in this book "obedient" uses of history. They look to history to find positive examples or precedents that we should follow today. But not all uses of history are obedient uses. Some historical arguments are very critical of people who lived in the past, including the founders and adopters of the Constitution. They deny that we should follow their practices and views and argue that we must redeem our system of government from previous injustices. These "critical" uses of history treat the past as a negative precedent that we must transcend, not as a positive example that we must follow. Both obedient and critical uses of history are "authority constructing" or "constructive" uses of history—they purport to offer relatively clear lessons from history that we can and should follow today. But still other uses of history are not designed to construct either positive authority or negative precedent. They are "deconstructive," in the sense that they try to show that the lessons of history are ambiguous and not easily adapted to our present situation.

A. Collective Memory

Some of the most important arguments in constitutional interpretation invoke collective memory. Collective memory is what a group— for example, a religion, a profession, a people, or a nation—remembers and forgets about its past.[6] This combination of remembering and forgetting helps constitute the group's identity and structures its values and its commitments. Precisely because memory is selective, it may or may not correspond to the best account of historical facts that we now have available.

The literature on memory uses several different terms—"collective memory," "cultural memory," and "social memory"—more or less interchangeably, as I will in this book.[7] However, some scholars treat cultural memory as a special case of collective memory.[8] Cultural memory refers to the narrative memory of now-distant events that help constitute a group's identity but that most people in the group did not live through. People commemorate or refer to these events—and the persons and stories connected to them—in cultural artifacts, documents, monuments, and artistic representations.[9] The collective memory of the founding and Reconstruction, for example, is cultural memory. People recall or invoke cultural memory in public rhetoric, art, and social rituals—and, most importantly for our purposes, in law and politics.

The use of memory in constitutional argument is *constitutional memory*, a term coined by Reva Siegel.[10] Constitutional memory shapes people's views about what the law means and why people have authority. "Because constitutional memory is employed to legitimate the exercise of authority," Siegel explains, "constitutional memory has a politics . . . [and] it can help rationalize all manner of governmental and societal relationships."[11] Lawyers and judges continually invoke and construct constitutional memory; judicial decisions both rely on constitutional memory and produce constitutional memory.

What is remembered and what is erased have powerful normative effects. They shape our understanding of who we are and how things came to be, what is traditional and what is an innovation, who has committed wrongs and who has been wronged, what we owe to others and what they owe to us. Memory provides resources for understanding the world around us and assigning praise and blame. What is erased from memory, by contrast, can make no claims on us.

Collective memory—and forgetting—affect all types of constitutional interpretation. All of the standard forms of constitutional argument may make use of collective memory, and lawyers and judges often use history in stylized ways. Arguments from collective memory take sides in historical events and often identify heroes and villains, positive and negative examples. Originalist arguments in American constitutional culture are often hybrids that invoke collective memory. They combine appeals to national ethos, political tradition, and honored authority with other modalities of argument.

Many of the most important forms of constitutional interpretation—arguments from precedent, arguments from tradition, and arguments from original meaning or understanding—involve a mixture of memory and erasure. They emphasize certain elements of the past while effacing others. Yet the selectivity and erasure of constitutional memory can have ideological effects, and can bestow on constitutional claims a legitimacy that they do not always deserve.

The scope of constitutional memory matters to legitimacy because many features of constitutional legitimacy depend, whether directly or indirectly, on implicit notions of societal consensus, majority opinion, and the consent of the governed. But if the consensus is not real, if the majority is artificially constructed, and if the consent of the governed is not genuine, this undermines assumptions about legitimacy.

At stake in constitutional memory is which historical figures and movements will count as makers of constitutional meaning for the present. If constitutional memory features only a small group of white men as the central actors, the American constitutional tradition belongs to them, and it is their views that matter. Women and racial minorities have constitutional rights only because these white men allowed them to have rights.

This is a false portrait of the country's history. When we engage in constitutional construction, therefore, we should embrace an expansive conception of collective constitutional memory. The constitutional tradition in the United States is a dialectical tradition full of disagreements and multiple perspectives from many different people and groups, from every period in the nation's history, and from every part of society. It constitutes a rich source of competing ideas that later participants can draw on. These include the views and experiences of people left out of formal constitution-making, as well as the claims of social and political movements that have shaped our constitutional tradition. These groups can provide both positive and negative examples for the present.

The makers of constitutional meaning in the American political tradition are much broader than the Constitution's framers and adopters, or even those who influenced the framers and adopters. In constitutional construction, we may look to the ideas of people whose views were unpopular or minority positions in their own time but whose constructions of the Constitution turned out to be far wiser than the dominant opinions of their day.

Not all of the lessons of constitutional memory are positive. Not everyone in the past was heroic, and even people and groups that we celebrate today had serious flaws and failings. Some of the lessons of constitutional memory are deeply ambivalent. But all can be grist for the mill of constitutional construction. When we implement and apply the Constitution in our own time, many different groups and many different people can be makers of constitutional meaning. What matters is what their ideas and experiences mean for the present and whether they can serve as positive or negative examples for us today.

B. Originalism and Living Constitutionalism

Much of the debate over the uses of history in constitutional interpretation is a debate about the merits of originalism. Originalism is a family of theories that argue that we should interpret the Constitution (and its subsequent amendments) consistent with its original meaning—or in some versions, consistent with the original under-standing of the ratifiers or the original intentions of the framers. People usually oppose originalism to living constitutionalism, which argues that the practical meaning of the Constitution adapts—and should adapt—to changing social conditions.

My own theory of constitutional interpretation, living original-ism or framework originalism, does not view originalism and living constitutionalism as opposed.[12] It synthesizes these two positions, seeing them as two sides of a single coin.

Living originalism has many advantages over the versions of originalism developed by the conservative legal movement. First, it is superior from the standpoint of constitutional theory: it has a bet-ter account of what constitutions are and how they actually operate in practice. Second, living originalism recognizes that the Consti-tution's democratic legitimacy depends on more than the moment of adoption, and that the work of political and social movements is crucial to the Constitution's legitimacy over time, even if—as in the case of the civil rights movement and the women's movement—their efforts do not result in new constitutional amendments. Third, liv-ing originalism is superior in its use of history. It is more compatible with the work of professional historians. It can accommodate dis-agreements among the ratifying public and the views of those shut out of formal constitution-making. It is better at avoiding historical anachronism. And it makes use of the entire history of the country rather than focusing solely on the history of adoption.

Some originalists claim that originalism is required by the phi-losophy of language or by the rule of law itself. But most countries outside the United States do not employ originalism as their stan-dard method of interpretation, even if their judges occasionally make arguments that Americans would call originalist. Nor, for that mat-ter, is originalism the dominant interpretive approach in the fifty state constitutions—although state judges, too, sometimes appeal to original purposes and meanings.

As I will show in this book, the best explanation for why Ameri-cans are attracted to originalism lies elsewhere. Originalism is a fea-ture of *national* political culture (which is why it appears less frequently in state constitutions and outside the United States). It arose in the United States because of American cultural memory and American national identity. You will find people making arguments about original purpose and meaning throughout American history. But the rise of originalism as a general or comprehensive theory of constitutional interpretation is the product of the twentieth century. Originalism was first taken up by liberals in the middle of the century and then by conservatives who were responding to what liberals had done.

Both originalism and living constitutionalism arose in response to constitutional modernity—the felt sense that the world of the framers had long since passed away, and that the problem for the present was how to be faithful to an ancient constitution in very different circumstances. Living constitutionalism arrived a little earlier in the twentieth century; originalism came a little later. But they are really twins separated at birth. They are complementary ways of dealing with the problem of ceaseless change and increasing separation from the past. Originalism emphasizes that we must restore what was lost, return to ancient verities, and respect long-standing traditions. Living constitutionalism emphasizes that we must accept the reality of change, adapt successfully to new conditions, and work to improve and redeem our political project from generation to generation.

When Americans argue about the Constitution, they employ *both* of these cultural narratives, although how and when they use these stories may vary from situation to situation and from person to person. Moreover, Americans use both of these narratives not only to forestall reform but also to justify reform. In the United States, originalism often serves as a doctrine of revolution. Franklin Delano Roosevelt invoked the framers to justify the New Deal. The Warren Court used originalism to overturn old precedents. And the conservative legal movement, which adopted originalism as its common language, has been devoted to remaking American constitutional law for the past half century.

C. History Is a Resource, Not a Command

This cultural account helps explain a great deal about how Americans actually use originalism—and history more generally—in constitutional argument. A recurrent theme of this book is that in constitutional interpretation, history is a resource, not a command. It is a way that we reason with each other in the present rather than a collection of mandates from the past.

When I say that history is a resource, I do not mean that it is merely a rhetorical resource for making arguments. History can also be a source of edification. But above all, it is a potent source of meaning. The past is constitutive of our world and what our world means to us. History can be a resource for argument because people's beliefs and worldviews are shaped by past causes of which they may be only dimly aware and, equally important, by their memory of the past. The rhetoric of history has power because memory has power. History is a resource for argument because we are made out of it.

Lawyers sometimes talk about history as if it could generate legal commands in the present. But this is a mistake. It is true that where the text of the Constitution announces a clear, unambiguous rule, people treat the text as the source of a legal obligation. But that is not because history itself commands anything; it is because duly enacted law remains in force until it is lawfully changed. This feature of the rule of law is as true of new texts as of ancient ones.

Most contested questions of constitutional interpretation, by contrast, arise when the text is not clear. This can happen, for example, when the text uses principles, standards, or other vague or abstract language, and we must apply it to new situations; or when the text points in contrary directions or is silent, and we must reason from principles of constitutional purpose and structure.

When this happens, we engage in *constitutional construction*. We must decide the best way to implement the Constitution through doctrines, practices, and institutions. Older constructions, in turn, generate new interpretive problems as new situations arise. These problems often lead to new constructions or modifications of older ones. Constitutional law in the United States is a history of successive constitutional constructions, which build on and apply older constructions, or modify and displace them with newer ones.

History matters to constitutional interpretation because history is a powerful resource for constitutional construction. People argue for and against proposed constructions by channeling history through the standard modalities of argument.

Because most contested questions occur in the zone of constitutional construction, most arguments that use history occur there as well—including arguments from adoption history. Most originalist arguments are really arguments about how to construct the Constitution—they are a special case of how people use history generally. That is why judges sometimes pay careful attention to originalist arguments and sometimes ignore them completely, and why sometimes they are quite persuasive and sometimes quite unpersuasive.

Most of the originalist arguments that lawyers and judges make about the Constitution are hybrids: They combine appeals to national ethos, tradition, and honored authority with the other modalities. This hybrid nature gives originalist arguments their distinctive character. Because originalist arguments appeal to ethos, tradition, and honored authority, they trade on our identification with the past and our willingness to accept the values of the past as our values and the decisions of the past as our decisions. This means that originalist arguments will normally not be persuasive unless we can plausibly accept the values of the framers and adopters as our own or can somehow recharacterize these values (for example, at a high level of generality) so that we can plausibly accept these values as our own. Conversely, when the values of the framers and adopters appear too alien or irrelevant, lawyers and judges generally avoid making originalist arguments.

This is why the actual practices of American lawyers and judges do not correspond to academic theories of originalism that argue that originalism is baked into the meaning of the Constitution and is always mandatory. Sometimes lawyers and judges pay no attention to originalist arguments and just argue about doctrines and precedents. Sometimes they are aware of originalist arguments but reject them as irrelevant or unworkable.

Because Americans have different values, they will also disagree about when we should identify with the values of the framers or adopters, and they will characterize the work of the framers or adopters in different ways. So although originalism presents interpretation as a matter of renouncing our own normative choices and simply following the commands of the framers or adopters, it often reconstructs and remembers what the framers or adopters said to better suit the interpreter's values. That is to say, originalism is both an inquiry into the past *and* a form of historical ventriloquism. We make the past speak our normative values in the form of commands so that we can then obey them.

Because originalist arguments are appeals to the nation's cultural memory, nonoriginalists should not avoid them. They can and should make originalist arguments too. In politics, cultural memory belongs to everyone, and everyone has a stake in the stories we tell about ourselves and about how things came to be. Everyone has a stake in what is remembered and what is forgotten, because memory is a source of political power. If people refuse to claim memory and tradition for themselves, they will be governed by other people's versions.

The country's history is far broader than just the history of its framers and adopters. There is also the history of social and political movements that succeeded and failed and the history of people from all walks of life who had views about the Constitution. They offer both positive precedents and negative examples that can instruct us in the present. Many people in the nation's history were excluded from political power and shut out of constitution-making but still made claims on the Constitution. They may not be as celebrated as our famous framers. But if they have something to teach us, they can still be makers of constitutional meaning for us today.

D. When Lawyers and Historians
Argue about the Constitution

One purpose of Bobbitt's original account of the modalities was to show how everyone, and not just lawyers, could make constitutional arguments. But of course, most of the people who use history in constitutional law are lawyers, judges, and legal academics. Lawyers and academic historians often quarrel about the right way to use history in constitutional interpretation. Some academic historians complain that lawyers misuse history, while the latter respond that historians do not understand legal argument. Although conservative originalists play a prominent role in these disputes today, the disagreements long predate the rise of originalism.

Lawyers try to escape the criticism of historians through two standard stories that emphasize the differences between what lawyers and historians do. According to the first story, lawyers employ specialized skills of legal exegesis that historians do not understand. According to the second, lawyers require a usable past that historians will not provide.

These two stories are familiar but a bit misleading. With respect to most of the modalities of constitutional argument, historians are as well equipped to make constitutional claims as lawyers are. In fact, plenty of disagreements between lawyers and academic historians do not concern the distinctive skills of lawyers at all. Rather, they arise from controversial theories of interpretation that many lawyers do not accept either. Emphasizing lawyers' professional differences from historians actually disguises disagreements *among* lawyers about how to use (and how not to use) history. So when lawyers try to stiff-arm academic historians, often they are actually engaged in long-running disputes with other lawyers who disagree with their interpretive theories, their methods, and their conclusions.

Part of the reason why lawyers quarrel with historians is that they want to assert law's methodological autonomy. But the more that lawyers try to assert the methodological autonomy of law from history, the more they will fail—ironically, because of law's distinctively adversarial professional culture. Lawyers want to persuade audiences and win arguments with their opponents. And in order to win those arguments, lawyers will search for ever new historical sources and approaches; they will insist on bringing the work of historians back in to undercut their opponents' claims.

It is certainly true that lawyers seek a usable past to persuade others and to litigate and decide cases. That is one reason why they are so attracted to historical arguments in the first place. But the best way to obtain a usable past is not to limit historical inquiry artificially. It is to recognize the many different types of historical argument and the many different ways to use history. Just as constitutional interpretation becomes better when it expands constitutional memory, it becomes richer when it embraces all that history has to offer.

CHAPTER TWO

History and the Forms of
Constitutional Argument

THERE IS A LARGE literature on the proper use of history in constitutional interpretation.[1] Much of this literature concerns adoption history: the history leading up to and surrounding the adoption of the Constitution and its subsequent amendments.

Adoption history has dominated scholarly debates about the uses of history because most of these debates have been, either directly or indirectly, about the merits of originalism, which gained increasing importance with the rise of the conservative legal movement in the past half century. I will have plenty to say about originalism in this book. But the predominant focus on originalism has had a cost: it has diverted our attention from the vast realm of history that is irrelevant to originalism.

Originalism cares about history to the extent that history sheds light on original meanings, understandings, or intentions. Judged from the standpoint of the originalist model, all other uses of history, all other periods of history, and, indeed, all of the other places on Earth where history occurred are of limited importance. Originalist theory has a bounded conception of constitutional memory, neglecting the history that is not relevant to its theoretical claims.

Yet most history—and most American history—is not adoption

history. The history and experience of groups shut out of formal constitution-making—women before the Nineteenth Amendment, free Black people before Reconstruction, Native Americans, and slaves—is irrelevant to originalism except to the extent that these groups influenced framers and ratifiers.

The history of social mobilizations, political movements, and institutional innovations that have dramatically changed America but have not led to the ratification of a new constitutional amendment are, by definition, not adoption history. Examples include the New Deal, the creation of the national security state in the 1940s and 1950s, the civil rights revolution of the 1950s and 1960s, the second wave of American feminism of the 1970s that led to modern sex equality law (but did not achieve an Equal Rights Amendment), and the gay rights movement.

These political transformations and social mobilizations have greatly affected how Americans understand their Constitution today. But from the standpoint of the originalist model, this history has limited importance because it did not lead to constitutional amendments. Indeed, for some originalists, many of these events produced departures from original meaning that must be explained, if at all, as exceptions and errors that we retain not because they are faithful to the Constitution but because too many people have relied on them and it is too difficult to fix the mistakes now.

In fact, most of the twentieth century is pretty much useless to the originalist model, except as a negative example—it is the period when everything went to hell in a handbasket. No less than eleven constitutional amendments—or twelve, depending on how you count— were adopted in the twentieth century, but these amendments have played a very small role in the great battles over constitutional interpretation that characterized the twentieth century.[2]

Post-ratification history—the history of the understandings of and struggles over constitutional norms after adoption—is also generally irrelevant to the originalist model except where post-ratification history might shed light on adoption history.[3] The practices of the Washington administration immediately after adoption of the Constitution are generally thought relevant to understanding the original meaning of the president's powers under Article II.[4] But the practices of the Roosevelt, Truman, and Eisenhower administrations—which did far more to shape the actual presidency that we have and the actual powers that contemporary presidents enjoy—are irrelevant.[5]

Even when nonoriginalists criticize originalism, they tend to do so on originalists' turf—and about the kind of history that originalists care about. Critics of originalism have argued that lawyers and judges should be more attentive to the complexities of history and pay more attention to the work of professional historians. The irony, of course, is that for the most part, these debates over methodology are debates over adoption history—and especially of the founding and the early years of the republic. They reinforce the notion that the central example of historical argument is originalist argument, and that the kind of research that is most relevant to constitutional interpretation is research that sheds light on the history of adoption.

But if we really want to understand the uses of history in constitutional argument, we must begin in a different place. Instead of debating the pros and cons of originalism, we should focus instead on how people actually make constitutional claims. And for that purpose, we should turn to the modalities.

A. Rethinking the Modalities of Constitutional Argument

People use a standard set of forms of argument to analyze constitutional problems and construct arguments about the best interpretation of the Constitution. In the language of rhetorical theory, they are the standard topics or *topoi* of constitutional law.[6] Philip Bobbitt famously called these standard forms of argument "modalities," and this term has become widely adopted in constitutional theory.[7]

Bobbitt argued that all constitutional arguments fall into six standard types: text, history, structure, prudence, precedent, and ethos.[8] It turns out, however, that Bobbitt's list of standard arguments is not very useful for thinking about how people use history in constitutional argument. First, he confusingly called one of his modalities "historical" argument.[9] That seemed to imply that there was a single modality of historical argument and that all the other kinds of arguments—from text, precedent, consequences, structure, and national ethos—did not use history. (Bobbitt himself did not believe this.) Second, even more confusingly, Bobbitt identified "historical" arguments with arguments from original intention.[10] This seemed to imply that the only ways that people use history in constitutional law is by making originalist arguments. It also seemed to suggest that all originalist arguments are arguments from original intention. This has not been true since at least the 1980s, when arguments from original public meaning became the dominant approach among originalists.

Some time back, building on the work of Bobbitt and Richard Fallon, I proposed a different list of standard constitutional arguments, better calibrated to the kinds of arguments that lawyers and judges make and better designed to explain the uses of history in constitutional argument.[11]

Most arguments about the proper interpretation of the Constitution fall into the following basic categories:

1. Arguments from *text*. These include arguments about definitions of the words and phrases in the text, arguments that compare and contrast different parts of the text, arguments that compare the text with other texts, arguments that look to dictionaries and corpus linguistics, and arguments that employ traditional canons of statutory interpretation.

2. Arguments about constitutional *structure*. These are arguments about how the constitutional system as a whole should operate and how the various parts of the system should interact with each other. These include arguments about the proper functioning of federalism, the separation of powers, democracy, and republican government.

3. Arguments from constitutional *purpose*. These are arguments about the point or purpose of the Constitution. They include arguments about the purposes, intentions, and expectations of the people who lived at the time of the adoption of the Constitution and its subsequent amendments, as well as purposes attributed to the Constitution over time.

4. Arguments from *consequences*. These are arguments about the likely consequences of interpreting the Constitution in one way rather than another. Arguments from consequences include arguments of institutional prudence: arguments that consider the political and practical consequences of a proposed interpretation (or implementing

doctrine), how other people and institutions are likely to respond to it, and how well or how badly other actors will be likely to administer the interpretation in the future.

5. Arguments from *judicial precedent*. These are arguments based on previous judicial decisions, whether from the United States or from Great Britain before the U.S. broke away. They include arguments about what is holding and what is dicta, about what is controlling authority and what is merely persuasive authority. They include familiar common-law arguments for distinguishing cases, generalizing from cases, reasoning from case to case, and reasoning by analogy. Arguments from precedent include arguments based on the doctrinal categories and tests that previous precedents have generated. Hence, arguments from judicial precedent collectively form a very large family of topics and subtopics. They are probably the most common form of legal arguments about the Constitution.

6. Arguments from *political convention*. These are arguments about political conventions and settlements that arise within institutions or branches of government (for example, within the executive branch) or among institutions or branches of government (for example, conventions that arise between the executive branch and Congress).

7. Arguments from the people's *customs* and lived experience. These arguments consider the public's customs, expectations, and ways of life and whether a proposed interpretation of the Constitution will conform to, vindicate, assist, defy, or disrupt them.

8. Arguments from *natural law or natural rights*. These arguments concern rights that governments exist to secure and protect (natural rights), as well as arguments about what kinds of laws are necessary to protect and promote human flourishing (natural law).

9. Arguments from *national ethos*. Arguments from ethos appeal to the character of the nation and its institutions and to important, widely shared, and widely honored values of Americans and American culture.

10. Arguments from *political tradition*. Arguments from political tradition appeal to the traditions and traditional values of the American people, to collective memory, to the meaning of key events in American political history (e.g., the Revolution, the Civil War, the New Deal), and to the lessons we should draw from those events. They often overlap with arguments about national ethos.

11. Arguments from *honored authority*. Arguments from honored authority appeal to the values, beliefs, and examples of culture heroes in American life. Examples of culture heroes include the founders as a group and key founders like George Washington and James Madison or important historical figures like Abraham Lincoln, Frederick Douglass, Susan B. Anthony, and Martin Luther King Jr. They often overlap with arguments about national ethos and political tradition.

These categories are not exhaustive, but they cover most examples.[12] All of the categories overlap to some degree; but the last three are very closely related, so I will sometimes refer to them together as arguments from ethos, tradition, and honored authority. They are the subject of chapter 4.

Each modality offers us a different way to claim authority for our proposed legal interpretation. And each modality comes with an implicit theory of why arguments of the type we are making are valid and persuasive. For example, textual arguments assume that we should interpret the Constitution consistent with its text and reasonable inferences from the text; arguments from purpose assume that we should interpret the Constitution in light of its purposes; arguments from structure assume that we should interpret the Constitution so that its various parts function properly in conjunction with each other; arguments from consequences assume that where the text is unclear, we should choose an interpretation that avoids bad consequences and promotes good ones; and so on.

In short, the modalities represent a series of commonplaces or widely accepted rules of thumb about how to interpret the Constitution.[13] The modalities give a rhetorical structure to legal reasoning— they provide a set of shared topics for argument that structure legal discourse and legal imagination.[14] The modalities not only shape how an argument is constructed but also connect the advocate's reasoning to claims of legal authority as naturally as tendons connect muscle to bone.

If you look at the preceding list of modalities I offered, you can immediately draw several conclusions about how people use history in constitutional argument.

First, there is no separate category of "historical" arguments. People can—and do—use history to support arguments from each of these modalities. Even arguments from judicial precedent often look to history.[15] These arguments may focus on the history of past doctrine, or they may employ doctrinal categories that require historical inquiries. For example, the test for a suspect classification under the Equal Protection Clause requires showing a history of previous discrimination.[16] Other doctrinal tests ask whether a practice is long-standing or traditional.[17]

Bobbitt's and Fallon's lists of constitutional modalities each featured a separate category of historical arguments, and each limited historical arguments to arguments from the original understanding or the intentions of the framers. Each, in effect, imagined "originalism" as a distinctive mode of argument, and each associated historical argument with originalism, and originalism with historical argument.

This is unhelpful for two reasons. First, it overlooks the possibility that lawyers might use history other than adoption history. Second, it overlooks the fact that lawyers use history in many different ways to buttress a wide variety of constitutional arguments. Indeed, thirty years after Fallon's initial article, he wrote an excellent piece showing how history was used in arguments from precedent.[18]

There is no single modality of "historical argument." Rather, arguments using all of the modalities may invoke history to support their claims. For each modality of constitutional argument—text, structure, purpose, consequences, and so on—there is a different way to use history.

Figures 2.1 and 2.2 show the differences between Bobbitt's approach and mine. Bobbitt's model treats historical argument as a separate modality; it concerns framers' intent or understanding. In my model, by contrast, there is no separate modality of historical argument; instead, history is available to support each style of justification. Moreover, history is not limited to the framers' intentions, meanings, or understandings, and the model applies to both adoption and nonadoption history.

B. The Interdependence of History and the Forms of Constitutional Argument

Each modality of constitutional argument involves a distinctive form of justification. Each offers a different kind of reason why people

Text	History	Structure	Prudence	Precedent	Ethos
	(the intentions and understandings of the Framers)		(primarily about judicial restraint, but also includes arguments from consequences)	(includes arguments about tradition, political settlement, political convention, and social custom)	(appeals to the country's basic values, especially the philosophy of limited government)

Figure 2.1. Bobbitt's modalities of constitutional interpretation

◄────────── History can be used to support all styles of argument ──────────►

Text	Structure	Purpose	Consequences	Judicial Precedent	Political Settlement/ Convention	Custom	Natural Law	Ethos	Tradition	Honored Authority

Figure 2.2. Historical argument in constitutional interpretation

should accept a particular reading of the Constitution. And each modality has an account of why that form of argument is or should be valid in American legal culture.

Constitutional argument treats history as useful to the extent that it helps people make claims of legal authority using one of the standard forms of justification. So, for example, people who make arguments from original intention view history as relevant to the extent that it shows us what the intention was. They view history through the lens of this particular modality. History that does not perform this function may be ignored or treated as irrelevant, even though it may be quite relevant for other purposes. Because there are many ways of making valid constitutional arguments, there are also many different ways of using history in constitutional argument.

Let us put these ideas together. Each modality rests on an implicit theory of constitutional argument—that is, a theory of why this kind of argument is an appropriate way to interpret the Constitution. So arguments from purpose assume that we should interpret the Constitution in light of its purposes; structural arguments assume that we should interpret the Constitution consistent with the proper functioning of its parts and their proper relationships to each other; and so on. People use history against the background of these theories of constitutional argument, even (and especially) when the theory (or the modality) is not explicitly articulated. Thus, history usually appears in legal arguments as an *enthymeme*—an argument with a suppressed premise.[19] That suppressed premise is the theory of argument that justifies the use of history, and that makes the use of history salient and relevant to constitutional interpretation.

This means that in constitutional argument, history and the modalities of argument are interdependent. Legal argument often depends on historical claims; conversely, what history is relevant to legal justification and how it is relevant depend on the underlying form of justification one is invoking (textual, structural, precedential, and so on). Theory makes history relevant.

History and forms of legal justification are related in a second way. What people look for in history and what they see in history are shaped by the background mode of justification: why a particular kind of constitutional argument is valid and the kinds of facts that would tend to support or constitute this argument. The way that people imagine history, look for things in history, deem historical evidence relevant or salient, and weigh competing historical claims will depend on their background modes of justification. For each theory or style of legal argument, there will be a corresponding way to use history to support that argument. And there will also be a corresponding lens or filter through which people perceive and interpret the significance and relevance of historical events. In short, history supports the different forms of legal argument, and the different forms of legal argument provide or impose a perspective on history.

These two ideas—that theory makes history relevant and that theory imposes a perspective or filter on history—are central to understanding how people use history in constitutional interpretation. Most historical arguments are enthymemes that suppress a theoretical premise. And an interpreter's use of history shapes the interpreter's perspective on history—the way that history is studied, remembered, understood as relevant or irrelevant, characterized, interpreted, and argued over.

Each modality of justification not only shapes how people use history but also provides ways of rebutting or critiquing that use. If you use history to make a structural argument, your opponents can invoke history on the same terms. Within each modality, people may criticize or rebut an argument on the grounds that the argument simplifies or distorts history, engages in anachronism, or simply gets the facts wrong. (They can also switch to another modality of argument to rebut their opponents.) That is why revealing the suppressed premise of historical argument is important to evaluating it and understanding its strengths and weaknesses. Legal argument often elides the theoretical assumptions that bestow authority on history. Bringing these premises to the surface helps us evaluate and criticize historical arguments on their own terms.

C. Constructive and Deconstructive, Obedient and Critical Uses of History

The culture of legal argument is an adversarial culture. Legal advocates try to establish their own claims of legal authority, and they also try to undermine claims of legal authority by their opponents. This suggests two different rhetorical postures—one that promotes certainty and one that promotes uncertainty. *Authority-constructing* (or constructive) uses of history employ history to construct claims of legal authority using the various modalities. They marshal historical facts and organize historical studies to build a convincing case and ward off potential objections. *Authority-deconstructing* (or deconstructive) uses of history use history to rebut, cast doubt on, or complicate other people's uses of history as they employ the modalities. The goal of authority-deconstructing arguments is not to build up but to tear down—to shift burdens of proof, to sow uncertainty, to deny clarity, to multiply complexity, and to assert that opposing arguments gloss over important facts, indulge in anachronisms, or are overly simplistic.

In addition, when advocates use the modalities, there are two different ways to invoke the past as authority for law. The first approach treats the past as a positive source of authority, as something we should follow in the present. The second treats the past as something we should avoid or transcend or whose unfortunate legacy we still suffer from.[20]

Obedient uses of history treat the past as a positive model for present-day behavior—because it reveals correct meanings, because it serves as honored precedent, because it is morally worthy, because it offers a positive example, because it tutors us in how to behave, or because it is consistent with our political traditions. *Critical* uses of history treat the past as something that we should not follow in the present and should reject, compensate for, or disown. Critical history is aversive history. It describes faults, sins, and errors. It shows us what we should never let happen again, what should no longer be part of us, and what we should strive to repair. Critical history may also show us the legacy of mistake, injustice, and oppression that we should react against, and that we should try to extirpate, compensate for, eliminate, or disestablish in our current practices.

Of course, the past is neither wholly one thing or its opposite. Good and bad, honorable and dishonorable, helpful and harmful are all mixed together, and what we see in the past reflects our current situation and perspectives. The meaning of the past continually changes, not because the facts change but because we change, pushed forward continuously into new situations, which form ever new perspectives and points of comparison with the old, and which cast a continuously changing light and shadow on what went before. Historical studies rightly emphasize the motley nature of the past, its richness and its ambiguity, as well as its difference from our current world. In distinguishing between obedient and critical uses of history, therefore, I am not claiming that the moral meaning of history is clear-cut. Instead, I am interested in how people use the past in legal rhetoric, as a positive model or a negative precedent.

Combining these rhetorical postures, we have a box of four (figure 2.3). In practice, a skillful advocate will use all four of these approaches in framing a legal argument, offering positive precedents to be followed and negative historical examples to disown, while simultaneously highlighting mistakes, confusions, complexities, and

	Authority-constructing *(using the modalities)*	**Authority-deconstructing** *(directed against opponents' use of the modalities)*
Obedient	Claiming legal authority from positive example or precedent Example: "Alexander Hamilton's views in *The Federalist* are a sure guide to the powers of the Presidency today."	Undermining claims to legal authority from positive example or precedent Example: "There is insufficient evidence that the founding generation believed that the Second Amendment guaranteed an individual right to bear arms outside of military service."
Critical	Claiming legal authority through aversive history or by negative example Example: "Today's voter identification laws are a continuation of the legacy of Jim Crow-era poll taxes."	Undermining claims to legal authority that use aversive history or negative examples Example: "It is a gross over-simplification to conclude that state bans on government aid to religion stem from anti-Catholic bigotry."

Figure 2.3. Rhetorical postures in using history

anachronisms in opponents' arguments. Advocates will pick the part of the past they want to honor, while disclaiming or glossing over other parts of the past. Their opponents, eager to rebut them, will try to flip the script, seizing on omissions and complications.

CHAPTER THREE

How Modality Shapes History

I N CHAPTER 2, I argued that the modalities people use in constitutional argument shape how they use history. This chapter offers two examples.

A. Structural Argument

My first example comes from Justice Robert Jackson's famous opinion in the *Steel Seizure* case, *Youngstown Sheet & Tube Co. v. Sawyer*.[1] Jackson explains why Article II does not give the president inherent emergency powers. He begins by making ritual obeisance to "the forefathers" and noting that they omitted adding such a power to the constitutional text.[2] But Jackson then goes on to reject the idea that the Court should infer such powers through constitutional construction. Jackson points to the experience of "many modern nations" with emergency powers:

> Germany, after the First World War, framed the Weimar Constitution, designed to secure her liberties in the Western tradition. However, the President of the Republic, without concurrence of the Reichstag, was empowered temporarily to suspend any or all individual rights if public safety and order were seriously disturbed or endangered. This proved a temptation to every government, whatever its shade of

opinion, and in 13 years suspension of rights was invoked on more than 250 occasions. Finally, Hitler persuaded President Von Hindenb[u]rg to suspend all such rights, and they were never restored.[3]

By contrast, Jackson points out,

> The French Republic provided for a very different kind of emergency government, . . . [in which] emergency powers could not be assumed at will by the Executive but could only be granted as a parliamentary measure. And it did not, as in Germany, result in a suspension or abrogation of law but was a legal institution governed by special legal rules and terminable by parliamentary authority.
>
> Great Britain also has fought both World Wars under a sort of temporary dictatorship created by legislation. As Parliament is not bound by written constitutional limitations, it established a crisis government simply by delegation to its Ministers of a larger measure than usual of its own unlimited power, which is exercised under its supervision by Ministers whom it may dismiss. This has been called the "high-water mark in the voluntary surrender of liberty," but, as Churchill put it, "Parliament stands custodian of these surrendered liberties, and its most sacred duty will be to restore them in their fullness when victory has crowned our exertions and our perseverance." Thus, parliamentary control made emergency powers compatible with freedom.[4]

Jackson summarizes the lessons of this history: "This contemporary foreign experience may be inconclusive as to the wisdom of lodging emergency powers somewhere in a modern government. But it suggests that emergency powers are consistent with free government only when their control is lodged elsewhere than in the Executive who exercises them. That is the safeguard that would be nullified by our adoption of the 'inherent powers' formula. Nothing in my experience convinces me that such risks are warranted by any real necessity, although such powers would, of course, be an executive convenience."[5]

Jackson's use of history is noteworthy in four respects. First, although he begins with a bow to the framers, he is not using history to determine original meaning, original intentions, or original understanding. Indeed, he finds appeals to original understanding singularly unhelpful: "Just what our forefathers did envision, or would have envisioned had they foreseen modern conditions, must be divined from materials almost as enigmatic as the dreams Joseph was called upon to interpret for Pharaoh."[6] Jackson focuses on relatively recent history, not the history of the late eighteenth century. And he is not even concerned with the history of the United States. His examples come from Europe.

Second, when Jackson discusses the historical experiences of Germany, France, and Great Britain, his argument is about structure and consequences. We should interpret the Constitution this way because it avoids bad consequences (a consequentialist argument) or because it is more consistent with important structural features of the Constitution that secure liberty and self-rule (a structural argument). Jackson uses contemporary European history to make his points, but he could also have drawn on a wide range of examples from around the world and from different periods in history, including, for example, the dictatorships of ancient Rome.[7]

Third, Jackson does not explicitly state or defend his theory of argument. He does not say, "I am making an argument from structure or consequences, and here are the reasons why you should accept these kinds of arguments." Rather, he uses history unselfconsciously—he leaves the background theory of argument unstated, and he simply assumes that his audience accepts the validity of appeals to structure and consequences. Jackson's argument is an enthymeme. It suppresses a crucial premise—namely, the theory of legal justification that underlies the history he presents.

Fourth, Jackson's argument offers a constructive use of history to establish authority, with both obedient and critical claims. He seeks to convince us that history offers relatively clear lessons that we should follow. Once we clarify the background theory of justification implicit in Jackson's argument, we can see exactly how a critic might dispute or correct Jackson's use of history. We could use the same modalities he does to offer rebuttals. These rebuttals will employ critical or deconstructive uses of history. They will argue that

his history offers the wrong model to follow or that the lessons he
wants to draw from history are unclear and contestable.

Critical: One might argue that Jackson's historical examples are
irrelevant because they are too different from our American experience, so we have no reason to follow them. Or one might argue that
we should not be guided by European constitutional ideas because
they are inconsistent with American constitutional values.

Deconstructive: One might dispute what the historical account tells
us about structure and consequences. Perhaps Jackson did not get
the history of Weimar right. Perhaps the constitutional provisions
were not the real cause or the most important cause of Germany's
slide into totalitarianism. Perhaps what saved France and Great Britain from Germany's fate was not legislative control over emergency
powers but other features of French and British political culture.

In short, to respond to Jackson's historical argument, we can
complicate the history, resituate and recontextualize it, and add counterexamples, counterinterpretations, and counternarratives.

B. Arguments from Judicial Precedent

Arguments from precedent frequently use history. These arguments
do not claim that interpretations are correct because of what the
adopters meant, thought, or understood. Instead, arguments from
precedent claim that an interpretation is correct because of previous
decisions by courts. They derive their authority from rule of law
values and from the institutional practice of stare decisis.

Arguments from judicial precedent may require historical inquiry because particular judicial tests within doctrine may depend
on history. For example, substantive due process jurisprudence protects substantive rights under the Due Process Clauses of the Fifth
and Fourteenth Amendments. This jurisprudence requires an inquiry into the historical importance of a right and evolving traditions of practice.[8] Courts decide whether a right should be protected
by looking to history. Equally important, courts may look at history
differently than they do when they inquire into original meaning,
intentions, or understanding.

McDonald v. City of Chicago offers a good example.[9] In a previous
case, *District of Columbia v. Heller*, the Supreme Court held that the

Second Amendment guaranteed a right to keep and bear arms in the home for purposes of self-defense.[10] The issue in *McDonald* was whether this Second Amendment right applied to state and local governments through the Fourteenth Amendment. The Court held that it did, but on the basis of two different reasons that employed history in two different ways.

Justice Clarence Thomas, concurring in the judgment, argued that the original meaning of the Fourteenth Amendment's Privileges or Immunities Clause included the Second Amendment right to keep and bear arms.[11] His opinion offers evidence of what the framers of the Fourteenth Amendment intended and the ratifiers expected.[12]

Justice Samuel Alito, writing for a four-justice plurality, canvasses much of the same history as Justice Thomas.[13] But his focus is quite different. Justice Alito argues that given the Court's current test for incorporation—as shaped by previous precedents—Second Amendment rights should be incorporated against the states.[14] The central question, Justice Alito explained, is "whether the Second Amendment right to keep and bear arms is incorporated in the concept of due process" in the Fourteenth Amendment.[15] To decide that question, "we must decide whether the right to keep and bear arms is fundamental to *our* scheme of ordered liberty" or "whether this right is 'deeply rooted in this Nation's history and tradition.'"[16]

The differences between the kinds of arguments that Justices Thomas and Alito make shape the history that is relevant to each. Justice Thomas wants to know what the adopters of the Fourteenth Amendment meant. Therefore, his focus is on adoption history and the meaning of "Privileges or Immunities of Citizens of the United States." Justice Thomas does not care what other generations of Americans thought about the right to bear arms except to the extent that their views elucidate the understandings of the adopting generation.

Justice Alito, by contrast, relies on the authority of judicial precedent. He therefore uses history in two different ways. First, he looks to the history of doctrinal development to derive the proper test. Second, he applies a doctrinal test that asks a historical question. The doctrine asks whether there is a long-standing tradition of treating a right as fundamental. If so, and if the Court has not previously decided the question to the contrary (that is, in the history of precedent), the right is protected by the Due Process Clause of the

Fourteenth Amendment. As he puts it, "Unless considerations of stare decisis counsel otherwise, a provision of the Bill of Rights that protects a right that is fundamental from an American perspective applies equally to the Federal Government and the States."[17]

Justice Alito therefore endeavors to show that the right to keep and bear arms has long been regarded as fundamental. He canvasses attitudes at the founding, during the early nineteenth century, and during Reconstruction leading up to the ratification of the Fourteenth Amendment.[18] He argues that the framers of the Fourteenth Amendment believed that the right to bear arms was fundamental.[19] But Justice Alito does not care that the adopters would not have understood the right in the same way as a modern court. The adopters would probably have considered the right to keep and bear arms as a right of citizens protected by the Privileges or Immunities Clause. But the Supreme Court long ago relegated that clause to irrelevance. Beginning in the early twentieth century, it began asking whether a right is "incorporated" into the Due Process Clause.[20]

An important weakness in Justice Alito's argument—which does not apply to Justice Thomas's—is that Justice Alito does not carry his story forward into the twentieth century. Having established that the right was viewed as fundamental in 1868, he pronounces it deeply rooted in the nation's traditions and stops his historical inquiry. Nevertheless, although the views of the Fourteenth Amendment's adopters may be good evidence that a right has long been regarded as fundamental, they cannot establish that proposition by themselves. Suppose, for example, that public attitudes that the right is fundamental faded away in the late nineteenth century because of concerns about political radicals, labor activists, and immigrants, that states and the federal government began to regulate arms regularly, and that the modern movement for gun rights did not begin in earnest until the second half of the twentieth century.[21] Rather than always being deeply rooted in our nation's traditions, the right's importance to Americans has oscillated throughout history. This history would tend to undermine Justice Alito's doctrinal argument that there is a long-standing tradition of viewing the right as fundamental, but it would have little effect on Justice Thomas's inquiry into original meaning.

Even when Justices Alito and Thomas focus on the same period of history—Reconstruction—they see different things. Justice Thomas asks whether the right to bear arms is a privilege or immunity of national citizenship protected by the Fourteenth Amendment's Privileges or Immunities Clause. He tries to show that the adopters meant to protect portions of the Bill of Rights through that clause, and he describes how early Supreme Court decisions like the *Slaughter-House Cases* and *United States v. Cruikshank* distorted the framers' design.[22] Modern case law uses the doctrine of "substantive due process" to incorporate fundamental rights into the Due Process Clause; but this clause, Justice Thomas explains, is about the protection of process, not substantive liberties.[23] Adoption history shows that the Court's precedents have betrayed the Constitution's original meaning, creating a "jurisprudence devoid of a guiding principle."[24]

Justice Alito finds these aspects of history irrelevant to his purposes. His source of authority is not original meaning but past precedent: "For many decades," he explains, "the question of the rights protected by the Fourteenth Amendment against state infringement has been analyzed under the Due Process Clause of that Amendment and not under the Privileges or Immunities Clause."[25] And that settles the matter. Whether or not the Supreme Court has strayed from the adopters' views, Justice Alito explains, it will "decline to disturb" its previous rulings.[26] Where Justice Thomas sees a betrayal of the original understanding, Justice Alito merely sees a line of precedents to be followed.

CHAPTER FOUR

Arguments from National Ethos, Political Tradition, and Honored Authority

S OME OF THE MOST important uses of history in constitutional interpretation involve the last three modalities of argument: these are arguments from national ethos, political tradition, and honored authority. What makes these arguments special is that they rely on stylized accounts of history and appeal to collective memory.

Collective memory lies in the background of almost all constitutional interpretation. But what makes arguments from ethos, tradition, and honored authority special is that they foreground what is often in the background. So these arguments are exemplary of the role that collective (or cultural) memory plays in constitutional interpretation.

Moreover, as I will argue in chapter 9, these three kinds of arguments often shape how people use adoption history in making constitutional arguments. In fact, most of the originalist arguments that lawyers and judges make are usually also arguments from political tradition, national ethos, or honored authority.

Arguments from national ethos and political tradition appeal to what is honorable about the nation's history and values judged from the standpoint of the present. They state what Americans stand for and, equally importantly, what they do *not* stand for and what they have rejected as not part of who they are. They are arguments about national values, national character, and the retrospective meaning of political, legal, and historical events. Arguments from ethos and political tradition are explicitly or implicitly narrative in character. The story that undergirds arguments from ethos and tradition may be framed in terms of sweeping narratives, canonical events, and cultural heroes. Or it may be a more down-to-earth account of the history of the common law and state statutes. In either case, the point of recounting the story is to draw a normative lesson for the present.

Arguments from tradition claim that our traditions constitute our political life and offer normative direction to our endeavors. Arguments from national ethos claim that a constitutional interpretation that betrays the deepest meanings of America's values and political traditions cannot be correct. Finally, arguments from honored authority claim that we should follow the model and the views of honored figures from our nation's past because (1) they represent important national values and norms; (2) they are central to or constitutive of important and valuable American traditions; or (3) their actions and beliefs display wisdom, courage, or other political virtues.

Because traditions are shaped and sustained over long periods of time and because new traditions can arise throughout the nation's history, arguments from ethos and tradition may invoke many different periods in American history, not just adoption history. Sometimes arguments from political tradition and national ethos may point in different directions than arguments from original meaning. Our present-day understandings about the meaning of America and its values may not have been obvious or uncontroversial to everyone at the time of adoption. Some features of the American experience that we see as central today were unknown to or would have been rejected by the adopting generation.

For example, because of the work of successive waves of social movements for equality, most Americans believe that equality and opposition to racism are central to the American creed. But many people in 1787—or even 1868—might not have seen it the same way. The American political tradition as it has developed may reshape or even reject the principles and values we derive from original meaning, original understanding, or original intentions.

Nevertheless, many arguments that people call "originalist" are better understood as appeals to ethos, tradition, and honored authority. A distinctive feature of American constitutional culture is its quasi-religious veneration of its framers and founders—not necessarily as they were understood in the past or in their own time but as they are understood in the present.

Arguments from national ethos and political tradition address fellow members of the political community through invoking the normative meaning of a shared past. They interpret the meaning of the past to show what we should do in the present—as well as what we should not do. Hence, arguments from ethos and tradition make certain assumptions about the speaker and audience. They assume that both the speaker and the audience identify with a common tradition, that the identities of both speaker and audience are partly constituted by that tradition, and therefore that both speaker and audience wish to continue to be true to it.

Note that these assumptions may be unfounded. If people do not identify with the country's traditions, arguments from ethos and tradition will have little purchase. If people do not look up to venerated figures as positive models, arguments from honored authority will carry little weight.

Arguments from ethos, tradition, and honored authority are similar to what Philip Bobbitt called "ethical" arguments.[1] In *Constitutional Interpretation*, Bobbitt suggested that ethical arguments are appeals to "the idea of limited government, the presumption of which holds that all residual authority remains in the private sphere."[2] Ethical argument concerns "those choices beyond the power of government to compel."[3]

This account of national ethos is too narrow, and Bobbitt did not mean for it to be exclusive.[4] In any case, Bobbitt offered another definition of ethical argument that is much broader: "constitutional argument whose force relies on a characterization of American institutions and the role within them of the American people."[5]

Many aspects of American political traditions and national ethos do not concern limited government and the protection of the private sphere. Two obvious examples are the idea of democratic egalitarianism and equality before the law, which apply regardless of the size of government. Moreover, some aspects of American ethos and political traditions, like those implicit in Social Security, the Homestead Act, the National Security Act, and Medicare, assume the beneficial exercise of government power in the public interest. Indeed, one of the central motivations for the creation of the 1787 Constitution was that the existing government's powers were too limited; government needed to be vigorous in order to protect liberty and provide security.[6] This example shows that what people call American traditions and American character are often subject to multiple and contrasting interpretations.

Arguments from ethos, tradition, and honored authority can overlap with arguments from social custom or political convention. Arguments from social custom assume that the people as a whole have settled on a set of mores that reflect mutual adjustment, solve coordination problems, and economize on collective wisdom. Arguments from political convention assume that political actors have settled on permissible courses of conduct that all relevant actors have either consented or acquiesced to; the authority of these conventions comes from mutual consent and/or continuous practice.

In like fashion, arguments from ethos and tradition can appeal to the collective wisdom of past generations. They may also implicitly rely on an imagined consensus of values or the consent of the governed to old laws and doctrines. At the same time, these arguments may also focus on key individuals and events like the Civil War or the New Deal as symbols of the country's values; they may emphasize great deeds and struggles, cultural heroism and cultural villainy, and narratives of progress, decline, restoration, and redemption.

Even so, there are important differences between these kinds of arguments. Appeals to social custom or political convention usually argue for retaining some version of the status quo, even if the nature of the status quo is disputed. But appeals to ethos, tradition, and honored authority may work quite differently. Lawyers' invocation of tradition need not be Burkean—it might be revolutionary. Judges might invoke tradition to chip away or overturn existing precedents and conventions. When Americans invoke the traditions of the past, they may be offering jeremiads or narratives of decline. They may call for restoration. Or they may urge the present to return to the wisdom and instruction of a forgotten past, newly excavated.

For example, when the Supreme Court eliminated the right to abortion in *Dobbs v. Jackson Women's Health Organization*, Justice Samuel Alito argued that the right to abortion had no basis in the country's traditions.[7] In overturning *Roe v. Wade*, he sought to eliminate half a century of constitutional rights protection, not preserve the status quo. And he specifically rejected the idea that the Court should maintain the status quo because generations of American women had come to rely on access to abortion when contraception fails.[8] Alito's argument from tradition is the opposite of an argument from custom.

A. Invoking Collective Memory

A good example of a constitutional argument from ethos and tradition appears in Justice Louis Brandeis's concurrence in *Whitney v. California*.[9] Justice Brandeis argues that government should not be able to punish seditious speech unless it poses a "clear and present danger."[10] To explain why, he appeals to the values and beliefs of the American revolutionaries, and he argues that we should remain faithful to these values and beliefs today: "Those who won our independence believed that the final end of the State was to make men free to develop their faculties; and that in its government the deliberative forces should prevail over the arbitrary. They believed liberty to be the secret of happiness and courage to be the secret of liberty."[11]

The courage to risk social disruption from political dissent, Justice Brandeis explains, is a central and honored American value: "Those who won our independence by revolution were not cowards. They did not fear political change. They did not exalt order at the cost of liberty. To courageous, self-reliant men, with confidence in the power of free and fearless reasoning applied through the processes of popular government, no danger flowing from speech can be deemed clear and present, unless the incidence of the evil apprehended is so imminent that it may befall before there is opportunity for full discussion."[12]

Although it might seem that Justice Brandeis is making an argument from original intention, he is really appealing to American ethos and tradition, drawing on features of American collective memory. (Of course, as I emphasize in this book, most originalist arguments are also appeals to ethos, tradition, and honored authority.)

First, note that Justice Brandeis speaks of "those who won our independence," that is, the American revolutionaries, rather than "those who framed our Constitution." The two groups overlap, but they are not identical; however, in American cultural memory, the two groups tend to merge into one. This is a sign that we are dealing with an argument from tradition or ethos rather than a technical argument about the meaning attributed to the Constitution by its framers or ratifiers. Arguments that appeal to the founders or the framers as an undifferentiated whole or that conflate different generations (revolutionaries, framers, politicians of the early federal period) are likely to be arguments from tradition or ethos.

From the nation's founding to the present, what is fundamental to American character and political culture has been contested. There is usually more than one way to characterize a country's political traditions and national ethos. Moreover, appeals to tradition are complicated by the fact that consensus in practice and belief often disappears when we inspect history more closely. Moreover, many practices and beliefs that were once widely accepted and considered traditional or valuable are now rejected as un-American.

When people argue from political tradition or national ethos, therefore, they must make interpretive judgments about what aspects of American history are central and valuable features of the country's traditions and what aspects are peripheral, exceptional, irrelevant, or have been dishonored or repudiated as time has passed.[13] That is, arguments from political tradition or national ethos claim that particular values or beliefs are characteristic of the nation and its traditions *rightly understood*. Such arguments are inevitably interpretive and normative—and therefore contestable.

Accordingly, Justice Brandeis's argument passes over many historical complications. He does not consider, for example, whether the founding generation disagreed about protecting politically unpopular speech, whether some of the founders were selective in their support of free expression, or whether some members of the founding generation actually *wanted* to suppress particular dissenters—for example, Loyalists during the Revolution or supporters of France during the early years of the republic. After all, the Federalists who supported the Alien and Sedition Acts *did* fear the effect of seditious advocacy.[14] It was the Jeffersonian Republicans—then the political minority—who articulated the need for civic courage.[15] And even Jefferson himself was not always a champion of free expression.[16] He was perfectly happy to have states regulate speech and press, for example.[17]

If Justice Brandeis's argument is an argument from original intention or original meaning, it is a pretty bad argument.[18] Charitably understood, however, Justice Brandeis is using history in a different way. If pressed, Justice Brandeis should have been willing to admit that not all of the founders—or the Americans who succeeded them—practiced civic courage. Nevertheless, he might emphasize, this ideal best represents our aspirations as a people.

Note, moreover, that Justice Brandeis is not invoking ethos and tradition in order to argue against change or to preserve the status quo. Quite the contrary: he wants the Supreme Court to protect the speech of dissidents, which the law of his day did not.[19] Justice Brandeis uses the cultural memory of the American revolutionaries to criticize the Court's existing doctrine. His use of ethos is reformist or revolutionary, rather than a defense of existing arrangements. We can generalize this point: although appeals to tradition may seem conservative on the surface, they are often calls for transformation or revolution. Movements for reform often try to persuade fellow citizens by appealing to shared premises and widely honored examples.[20] If the speaker believes the country has strayed from the correct path, then a call for fidelity to ethos or tradition is an argument for change, not stasis.

B. Selection and Simplification

Justice Brandeis invokes a heroic past; he calls on Americans to live up to their ideals and to their highest aspirations as a people. And he tells his story from a present-day perspective, describing how matters appear—and what they mean—in hindsight. His portrait of the past is deliberately selective. He equates Jefferson's vision with American values and he treats Jefferson's Federalist opponents as false prophets. He identifies with some members of the founding generation as reflecting the best in the American tradition and neglects or simply refuses to identify with others.

These features of Justice Brandeis's argument are characteristic of appeals to ethos and tradition. Such arguments assume that history has a purpose or meaning that vindicates or critiques the present and points to the proper direction of action in the future.[21] Arguments from ethos and tradition both explain and invoke the meaning of events in the country's history, including the normative lessons we should draw from these events. Hence, arguments from ethos and tradition may simplify or select from a more complex history in order to demonstrate how the past exemplifies key values or lessons.

Because arguments from ethos and tradition draw meaning from history, they often take a narrative form. They may employ, either overtly or implicitly, narratives of progress, decline, stasis, upheaval, restoration, or redemption. They explain who Americans are by explaining where they have come from and where they are going. They are arguments about Americans' deepest values as symbolized by the struggles, commitments, successes, and failures of the past.[22] They are appeals to a transgenerational subject, "We the People," who possess certain traditions, values, and features of character that we come to understand in retrospect.

Arguments from ethos and tradition attempt to explain the trajectory of events in American history. That trajectory may not be one of progress. Americans may have missed opportunities for redemption or fallen short of their ideals. They may have strayed from the wisdom of tradition and must be urged to return to it.

Because arguments from ethos and tradition explain the meaning of history from the standpoint of the present, they are often anachronistic. People in the past did not know how the future would turn out; therefore, they did not understand themselves or their actions in terms of the narratives we craft today. The defenders of slavery did not know that they would lose, and the defenders of abolition did not know that they would ultimately win. Neither side's adherents knew what use later generations would make of them or how their story would be represented as part of the country's political traditions.

Arguments from ethos and tradition tend to treat history in a stylized fashion. Sometimes they purposefully condense events and smooth over complexities and complications. They seek to understand the past, not for its own sake but in the service of the present and the future. History that explains American values may be heroic or tragic, but it is always didactic.[23]

There are many ways to do this. Justice Brandeis's approach in *Whitney* is schematic and abstract, emphasizing the founders' larger and deeper commitments rather than their specific laws and doctrines. Brandeis argued that there was a tradition of free speech in the United States despite the history of official regulation of speech. In the middle of the twentieth century, the historian Leonard Levy sharply criticized this account. He argued that there had actually been a "legacy of suppression" in early American law.[24] Levy's critics defended the American free speech tradition by pointing out that the actual practices of free speech and press at the founding were far more libertarian than the law on the books.[25] This way of constructing tradition looks not to positive law but to popular practice and statements of principle.

In *Obergefell v. Hodges*, Justice Anthony Kennedy argued that the American tradition of liberty justified the extension of the right to marry to same-sex couples.[26] The question, he argued, was not whether there was a history of specific legal guarantees of same-sex marriage in American law.[27] Rather, the correct question was whether the reasons why Americans had traditionally protected the right to marry applied to same-sex couples as well.[28] Thus, *Obergefell* does not involve a rejection of tradition—as the dissenters contended—but rather a particular way of constructing and applying it. In Kennedy's hands, history offers us a set of reasons for our traditional practices that we can apply by analogy to new situations and circumstances. In this way, we might alter or even reject existing practices while being faithful to the country's traditions of liberty.[29]

In *Dobbs v. Jackson Women's Health Organization*, Justice Samuel Alito took the opposite approach. He sought to show that the right to abortion was not deeply rooted in the nation's history and traditions because there was no history of specific legal protections for abortion.[30] He offered a history of specific laws, doctrines, and regulations. He argued that beginning in the nineteenth century state legislatures began criminalizing abortion and that there was no legal protection for abortion until the 1970s.[31]

In Alito's version, American traditions are not principles or reasons; rather, we find them in specific laws passed by state legislatures. The meaning of tradition is not an abstract idea or commitment but a set of positive enactments and ancient common-law doctrines. For Alito, the central question is whether state statutes have specifically protected an asserted liberty; if the practice has been criminalized, a fortiori there is no tradition of protecting it. In constructing tradition this way, he rejects the possibility that the law on the books did not match Americans' actual practices or beliefs with respect to abortion and contraception.[32] This is the opposite of the way that people have constructed the American free speech tradition; as noted earlier, in the case of free speech, the official law was much more restrictive than people's practices or beliefs.

Alito's approach identifies American values and traditions with the positive law of the past, rather than actual practices of liberty or general principles and commitments.[33] Construing tradition in this way is well designed to make it hard for courts to recognize new constitutional rights that could challenge old laws. In the specific case of abortion, Alito's construction of national tradition was designed to eliminate fifty years of protection on the ground that the recognition of liberty arose mostly from court decisions in the 1970s. It treats the law from the 1970s onward not as part of America's traditions but rather as a wrong turn. Alito does not regard *Roe v. Wade* and later cases as evidence of American traditions of liberty even though they were part of American law for half a century and enjoyed significant public support. Instead, he constructs an earlier account of positive law that he treats as the real or true tradition.[34]

In *New York State Rifle & Pistol Association, Inc. v. Bruen*, the Supreme Court struck down New York's limitation on carrying weapons outside the home.[35] Writing for the majority, Justice Clarence Thomas also looked to positive law to construct tradition, but in the opposite way that Justice Alito did in *Dobbs*. (Even so, the two justices joined in each other's opinions, which abolished abortion rights and expanded gun rights.)

While Justice Alito argued that no right was fundamental unless there was a tradition of statutes protecting it, Justice Thomas argued that governments may not regulate the right to keep and bear arms in common use unless the state's regulation is consistent with the history of gun regulation that can be traced back either to 1791 or 1868. (He does not decide which date matters.)[36]

Justice Alito constructs tradition by using positive law to prevent the recognition or expansion of rights. Justice Thomas constructs tradition by using positive law to prevent new government regulations of rights unless those regulations are comparable to those enacted in the past.[37] Moreover, the comparison must be to laws enacted very early on in the history of the republic; the fact that the predecessors of New York's licensing law dated back over a century does not count.[38]

As you can see from these examples, lawyers and judges can construct tradition in many different ways. They can identify tradition with the history of positive law, or they can identify tradition with historical principles, understandings, or practices that transcend positive law and contest or critique it. They can describe tradition broadly in terms of general principles or narrowly in terms of specific legal rules and prohibitions. Finally, they can construct traditions of *rights* or traditions of government *regulations* to support their desired outcome.

In each case, however, the rhetorical power of arguments from tradition depends on how lawyers and judges tell the story that constructs the tradition and shows its normative lessons for the present. And the normative lesson that lawyers and judges draw from history depends on how they select and characterize some facts while omitting others.

C. Arguments from Honored Authority

Many constitutional arguments feature the nation's cultural heroes. As I explain in chapter 6, a culture hero is a figure of history or legend to whom a people attributes its greatest or most essential achievements or values, or someone who symbolizes a people's characteristics or aspirations.[39] The use of culture heroes is characteristic of a special kind of constitutional argument from cultural memory. I call these *arguments from honored authority*.[40] If an honored figure— say Madison, Jefferson, Washington, or Lincoln—expresses or demonstrates a view about a constitutional question, the argument has greater persuasive authority simply because the honored figure expressed it or supported it. That is because one way of being faithful to tradition is to adopt the same practices or beliefs as a culture hero, who acts as a paragon and as a model for appropriate action.

When the culture hero does not come from the founding period, it is easy to see that the argument is not one of original meaning. But quite often arguments from honored authority do invoke members of the founding generation. In these situations, arguments from honored authority resemble and overlap with arguments from original meaning, original intention, or original understanding. But their claim to authority involves more than a simple appeal to original meaning, intention, or understanding.

Originalist theories generally assert that a particular meaning, intention, or understanding was both fixed *and* widely shared at the time of adoption. That is why current generations must follow this meaning, intention, or understanding today. But an honored authority's views (or practices) may not have been the consensus view. They may not have been representative of what most other founders, framers, ratifiers, or citizens believed, and on certain questions, there may have been no consensus view. So the claim to authority is not that the honored authority's views were widely shared in that person's own time but that they are important to our present-day political traditions or otherwise worthy of emulation. To be sure, people may quote honored authorities in the mistaken belief that their views are a good proxy for those of the adopters in general. But doing so may confuse salience and honored status with representativeness.[41]

For example, James Madison's views on constitutional issues evolved through decades of public life as he served in multiple capacities and confronted a wide range of political problems and controversies.[42] He and other founders—including many of the early Federalists—were often on different sides of political and legal issues as time went on. Merely citing Madison's views—as lawyers and judges are wont to do—does not mean that one has correctly captured the views of the framers or adopters. Madison offered opinions on constitutional questions throughout his life that the adopters may never have considered or on which there was no generally agreed view.

Nevertheless, statements by James Madison on almost any subject are treated as having persuasive authority because he is regarded as the father of the Constitution. Here again, *why* we use history matters greatly to assessing the strength and relevance of particular arguments. Often Madison's views may not be a reliable guide to original meaning, original understanding, or original intention, and yet they may still be important to us today because of his preeminent place in American political traditions.

George Washington's decisions and actions as the first president of the United States offer a particularly complicated form of authority. Some of Washington's decisions as president may have been followed by most or all of his successors and therefore have the authority of nonjudicial precedent or convention. Indeed, Akhil Amar has argued that the framers, knowing that Washington would be the first president, assumed that he would fill out many of the details of the office.[43] In other cases, however, people may look to what Washington did to elucidate the meaning of executive power today because of Washington's symbolic status in American history. Arguments that his actions demonstrate the original meaning of Article II may actually be better characterized as arguments from honored authority, using Washington as a sort of constitutional paragon and a model for constitutional virtue. Although Washington was greatly honored and admired in his lifetime, not all of his contemporaries agreed with everything he did as president or would have agreed that what he did fixed for all time the correct meaning of Article II. As with most political leaders, many of Washington's decisions were controversial in his own day and may not reflect a consensus of meaning, understanding, or intentions. Although his actions might not be a reliable guide to original meaning, they still might be important as arguments from an honored authority who holds a central place in the American political tradition.

D. Selective Identification and Disidentification

Arguments from ethos and tradition often call for us to remember what "we"—a transgenerational subject—fought for, what we stand for, what we promised we would do, and what we promised we would never let happen again.[44] They explain the meaning of history in terms of what has been lasting, honorable, and worthy of continuation in our political traditions. Often they do this as a critique of the status quo. One of the most common forms of argument is the American jeremiad, which asserts a decline or a falling away from political virtue and proclaims the need for reform and renewal.[45]

Such judgments may offer a selective view of history. But they are also partial in another sense. They identify people and ideas that history has hallowed through time, as well as people and ideas that history has judged mistaken. They refer, either implicitly or explicitly, to who was on the right side of history as judged from the present and who was on the wrong side. Those on the right side should be emulated; those on the wrong side serve as negative examples. Thus, arguments from ethos and tradition pick history's winners and losers, regardless of how these people understood themselves or were understood by others in their own day.

Arguments from ethos and tradition engage in *selective identification* and *disidentification*.[46] They identify Americans in the present with only some of the people who lived in the past and only some of the events that occurred in the past. Equally important, they also *disidentify* Americans in the present from certain people and events in the past, because those people and events have proven not to be representative of America at its best or because they exemplify ideas and traits that Americans today should denounce or repudiate.[47]

Thus, a contemporary argument about the constitutionality of the Voting Rights Act would identify with President Lyndon Johnson and Martin Luther King Jr., and his followers and disidentify with the police who rioted on the Edmund Pettus Bridge. An argument about the proper interpretation of the Fourteenth Amendment might identify with social movements for abolition, Black civil rights, and women's rights and disidentify with their opponents, who lost a political struggle over the nature of America. For similar reasons, people may prefer to quote the views of those who supported the Constitution rather than their anti-Federalist opponents. The reason is not because the former had a better insight into original public meaning of the words in the Constitution than the latter—after all, both sides spoke the same English language—but because the supporters were on what people now consider the right side of history.[48]

In such arguments, disidentification is as important as identification. American constitutional culture includes both a list of canonical cases and a list of anticanonical cases, like *Lochner v. New York*, *Dred Scott v. Sandford*, *Plessy v. Ferguson*, and *Korematsu v. United States*.[49] A familiar form of constitutional argument is to associate one's opponents with the positions taken in these anticanonical cases, because people think that the decisions were on the wrong side of history.[50]

Arguments from ethos, tradition, and honored authority need not concern adoption history or the framers. A good example is the hallowed status of *Brown v. Board of Education* and the civil rights movement in the American political tradition.[51]

In *Parents Involved in Community Schools v. Seattle School District No. 1*, the members of the Supreme Court fought over the legacy of *Brown* and over who was most faithful to the values of the National Association for the Advancement of Colored People (NAACP) and the members of the civil rights movement that fought for racial equality in the 1950s and 1960s.[52] Notably, the Court's originalist justices did not look to the original meaning of the Reconstruction Amendments to justify their conclusions. Instead, they turned to the meaning of *Brown v. Board of Education*.[53]

The issue in *Parents Involved* was whether school districts in Seattle and Louisville could assign students by race in order to promote greater racial integration.[54] The plurality opinion, written by Chief Justice John Roberts, held that they could not, invoking the legacy of *Brown* and arguing that the school districts were attempting to return to pre-*Brown* ideas.[55] Justice Clarence Thomas's concurrence emphasized that his approach was especially faithful to the values and arguments of the plaintiffs in *Brown*.[56] Moreover, Justice Thomas argued, the dissenters and the school board, who would allow local authorities to use race to promote integration, were like the people who attempted to defend racial segregation in the public schools and who opposed the result reached in *Brown*.[57] (Here Justice Thomas both identifies with culture heroes and identifies his opponents with the collective memory of antiheroes.) Conversely, the dissenters argued that they were actually faithful to the legacy of the civil rights revolution and *Brown* and that the plurality and Justice Thomas were misreading and dishonoring *Brown*.[58]

The contrasting opinions in *Parents Involved* were not simply arguments about *Brown* as a legal precedent. Rather, they were arguments about the meaning of *Brown* as a central symbol of America's constitutional traditions. The arguments in *Parents Involved* made much use of history, but not adoption history. Their focus was not on the original meaning of the Fourteenth Amendment but on the original meaning of *Brown* and the struggle over Black civil rights.[59]

Both sides identified with Thurgood Marshall, the NAACP, and the civil rights movement, and both disidentified with the defendant school boards in *Brown* and with the many powerful and influential national politicians who believed that overturning the separate but equal doctrine of *Plessy* was a mistake. Each side claimed that they were being faithful to *Brown* and the civil rights revolution and that the other side had betrayed its principles.

Much of *Parents Involved* is an invocation of ethos and tradition, articulating the meaning of history in hindsight and identifying history's winners and losers. The decision also demonstrates the multiple interpretations and meanings available to people who call on a historical tradition. Not only did both sides engage in selective identification and disidentification, but both drew very different lessons about the meaning of history and the principles that the civil rights movement fought for. For the plurality and for Justice Thomas, the NAACP's campaign to overturn *Plessy* was centrally about the achievement of a colorblind Constitution; for the dissenters, it was a struggle to end racial subordination and to achieve a racially integrated society.[60]

E. Evaluating Arguments from Ethos, Tradition, and Honored Authority

Arguments from ethos, tradition, and honored authority are as important as they are ubiquitous in American constitutional culture. One responds to these arguments through a combination of constructive, obedient, critical, and deconstructive uses of history. If we offer an alternative account of national ethos and tradition with different normative lessons, that is our own constructive and obedient use of history. If we show that our opponent's historical account is incorrect, incomplete, or oversimplified, we are using history deconstructively. And if we argue that our opponents' invocation of tradition and ethos conceals or downplays events that are unjust, unworthy, and dishonorable, we use history critically.

These responses generally do one of three things. First, they offer counternarratives. Second, they complicate history. Third, they draw competing normative lessons from history. These three tasks are related, and they clarify how people argue about history—and with history—in politics and law.[61]

Because arguments from ethos and tradition look for something that can be called national meaning, national character, or national tradition, they tend to view history as relevant to the extent that it yields what they are searching for. That is, these arguments go into history *looking* for coherence, determinacy, and order in a past that may lack these features, or may have less of them than the advocate is looking for. That is one reason, although surely not the only one, that lawyers' history tends to wipe away complications and difficulties. The three-pronged strategy of counternarratives, counterlessons, and complications offers a corrective to the ways that lawyers' arguments tend to reshape (and possibly deform) the historical record.

People employ the past to contend about important values in the present and to assert the proper direction of future action. Offering counternarratives, counterlessons, and complications helps bring these normative elements of historical use to the surface. They expose the normative choices we make in constitutional argument when we invoke history. And so they also make more salient our own responsibilities for the choices we make in the present.

Appeals to ethos, tradition, and honored authority may obscure these responsibilities by arguing that our proper path is to emulate the past and submit to the authority of the past. We treat individuals, institutions, narratives, and traditions as theoretical and practical authorities that give us reasons to follow their example and adopt their reasons as our own.

The point of historical complication, counterinterpretation, and counternarrative is to reassert our responsibility for the choices we make in the present. The point is not to undermine the value of tradition, ethos, or honored authority in moral and political argument generally. Rather, it is to demonstrate that there are multiple paths that might constitute a proper continuation of tradition and multiple

ways to continue and honor the constitutional project of past generations. In addition, complication, counterinterpretation, and counternarrative can help us see that the failings of the past, the legacy of
past mistakes and injustices, and the limitations of even our most
honored culture heroes are vitally important to making sound judgments in the present.

These critiques may demystify certain uses of ethical authority,
but they do not eliminate ethical authority itself. They may complicate history so that tradition seems far more equivocal and multi-
vocal, but they do not eliminate the constitutive power of tradition
over people who live within it. Rather, these critiques bring to the
surface what is at stake in our use of history to persuade each other—
that what we are actually doing is fighting about values, norms, and
ethos using the past as a common point of reference. This is part of
what it means to say that history is a resource and not a command.

Lawyers must often persuade people who may lack deep historical knowledge, let alone professional historical training. In this task,
they should never make historical arguments that they know to be
false, misleading, or oversimplified. Didactic history often engages
in narrative construction, simplification, and selective identification,
but these rhetorical devices must always be in the service of helping
explain what one knows to be true to an audience who is thereby
better able to understand its truth. This does not excuse us from having to address and respond to factual complications and contrasting
interpretations.

Some arguments from ethos, tradition, and honored authority
are deflated when we complicate the historical picture. Others are
not. They may become richer and more complex by absorbing complicating information, but they need not entirely lose their ability to
persuade. What they will probably become, however, is more clearly
about norms and political visions than purely about historical facts
and descriptions. They will be more clearly revealed as arguments to
adopt certain norms because this is the best way of carrying on American political traditions that are *properly* honored and understood.

A successful argument from ethos, tradition, and honored authority can withstand the introduction of complication and complexity
and still be persuasive to its audience. But what makes the argument
persuasive is that the audience believes that it correctly captures the

country's shared values and commitments—what the country *should* stand for rather than what particular people have actually done in the past. The argument remains persuasive because the historical complications do not undermine the audience's judgment about what the country's true traditions are. Despite the contrary evidence and counterexamples, the lessons of the past continue to shine through.

For example, Justice Brandeis's argument about civic courage is likely to remain persuasive because most Americans today broadly agree with protecting the value of freedom of speech, even for unpopular views. So it does not matter that the founders were quite inconsistent in their views about freedom of speech and protected far less speech than Americans would today.

But suppose we made the same argument about the American free speech tradition in the context of a more specific dispute—for example, whether the law should offer very strong constitutional protection for defamation of celebrities and other public figures. Then consensus might quickly evaporate. People who oppose strong First Amendment protections for defamation might point out that the founders themselves had different practices. Justice Thomas, for example, has recently criticized the highly protective actual malice standard of *New York Times v. Sullivan*, which, he asserts, flies in the face of the founders' practices.[62] Similarly, in *Dobbs v. Jackson Woman's Health Organization*, Justice Alito argued that there was a tradition of abortion prohibition dating back to the thirteenth century. Critics responded that Alito wrongly dismissed the historical protection of abortion before quickening (roughly five or six months into the pregnancy) and half a century of modern protection.[63]

These examples point to a more general problem with stylized accounts of history used to generate clear normative lessons for law. Such arguments succeed to the extent that, even after acknowledging the complications and counternarratives, the normative lesson of history remains persuasive. But this begs the question: persuasive to whom? People with different normative values will differ about what features of history are irrelevant, exceptional, or inconsequential to the argument and about whether factual complications explode it. Moreover, if people do not accept that the tradition expresses their values, they may refuse to accept that the law should enforce it. Hence, people with different values and experiences may feel quite differently about whether an argument from tradition succeeds and whether historical complications and counterexamples undermine it.

This does not show that these arguments are worthless. Rather, it shows that arguments about ethos, tradition, and honored authority are always as much about present-day values as they are about history. As with many other historical arguments we will encounter in this book, people use competing constructions of the past to argue about what the country's values are and should be in the present.

PART II

Originalism and Living Constitutionalism

CHAPTER FIVE
Twins Separated at Birth

A. Introduction

During an oral argument before the United States Supreme Court in 2010, Justice Samuel Alito poked fun at his usual ideological ally, Justice Antonin Scalia. The issue before the Court was whether violent video games were protected by the First Amendment's guarantee of freedom of speech. "I think what Justice Scalia wants to know," Alito deadpanned, "is what James Madison thought about video games. Did he enjoy them?" Scalia, who did not seem to find this at all funny, growled in response, "No, I want to know what James Madison thought about violence. Was there any indication that anybody thought, when the First Amendment was adopted, that there—there was an exception to it for—for speech regarding violence? Anybody?"[1]

This exchange symbolizes one of the most distinctive features of American constitutional culture: its fascination with (and debates over) originalism in constitutional interpretation. The term "originalism" refers to a family of theories and rhetorical approaches. What they have in common is the idea that people should interpret the U.S. Constitution according to the meanings, purposes, intentions, or understandings of those who framed or adopted the Constitution or who lived at the time of its framing and adoption. (For convenience, I will sometimes use the phrase "founders, framers, or adopters.")

57

One must offer all of these alternative formulations because, among American legal academics at least, the theory of "originalism" has split into multiple competing versions.[2] Among the general public, however, the idea of originalism is captured by the deceptively simple notion that judges should interpret the Constitution according to "what the framers wanted." In popular discourse, this advice is primarily directed at judges, who, it is feared, are repeatedly tempted to stray from the framers' vision and substitute their personal political predilections for the country's basic law.

Most Americans know comparatively little about what the framers and adopters actually wanted or sought to achieve in creating the Constitution. Even seemingly noncontroversial statements phrased at an abstract level, such as "the founders believed in limited government," may turn out to be seriously misleading.[3] On some issues, there was no consensus among the adopters, and in still other cases—due to significant changes in technology and society—the adopters could not have had any intent at all. This was the premise of Alito's little joke at Scalia's expense. Finally, some of the most important features of American constitutionalism were put in place after the Civil War during Reconstruction, but the Reconstruction framers and adopters are almost unknown to most Americans and are rarely invoked. (The notable exception is Abraham Lincoln, who pressed for adoption of the Thirteenth Amendment but was assassinated before it was ratified by the states.)

Nevertheless, the idea of fidelity to the founders and a desire to follow their example and their wisdom—even when wholly imagined—is a powerful trope in American constitutional argument, although not in most other constitutional democracies.

In this chapter and the next, I will explain why Americans are attracted to originalism—and also to its opposite, the idea of a living Constitution. People often think of these two approaches to constitutional interpretation as irrevocably opposed. But in fact they are just two sides of a single coin. Americans have embraced them because they offer complementary stories about how to negotiate an ever-changing present with a centuries-old Constitution.

Although originalism presents itself as a theory of how judges should decide cases, originalism appears most prominently in legal and political rhetoric *outside* of courts. So we should distinguish the

practice of originalist argument in the courts (call it "judicial originalism") from originalist theorizing and argument in the legal academy ("academic originalism") and the frequent rhetorical use of
originalist tropes in American politics and popular culture ("popular
originalism").

Although legal academics, lawyers, and judges mutually influence each other, there is a significant gap between academic originalism and the way that lawyers and judges actually make originalist
arguments in the United States. Generally speaking, originalist academics treat originalist practice as an imperfect copy of what theory
requires; they may even argue that we cannot fully assess the merits
of originalism because it has never actually been put into place sys-
tematically.[4] In this book, however, I treat the actual practices of
originalist argument (judicial originalism) as telling us something
important about how originalist argument actually works in American legal culture and, in particular, about how people use history in
constitutional interpretation.

Academic justifications of originalism often rest on claims about
the philosophy of language, democratic legitimacy, or the rule of law.
These theories, which are often quite complex, may be important to
academics, but they do not explain originalism's larger appeal in the
United States. Nor do these theories explain why originalism has
failed to become the dominant approach to constitutional interpretation in democracies around the world or even for the constitutions
of the fifty states, since, presumably, the philosophy of language, democracy, and the rule of law apply there as well. To understand the
attractions of originalism in the United States, one must stop thinking of it primarily as a theory of interpretation and start thinking
about it as a cultural narrative. Cultural memory, not philosophical
theory, is the best explanation for Americans' attraction to originalism in politics and law.

Accordingly, in this chapter and the next one, I discuss originalism and its opposite number, living constitutionalism, as cultural and
political phenomena, rather than offering normative criticisms. Later
in this book, I will say more about the pros and cons of originalism
and living constitutionalism as interpretive approaches. In this chapter and the next, however, I consider their relationship culturally
and sociologically. The same historical forces produced both origi-

nalism and living constitutionalism in twentieth-century American culture, and so the two approaches are, in fact, twins separated at birth.

B. Thirty-One Flavors of Originalism

Originalist theories of interpretation generally hold that constitutional interpretation should be based on something that is fixed at the time of adoption of the Constitution or an amendment to the Constitution.[5] Different originalists have different views of what is fixed at the time of adoption or amendment. It might be (1) the original intentions of the framers of the Constitution, (2) the original understandings of those who ratified the Constitution in the various states, or (3) the original public meaning of the Constitution's text to a suitably informed (or idealized) individual living at the time of adoption. These different criteria produce, respectively, original intention originalism, original understanding originalism, and original public meaning originalism. Original public meaning originalism is probably the dominant view among academics these days, but it, too, has many different versions.

You might think that original public meaning originalism would focus primarily on what ordinary individuals—most of whom were not lawyers—understood the Constitution's words and phrases to mean.[6] But many conservative originalists—who are also lawyers— identify original *public meaning* originalism with what is actually original *legal meaning* originalism. That is, they try to figure out how lawyers, viewing the Constitution as a legal text, would have construed it at the time of adoption, and they equate this with the original meaning to the public.[7]

Equating public meaning with legal meaning allows originalist lawyers to focus on what lawyers like to focus on most—legal materials. Accordingly, they attempt to derive original public meaning from adoption-era debates over the Constitution and its amendments, old judicial precedents and statutes, histories of which activities were regulated or criminalized prior to adoption and which were not regulated or criminalized, contemporaneous state constitutions, the history of British constitutional law before the founding, treatises like Blackstone's *Commentaries*, and the writings of founding-era legal and political elites. Originalist lawyers may also include structural arguments in their accounts of original public meaning.[8] As a result, the term "original public meaning" often stands for a broad range of legal sources, many of which most members of the actual public would know little to nothing about. I call this general approach to original meaning a "thick" account of original meaning. I contrast it to my "thin" account of original meaning defended later in this book.

Some legal originalists have turned to corpus linguistics—surveys of founding-era texts—to try to figure out how the public used particular words and phrases in the Constitution.[9] Lawyers with a thick account of original meaning may sometimes look to these studies as well. Corpus linguistics tries to derive linguistic *meaning* from frequency of historical *use*, looking at documents that may have little to do with constitutions or constitution-making, much less the political or regulatory contexts that might arise in the future. The frequency of use in diverse texts, however, may not reflect the particular use in a constitutional provision.[10] What people mean by their words, moreover, outstrips how people have used them in the past, because people must be able to employ them and combine them in ever new contexts and situations. For these reasons, the historical frequency of the use of words in the English language can only be evidence of original public meaning, rather than conclusive.

After the Supreme Court held that the Second Amendment right to "keep and bear arms" applied to general self-defense and not merely to military uses of weapons, a group of linguists, legal scholars, and historians used corpus linguistics to decide whether the phrase was in fact limited to military uses, producing a series of conflicting answers.[11] Corpus linguistics does not put an end to disputes about original public meaning; it simply adds grist to the mill of constitutional debate.

Original *law* originalism, recently championed by William Baude and Stephen Sachs, is less textually focused than most other conservative originalisms. For Baude and Sachs, originalism simply means following the law and the interpretive methods in place at the time of the Constitution's ratification, as modified by any legitimate changes in legal doctrine and legal interpretive methods since then.[12] This includes whatever rules courts have legitimately adopted from the founding to the present day that instruct them when they should continue to adhere to otherwise nonoriginalist or mistaken precedent.[13] Essentially, their approach is captured by the slogan: the founders' law, as lawfully changed.[14] Baude and Sachs are less interested in the fixed meanings of words than in the state of the law at the founding.[15] So if legal doctrine legitimately evolved through common-law reasoning, the results may be consistent with their version of originalism even if they are not consistent with some other versions of original meaning originalism.[16]

My own theory of constitutional interpretation, living originalism or framework originalism, also differs from most conservative versions. It has a thin account of original public meaning, and it is compatible with living constitutionalism. I discuss it in chapters 7 and 8.

As you can see from this brief survey, academic originalism is a mansion with many rooms, and its adherents can find ever new ways to argue with each other about which is the best approach. Practicing lawyers and judges who embrace originalism, meanwhile, do not trouble themselves too much with these theoretical disputes, and politicians and the members of the public do not trouble themselves at all.

C. Originalist Arguments versus Originalist Theories of Interpretation

All American lawyers draw from the same basic styles of argument—the modalities. Originalists and nonoriginalists can exist in the same legal culture because both use the same basic kinds of arguments but simply accord them different weight and importance. Originalists make lots of legal arguments that are not based in original meaning—for example, doctrinal arguments, consequentialist arguments, and arguments from tradition and practice. Conversely, nonoriginalists often make arguments from original meaning, original purpose, original intention, and original understanding, without thereby becoming converts to originalism.

Thus, it is very important to distinguish the originalist *arguments* that people make from originalism as a *comprehensive theory of interpretation* that tells you the only correct way to interpret the Constitution.

Regardless of people's commitments to particular constitutional theories, people use all of the modalities of legal argument when they want to persuade others. Accordingly, almost everybody makes arguments from original intention, original meaning, original purpose, or original understanding from time to time, whether they are devoted to originalism or fervently opposed to it. Lawyers, judges, and legal academics will quote *The Federalist*, Madison's notes of the Philadelphia Convention, statements by members of the founding generation, and legal materials and legal understandings contemporaneous with the founding and Reconstruction. That is because these are part of the standard topics of legal argument in American constitutional culture.

Invoking the wisdom of the founders, digging up the history of habeas corpus in England, quoting Blackstone's *Commentaries*, or reminding people of what Washington did or Hamilton said or Madison wrote does not make you an originalist. It does not mean that you think that originalism is the only legitimate theory of constitutional interpretation or even the best theory. It just means that you think, in a particular context, that this kind of argument will be most plausible or convincing to your intended audience.

For example, when lawyers face legal issues for which there are very few precedents—for example, presidential impeachment—they will immediately turn to originalist styles of argument.[17] That is because lawyers latch on to whatever sources of argument are available to them. And when the Supreme Court creates doctrinal tests that look to how things were at the founding, lawyers naturally follow suit and produce this evidence.[18] But the fact that lawyers sometimes make originalist arguments does not mean that they accept that originalist analyses are the only or the best way to do constitutional interpretation. Appeals to founders, framers, and adopters are just tools in their rhetorical arsenal.

Conversely, self-styled originalist lawyers and judges make many different kinds of legal arguments that are not at all originalist. That is because most legal arguments in American courts are doctrinal. They reason from the authority of previous precedents, not from the authority of the framers or founders. That is especially the case in federal trial and intermediate appellate courts, because these courts must apply the law of higher courts.[19]

Lawyers and judges will tend to rely most on originalist arguments in three situations.

The first situation is when there are relatively few precedents on point; presidential impeachment is an example. Where judicial precedents are plentiful, originalist arguments rarely dominate judicial analysis; they are mostly added as spice or seasoning. A judicial opinion may throw in a quote from *The Federalist* or a letter from a famous framer, but it will probably decide the case on other grounds.

The second situation is when judge-made doctrines specify that one must use a historical test that looks to founding-era practice. That is what the Supreme Court does, for example, in interpreting the Seventh Amendment right of trial by jury in the federal courts.[20]

The third and most interesting context in which lawyers and judges make originalist arguments is when they want to discard existing bodies of precedent and go off in a new direction. The best way to displace existing authority is to gesture to an even older and more honored authority. That is why the turn to originalism is often part of a law reform project. American movement conservatives, for example, have sought to attack liberal precedents and move the law in their preferred direction. Originalism comes in very handy in these situations.

Although today people mostly associate originalism with conservatives, at different points in history, both liberals and conservatives have used the framers, founders, and adopters to critique the status quo.[21] Whatever one's politics, originalism can be a useful rhetorical stance for would-be legal revolutionaries. And that is one reason why originalism is so attractive to American lawyers, judges, and politicians.

Not all reform projects view the founders as positive examples, of course. When people criticize the founders, for example, by denouncing them as slave owners or as complicit with slavery, they are not engaged in originalist argument, even though they are talking about the founding. The famous 1619 Project that emphasizes the role of slavery and racism in the country's origins is not engaged in originalist rhetoric, even though it is very much about the founders.

It is a *critical* use of history; we might even call it *antioriginalist* argument. And there is a long history of rhetoric critical of the founders that exists alongside the dominant strains of founder reverence in American political culture.[22]

Yet despite the moral failings of the founders—detailed at length by historians—movements for political reform and revolution in the United States have often turned to originalist rhetoric. American politicians regularly refer to the values of the founders and framers; so too do social and political movements like the first wave of American feminism in the nineteenth century and Tea Party conservatives in the 2010s.[23] Politicians, political activists, and media pundits quote the framers and founders frequently, sometimes with an almost religious zeal. Some conservative Christians, in fact, have argued that the Constitution, like the Bible itself, is divinely inspired.[24]

Political originalism is primarily an appeal to national ethos and to an imagined tradition. Often it does not seriously engage with the historical record, which may be quite complicated and equivocal and in some cases not particularly flattering. Popular originalism is a way of attacking the (imagined) status quo, pressing for reform, or reacting to undesirable change; it is a mood rather than an enforceable dogma, much less a coherent theory of judicial practice.

Above all, it is important to keep in mind the distinction between individual uses of originalist argument—that is, arguments that employ adoption history as one source among many for persuading audiences—and a general commitment to originalism as a theory of constitutional interpretation. You can find arguments about original purpose or original intention from the earliest years of the American republic. But originalism as a comprehensive theory of interpretation—that is, a general theory about the correct way to do constitutional interpretation—is a rather late development. It is a product of the twentieth century, for reasons I shall explain shortly.

D. Originalism's Twin: Living Constitutionalism

The position usually opposed to originalism is living constitutionalism. What is the idea of a living Constitution? Again, like originalism, there are many different versions. Essentially, living constitutionalism is the view that we must interpret the Constitution in accordance with changing times and circumstances.[25] As the nation grows and changes, so too does the practical meaning of the Constitution, even if its text does not change. As new events overtake older ones and as people's values evolve in response, one must interpret the Constitution to take these changes into account. The metaphor of a "living" constitution suggests an organic process of evolution and adaptation to a changing environment. It invokes the familiar idea that life involves change and therefore requires adaptation to change.[26]

Much of what I have just said about originalism also applies to living constitutionalism as well. One can find arguments that the Constitution must be interpreted flexibly, or that it must adapt to changing times and circumstances, in politics, in popular culture, in judicial opinions, and in academic theories of interpretation. Lawyers and judges invoke the idea of a Constitution that changes with the times to justify changes in legal doctrine.[27] And people in political movements often make connections between a living Constitution and their arguments for political and social reform.

As with originalism, there are many different academic theories that presuppose some form of a living Constitution.[28] In fact, living constitutionalism is not, strictly speaking, an interpretive theory at all—instead, it is a basic assumption that underlies many different constitutional theories.

As with originalism, it is also important to distinguish individual uses of arguments for constitutional adaptation from a commitment to living constitutionalism as a general approach. One can find arguments that resemble living constitutionalism throughout American history. To be sure, the founding era, influenced by Newton rather than Darwin, was attracted to mechanical rather than biological metaphors.[29] So people in the founding era would not have spoken of the Constitution evolving as people do today. Instead, like John Marshall, people in the early republic would have borrowed familiar ideas about the British constitution—that it was meant to be flexible and adaptable and therefore enduring and timeless.[30] The use of biological metaphors to describe the Constitution and the self-conscious invocation of a living Constitution as the proper approach to interpretation is also, like originalism, a product of the twentieth century.[31]

Originalism and living constitutionalism take opposing views about change. One theory is about what does not and must not change.

The other theory is about what does and must change. As a result, most people think that originalism and living constitutionalism are irreconcilable opposites. But these two positions have more in common than their adherents would like to admit. What some achieve through originalist rhetoric and demands for a return to origins others achieve through the rhetoric of adaptation, and vice versa.

Movement conservatives use originalist rhetoric to justify change and reform in American institutions. In this way, originalism performs the same function that the rhetoric of living constitutionalism performs for progressives and liberals. Conversely, living constitutionalism meshes well with liberals' and progressives' standard story about the meaning and purpose of America, the source of its values, and its proper direction for the future. In this way, living constitutionalism performs the same function for progressives that originalism and calls for fidelity to the founders perform for conservatives. And given this symmetry, it should not be surprising that Americans employ *both* rhetorical styles at different times and in different contexts.

The fact that these two approaches are so similar in so many ways is not an accident. They really are twins separated at birth— the birth of modern constitutionalism, that is.

E. Originalism, Living Constitutionalism, and Constitutional Modernity

To see why originalism and living constitutionalism have so much in common, we must understand them as cultural narratives. The two approaches represent two aspects of a single phenomenon: how Americans deal with the problem of constant change in the context of an ancient constitution.

Americans live under a very old constitution. Around the world, written constitutions last for a median age of approximately nineteen years; by that point, half of them have been replaced by a new constitution.[32] The U.S. Constitution is an outlier; it dates back to the 1780s.

A very old constitution has benefits but also disadvantages. Its benefits are the degree of reverence that it is likely to generate over time.[33] Because one of the most important purposes of a constitution is to foster a stable politics, creating incentives for people to work for political change within the constitutional order can often be a very good thing, at least if the constitution is not too inflexible.

And it turns out that the American Constitution is quite flexible, although people sometimes like to pretend otherwise. It is true that there are hard-wired parts of the Constitution that cannot easily be changed through interpretation. And at different times, these hard-wired features can make the system unwieldy and antidemocratic.[34] Nevertheless, the adaptability of the constitutional system has encouraged Americans—for the most part—to domesticate their repeated impulses for revolutionary political change and to work them out peacefully within the confines of their ancient constitution. The major exception, of course, is the constitutional failure that led to the American Civil War, which was followed by new constitutional amendments and a constitutional reconstruction.

As I write these words, America's ancient constitution is undergoing yet another test of its durability: the United States is undergoing political strains as severe as those faced during the years before the Civil War. I have argued that the American political system is suffering from an advanced case of "constitutional rot," and what the future holds for our experiment in democracy is quite uncertain.[35] The country may become increasingly less democratic, or pent-up public frustration may lead to a rebirth of constitutional innovation, as there was during the early twentieth century.[36] Reforming our political institutions is crucial to our democracy's long-term survival, but that is a topic for another book.[37]

Americans have constructed a modern state—which does all of the things that modern states do—atop their ancient constitution. For the most part, this was necessary and perhaps even inevitable. But eventually it produced a crisis of modernity. By a crisis of modernity, I mean the recognition that one is losing—or has already lost—crucial connections to the stabilizing and legitimating authority of the past and the institutions and traditions of the past. Modernity is the sense that these forms of authority are outdated, are slipping away, or can no longer perform their customary function. Such crises, of course, are not only features of relatively recent times; they have occurred repeatedly throughout human history.[38]

The 1787 Constitution was designed for a different world and a different country than the American democracy of the twentieth century. It was not designed to accommodate a global superpower that was also a modern regulatory and welfare state. During the twentieth century, people repeatedly recognized that the world that produced the old constitution was long gone and that they were living in a different age.

There are two standard responses to this sense of modernity and loss of organic connection to the past, in culture and in politics. The first response is to accept that we are modern and embrace our separation from the past and from tradition. We deliberately reject the past, exaggerate our distance from it, and define ourselves against it. The second response is precisely the opposite. We deny that we are separated, or we attempt to prevent any further separation. We cleave to the past and attempt to regain it. To the extent that the past seems lost to us, or its loss is threatened, we cling to its concrete manifestations, practices, and rituals, and we pledge faith in them and through them.[39] That is why fundamentalism is a recurrent feature of modernity and crises of modernity. People often think of fundamentalisms as the very opposite of modernity, but this is an illusion, viewed from the perspective of people who have adopted the first response. Modernity is the sense of separation from the past, and fundamentalism is one possible—and frequent—response to this separation.

The American federal government was thoroughly transformed during the twentieth century. It became strong and powerful, and it seemed increasingly loosened from its moorings in the eighteenth century. With the New Deal and the creation of the national security state, it was no longer possible to pretend that the Constitution-in-practice bore much resemblance to the Constitution of 1787 or even the post–Civil War Constitution of 1868.

This recognition creates a crisis of *constitutional modernity*. Like other crises of modernity, this recognition produces two equal and opposite reactions. Both of them feature in American constitutional culture and in the views of American liberals and conservatives alike.

One reaction is the embrace of a living Constitution. The idea of a living Constitution argues that the Constitution must adapt to changing times. It is a version of the first response to modernity. We must accept change, even if this means abandoning the values and assumptions of the past. The framers' world is not our world, and we cannot return to it. The other reaction is originalism. It is a version of the second response to modernity. We have lost—or are in danger of losing—our connection to the Constitution that sustains us. Therefore, we must regain the past. We must pledge faith in the wisdom of the framers and the laws they bequeathed to us. We must return to the place from which we strayed and restore the Constitution that has been lost.[40]

These reactions to constitutional modernity describe two basic features of American constitutionalism today. They are cultural as much as they are political or legal. Americans have repeatedly employed these cultural approaches to deal with constitutional change, especially since the beginning of the twentieth century. Perhaps equally important, these approaches do not map neatly onto political liberalism versus political conservatism. *Both* liberals and conservatives have used these tropes—the need to adapt to a changed world and the need to return to the wisdom of the framers—at different times with respect to different subject matters.

F. Cafeteria Originalism

Americans like to talk a lot about the wisdom of their framers and of the founding generation generally. But this does not mean Americans accept the thicker versions of originalism that I described earlier. Most Americans do not actually believe that we should always adhere to the original understandings of the adopting generation or apply the Constitution in the same way that founding-era lawyers would. They do not want to strip married women of their rights, enforce the free speech doctrines of the 1780s, or outlaw a host of popular federal government programs. And it goes without saying that most Americans—including most American lawyers and judges— do not bother themselves much with the many different varieties of academic originalism or the complicated and convoluted disputes among academic originalists.

American lawyers and judges, even self-described originalist ones, do not consistently apply originalism. Instead, American lawyers and judges invoke the framers and adopters selectively, often describing their views and principles at varying levels of generality so that they cohere with most of current practice but also justify legal reform. In other words, understood as a rhetorical practice of lawyers and judges, originalism is a far more flexible and pragmatic phenomenon than originalism understood as an exclusive theory of legitimate constitutional interpretation. To understand why Americans engage in originalist rhetoric, we must understand originalism as a set of cultural practices of justification in politics and in law as well as an academic theory of correct legal interpretation. Originalist rhetoric is a distinctively American way of invoking cultural memory and arguing about the nation's political and legal traditions.

Although Americans often have idealized conceptions of their framers, they are also very pragmatic. To the extent that people can identify the framers' values (as they imagine them) with their own values, they endorse the framers' views, and they insist that their fellow citizens should do likewise. But to the extent that they find the framers' values unjust or irrelevant to their lives, they simply ignore the framers, or, equally likely, they reinterpret or recharacterize what the framers said and did so that they can identify with it. This should hardly be surprising. It is what every tradition does with the hallowed symbols of its past.

Thus, American lawyers and judges do not feel obligated to consult or follow the views of the founders, framers, or adopters in every case. And when lawyers and judges do invoke the founders, framers, or adopters, they do not treat their views as binding when there are more pressing considerations. Thus, in practice, American originalism is not really an exclusive theory of interpretation, no matter what particular academic theories might suggest or American politicians might claim.

We might make an analogy to American religious practice. American Catholics are sometimes called "cafeteria Catholics" because they pick and choose which parts of the Church's teachings to accept and under what conditions. Many American Catholics, for example, disregard the Church's admonitions against contraception and divorce. In the same way, although American culture is saturated with references to the founding and the wisdom of the framers, Americans are essentially "cafeteria originalists." They pick and choose when to follow the views of the founders, framers, or adopters (as they understand them) and often artfully recharacterize these principles to support contemporary political and legal arguments.

The same point applies even to self-consciously originalist lawyers and judges. Although they may be committed to originalism as a method of interpretation, they do not, in practice, treat it as an exclusive method for analyzing constitutional questions. When originalism proves useful to articulating their views about the best reading of the law, they make originalist arguments. But when originalism is not useful—which is true of a wide range of different areas of constitutional law—originalist sources and arguments are quietly shelved, and the debate focuses on other kinds of legal arguments, for example, precedent, tradition, and consequences.[41]

At the same time, people often see in history what they want to see, and because people may begin with the assumption that the historical materials, rightly construed, are on their side, it is often possible for clever lawyers to come up with originalist arguments for a wide range of contemporary views and positions. And these days, there are enough agile lawyers to ensure a steady supply of originalist arguments for almost every contemporary controversy. To be sure, academic theories will not always allow this degree of flexibility. But in litigation, lawyers and judges do not always commit themselves to the strictures of particular academic theories. Instead, they make the kinds of originalist arguments that they believe will be most useful to their cause and most persuasive to their audiences.

Obviously, this flexibility is useful for accommodating existing political and legal practices. But it is more important for another reason. Strange as it may seem, one of the most important uses of originalist rhetoric in the United States is not to *preserve* existing traditions but to *transform* them. Americans regularly invoke the memory of the founders and their principles to justify political and constitutional reform. That is why they use the founders to criticize contemporary politicians and especially contemporary judges. Americans employ originalism as a political practice for critiquing the status quo (whether in a liberal or conservative direction) and arguing for change. In order to do this, however, one must be able to invoke the founders, framers, and adopters on only some subjects but not others. And one must be able to read their insights selectively, abstractly, and creatively, so that they appear directly relevant to contemporary political and social contexts that few of the founders, framers, and adopters could have imagined.

What is interesting about American constitutional culture, then, is not that it is thoroughly and uncompromisingly originalist. It is not. Americans are as pragmatic about their originalism as they are about almost everything else. What is interesting is that American constitutional culture takes originalist arguments seriously in a way that most other constitutional cultures rarely do.

G. Originalism and National Political Identity

State courts, like federal courts, often make originalist arguments.[42] Because appeals to purpose (and intention) are a standard modality of legal argument, lawyers often make arguments about the original purpose, intention, or understanding of a state constitutional provision. That is especially true when state court judges construe recent amendments to state constitutions, which are far more frequent than amendments to the federal constitution. Yet state courts will often interpret state constitutional provisions in the same way as the corresponding provisions of the U.S. Constitution, regardless of the history that led to the adoption of the state provision.[43] So state judges, just like federal judges, use originalism opportunistically. Like all Americans, they are cafeteria originalists. However, because originalism has become the basic interpretive stance of the conservative movement, conservative state judges with connections to the Federalist Society have started to apply originalist methods to state constitutions more frequently.[44]

In any case, you will rarely see the framers of *state* constitutions treated with the same respect as the framers of the American Constitution. Nor do politicians or social movements routinely invoke the founders of individual states as justification for their positions. Unlike the federal Constitution, which was originally drafted in 1787, the fifty state constitutions have a variety of different ages, and most states have had multiple constitutions. Moreover, unlike the federal Constitution, most of these state constitutions, regardless of their age, are constantly being amended, sometimes by the legislature, and sometimes by the public through propositions, initiatives, and referenda.[45]

State courts are especially likely to engage in forms of "living constitutionalism," interpreting their constitutions according to evolving contemporary mores.[46] That is because state courts are often the initial venues for promoting legal theories that are later introduced in the federal courts—involving such diverse issues as race relations, sex equality, property rights, gun rights, and positive rights of education and housing.[47] The litigation campaign to secure equality of marriage rights for gays and lesbians is only the most recent example.[48] This is not surprising, given how constitutional development operates in the United States. Political mobilizations (and countermobilizations) often turn to local venues—city councils, state legislatures, and state courts—to win converts for their novel constitutional claims. As they succeed in state and local jurisdictions, they attempt to extend their influence nationally, through litigation in the federal courts and through pushing for new legislation and new administrative regulations. Originalist argument is not always useful in this process, and sometimes it is almost entirely beside the point.

These features of state constitutional practice tell us a great deal about originalism as a cultural phenomenon. They suggest that originalism is primarily a feature about the interpretation of the *national* constitution and that reverence for the views of the founders is an aspect of national culture and national political identity. Americans are attracted to originalism not because democracy and the rule of law compel it, but because originalism is a political practice that draws on cultural memories about America as a nation. This is especially so when the issue is federalism. Disputes about state prerogatives and limits on federal power are debates about the nature of the national Constitution and about the nature of the American nation; hence, it is not surprising that originalist rhetoric frequently appears in such debates. American originalism, in short, is a product of the construction of American *national* identity and a feature of *national* constitutional culture.

H. Originalism Outside the United States

Given what I have just said, it should come as no surprise that originalism, as a general or comprehensive theory of interpretation, is not widely adopted outside of the United States. There is a textualist version of originalism occasionally used in Australia, but originalism as a general—much less an exclusive—theory of interpretation has not taken hold in very many other places.[49] By contrast, you will sometimes find originalist *arguments*—that is, arguments that refer to the purposes or values of the founders of a country or the framers of a constitution—in courts outside the United States. Yvonne Tew has identified examples of originalist arguments in Malaysia and Singapore.[50]

It is likely that we can find many more examples around the world, because appeals to purpose, intention, political tradition, and honored authority are very familiar kinds of arguments both in law and in politics. After all, nonoriginalists in the United States make originalist arguments all the time. But, as I have explained before, the occasional use of originalist arguments is not the same thing as adopting originalism as a general theory of interpretation.

Defenders of originalism sometimes argue that originalism is required by democracy, the rule of law, the nature of interpretation, or constitutional fidelity. If that were so, we would expect to see originalism as the dominant practice of constitutional interpretation around the world, which it is not. (Similarly, we would expect to see originalism as the dominant practice in the interpretation of the fifty American state constitutions, which, as I have just noted, is also not the case.)[51] On the other hand, if arguments from purpose or intention are standard *topics* or *modalities* of legal argument, we would expect to see them used on occasion in the fifty states and in other countries, which we do.

The most widespread approach to constitutional interpretation in constitutional courts in contemporary democracies is proportionality review, which is decidedly not an inquiry into original meanings, intentions, or understandings.[52] Similarly, Kim Scheppele explains that although purposive interpretation is common in "advanced constitutional systems," constitutional courts do not generally inquire into original meanings or original intentions.[53] "In Europe," Michel Rosenfeld tells us, "recourse to originalism is virtually nonexistent," and "even implicit references to originalism in substance are quite rare."[54] And Canada, the country perhaps most similar to the United

States culturally, nevertheless has a very different *constitutional* culture.[55] Canada's constitutional culture is perhaps most famous for developing the doctrine of the constitution as a "living tree."[56]

"Originalism," Peter Hogg assures us, "has never enjoyed any significant support in Canada."[57] That is not quite true. There has been a growing interest in originalist theory among Canadian academics and judges.[58] It is not hard to see why. American culture is very influential around the world—especially in Canada—and that includes American political and legal culture. Therefore, it is hardly surprising that, over time, lawyers, judges, and law professors in other countries will draw from interpretive debates in the United States and even import elements of American originalism into their legal cultures.[59]

Because legal cultures differ, however, lawyers, judges, and legal academics in other countries will probably use originalist ideas in ways that are importantly different from the ways that Americans use them. Moreover, some kinds of originalism will probably prove more useful than others. For example, there is nothing particularly difficult about occasionally making arguments about the purposes or goals of the drafters or adopters of a country's constitution, or about the values of those who founded the country. And my own version of living originalism is fairly easy to adapt to other countries with a written constitution. By contrast, it is somewhat harder to employ the thicker versions of originalism associated with the modern conservative movement, at least as a general or comprehensive approach.

Since most judges in other countries are not originalists in the American sense, we cannot assume that a thick conception of originalism is necessary to protect the rule of law or democracy, or somehow follows ineluctably from the very fact of a written constitution. It is quite possible to have the rule of law, democracy, and a written constitution without subscribing to originalism. Not only is it possible; it is the usual situation around the world. The reason why Americans are especially attracted to originalism lies elsewhere; I take up that question in chapter 6.

CHAPTER SIX

Why Are Americans Originalist?

S O F A R I H A V E argued that American originalism cannot be
explained by the nature of language, by respect for democracy, or by the requirements of the rule of law, because many
other democracies that have written constitutions and respect the rule of law are not originalist. Instead, I have suggested
that American originalism has more to do with features of American
political culture and American cultural memory. In this chapter, I
consider why originalism took hold in the United States but not in
most other Western constitutional democracies.

My argument will proceed in two steps. First, I will explain why
the Constitution and its framers have become such a powerful feature of national identity. Second, given these features of American
culture, I will explain why a particular approach to constitutional
interpretation, originalism, arose in a particular period in history, the
twentieth century. As noted in chapter 5, this same period also produces living constitutionalism, and for related reasons.

The culture of a nation affects how its people argue about its
laws.[1] So it is hardly surprising that American society and culture
have had powerful effects on American jurisprudence.

For example, in most countries, the framers of the current constitution are not especially revered by the general public. But they
are revered in the United States. The reason, I think, concerns the

story that Americans tell about their creation as a distinct nation and people. This national narrative helps explain the special power that the Constitution's framers hold over the political imagination of Americans.

In fact, Americans' attraction to originalism is overdetermined. Here is a list of historical and cultural factors, which, taken together, have helped generate Americans' attraction to originalism:

(1) America's revolutionary tradition;

(2) the long dominance of a Protestant religious tradition, with its emphasis on close reading of scriptural texts and redemptive calls for a return to origins;

(3) the emergence of the American state, nation, and people (at least in the popular imagination) roughly contemporaneous with the creation of the American Constitution;

(4) the fact that the Constitution is strongly identified with American nationhood and peoplehood;

(5) a long tradition of reverence for the Constitution and the Declaration of Independence as foundational scriptures in the American civic religion; and

(6) Americans' special veneration of the founding generation and particular figures within that generation (like George Washington and James Madison) as culture heroes.

A. The Revolutionary Story: Born in the USA

In American cultural memory, the revolutionary founders of the American nation and the framers of the American Constitution are conflated as "the Founding Fathers," the "founders," or the "framers." Americans share an origin story about how they came to be Americans. This cultural memory deeply affects American legal and political discourse.

According to this story, the American state (the United States of America), the American nation (America), the American people ("We the People of the United States"), and the American Constitution (whose preamble begins with that famous phrase) were born virtually at the same time. America was created through an act of political revolution. Equally important, this revolutionary act was a *self-creation*, in which Americans acted as the midwife to their own birth. Through political revolution, the American people brought themselves into being as Americans and created a state and a Constitution under which they still live.

The American political mythology is one of self-birth (autochthony); yet Americans, as a settler nation, were clearly *not* the indigenous inhabitants of the land that came to be called America. They may claim to have made themselves, but they did not spring from American soil. In fact, the very presence of indigenous peoples and a forcibly imported slave population may have led Americans reactively to overemphasize how much they created themselves and their nation out of a wilderness.[2]

The story of American origins ties the creation of American national and political identity closely to the creation of the American Constitution. The fate of America is linked to the fate of its Constitution, and vice versa. The members of the revolutionary generation and the framers and adopters of the American Constitution (who are not always the same people) become the veritable symbols of American identity, American statesmanship, and American values. Particular individuals in the story—George Washington, Benjamin Franklin, Alexander Hamilton, Thomas Jefferson, James Madison, and John Adams—stand metonymically for the entire generation that produced the nation and the Constitution and are especially venerated. These men—the "Big Six" founders—are among the most prominent culture heroes in American mythology. Perhaps ironically, Jefferson and Adams did not even attend the Philadelphia Convention—they were engaged in overseas diplomacy—and Hamilton was absent for long stretches of time.

The creation story that connects the creation of the Constitution to the creation of the American state, nation, and people is a fiction, omitting the presence of Native Americans and slaves, who were not originally counted as part of We the American People. It also conveniently collapses time frames. From 1776 to 1781, the American government (such as it was) was the Continental Congress. From 1781 to 1789, the country was governed by the Articles of Confederation, which proved unworkable; the failure of the Articles led to the Philadelphia Convention.

Americans' cultural memory tends to collapse these events. Most

Americans have never even heard of the Articles of Confederation; those who have probably do not regard the Articles as America's first Constitution. Instead people tend to think of the Articles as a sort of transitional document or trial run that led to the real Constitution, the Constitution of 1787.

The irony is that the Articles were anything but a transitional document. They were styled as "Articles of Confederation and perpetual Union" and were unamendable without the agreement of all the states. Article XIII provided that "the Union shall be perpetual; nor shall any alteration at any time hereafter be made in any of them; unless such alteration be agreed to in a Congress of the United States, and be afterwards confirmed by the legislatures of every State."[3]

The Philadelphia Convention, convened under the pretense of suggesting amendments to the Articles, was in fact a "runaway" convention, which eventually jettisoned the Articles completely and proposed a new Constitution that would become effective on ratification by conventions in nine states rather than the thirteen required by the Articles. It was, therefore, a revolutionary act of its own, breaking from the previous revolutionary government.

In sum, American cultural memory is the memory not only of a revolution but of political autochthony or self-birth, in which key documents—the Declaration and the Constitution—emerge with the formation of "We the People" and are bound up with its identity and political self-conception. These documents are more than merely the birth certificate of a nation and a people; in the American imagination, they become akin to scripture in an American civic religion based on this powerful myth of origin.

In his study of comparative originalism, David Fontana has suggested that originalist rhetoric is most likely to appear in countries in which a constitution is strongly identified with the creation of the nation itself. "[T]he most relevant" feature that explains whether a country's constitutional culture will embrace originalism "is whether . . . its constitution created the nation that lives under the constitution, or . . . merely reorganized the institutions of the country." Countries with "revolutionary" constitutions, Fontana explains, are more likely to have originalist cultures than countries with "reorganizational" ones.[4]

This helps explain important differences between the United States and Canada. Despite Canada's many cultural affinities to the United States, Canadian cultural memory is quite different. Canada does not have a revolutionary tradition, and Canadian nationhood and the Canadian Constitution emerged in phases, beginning with the 1867 British North America Act, which was passed by the British Parliament and not by "We the Canadian People."

Moreover, although many countries have revolutionary traditions, very few have a revolution that—in the nation's cultural memory, at least—simultaneously creates the people, nation, state, and constitution.[5] Compare the United States with France. Both countries have a revolutionary tradition—indeed, their two revolutions were roughly contemporaneous. And in both countries, the revolution is strongly tied to national self-identity and to national ideals. But there are also important differences. There was a French state before the French Revolution. There were French people before the French Revolution. There was a French nation before the French Revolution. The French Revolution did not create the French state; it did not create the French people, and it did not create the French nation. Moreover, although the French Revolution led to a constitution, it is not the constitution under which the French people now live. The ideas of state, nation, and people are distinct, both historically and logically, from the current French Constitution of the Fifth Republic.

The French do not consider their current 1958 constitution as the very essence of what it means to be French. Nor could they, given the many changes in French government since the Revolution. France has had five republics and multiple constitutions; Americans claim to have had only one republic and one Constitution, despite the previous failure of the Articles of Confederation, the constitutional breakdown of the Civil War, and the twentieth-century transformations of the New Deal and the national security state. No matter how much America changes, Americans continue to insist that they have had only one republic, one Constitution, and, as the Pledge of Allegiance explains, "one nation, under God, indivisible, with liberty and justice for all."

Before the American Revolution, there were British colonies but no American state, and no American nation. There was not even a single American people, although some American patriots devoutly wished for it.[6] The general acceptance of Americans as a single people took longer, and perhaps was not fully established until after the Civil War.

Nevertheless, according to the story that Americans tell themselves, the American Constitution, the American state, the American nation, and the American people came into being at almost the same time and are the work of a single generation. For this reason, the American nation and, indeed, the American people themselves are strongly identified with the national Constitution. Indeed, the Constitution begins with the words "We the People of the United States . . . do ordain and establish this constitution for the United States of America." Americans pronounce the Constitution as theirs by announcing themselves as the people of a nation, the United States of America. There is something magical at work in this phrase—the people and the Constitution seem to call each other into being. The Constitution symbolizes the country, and the generation that creates it stands for Americans as a whole.

Of course, this story—that the Constitution, state, nation, and people—all came into being at the same time—is a myth. But it is a powerful myth, just the same. The Articles of Confederation are the real first American Constitution. They, and not the Constitution, state that there shall be a "perpetual union" between the former colonies, which in 1776 had declared themselves to be "free and independent states." But in American cultural memory, the Articles, if they are remembered at all, play the role of a temporary measure, a stopgap, a feckless failure that led to the real constitution, the Constitution of 1787.

B. The Constitution and Culture Heroes

When Americans speak of the framers or the Founding Fathers, in fact, they tend to run together the generation that fought the Revolution with the generation that ratified the Constitution. These people overlap, but they are not quite the same.

Although the founding generation is revered collectively, not all its members receive the same degree of attention. Members of the founding generation thought to have key roles in the creation of the American nation take on a mythic status.

Take, for example, the six people who are most honored as Founding Fathers—the "Big Six": George Washington, Thomas Jefferson, James Madison, Benjamin Franklin, John Adams, and Alexander Hamilton. These people stand for the entire generation that produced the Constitution even though they were of different ages and played very different roles. Recently the National Archives began a project on the collected papers of the Founding Fathers—and not surprisingly, the papers they collected are of these six men.[7]

In American mythology, these six figures, and the founding generation considered collectively, are treated as *culture heroes*. In the study of mythology, a culture hero is a figure of legend that stands for a people's values, characteristics, and aspirations. With respect to a nation, a culture hero is a person from the past who symbolizes the nation, its ideals, hopes, values, and achievements.[8]

Culture heroes are often credited with important innovations or achievements. King Arthur stands for British unity and chivalry; the legendary Chinese emperor Fuxi is said to have invented the arts of writing, trapping, and fishing. As these examples demonstrate, culture heroes are often people of high rank or status (including kings or demigods), but they can also be pioneers or explorers (like Daniel Boone or Davy Crockett), artists (like Homer or Hesiod to the ancient Greeks), or people who symbolize extraordinary achievements (like Alexander the Great or Aeneas) or virtues (like Cincinnatus). Jeanne d'Arc, an illiterate farm girl who helped defeat the English, is a culture hero in France. Culture heroes need not be perfect in all respects—indeed, their failures and defects may themselves be topics of legend—but they are often held up within the culture as sources of wisdom and examples for emulation.

A cultural antihero, by contrast, is a person who embodies values or achievements that the culture currently rejects (but may once have accepted). Culture antiheroes also include people who make a great mistake or transgression that is important to the culture or defines the culture. Thus, the same person can be both a culture hero and an antihero; an example from Christianity is Adam and Eve, who are the progenitors of humankind but whose mistake results in humankind's fall from grace.

In America, culture heroes include the Founding Fathers as a group and, individually, key figures like the Big Six. In the nineteenth century, they include Abraham Lincoln, Frederick Douglass, and Susan B. Anthony; and in the twentieth century, Rosa Parks and Martin Luther King Jr. Like all culture heroes, their salience and prominence may wax and wane over time.

Culture antiheroes in American mythology include King George III, Chief Justice Roger Brooke Taney, and Sheriff Bull Connor. Interestingly, the Founding Fathers (and particularly Thomas Jefferson) may also play the role of antiheroes when people think of them as slaveholders or accommodators of slavery.[9]

What is interesting about the United States is that several of its most important culture heroes are also the framers of its Constitution—along with Abraham Lincoln, who symbolizes the preservation of the Union and its victory against slavery in the Civil War. Culture heroes do great things. The creation of the Constitution—which is identified with the creation of the American nation, state, and people—is, for Americans at any rate, among the greatest of achievements.

In explaining America's attractions to originalism, the country's conception of its founders as culture heroes is probably as important as its revolutionary tradition. In his study of the secularism provisions of the Turkish Constitution, Ozan Varol has suggested that "originalism blossoms when a political leader associated with the creation or revision of the nation's constitution develops a cult of personality within the nation."[10] This would explain another difference between the United States and France. Not only does the French nation predate the French Constitution(s), but the French Revolution is the central object of civic devotion, rather than particular revolutionaries like Danton or Robespierre, who are admittedly complicated figures.

Because Americans think of the same group of people as responsible for creating the American state, the American nation, and the American Constitution, the ethos of American constitutionalism, statehood, and national identity are all projected onto a single group of culture heroes—a phenomenon we might call the "ethical trifecta." It is therefore no wonder that Americans imbue the generations that produced the American Revolution and the American Constitution with enormous symbolic and ethical significance.

C. Constitutional Protestantism and the Return to Origins

A third factor in the American embrace of originalism is its cultural Protestantism.

The characteristic American response to—and justification for—constitutional change during the twentieth century has been to call for a return to origins and fundamental principles, using the culture heroes of the founding (and Abraham Lincoln, savior of the Union) as sources of quotable wisdom. In fact, this rhetorical and cultural gesture of return to origins predates the American Revolution—it emerges out of the radical Protestantism of American Puritanism.

As Sacvan Bercovitch famously explained, the characteristic American complaint is the jeremiad—the fervent denunciation of corruption and decline in American institutions, coupled with a stirring call for return and renewal. "In virtually every area of life," Bercovitch argued, "the jeremiad became the official ritual form of continuing revolution" in the United States.[11] In politics, the cultural memory of the Revolution and the founding has allowed Americans to engage in a series of constitutional jeremiads, making originalism a potent vehicle for justifying continuing revolution in American constitutional law.

That is only one of the many cultural connections between originalism and Protestantism. In one of my previous books, *Constitutional Redemption*, I emphasized—following the work of Sanford Levinson—that Americans have a Protestant constitutional culture.[12] It is Protestant in two respects. The first is the idea of *sola scriptura*—the idea that we should appeal to the text, and not to learned intermediaries like the church, to decide what God wants of us. In the same way, the text of the Constitution and the Declaration of Independence become the scripture, symbol, and language of American civic faith. Learned intermediaries—that is, federal judges—may sometimes get it wrong, so the people must correct them.

A second "Protestant" idea is the rejection of the established church in order to return to, restore, and renew the true faith. This, too, is a feature of American constitutionalism: repeated attempts to renew, restore, and redeem the true Constitution in the face of the established order and political leaders—especially judges—who have caused the Constitution-in-practice to stray from the true path.

America's Protestant constitutional culture is not necessarily conservative. Indeed, it is often quite radical. Calls for return and renewal are arguments for change, not stasis. That is because the past that we hope to return to is often a product of our own dreams and aspirations. We seek to return to the purity of an imagined world of earlier times. As the historian Sir Lewis Namier once put it, we imagine the past so that we can remember the future.[13]

I do not mean to suggest that this feature is unique to American constitutional culture or American originalism. My point is that, because of America's national narrative, Americans identify these tropes of return and restoration strongly with the Constitution and its framers.

D. Originalism in Constitutional Modernity

So far I have described some key elements of American political culture: America's revolutionary tradition; its treatment of the Constitution and the Declaration as foundational scriptures in the American civic religion; America's Protestant tradition of textualism and redemptive calls for a return to origins; the myth that the American Constitution, nation, and people were created together; and the long history of reverence for the founding generation and its culture heroes.

Most of these features of American culture, however, have been around for a long time. For example, Americans' reverence for the founding generation as culture heroes was already present in the antebellum era.[14] So why did originalism arise as a general theory of interpretation when it did—not in the first decades following the founding, but during the twentieth century?

Throughout American history, lawyers and judges have made claims about the purposes and intentions of the Constitution's framers.[15] But they made these arguments in conjunction with a wide range of other legal arguments about text, structure, purpose, precedent, and consequences.

By contrast, American originalism—as a self-conscious and general theory of legal interpretation—is a relatively recent invention. It arose from the way that first liberal and then later conservative political movements from the middle of the twentieth century onward have explained and justified their constitutional projects of reform. The key to understanding the rise of originalism is the problem of the twentieth century.

During the twentieth and early twenty-first centuries, the United States experienced multiple upheavals and changes in the constitutional order. These include the New Deal and the rise of the administrative and regulatory state, the creation of the national security state, the Great Society and the creation of the American welfare state, the civil rights revolution, the sexual revolution, the second wave of American feminism, the gay rights movement, and a series of conservative countermobilizations that reacted to these changes.

The twentieth century was an age of constitutional modernity, in which actors became increasingly self-conscious about how much social, economic, and legal change had deviated from traditional understandings.[16] With modernity usually come modernist crises of belief, and one of the standard cultural effects of modernity is a schizophrenic attitude toward the past. On the one hand, the past is increasingly left behind, sometimes proudly or deliberately. This is the view that I have identified with living constitutionalism. On the other hand, there is a repeated longing to regain the past and its authority, even in an imagined form, which I have identified with originalism.

The experience of modernity is *both* about transcending the practical and cultural constraints of the past *and* the anxiety that this freedom creates. One way to help relieve that anxiety is by calling on the past and employing it as a powerful source of authority in uncertain times. And this is so whether one is a conservative or a revolutionary.

It is no accident that many fundamentalist movements emerge from modernist challenges to belief and practice; they respond to periods of change when, in Marx and Engels's famous words, "everything solid melts into air."[17] But in constitutional modernity, the invocation of the past—and the great deeds, principles, and commitments of the past—is useful not only as a means of forestalling change but also as a way of justifying change and consolidating change.

In America, originalism is like the spoonful of traditionalist sugar that helps the modernist medicine go down.

In a period of continuous constitutional struggle and change, both liberals and conservatives have sought to invoke the past as a justification for moving constitutional understandings in their favored direction. Hence, the founders, framers, and adopters have increasingly been mobilized on both sides of these debates, first by political liberals in the middle of the twentieth century and then by the conservative legal movement in the latter part of the twentieth century.

What is remarkable about liberal constitutional rhetoric in the middle of the twentieth century is that it featured *both* arguments for progressive adaptation to changing times and circumstances *and* appeals to the wisdom of the framers. During the constitutional crisis over the New Deal, for example, President Franklin D. Roosevelt argued that a conservative Supreme Court had strayed from the founders' design of a flexible, pragmatic Constitution that gave the federal government power to solve national problems. He compared the Constitution to the Bible and argued that, "[l]ike the Bible, it ought to be read again and again."[18] He extolled the framers' wisdom in providing for a flexible document that provided "all the powers needed to meet each and every problem which then had a national character and which could not be met by merely local action."[19]

Roosevelt denounced the conservative justices of the Supreme Court for disregarding the framers' meaning. The justices were "reading into the Constitution words and implications which are not there, and which were never intended to be there."[20] He called for the restoration and the redemption of the true Constitution created by the framers: "We must take action to save the Constitution from the Court and the Court from itself. We must find a way to take an appeal from the Supreme Court to the Constitution itself."[21]

Roosevelt's speeches are eye-opening today precisely because he is widely regarded as a prominent liberal symbol of living constitutionalism, which is generally assumed to be the very opposite of originalist thought. Yet Roosevelt's argument was a characteristically liberal use of the founding. He claimed that the constitutional text was *designed* to be forward-looking and sufficiently adaptable to deal with new national problems then unforeseen. The Constitution was a wise and flexible document written by wise and pragmatic men. It was, in Roosevelt's words, a "layman's document, not a lawyer's contract," and "a charter of general principles."[22] The framers, Roosevelt explained, "used broad and general language capable of meeting evolution and change when they referred to commerce between the States, the taxing power and the general welfare."[23] The founders were political experimentalists, just like the New Dealers.

It is therefore fitting that Roosevelt's first appointment to the Supreme Court was Hugo Black, an Alabama senator who became the most famous liberal advocate of original intention and one of the Supreme Court's greatest civil libertarians. Black was truly an originalist *avant la lettre*, for the word "originalist" would not be coined until 1980 by Paul Brest, a liberal critic of conservative originalism.[24] From the 1940s to the 1960s, Justice Black and, later, various justices on the liberal Warren Court repeatedly invoked the framers to legitimate elements of the New Deal/civil rights regime, to secure equality in voting rights, to reform police practices, to require separation of church and state, to protect civil liberties, and, above all, to justify overturning many existing legal doctrines.[25]

In Alfred Kelly's famous critique of how American lawyers use (and misuse) history, *Clio and the Court: An Illicit Love Affair*, he accused Black and other liberal justices of "law office history"—that is, of using history selectively to justify politically desirable results.[26] Moreover, he pointed out that throughout American history, people had used appeals to the framers as a "precedent-breaking device." By breaking with existing doctrine and returning to the original meaning of the Constitution, a court could claim that it was actually preserving constitutional continuity.[27] "In search of some adequate guiding principle upon which to support their libertarian interventionism in the social order," Kelly argued, "the reformist activists on the Court initiated a new era of historically oriented adjudication."[28] The Warren Court turned to history to justify its increasingly muscular exercise of judicial review. Thus, it is no accident that, as Frank Cross has shown, the liberal Warren Court cited *The Federalist* "more than any previous Court [in] American history."[29] In short, to justify constitutional transformation midcentury, American liberals employed *both* a rhetoric of change and evolving social values *and* a rhetoric of return to founding-era verities.

The work of the Warren Court and the early Burger Court, in

turn, served as targets for powerful conservative countermobilizations that dominated American political culture through the end of the twentieth century and into the early twenty-first century. Far more than midcentury liberals, conservative social and political movements adopted originalism and fidelity to the founders' Constitution as key rhetorical justifications for political and legal revolution. Conservatives like Reagan Attorney General Edwin Meese and Judge Robert H. Bork denounced the living constitutionalism of legal liberalism and promoted originalism as the sole legitimate method of constitutional interpretation.[30] Moreover, conservatives sought to identify originalism and fidelity to the founders with conservative political and legal ideals.[31] So effective were these attacks that most Americans today have forgotten that legal liberals both before and during the Warren Court had themselves often invoked adoption history to justify many of their most celebrated innovations.

Originalism in American constitutional law, therefore, is a product both of the distinctive construction of American cultural memory and of the way that political and legal actors in the twentieth century have built on that cultural memory to struggle over American politics and American constitutional law. Although Americans pride themselves on being cultural innovators and repeatedly breaking with past traditions, there are deep strains of traditionalism in American thought and life. Founder and Constitution worship is Americans' characteristic way of articulating American traditions and arguing about how to adapt those traditions to contemporary problems. Originalism allows Americans to argue about American ethos and political tradition in the present by reference to honored founders and framers. Although it may offer itself as a jurisprudential theory about correct legal interpretation, originalism's roots are political and cultural.

As noted previously, contemporary conservative originalism is the result of conservative political mobilizations that began in the late 1960s and early 1970s and came to fruition with the election of Ronald Reagan in 1980. Movement conservatives adopted originalism as a way of explaining what they believed was wrong with legal liberalism and, in particular, the decisions of the Warren and early Burger Courts in the 1960s and 1970s.[32] These decisions had revolutionized criminal procedure; created guarantees of sexual autonomy,

the right to abortion, and women's equality; mandated racial integration of public schools; and increased judicial oversight of prisons,
schools, and hospitals. Originalist appeals helped conservatives explain how liberal federal judges had strayed both from the correct
interpretation of the nation's charter and from their proper role as
unelected judges.

Thus, modern conservative originalism has been a call for reform through the rhetoric of return and restoration. It was also, at
least in its early years, a call for judicial restraint and for respect for
democracy.[33] Conservatives argued against liberal ideas of a "living
Constitution," which, they claimed, gave insufficient deference to
democracy and failed to restrain judges from imposing their personal political views on the law.

Nevertheless, as conservatives won elections, they began to control the federal courts, and they soon achieved a conservative majority on the United States Supreme Court. In this changed political context, arguments for judicial abstention increasingly made less
sense. Conservatives wanted courts to strike down liberal legislation,
rein in federal power, and protect the kinds of rights that conservatives favored—the rights of property owners against environmental
regulation, the rights of corporations and wealthy donors against
campaign finance regulation, the rights of gun owners against gun
control, the rights of states against guaranteed federal health care
and federal protections of voting rights, the rights of whites against
affirmative action programs, the rights of conservative Christians to
promote religion in the public square and in public expenditures, and
so on. Promoting these kinds of rights required a muscular judiciary
unafraid to exercise the power of judicial review in order to protect
important constitutional values.

In this new world of conservative judicial hegemony, originalism
could no longer serve primarily as a justification for judicial restraint.
It had to be reconceptualized in order to legitimate conservative
judicial activism.[34] The difficulty was that the term "judicial activism"
had been rendered politically radioactive by continuous assaults by
conservatives against liberal decisions and liberal jurists. Therefore,
new euphemisms like "judicial engagement" or "judicial fidelity to
text, history and structure" explained the role appropriate for conservative judges.[35] In this way, conservative originalism gradually shed

its associations with judicial restraint and respect for majoritarian politics. Once conservatives solidified control over the federal courts, they once again become defenders of robust judicial review to protect important constitutional values, just as they had been before the New Deal.

The earliest versions of originalism in the twentieth century, those of Hugo Black, Raoul Berger, and Robert Bork, focused on the original intentions of the framers. So it was easy to connect reverence for the framers to a theory of interpretation that focused on their intentions. Nevertheless, as academics began to make theoretical arguments for originalism in the 1980s and 1990s, the theory of originalism mutated, creating many different versions. Some of these versions do not technically depend on reverence for the framers at all. For example, original public meaning originalism asks what a reasonable person at the time of adoption would have understood the text to mean. So an eighteenth-century dictionary or a letter from a tradesperson might be evidence of original meaning that is just as good as an essay written by James Madison. In practice, however, originalist lawyers, judges, and academics prefer to cite the framers, especially *The Federalist* and the writings of the Big Six. This shows that reverence for culture heroes continues to underwrite originalism politically and culturally even when particular academic theories formally depend on other considerations.

Originalism and appeals to the values of the framers are among the most familiar tropes of American movements for political change. They are standard ways that Americans advocate change and accommodate change under the sign of permanence, continuity, and tradition. This point offers yet another way of seeing why originalism and living constitutionalism are two sides of the same coin. Many American movement conservatives today do not simply want to preserve the status quo. They are often quite critical of the country's direction. They want to change society and culture, often quite drastically. To support their political project in constitutional law, they naturally turn to the language of originalism, with its reverence for the founding and its construction of an imagined past.

In this way, as Robert Post and Reva Siegel have explained, originalism can play the same reformist role for American movement conservatives that living constitutionalism plays for American progressives.[36] Originalism justifies overturning liberal precedents and hobbling or striking down liberal legislation. Originalism provides a common constitutional discourse for articulating conservative claims. Originalism is the living constitutionalism of movement conservatives.

Every political culture must deal with change, but different countries articulate and struggle over their traditions in different ways. In some countries, political tradition can be associated with a common culture, a shared religious or ethnic identity, or the shared memory of wars, struggles, victories, and defeats. In the United States, however, national identity is bound up with the memory of the American Revolution and the enactment of the American Constitution. American political identity is strongly shaped by what Sanford Levinson has called America's constitutional faith.[37]

Americans like to imagine themselves as forward-looking pioneers—itself a quasi-originalist image. They celebrate American dynamism. Yet at the same time, Americans need to believe that something remains constant about themselves in the face of constant change. Constitutional originalism offers Americans a language to express their longing for continuity as well as pride in their past achievements. Originalism, which on its surface appears to defy the very idea of a continuously changing Constitution, is actually a key device through which Americans articulate and justify political change to themselves and to each other. It is the language of revolutionaries as well as defenders of the old order, of constitutional reformers as well as constitutional conservatives. It offers a familiar language through which Americans can argue with each other and remember who they are in the midst of constant political transformation.

PART III

Interpretation and Construction

CHAPTER SEVEN

Living Originalism

HAVING INTRODUCED ORIGINALISM AND its twin, living constitutionalism, as cultural themes, I now turn to how they operate in constitutional interpretation. To do this, I will draw on my theory of framework originalism, developed in my 2011 book, *Living Originalism*.[1] As the name implies, framework originalism argues that the Constitution creates a basic framework or plan for politics that is not complete at the outset but must be filled out and built on by later generations. And as the title "living originalism" implies, I believe that originalism and living constitutionalism are fully compatible positions. You do not have to be one or the other. You can be both. And not only can you be both, but that is the best and the most attractive understanding of the American constitutional tradition.

A. Framework Originalism, Interpretation, and Construction

Framework originalism argues that a constitution is a framework for making politics possible. Successive generations build on the constitutional framework over time through constitutional construction.

Framework originalism distinguishes between *constitutional in-*

terpretation, which tries to ascertain the original meaning of the Constitution's words and phrases, and *constitutional construction*, which applies and implements those words and phrases in practice. This distinction is characteristic of a family of approaches called the "New Originalism."[2] As I will argue in this book, the distinction between interpretation and construction has important consequences for how constitutions grow and develop over time. It also has important consequences for how people use history in constitutional argument.

What most people think of as constitutional interpretation is actually a combination of interpretation (in the narrow sense just described) and constitutional construction. Constitutional interpretation involves figuring out the original communicative content of the Constitution's words and phrases. The original communicative content includes the original semantic meaning of the words and phrases in the text, any generally recognized legal terms of art, and any inferences from historical context necessary to understand the words and phrases in the text. In most cases, the Constitution's words mean today what they meant at the time of adoption; but there are a few exceptions, and we want to be sure that we do not unwittingly engage in a pun or a play on words.[3]

There is far more to constitutional interpretation, however, than ascertaining original meaning. Interpreters have to give effect to the Constitution through creating and applying doctrines, practices, and conventions. Hence, there is a second activity of constitutional interpretation, called constitutional construction.

When the Constitution is silent, or when it uses vague or abstract language, standards, or principles, an inquiry into original meaning will not be sufficient to decide most contested questions. Constitutional construction fleshes out and implements vague and abstract language through creating and applying doctrines, conventions, practices, laws, and institutions to implement the Constitution's provisions and further constitutional values.[4]

All three branches of government engage in constitutional construction, responding to each other and to continuous waves of social and political mobilizations in politics and civil society.[5] These tasks are the work of multiple generations; the adopters only begin a transgenerational project of governance that others must continue.

Each generation has a duty to keep the constitutional project going by building out and implementing the Constitution in its own time.[6]

The need for constitutional construction is an inevitable consequence of a written constitution. Written constitutions contain different kinds of legal norms. They contain hard-wired rules, which are designed to require relatively little practical judgment to apply. But they also contain standards like "unreasonable searches and seizures" and principles like "freedom of speech." Standards and principles usually require considerably more practical judgment to apply in changing contexts and often lead to the creation of doctrines and subdoctrines. In addition, the meanings of some terms in the Constitution, such as "search," "seizure," and "speech," may become uncertain or vague as social, political, and technological contexts change. Deciding what these terms mean in practice also requires the exercise of practical judgment. Finally, the Constitution sets up competing centers of power—between the federal government and the states or among the various branches of the federal government. These different power centers complete and contend with each other over time, leading to evolving practices and conventions that pose ever new questions for constitutional construction.

In sum, a written constitution's allocations of power, its use of words and phrases, and its choice of rules, standards, principles, and silences leave many issues for future generations to work out. The Constitution is always an unfinished project, and there is always more work to do to build out and implement the Constitution under changing circumstances.[7]

The members of each generation, operating within the basic framework, must construct the Constitution in their own time. Successive generations will build on previous constructions—adding to some, modifying others, and replacing still others. Thus, much of what people call "constitutional interpretation" is really constitutional construction or involves building on previous constitutional constructions. People must exercise practical judgment to decide the best way to build out the Constitution faithfully.[8] Reasonable minds can differ on which constructions are the best ones, and over time, people's views of the best constructions may change.

People argue for and justify proposed constructions by using the standard forms of argument described in part 1 of this book. People use the modalities to analyze constitutional problems and to explain why their proposed constructions are faithful to the Constitution and are the best way to continue the constitutional project. Thus, the standard modalities of argument are the basic toolkit for analyzing and justifying constitutional constructions. Because there are many different kinds of legal arguments, people engage in a sort of reflective equilibrium among different approaches.[9] Moreover, people do not do this in isolation. They are also influenced by other people's judgments about which arguments are best. Deciding among different kinds of arguments is a process of reflective equilibrium in a community of mutual influence.[10]

Building out and implementing the Constitution through successive constructions produces the *Constitution-in-practice*. The Constitution-in-practice is different from the text of the Constitution. And usually it differs from what lots of people think is the best construction of the Constitution. The Constitution-in-practice is the Constitution considered as an institution, the Constitution we have to work with and argue about every day. Social and political movements try to move the Constitution-in-practice closer to their ideal of what the Constitution should mean.

Even if the text of the Constitution remains the same—because there are no new amendments—the Constitution-in-practice is always changing. When we study constitutional law today, for example, we study the current doctrines of the Constitution-in-practice, which may be different from the doctrines in place a decade or fifty years ago and may be quite different in the future.

Framework originalism argues that we must be faithful to the basic framework of the Constitution. The basic framework consists of the original meaning of the Constitution and its subsequent amendments, and the Constitution's choice of legal norms—rules, standards, and principles—to constrain and delegate future constitutional construction. The basic framework does not change without a constitutional amendment or a new constitutional convention. Constitutional constructions, however, may change without a new amendment. They are the part of the Constitution-in-practice that changes, while the basic framework remains the same. In this way, framework originalism is fully consistent with the idea of a "living Constitution" whose application may change over time in response to new problems and circumstances. That is why it is also called "living originalism."

B. The Thin Theory of Original Public Meaning

Originalist theories generally hold that (1) something (original meaning, intention, or understanding) is fixed at the time of adoption and cannot be changed without a constitutional amendment and (2) what is fixed at the time of adoption constrains constitutional interpretation in some way. The first claim is called the "fixation thesis"; the second claim is the "constraint principle."[11]

For framework originalism, what is fixed at the time of adoption (and subsequent amendment) is the basic framework: the original meaning of the Constitution's words and phrases along with the text's choice of rules, standards, and principles. Because framework originalism argues that original public meaning is fixed at the time of adoption and that it constrains interpretation, it is a kind of originalism, although, to be sure, it is different from most versions of conservative originalism.

Framework originalism has a "thin" theory of original meaning. "Original meaning" refers to (1) the original semantic meaning of the text, (2) any generally recognized legal terms of art, and (3) inferences from background context necessary to resolve ambiguities and make sense of the text.[12] Let me address each of these in turn.

In an ancient constitution like America's, the semantic (i.e., definitional) meanings of words may change over time. Imagine, for example, a constitution written in Chaucerian English—many of the words would have acquired new or different meanings over the years, not to mention different spellings. In the case of the U.S. Constitution, largely written in the eighteenth and nineteenth centuries, most words and phrases have the same semantic meanings as they did at the time of adoption. But there are a few exceptions or possible ambiguities. Article IV, section 4, of the Constitution, for example, speaks of the federal government's duty to respond to "domestic violence" in the states, which refers to riots or insurrections, not interspousal battery; the same clause requires the United States to guarantee the states a "Republican form of government," meaning a representative government, not a government controlled by the Republican Party (founded many years after those words were written). Article I, section 8, speaks of "magazines," which are places for storing ammunition, not glossy publications, and the Second Amendment speaks of the right to keep and bear "arms," which refers to weapons, not limbs or appendages.

In addition, some terms in the Constitution, like "letters of marque and reprisal" in Article I, section 8, are legal terms of art. To apply the text today, it is important to know what these terms of art meant at the time of adoption. However, many of these terms were taken from the common law. Because the Constitution does not freeze the common law in time, these terms are subject to common-law evolution through successive decisions.

Finally, some features of the text require an understanding of the background context. We look to context to decide what pronouns and indexicals like "it" or "this" refer to in the text. We look to context to decide whether the text uses a generally recognized term of art. We look to context to recognize when the text uses words or phrases nonliterally—for example, as a metaphor or a synecdoche. For example, the word "speech" in the First Amendment and the word "writings" in the Progress Clause of Article I, section 8, are examples of synecdoche, a literary figure in which an example stands for a larger category of things.[13] From context, we also understand that when the constitutional text refers to "the Senate," it is talking about the U.S. Senate and not the Roman Senate, that when the Constitution mentions dates and months it refers to the Gregorian Calendar and not a lunar calendar, that all numbers mentioned in the text are in base ten rather than in base twelve, and so on. These features of the constitutional text, although not expressly stated, require us sympathetically to understand the text in context.[14]

Consider these three ideas together: that interpreters should pay attention to linguistic change in order to avoid unintended puns and plays on words, that interpreters should recognize the existence of legal terms of art, and that interpreters should read the text consistent with basic assumptions about background context. These three requirements are fidelity to "original meaning" or "original communicative content" in a thin sense.[15]

C. Original Meaning and
Original Expected Applications

Because framework originalism has a thin theory of original meaning, it leaves most important constitutional controversies in what Lawrence Solum calls the "construction zone."[16] The first people who work with the Constitution have various assumptions and expectations about how it will work in practice; based on these assumptions and expectations, they create an initial set of constructions. Later generations may continue, elaborate, modify, or even replace these constructions over time. That is because the initial legal constructions of the text are not part of the original public meaning.

For example, the initial legal construction of the Fourteenth Amendment did not protect women (and especially married women) from many forms of legal discrimination. In particular, the framers and adopters of the Fourteenth Amendment did not expect or intend that it would disturb the common-law coverture rules, by which women lost most of their rights upon marriage.[17] But the original public meaning of the words in the amendment—"equal protection of the laws," "due process of law," and "privileges or immunities of citizens of the United States"—does not mention the coverture rules and does not require this result. The framers' view that the amendment does not disturb the common law is only the initial legal construction of the amendment by people who lived at the time of adoption, and we do not have to accept it today.

Here is another example: the Eighth Amendment prohibits "cruel and unusual punishments." The text offers a standard. The proper question is how to apply this standard in our own time. So even if the adopting generation did not think that a certain punishment was cruel and unusual, it might be cruel and unusual in today's world and is therefore prohibited by the Eighth Amendment.

These are two examples of a more general point. Although we must follow the *original meaning* of text, we are not bound by the *original expected application* of the text. The original expected application concerns how people living at the time the text was adopted would have expected it would be applied. The original expected application includes not only specific results that people expected but also the way that the adopting generation would have articulated and

applied the relevant legal principles, as well as the initial constructions that contemporary lawyers would have given to the text.[18]

Because lawyers are creatures of their time, the initial legal constructions of a text will often reflect the public's—or political elites'—
assumptions about how the text should be applied in practice. Thus,
the sexism of the framers and adopters of the Fourteenth Amendment was reflected in the initial legal construction of the amendment,
which mirrored their worldview about women's special and inferior
status and justified denying women the same rights as men. But according to the thin theory of original meaning, those contemporary
legal constructions of the Fourteenth Amendment are not part of the
original meaning of the text.

In short, the thin theory allows us to build on previous constructions, but it does not require us to accept them if they are unjust or
unworkable. At the same time, it takes seriously the norms in the
text of the Constitution. When the Constitution states a rule, we
apply the rule because that is what the text says. When the Constitution states a standard, we apply the standard because that is what
the text says. And when the Constitution states a principle, we apply
the principle because that is what the text says. We must apply these
rules, standards, and principles in our own time, building on and,
where necessary, modifying the previous constructions of earlier
generations.[19]

When we engage in constitutional construction, we are guided
by what the adopting generation believed, as well as by the history
of past practices, conventions, and doctrinal constructions. Because
the Constitution is an intergenerational project, we normally do not
write on a blank slate. The history of past constructions—some dating back all the way to the beginning of the republic—is an important element in deciding how to apply the Constitution today. But
these early constructions are not part of the original public meaning. Therefore, if they are unhelpful or unjust, later generations can
modify them and create new constructions to replace them. What
later generations may not modify—at least not without an Article V
amendment—is the basic framework: the original public meaning of
the words and phrases used in the Constitution and the Constitution's choice of rules, standards, and principles.

D. Framework Originalism
and the Living Constitution

My theory of interpretation has a distinctive view about what we mean by a "living" Constitution. The processes of constitutional construction through politics and law are living constitutionalism. The American Constitution is "living" in the sense that people engage in successive constitutional constructions in order to meet the problems of their time, creating new constructions that may supplement, displace, or reinterpret older ones. This is how the American people build out the Constitution-in-practice over time. That is all that is meant by a living Constitution.

People sometimes argue that a living Constitution is a normative theory that requires that judges make the Constitution responsive to changing times. But there is almost always more than one way to respond to change, and people with different values will want to respond in very different ways. (For example, some people will argue that the best way to respond to change is to continue to apply the same rules as before.) So the injunction to respond to the times is no more than a slogan. It tells us nothing about what to do.

Living constitutionalism is not a distinct theory of interpretation that gives advice to judges or that judges might consciously follow. Rather, it is an account of the processes of constitutional construction over time.[20] That is why living originalism is both originalist and compatible with a living Constitution. Indeed, because constitutional construction is an inevitable part of constitutional interpretation, and because the Constitution-in-practice is always changing, we cannot help but have a living Constitution.

In sum, with respect to the constitutional text, I am an originalist—a framework originalist, that is. But with respect to the entire Constitution as an institution for governance—what I call the Constitution-in-practice—I am a living constitutionalist.

My adherence to the basic framework and my belief in the continuous development of the Constitution-in-practice are simply two sides of the same coin. They describe different features of the same phenomenon.

Of course, my version of originalism is not a particularly controversial position in the United States. Many nonoriginalists could accept it, although they wish I did not go on about original meaning so much. Many originalists could accept it too, although they wish I did not emphasize the Constitution's flexibility so much.

Nor would living originalism be a particularly controversial position to take about most constitutions in most countries around the world. I often meet judges and legal scholars from other countries, and when I mention to them that I am originalist, they are horrified! Then I explain my views in more detail, and they say, "Well, that's not so unreasonable. Why did you frighten me by saying that you were one of those crazy American originalists?"

E. Thick Originalism

What makes originalism controversial both within and outside the United States is a far stronger claim than living or framework originalism. When most people think of originalism, they usually have in mind a thicker, more restrictive conception. Often they have in mind the idea that today's judges must interpret the Constitution in the way that people at the time of its adoption would have interpreted it or that judges must give the provisions of the Constitution the same legal effect that lawyers at the time of adoption would have given them. Conversely, to the extent that judges decide cases or create doctrines inconsistent with these criteria, their interpretations are illegitimate.

This kind of originalism is an exclusive approach to constitutional interpretation; judges who adopt a different approach act illegitimately and lawlessly.[21] As the title of one of Judge Robert Bork's pieces from the 1980s argues, originalism is "The Only Legitimate Basis for Constitutional Decision Making."[22] This version of originalism has a much thicker account of original meaning (or intention or understanding) than the thin version of original meaning I argue for. And it is this thick version of originalism that generates such opposition from other lawyers and judges in the United States and mystifies lawyers and judges in other parts of the world.

Because living originalism has a relatively thin conception of original meaning, it has a wide zone for constitutional construction. By contrast, the "thick" conception of original meaning favored by most conservative originalists has a correspondingly narrower zone for construction. In fact, some conservative original meaning originalists object to the very category of constitutional construction; for them, all constitutional issues are questions of interpretation, and the Constitution's original meaning settles—or at least significantly bounds—the majority of constitutional questions.[23]

Much historical research and debate about adoption history concerns the original legal constructions that people around the time of adoption would have given to the Constitution's words and phrases. It involves what I call "original expected applications"—how the relevant adopters understood the principles and purposes behind the Constitution, the cases and situations that would be covered by the Constitution's terms, and how the Constitution's words would apply to the controversies of their day.[24]

In *Living Originalism*, I point out that there are many different meanings of "meaning"—including semantic meanings, inferences from context, intentions, purposes, expectations, and cultural associations—and that it is a mistake to assume that the act of adopting a constitution fixes all of these meanings permanently into the law. Instead, what is fixed at the time of adoption—and is binding on later generations—is original meaning (in the thin sense described earlier) and not the purposes, intentions, expectations, initial legal constructions, psychological states, or cultural associations of the adopters. Fidelity to original meaning does not require fidelity to original expected applications.[25]

For a long time, conservative originalists tended to run together original meaning with original expected applications.[26] That is because when most of them moved from original intention to original meaning originalism in the 1980s, they did not expect that this would alter the results that originalism produced. As Justice Antonin Scalia put it, there was not much difference between the two formulations.[27] Nevertheless, after several decades of academic debate, many conservative originalists today would agree with me that the original public meaning is different from original expected applications.[28] They would acknowledge, for example, that applying the same text under changed factual circumstances may sometimes produce different results than the adopting generation would have expected.

Nevertheless, when conservative originalists develop their thick

conceptions of original meaning, they usually look to original expected applications as a guide.[29] For example, they may identify the
original public meaning with the initial legal constructions of the
Constitution's words and phrases. Or they may try to figure out how
people who lived at the time of adoption would have understood
and formulated the relevant legal principles and applied them to
particular cases. Or they may ask how a hypothetical individual living at the time of adoption would have formulated and applied these
legal principles.

The reason why conservative originalists usually do this is that
they want a relatively narrow zone of constitutional construction—
or they simply reject the idea of constitutional construction altogether. They do not accept that later generations must build out the
Constitution through subsequent constructions and that later generations must exercise judgment in doing so. Conservative originalists prefer an original meaning that already resolves most contested
issues.

If the zone of constitutional construction is very narrow—or
nonexistent—then it seems as if later interpreters do not have to
make as many normative choices. They simply have to follow the
rules already laid down. That is why in practice conservative versions
of original meaning originalism often hew closely to original expected
applications even though the concepts of original meaning and original expected applications are distinct.

I think that the quest for a theory of interpretation that tries to
resolve difficult normative questions in the present by unearthing
comprehensive accounts of adoption history is unlikely to succeed.
Nor is it likely to relieve judges from the responsibility for making
difficult normative judgments in the kinds of contested cases that
regularly come before the courts. Quite the contrary: people's normative judgments affect how they characterize the meaning of the
past, what they select from the past, and what they find relevant in
the past. Equally important, people's normative judgments affect how
they understand, apply, extend, or make analogies to legal doctrines
and materials from the past. People often read the past in confor-
mity with their normative priors and their assumptions about what
the past must have been like. Even people who spend their entire ca-
reers immersed in archives are prone to these tendencies; how much

more so are people who lack the time and industry and simply want to decide the next legal controversy. Thick accounts of original meaning may disguise ideological predisposition behind a cloud of learned citations, but they will not eliminate the need for normative judgment.

Here is an example: Suppose we want to know whether today's very strong protection of commercial speech is required by the original public meaning of the First Amendment. To demonstrate this, we might note that advertising was part of colonial-era practice, that colonial-era printers regularly printed advertisements, that revenue from advertising supported the colonial press, and that no less a figure than Benjamin Franklin defended the right of printers to print commercial advertisements as part of his arguments for a free press in 1731.[30] We then use this evidence to conclude that limitations on advertising in any medium are inconsistent with the original public meaning of the First Amendment.[31] Armed with this general principle, we might go on to argue that if an advertisement does not engage in common-law fraud or advertise illegal products, it is protected by the First Amendment, that the Federal Food and Drug Administration may not prevent drug companies from advertising off-label uses of prescription drugs without doing FDA-approved safety studies, and so on.[32]

This argument uses the language of originalism, but it makes many leaps of logic. First, it tries to read a general constitutional principle off founding-era practice—what was regulated and what was not regulated in everyday custom, in early state statutes, in English common law, and so on. But there are many possible principles that could explain founding-era practice. These might include conceptual distinctions that would have made sense to people in 1791 but that we do not think of today. Our attempt to read legal principles off founding-era practice—including founding-era legal practice— involves creative legal analogy. For example, the founding era might not even have had a concept of "commercial speech" that corresponds to today's doctrinal categories, which were created in the 1970s.

Second, founding-era practice may have assumed very different notions of how the state could regulate individual rights for the common good that are quite different from the libertarian assumptions of contemporary free speech law. Jud Campbell has pointed out that natural rights were always subject to reasonable regulation for the common good, so that we cannot read today's high level of speech protection back into the founding era's protection of freedom of speech or freedom of the press.[33] So even if the First Amendment protected some of what we would now call "commercial speech," it might have been subject to considerable regulation in ways that current doctrine does not comprehend.[34]

Third, we may not be able to read constitutional rights directly from founding-era practice because the founding era faced different problems and the law may have been underenforced.[35] In particular, we cannot take the lack of regulation of commercial advertisements before the Civil War as proof of the original public meaning of the Free Speech or Free Press Clauses. Even if a practice was not criminalized, state legislatures might still have had the power to reach it under their police power to promote the public's health, safety, and welfare. That point is especially important because the reasons we might want to regulate advertising today may be different from those that could have existed during the founding era. The founding era was not a consumer society, advertising did not pervade popular culture, there were no digital technologies for targeted advertising on social media that promoted the pathologies and social problems of our contemporary attention economy, and so on.

Fourth, we must decide how abstractly or broadly to articulate the legal principle that encompasses founding-era practice. There are many ways to do this, especially since we are creating doctrines for a very different era using very different doctrinal categories. Moreover, even if we think that a certain principle follows logically from historical practice, we must remember that "people in the past may reject or ignore implications we find self-evident while insisting on conclusions we think untenable."[36]

Fifth, whatever principle we come up with, we must then extend it to very different social and technological contexts in situations that the founders could never have dreamed of. Did founding-era free speech and free press concepts reach advertising of off-label prescription drugs? The question is as beside the point as asking whether James Madison enjoyed video games.

My argument is not that we cannot or should not draw these analogical extensions from the past; lawyers do this all the time. Nor is my argument that lawyers must avoid all anachronism in solving contemporary problems. The application of old law to new situations inevitably requires this.

My argument is rather that it is folly to say that the argument for protection of commercial speech is *required* by fidelity to original public meaning. To be sure, it may be an argument *from* original public meaning in the sense that it begins with the historical record and works outward from there. But original public meaning does not compel the conclusion. Rather, the conclusion is an imaginative extension from founding-era sources and legal materials.[37] It is an example of constitutional construction that uses adoption-era history to derive contemporary legal principles that we can use in the present. And there is nothing wrong with this use of history, as long as we recognize—and admit—that we are exercising normative judgment in the present. When done well, such arguments can be persuasive. Of course, people who disagree with us may make counter-arguments, also using history, and the legal debate goes forward.

I repeat: to say that an argument employs an imaginative extension from the past does not mean that it is a bad argument or an improper use of history. It simply means that it is a creative act of legal reasoning from an incomplete historical record to draw conclusions in a vastly different context of judgment. It is constitutional construction. That is what constitutional construction often does, and often what it must do. Constitutional construction is creative: it builds on the past to deal with the problems of the present and the future.

One should not try to pass off what is actually constitutional construction as the simple command of the text's original public meaning. For that is an attempt to deny normative responsibility for one's legal arguments. It is an attempt to deny the necessity of creative thinking and analogical extension under the guise of "just following the law."

F. Our Nonoriginalist Constitution

A thick version of originalism has many theoretical problems, which have produced a substantial academic literature.[38] But quite apart from the various theoretical problems, thick accounts of originalism also face a practical problem. Thick conceptions of original meaning cannot account for a very large proportion of our current practices, including practices that most Americans regard as valuable and would be reluctant to abandon. These include the modern administrative and regulatory state; federal protections for workers, consumers, and the environment; many aspects of the modern social safety net, including Social Security and Medicare; the modern conception of the presidency and the national security state; and large swaths of constitutional civil rights and civil liberties. Under thick accounts of original meaning, Americans have not been faithful to the Constitution in many ways, and for a very long time. Many, if not most, of the federal protections and programs that citizens rely on today are unconstitutional.

For some conservative originalists, this is a feature as much as a bug. They are not very happy with the New Deal, the administrative state, and significant parts of modern civil rights and civil liberties law. Many of them have never been fans of protecting sexual freedom or reproductive rights through the Constitution. Even so, there are many precedents and practices that they would find it embarrassing to disavow as constitutionally illegitimate. Thick accounts of original meaning or original understanding threaten to place many of the federal programs and protections that Americans rely on today beyond the Constitution. It is a theory of American constitutional interpretation that renders much of modern American governance unconstitutional.

Conservative originalists can make peace with some of these nonoriginalist practices and precedents. They can argue that generations of people have gotten used to these deviations from originalism and have come to rely on them, or that eliminating them would have enormous costs. Conservative originalists can argue that longstanding precedents inconsistent with (their thick account of) original meaning are an exception to the originalist account of authority.[39] They are illegitimate from the perspective of that model, but we should retain them anyway because of reliance interests.[40]

There are three problems with this strategy. First, the exceptions to originalism are so prevalent that they threaten to swallow the rule. If original meaning is as thick as some conservative originalists believe, much of contemporary constitutional practice will be inconsistent with originalism.

Second, it mischaracterizes the nature of American constitutional development. According to this picture, originalists must treat many modern features of the American state and contemporary understandings of American civil rights and civil liberties—for example, constitutional guarantees of equality for married women—as *mistakes* that we are stuck with and must grudgingly accept, rather than as *achievements* to be proud of.[41] The history of American constitutional development, conservative originalists tell us, is a history of errors piled atop more errors, an endless succession of deviations from the true Constitution. But, reluctantly, we have to keep most of it.

Third, in these and many other areas of the law, most conservative originalists reason from judicial precedents and other modalities of argument in much the same way that nonoriginalists do. They engage in what is essentially constitutional construction, because they recognize that adoption history cannot always be conclusive and that sometimes it must simply be ignored.[42] To be sure, conservative originalists may want to move the law closer to what they think originalism actually requires. But they must always balance their theory against other considerations that are not originalist. In and of itself, originalism does not explain why such a balance is necessary, when it should be invoked, how it should be conducted, and the relevant factors that this balancing should take into account. Individual judges have to decide these questions for themselves, based on their values and on what they think is currently canonical and durable in existing constitutional practices. As a result, there is wide room for differing judgments.[43]

G. Keeping Up with the Past

Many conservative originalists do not like this approach. They do not want to concede that there are a wide range of nonoriginalist precedents that fly in the face of their theory and that they nevertheless must simply accept. Instead, they would like to show that original meaning already produces most, if not all, of the necessary results. But this means that conservative originalists have to continually retrofit their theories of original meaning to make sure that they can accommodate canonical precedents, practices, and results. And what they have to explain changes over time, too, as new positions and precedents become canonical. Early originalists did not think that *Brown v. Board of Education* was consistent with originalism, and indeed, some racial conservatives turned to originalism because they believed that it showed that *Brown* was illegitimate.[44] But later originalists understood that no theory of constitutional interpretation would be taken seriously if it did not explain *Brown*, and so they worked hard to discover originalist justifications.[45]

This did not end the problems, of course. The justifications that originalists came up with to explain *Brown* did not explain *Bolling v. Sharpe*, which held that the federal government could not segregate on the basis of race, or *Loving v. Virginia*, which overturned laws against racial intermarriage.[46] For that matter, originalists were not able to explain why the federal government could not engage in race-conscious affirmative action, which violated conservatives' views about a color-blind Constitution. In 1791, when the Fifth Amendment's Due Process Clause was adopted, and many Americans were held in slavery, there was no constitutional ban on racial classifications. So later originalists came up with proposals explaining why results that seemed contrary to originalism were actually consistent with it.[47] Some conservative originalists have tried to explain why originalism is consistent with sex equality and even LGBTQ rights.[48] As society changes in ways that older originalists once opposed, later originalists have to find new originalist explanations. They must find justifications for contemporary values buried somewhere in the archives.

Conservatives want to do more, of course, than come up with originalist explanations for liberal constitutional doctrines. They would also like to make constitutional law more and more conservative. For example, contemporary conservatives would like a strongly libertarian First Amendment that can sweep aside business regulations, protect corporate political contributions and expenditures, exempt people from antidiscrimination laws, and cripple public-sector unions.[49] But the original meaning of the First Amendment—at least under a thick account—does not really support these conclusions.[50] One must read the history selectively and tendentiously to show that the eighteenth-century First Amendment matches the values of contemporary conservatives. Or one must jettison a thick account of original meaning in this area of the law and adopt a thin account.

The perpetual retrofitting of originalist theory to reach particu-

lar results leads to the sneaking suspicion that what really has constitutional authority in the United States is not the original meaning
of the Constitution itself but rather contemporary social and political values, to which originalist theories must continually conform.
The tail of social and political change is wagging the dog of originalist inquiry.

We can make much better sense of Americans' actual practices
of constitutional interpretation if we adopt the distinction between
interpretation and construction and recognize that fidelity to original meaning commits us only to a thin theory of original meaning.
That is, we can make better sense of the American constitutional
tradition if we adhere to something like framework originalism. And
in fact, framework originalism should not be especially difficult for
conservatives or liberals, originalists or living constitutionalists to accept. Indeed, even in countries that reject American-style originalism, it offers a plausible account of constitutional interpretation.

Since the 1980s, conservative originalists have tried to argue that
original intention, original understanding, or original public meaning should be the touchstone for legitimate constitutional interpretation, even if one must make exceptions for precedents of long
standing.[51] The interpretation-construction distinction suggests that
this project runs together what is *mandatory* with what is merely *persuasive*. Americans make originalist arguments because they like to
call on the nation's long-standing traditions and invoke the authority
of its cultural heroes. But they do so selectively. They are cafeteria
originalists.

The problem of thick theories of original public meaning is that
they attempt to leverage merely persuasive authority into mandatory authority, and appeals to the past into commands from the past.
Even originalist judges themselves cannot live up to this standard. It
is no wonder, then, that such a rigid approach to interpretation is
honored in the breach as much as in the observance.

H. The Originalist Model of Authority and Its Limits

Originalist theories of interpretation generally share a distinctive
view of constitutional authority: the proper interpretation of the Constitution depends on what was fixed at the time of adoption, whether

that thing is original meaning, intention, or understanding.[52] Constitutional interpretations are legitimate to the extent that they are consistent with what was fixed at the time of adoption; they are illegitimate to the extent that they are not. I will call this the *originalist model of authority*. History is important to constitutional interpretation because it is evidence of what was fixed; and the result of historical inquiry, when properly conducted, points to a legal norm that we must follow in the present if we want to continue to be faithful to the Constitution.

Originalists offer different theories for why we must follow what is fixed at the time of adoption.[53] A common explanation, however, is that the American people created the Constitution as an act of popular sovereignty; and the law they created must remain in force until it is altered or the people create a new constitution.[54] This argument combines elements of popular sovereignty (for the initial creation of the law) and the rule of law (for why the law should continue unchanged over time).

Once we introduce the distinction between interpretation and construction, however, it becomes clear that the originalist model of authority cannot explain why lawyers and judges make most of the arguments from adoption history offered in American legal culture. To be sure, the originalist model explains why we must always make arguments about adoption history in every case and why the best versions of these arguments are always *mandatory*; but it does not explain why arguments from adoption history could be merely *persuasive* authority, sometimes invoked and sometimes ignored. It does not explain why lawyers do not always try to make originalist arguments in every constitutional case and why judges do not always accept them. It does not explain why in a wide range of cases, even self-described originalist judges simply ignore adoption history and spend their time arguing about doctrine. Under the originalist model of authority, to knowingly reject what was fixed at the time of adoption is illegitimate.

This raises two related questions. First, why do American judges and lawyers sometimes ignore arguments from adoption history? Second, why do American judges and lawyers sometimes consider arguments from adoption history but only sometimes find them persuasive? The originalist model of authority by itself cannot answer these questions.

These practices, however, are completely consistent with living originalism. We interpret the Constitution according to its original meaning (in the thin sense), which is fixed at the time of adoption.[55] But the basic framework does not settle most disputed questions of constitutional interpretation. These require constitutional construction. Thus, living originalism accepts the originalist model of authority with respect to the content of the basic framework, but not with respect to questions of constitutional construction. That describes how most lawyers and judges actually operate in practice.

There are many possible ways we might build out the Constitution-in-practice. History—including adoption history—will normally be very important to construction. But it will be important in different ways than the originalist model of authority prescribes. Sometimes adoption history will give us the best construction. Often we can trace a line of gradual development from the original construction to the present day. But sometimes that line of development takes us very far from the original construction. And sometimes our country has made decisive breaks with the past. Therefore, in many cases, the best construction today is not the original construction. That, too, describes how most lawyers and judges actually operate in practice.

I. The Consequences of the Interpretation-Construction Distinction for Historical Argument

In order to accept these arguments, one does not have to agree with my theory of living originalism in all respects. The only idea that one has to accept is the distinction between interpretation and construction. This idea has far-reaching consequences for constitutional theory generally. In particular, it has important consequences for how constitutional interpreters use history. Let me list a few of them.

First, because construction, not interpretation, is the central case of constitutional argument, most historical argument—including arguments about adoption history—also occurs in the construction zone. And once we are in the construction zone, nonadoption history is as important as adoption history. Much historical argument is about cultural memory, and cultural memory spans the entire history of the country.

Second, the distinction between interpretation and construction explains why most arguments from adoption history do not behave in the way that the originalist model of authority assumes. American constitutional culture does not treat originalist arguments as mandatory; judges sometimes reject originalist arguments or do not even mention them at all. There is not even a single kind of originalist argument. Instead, there are a variety of originalist claims, corresponding to different modalities of justification.

Third, in constitutional construction, arguments from adoption history are usually hybrids: they also involve appeals to national ethos, political tradition, or honored authority. Many scholars, including Jamal Greene, David McGowan, Robert Post, and Michael Dorf, have pointed out that originalist arguments either explicitly or implicitly appeal to national ethos.[56] Lawyers and judges treat the founding era and members of the founding generation as having special *ethical authority* in constitutional argument.[57]

However, because originalist arguments usually appeal to ethos and tradition, they will normally not be persuasive unless people can plausibly accept the values of the adopters as their own, or can recharacterize them so that they can plausibly accept them as their own.[58] By contrast, when the values of founders, framers, and adopters seem too alien or irrelevant to contemporary values, lawyers and judges generally avoid making originalist arguments. As a result, much of originalist argument operates as a kind of historical ventriloquism, in which advocates make the founders, framers, and adopters speak their values.

Fourth, the distinction between interpretation and construction helps us understand why *opponents* of originalism generally accept the basic framework as binding and regularly make originalist arguments.

Nonoriginalists often criticize originalists on the ground that we should not be bound by the dead hand of the past. Nevertheless, they usually accept that the clear textual rules of the Constitution are binding—for example, that there are two houses of Congress and that each state gets two senators—even though these rules also represent the dead hand of the past.

Nonoriginalists also often complain that originalist arguments are anachronistic and that lawyers and judges cannot reliably discern original meaning, original understanding, or original intention. Even so, nonoriginalists often make arguments from adoption history themselves—in briefs, in public statements, and in open letters.[59] And of course, nonoriginalist lawyers have no problem serving up originalist arguments to persuade originalist judges on the bench.

The interpretation-construction distinction makes sense of these practices. Most nonoriginalists accept that the basic framework is fixed and cannot be altered without Article V amendment.[60] In the construction zone, nonoriginalists agree that arguments from adoption history can be persuasive authority and often highly persuasive authority. They understand that appeals to ethos, tradition, and honored authority are valuable and important features of American constitutional culture. And, like conservative originalists, they may work to characterize the constitutional tradition in ways that reflect their values. This should not be surprising. A living tradition of constitutionalism needs cultural memory and the resources that go with it, even—and especially—because the tradition is constantly changing.

CHAPTER EIGHT
Why It's Better to Be Thin

I N CHAPTER 7, I contrasted thick and thin conceptions of original public meaning. There is more than one version of original public meaning because the concept of the "original public meaning" in constitutional law is a theoretical construction rather than a simple report about social facts, and there is more than one way of cashing out this concept in constitutional law. In this chapter, I explain why a thin theory of original meaning is superior. It is better as a matter of constitutional theory. And it is also better able to accommodate a rich historical record and the work of professional historians.

Some scholars have tried to derive a theory of original public meaning from the philosophy of language alone.[1] But what we are interested in is not a general philosophical conception of meaning but those elements of meaning that are relevant to constitutional argument and constitutional interpretation.

An analogy may be helpful here. The ideas of causation or intention in tort and criminal law do not simply reflect physical events and psychological processes. What the law deems "intention" or "causation" in criminal law or tort law are shaped by and adapted to the policies, purposes, and concerns of these bodies of law.[2] In the same way, the concept of "original public meaning" will not be fully determined by general theories of meaning and communication.

While these theories may be helpful in understanding what a constitution communicates, they are also incomplete. What we want to know is not what meaning is in general, or even what meaning is in the ordinary circumstances of conversation, but what meaning is *for purposes of constitutional interpretation*. And the version of original public meaning we adopt—whether thick or thin—will depend on underlying views about constitutional theory: what constitutions are, how they work, what we expect from them, and what we want them to do.[3]

A. Original Public Meaning as a Theoretical Reconstruction of the Past

The concept of original public meaning is fashioned in the present for present-day use. It selects certain features of the past as relevant to constitutional interpretation and renders other features of the past irrelevant. It then reconfigures those features of the past that it regards as relevant through the perspective of a particular view about law and legitimacy. It then dubs that reconfiguration "the original public meaning of the text."

That does not mean that original public meaning has nothing to do with historical facts. Quite the contrary: in their quest for original public meaning, originalists are searching for facts.[4] An account of original meaning should rest on facts that we believe to be true, and it should be different if those facts turn out to be different.

But articulating the original public meaning is not a simple job of reporting what happened at a certain magical moment in time. It is a theoretical and selective reconstruction of elements of the past, brought forward to the present and employed for present-day purposes. Behind originalist claims are theoretical and practical commitments, even if lawyers and judges do not always recognize them. These theoretical and practical commitments shape which facts are relevant and important, and how and why they are relevant and important. These commitments prefigure what we look for in the past, how we evaluate what we find, what we discard as peripheral or not germane, and what we will do with the evidence that we bring forward with us into the present. Theories of original public meaning—

for there are more than one—carefully configure the past to serve the values of the present. And that is not a problem, as long as we are candid about those values, and willing to defend them openly.

Take, for example, one of the most frequently quoted tests of original public meaning—what a hypothetical speaker of the English language at the time of adoption would understand the officially adopted text to mean.[5] Under this approach, the actual views of actual speakers of the English language are evidence of this hypothetical speaker's views, but they are not conclusive. After all, this hypothetical person has no particular race, gender, or political party, has no particular political axe to grind, is not from any particular part of the country, and knows much more about history and law than most actual individuals would.[6] We must sift through history to imagine and construct what this hypothetical speaker of English would have thought. We must filter historical evidence through the sieve of a jurisprudential theory.

Gary Lawson and Guy Seidman are explicit on this point: "[W]hen interpreting the Constitution," they explain, "the touchstone is not the specific thoughts in the heads of any particular historical people—whether drafters, ratifiers, or commentators, however distinguished and significant within the drafting and ratification process they may have been—but rather the hypothetical understandings of a reasonable person who is artificially constructed by lawyers. The thoughts of historical figures may be relevant to the ultimate inquiry, but the ultimate inquiry is legal."[7]

This theory of original public meaning filters and reconfigures the past because it is designed to produce a legal meaning that constitutional interpreters living today might actually use. If, as originalists believe, original meaning should be binding on later generations, it cannot be plural and diverse. It must be unitary or, at the very least, significantly bounded. For most originalists, an account of original public meaning that regularly produced a plethora of potential original public meanings for every important controversy before the courts would be far less useful. Many originalists hope to use originalist theory to constrain judges—but a theory that regularly generated multiple original public meanings would simply not do the trick.

John McGinnis and Michael Rappaport's theory of original legal methods offers an example of how what purports merely to be a historical description of original public meaning actually reconstitutes history to serve practical and theoretical ends. Although they are less candid about this than Lawson and Seidman, their conception of original meaning is no less artificial and constructed.

McGinnis and Rappaport argue that the Constitution is written in the language of the law.[8] Therefore, we should determine the original meaning of the Constitution by using the interpretive rules and methods that adoption-era lawyers would have applied to the Constitution.[9]

Their theory imposes several different frames and filters on history. First, they focus on the views of lawyers, not the general public.[10] Interestingly, their theory rejects the Supreme Court's own theory of original public meaning, stated most prominently by Justice Scalia in *District of Columbia v. Heller*, that "'[t]he Constitution was written to be understood by the voters; its words and phrases were used in their normal and ordinary as distinguished from technical meaning' . . . [and] excludes secret or technical meanings that would not have been known to ordinary citizens in the founding generation."[11] In fact, conservative originalists often conflate original public meaning with original legal meaning, but McGinnis and Rappaport are clear that the meaning *to lawyers* is what counts.

Second, McGinnis and Rappaport argue that to produce original meaning, we should employ the methods of legal interpretation that adoption-era lawyers would have used, using them as adoption-era lawyers would have applied them.[12]

Third, McGinnis and Rappaport acknowledge that adoption-era lawyers may have disagreed about how to interpret the Constitution, and they also may have disagreed about what interpretive methods to use. In that case, McGinnis and Rappaport propose that present-day interpreters use a "51–49 rule."[13] Interpreters should designate as the original legal meaning "the better interpretation of a provision, even if it is only slightly better."[14] By this, they mean the interpretation that is "better supported" or "the meaning that was more likely than not."[15] "That rule," they assert, "should resolve almost any ambiguity, once the evidence for [one] interpretation is weighed against another."[16] They believe that even the meaning of seemingly vague terms can be resolved in this way.[17]

In short, even if adoption-era lawyers disagreed about what interpretive methods to use and also disagreed about how to apply those methods to particular issues, McGinnis and Rappaport argue that lawyers today, looking at the available historical evidence, can decide which interpretation was better supported. And that interpretation, they conclude, *is* the original meaning of the Constitution.

McGinnis and Rappaport assert that their 51–49 theory is purely descriptive—that is, it is concerned only with historical facts about meaning; and it is distinct from the question of what interpretive theory is normatively desirable.[18] Nevertheless, their descriptive theory conveniently meshes with their normative theory of why judges should be originalists.[19]

McGinnis and Rappaport believe that originalism is the best theory of interpretation because it produces the best consequences.[20] It produces the best consequences because constitutional provisions must be ratified by supermajorities, and McGinnis and Rappaport argue that supermajorities tend to produce rules that will produce the best consequences over time.[21] But in order to enjoy the benefits of supermajority rules, the rules must have determinate content and not be later subject to what McGinnis and Rappaport call "judicial updating."[22] They believe that once we take original legal methods into account, it is very unlikely that most constitutional provisions will turn out to be vague or unclear. That is because "citizens are risk-averse when it comes to constitutional provisions,"[23] and they would probably not agree to adopt abstract or vague provisions that would delegate responsibility for implementation to later generations. "[W]hat supermajority rules encourage are not broad delegations to the future, but determinate principles about which there is a broad consensus."[24] For this reason, they argue that once we apply the appropriate original legal methods, there is very little about the Bill of Rights that is vague or requires constitutional construction because these amendments "did not focus on deeply contested matters."[25]

In short, McGinnis and Rappaport's descriptive account of original meaning, with its 51–49 rule, is designed to generate the kind of determinate content that will, in turn, produce the admirable benefits of supermajority rules. Their theory of how to interpret the Constitution is designed to mesh with their theory of why constitutions produced through supermajority rules produce good results.[26] And it depends on their assumption that today's lawyers, looking at the evidence of legal meanings, can resolve almost all ambiguities and problems of vagueness and decide on a single original meaning, even if there was no consensus about either original meaning or original interpretive methods among adoption-era lawyers.

There are good reasons to think that their "descriptive" theory of original meaning has little to do with historical accuracy.[27] First, there was no general agreement in 1787 that lawyers' views rather than the views of the general public determined the meaning of the new Constitution.[28] In any case, what it meant to be trained as a lawyer in 1787 was quite different from what it means to be trained as a lawyer today. People did not go to graduate schools of law, and many picked up their legal training haphazardly or through apprenticeships.[29] Second, there was no consensus about what legal methods people should use to interpret the new Constitution.[30] Third, there is little reason to believe that lawyers would have reached consensus on how to read the new Constitution, judging from the constant disputes between lawyers about virtually every important question that arose both before and after ratification. For example, among those with legal training, interpretive controversies immediately broke out over the Jay Treaty, the First Bank of the United States, and the Alien and Sedition Acts.[31] In particular, the early dispute between the Federalists and Jeffersonians about what the First Amendment protected seriously undermines McGinnis and Rappaport's assurance that risk-averse citizens will only adopt "determinate principles about which there is a broad consensus."[32]

Fourth, McGinnis and Rappaport's 51–49 rule seems like a transparent attempt to manufacture a single answer and simply call it "original meaning" even where no consensus among adoption-era sources actually existed. McGinnis and Rappaport argue that since founding-era lawyers would have chosen the best supported interpretive rules and the best supported interpretations, so should we.[33] What other rule, after all, should we use? But the fact that we in the present are deciding what interpretive rule is "better supported" and what interpretation is "better supported" does not mean that our conclusions reflect the original legal meaning of the Constitution to its adopters, much less their own judgments about which interpretation was better supported. After all, by hypothesis, the adopters *disagreed* about what interpretive rules were best and what interpretations were best. And it is implausible to assume that the way that professionally trained lawyers with graduate educations read legal documents today is the same way that people with very different legal training would have read them in 1787. McGinnis and Rappaport's 51–49 percent rule is historical ventriloquism.

Once we concede that adoption-era lawyers often did not actually agree on what the Constitution meant or how to interpret it, McGinnis and Rappaport's supermajority justification of originalism also falls apart. First, most ordinary citizens who voted to adopt the Constitution may have known little about how lawyers would read the document, either in the near term or in the future, or what future lawyers would consider the "better supported" view. Second, if adopters disagreed about what the document meant—which they most certainly did—they could not be sure that the document would be interpreted according to their understandings. Therefore, they were not voting on a document involving "determinate principles about which there is a broad consensus."[34]

McGinnis and Rappaport respond that where adopters disagreed about what the new Constitution would do, they would engage in a probabilistic assessment of how the document would likely be interpreted in the future and then decide whether to support it based on "whether the expected net benefits of the document outweighed the uncertainty that they had about its meaning."[35] But this concession undermines McGinnis and Rappaport's central argument for originalism: that a determinate Constitution backed by supermajority support will produce good consequences centuries later, and that in order to realize those benefits, we must strictly follow the adopters' original meaning.

If all that is so, then McGinnis and Rappaport's theory of original methods originalism cannot really get off the ground. But even assuming that I am wrong about this and that the theory can be made workable, what the theory offers is not a mere description of original public meaning but a carefully constructed reconfiguration of the past that serves McGinnis and Rappaport's larger theoretical project.

B. The Advantages of a Thin
Theory of Original Meaning

So far I have argued that thick accounts of original meaning are not simply descriptions of the past but are constructed to serve theoretical and practical ends. They are choices about what to take from the past rather than merely descriptions of the past.

But the same is also true of framework or living originalism. Living originalism has *both* a thin theory of original public meaning *and* a division of labor between interpretation and construction. The thin theory treats only some history as relevant, because it is looking for original semantic meanings, generally recognized legal terms of art, and those features of background context necessary to understand the text and avoid plays on words. The rest of history is relevant to constitutional construction—the area in which most constitutional disputes occur.

Why is this way of using history better than a thick theory of original meaning? Living originalism is superior in four respects.

First, living originalism has a better theory of what constitutions are and how they work. It better accommodates the multiple sources of the Constitution's democratic legitimacy.

Second, living originalism better captures how people actually use adoption history in constitutional interpretation—sometimes employing it but sometimes rejecting or ignoring it. Living originalism better explains why Americans are cafeteria originalists.

Third, because living originalism features a wide zone for constitutional construction, it is better able to learn from and make use of the work of professional historians that conservative originalists often downplay or ignore. Living originalism does not insist, as some originalists do, that historians ask the wrong questions or look at the wrong evidence.[36] (I return to this criticism in part 5.) Living originalism has no problem when historians point out multiple viewpoints and assumptions among the ratifying public, because all of this history can be useful in constitutional construction.

Fourth, because living originalism features a wide zone for constitutional construction, it can also accommodate and make use of many different kinds of history from many historical periods, and the views and experiences of many different kinds of people. That is because the goal of construction is to use history to advise and tutor the present rather than to uncover decrees from the distant past.

Thick theories of original meaning exclude a great deal of what historians think is important because these theories hope to converge on a single legal answer or a limited range of possible legal answers. By contrast, living originalism can consider all of this history in constitutional construction. Because thick theories must be thick to do their jobs, they constrict constitutional memory and eschew historical complexity and lack of resolution. But because the thin theory is thin, it has plenty of room for what historians have to offer.

For example, living originalism can pay attention to the views of those who held minority positions about the Constitution that did not win out in their own time but that are relevant for us today. It can accommodate the stories and constitutional claims of people who were not officially part of the constitution-making process or were shut out of that process entirely. The views of enslaved and free Black people before the Civil War, and of women before the Nineteenth Amendment, are part of the dialectical tradition of American constitutionalism. Their views and experiences can be resources for understanding our Constitution and creating the best constructions for our own time. The views of suffragists about sex equality or of Wobblies and labor activists about the First Amendment can be grist for the mill of constitutional construction. Their experiences, and their wisdom, can tutor us in how we implement and apply the Constitution today.

Post-adoption history matters in constitutional construction. To interpret the Fourteenth Amendment, we do not have to rely solely on the views of Reconstruction framers and adopters. We can acknowledge that the social and political movements of the Second Reconstruction of the 1950s and 1960s, the movement for women's liberation in the 1970s, and the gay rights movement also shaped the Constitution's practical meaning.

In sum, living originalism makes many more people and groups potential resources for constitutional construction. We can care more about the complexities of history and the many groups and persons who can offer both positive and negative lessons from our past. Thus, in chapters 12 and 13, I argue that living originalism *expands* constitutional memory, while thicker versions of originalism *contract* or *erase* constitutional memory.

C. Frameworks and Skyscrapers

Framework originalism's division of labor between interpretation and construction—and the role that history plays in each—is based on a larger set of ideas about what constitutions are and how they work.

Most conservative originalists with a thick theory of original meaning view constitutions primarily as constraints on politics. I call this a skyscraper view of constitutions.[37] In the skyscraper model, the Constitution is like a finished building, and people engage in politics within its structures. They can only change the building through Article V amendment.

By contrast, I view constitutions as frameworks. They are a basic set of rules, standards, and principles that are designed to create institutions and channel political action in order to make politics possible.[38] Constitutions are designed to put politics in motion and cause people to solve their problems through politics as opposed to through violence and civil war.[39] But because constitutions are only frameworks, they need to be built out over time through constitutional construction by both the judiciary and the political branches. And as people struggle with each other in politics, they also construct the Constitution-in-practice as well.

For skyscraper originalists, who have a thick version of original meaning, the Constitution is mostly finished, and we engage in ordinary politics within its boundaries. For framework originalists like me, the Constitution is never finished, and we continue to construct many of its features through constitutional politics even as we live and work within it. For skyscraper originalists, the Constitution's democratic legitimacy comes from acts of popular sovereignty that adopt the Constitution or amend it through Article V's supermajority rules. For framework originalists, the Constitution's legitimacy comes from two sources, not one. The first source is, as before, adoption or amendment. But adoption and amendment are infrequent, and they do not explain most constitutional change in the United

States. The second source of the Constitution's legitimacy comes from successive constitutional constructions that respond, in the long run, to the forces of democratic politics.[40]

The way we construct our concept of original public meaning has a lot to do with our background assumptions about what constitutions are and how they work. If you hold to the skyscraper view of constitutions, you will be attracted to a relatively thick view of original public meaning, because you assume (or you hope) that original meaning can and will resolve a relatively high percentage of constitutional questions. Accordingly, there will be relatively less need for constitutional construction. In fact, McGinnis and Rappaport take this idea to its logical conclusion. They oppose the very idea of constitutional construction.[41] For them, everything, or almost everything, can be achieved through using original legal methods.[42]

Conversely, if you view the Constitution as a framework, always unfinished, and always being built out through constitutional construction, you will be more attracted to a thin theory of original public meaning. A thin account of original public meaning makes the most sense given that the democratic legitimacy of the Constitution, over time, depends on more than the initial act of lawmaking. It also depends in part on each generation's contribution to the constitutional project. The initial framework guides and channels how those contributions may be made, but it leaves a great deal to be worked out in the future.

The nature of language alone will not tell us which version of original public meaning we should choose. Instead, our view of original public meaning—and therefore the way we will use history to discover and expound that meaning—will depend on deeper debates about the nature of constitutions and the sources of their legitimacy.

The thin theory is superior as a matter of constitutional theory because constitutions are frameworks, not skyscrapers. They do not simply contain politics. They are built out and elaborated through politics. A constitution is an intergenerational project of governance that aims to create and preserve a decent politics but that is never fully completed.[43] A thin theory of original meaning, therefore, is most consistent with how written constitutions work and what they are for.[44]

D. The Thin Theory and Democratic Legitimacy

Not only is a thin theory of original meaning more consistent with how the U.S. Constitution actually operates, but it also better preserves the democratic legitimacy of the Constitution over time.[45] As noted earlier, for a skyscraper originalist, the Constitution has only one source of legitimacy—the act of popular sovereignty that produces a constitution or an amendment. But for the framework originalist, the Constitution has two sources of legitimacy. The first is the moment of adoption or amendment. The second is the succession of constitutional constructions that emerge from democratic politics and respond to waves of political and social mobilizations and countermobilizations.[46]

This second source of legitimacy is crucial to the American constitutional system. Huge changes occurred in the Constitution-in-practice during the twentieth century. But most of these changes cannot be traced to new constitutional amendments.[47] The New Deal; the rise of the administrative and regulatory state; the civil rights and civil liberties revolutions that protected accused persons and generated modern doctrines of freedom of speech and press; the voting rights revolution, with its principle of one person, one vote; and many constitutional protections for women and minorities were not the result of new constitutional amendments. Instead they were the result of successive constitutional constructions by the political branches and by the courts.

These constructions greatly improved the democratic legitimacy of the Constitution, and without them, many Americans would regard their system of government as deeply unjust and illegitimate. Skyscraper originalism often has considerable difficulty explaining and justifying these constructions. But framework originalism does not. Quite the contrary: it views them as exemplary of how the American Constitution actually works.

The Constitution becomes law through an act of popular sovereignty. For rule of law reasons, the Constitution continues as law until it is lawfully changed. It does not follow, however, that the Constitution maintains the same degree of democratic legitimacy over time.

The democratic warrant of the Constitution is greatest in the early years after its adoption, because the people who adopted it are still alive. But as time goes on, the adopting generation dies off; it is replaced by later generations who had no say in creating or adopting the Constitution. The "We the People" of the United States today are not the same human beings as the "We the People" who adopted most of the Constitution's text. In fact, most of the present generation may not even be related to the adopting generation.

Moreover, even if the process by which the Constitution or its amendments was adopted seemed democratically legitimate at the time, that process may look far less legitimate in the eyes of later generations. For example, the 1787 Constitution was adopted by popular conventions that were, by the standards of the eighteenth century, quite inclusive.[48] But that process would be considered very undemocratic today. Women, Native Americans, African Americans, and many poor white men were excluded from official constitution-making, and they constituted most of the population. If they had been included—almost unthinkable, given the politics and power relations of the time—the Constitution might have looked quite different.[49]

In short, as time passes, the Constitution's text may be no less law, but it may become less democratically legitimate law. A long-lived constitution has a democratic deficit, because the people who live under the Constitution cannot say that they or their elected representatives made it the law. That democratic deficit may become larger and larger with each passing generation, attenuating the Constitution's democratic legitimacy.

The standard response to this problem is to point out that the Constitution was adopted by "We the People of the United States" and that "We the People" is not simply the people living at the time of the founding but a transhistorical subject that continues over time.[50] "We the People" consists of the successive generations of individuals who inhabit the same nation—even if the boundaries of the nation and the people who live there change over time. (Think of all the land and the populations that the United States added through wars and treaties between 1787 and the present, not to mention the many waves of immigration from other countries.) The Constitution is a transgenerational project of this transgenerational subject.

Because we are part of the same "We the People" who created the Constitution, we created it, and so there is no democratic deficit. Until the present generation amends the Constitution or adopts a new one, We the People continue to be governed by our own past work.

For some, it may be flattering to be considered the same people as the founders. But if this answer is to be more than a convenient fiction, each generation must actually have a hand in building out the Constitution they live under. If we are going to claim that the Constitution is a transgenerational project of a transgenerational subject, we should take the consequences of that claim seriously. The Constitution-in-practice must be produced over time by many different people living at different times; it must be the work of many generations, not merely the adopting generation. The constituent or constitution-making power of the people must be exercised not only at the comparatively rare moments of initial adoption and amendment but continually in constitutional development, that is to say, through constitutional construction.

If the Constitution is to retain its democratic legitimacy over long periods of time, the initial act of popular sovereignty and the rule of law will not be sufficient. Democratic legitimacy must flow from a source that is continually refreshed. That source is constitutional construction, which, in the long run, responds to democratic processes. And if the legitimacy of the system depends on people exercising their constitution-making power through constitutional construction as well as adoption and amendment, this argues for a relatively broad zone of construction, and this, in turn, argues for a relatively thin version of original meaning.

Taking seriously the idea that the Constitution is a transgenerational project of politics has yet another consequence. It concerns institutional capacity.

The adopters of a constitution have limited capacities for predicting and controlling the future. They cannot foresee everything that will happen in political life; they cannot predict how technology, foreign affairs, demographics, and social change will drastically alter the world and wreak havoc on their best-laid plans.

Because human capacities for knowing the future are limited, the adopting generation must rely on the work of subsequent generations in order to make the constitutional project a success over time. It cannot do everything itself; it needs the assistance of many people devoted to the project who are strewn throughout time.

What the adopting generation can do, however, is to structure and channel the political choices of later generations in the hope that these people will become attached to the project and work to make it succeed. A transgenerational project, in short, must make the most of each generation's limited capacities to understand the challenges of the future, and it must rely on the contributions of each succeeding generation to keep the project going. Later generations may fail us, of course; that is why legitimacy also depends on constitutional faith. Constitutional faith is faith that the constitutional project can sustain itself over long periods of time and, in the words of the Preamble, become a more perfect union.[51]

If the constitutional constructions of successive generations are necessary to give the Constitution its continuing democratic legitimacy, and if the efforts of successive generations are necessary to compensate for the limited capacities of any single generation, then the best account of original meaning is a thin theory with a fairly broad zone for constitutional construction. Now the U.S. Constitution is not only among the most long-lived in history but it is also among the most difficult to amend in the world. A theory of original meaning that is too thick will exacerbate the democratic deficit of a long-lived constitution and will undermine democratic legitimacy as time goes on. Too thick an account of original meaning will also fail to economize on the collective wisdom of successive generations; it will make far less use of the institutional capacities of later generations to adapt government to technological, social, and economic change and to new crises and unexpected needs.

In sum, we best compensate for the increasing democratic deficit of originalism over time and the limited capacities of founders, framers, and adopters if we adopt a thin theory of original meaning that leaves ample room for constitutional construction. Living constitutionalism is nothing more than the processes of constitutional construction working out over time. That is why I argue that framework originalism and living constitutionalism are not opposed but mutually dependent; they are two sides of the same coin.

E. The Thin Theory and History

Living originalism's combination of a thin theory of original meaning and a broad zone of constitutional construction is also superior in how it handles history.

First, a thin theory of original meaning is better equipped to deal with disagreements among different actors and different publics about original intentions, understandings, public meanings, and legal meanings.

Second, a thin theory with a broad zone for construction is better able to avoid anachronism; thick theories of original meaning tend to encourage anachronism.

Third, because most historical arguments concern matters of constitutional construction, living originalism allows contemporary interpreters to decide that some historical interpretations were better than others, even if they were minority positions in their day.

Fourth, thick theories attempt to ground the legitimacy of constitutional interpretation solely in the Constitution's original public meaning. But living originalism can acknowledge that the actual sources of constitutional legitimacy—for example, the civil rights revolution—come from post-adoption history.

1. Dealing with Disagreement and Multiple Publics

During periods of constitutional adoption and amendment, we are likely to find a variety of different views circulating, along with an almost complete lack of attention to many questions that turn out to be important to later generations. On many issues, including both issues that people paid little attention to and issues about which people cared the most, a consensus about constitutional meaning—in the thick sense—is likely to be an illusion. With respect to these questions, it is misleading to assume that there would be a single view held by all reasonable persons, even hypothetical reasonable persons. This problem occurs whether we focus on original intentions, understandings, public meanings, or legal meanings. And if we construct a hypothetical individual to create consensus where there is none, we do both ourselves and the past a disservice.

Note, moreover, that if we really care about the meaning of the Constitution to the *public*, and not simply to framers or adopters, we should also be interested in the meaning of the Constitution to people who were excluded from the ratification and adoption process—women, free Black people, Native Americans, and enslaved people. If we include the views and understandings of these people, disagreements among the public (or more correctly publics) are likely to be even greater. We might well expect, for example, that free Black people and white plantation owners would disagree about many parts of the Constitution, including not only individual rights but also questions of federalism and national power.

To be sure, we can define the "public" in original public meaning to exclude groups shut out of governance—which includes most of the population at the founding. But then we must confront severe problems in the democratic legitimacy of the process. These defects in legitimacy will not be cured, as some originalists think, by women or Black people obtaining the vote a century or a century and a half later. By the time women and Black people gained the vote, most of the basic constitutional edifice had already been constructed.

In any case, however we define the "public," a thick theory of original public meaning cannot fully eliminate the fact that a sufficiently large population will have many different ideas about what the Constitution means—and especially so during periods of adoption and amendment.[52]

Professional historians often criticize lawyers' concepts of original public meaning for this very reason. Jack Rakove, for example, argues that original public meaning originalism depends on the views of imaginary people who never existed.[53] He points out that the framers themselves recognized that understandings of texts are rarely unitary and that people's views about what terms mean are likely to evolve in the heat of political confrontation.[54] Participants in constitutional debates will differ not only as to party and ideology but also as to class, education, experience, skill, and interest.[55] Moreover, their understandings emerge from a complex history of readings and counterreadings, traditions and countertraditions, goals and motivations, which reach backward indefinitely into the past.[56] What original public meaning offers us, Rakove argues, is but a pale copy of that rich historical texture.

When a proposed constitutional text is laid before the public, there are almost certain to be multiple understandings of its meaning and import. In a political process like the ratification of a constitution, different people will take away different things from the same document. This feature of legal texts was as true in 1787 as it is in our own day. Today lawyers and judges often disagree vehemently in ordinary cases of statutory construction, to say nothing of constitutional construction.[57] These disagreements are no doubt shaped by the political and ideological controversies of our day. But the period of ratification was filled with political and ideological disagreements every bit as fierce as those of the present. The notion that the late 1780s were a period of placid consensus about the meaning of words in legal texts, about the political principles behind them, or about their proper application to real-world controversies, is more than naive—it is simply ridiculous.[58]

The more that we demand of original public meaning *by itself* to resolve contested questions in the present, the more disagreement and the more variations of understanding we will find among the ratifiers of the Constitution and its amendments, not to mention among the general public—and we may find that for certain issues, there was no consideration at all. Originalists may hope to discover what a reasonable person would have understood the constitutional text to mean. But in any age or era—as in our own—reasonable people often differ about many things, especially where politics is involved.

If, undaunted, we nevertheless insist on a thick version of original meaning, we will discover that we will only be able to draw out a single answer from the past by reading the evidence selectively and opportunistically, by ignoring many members of the public, or by declaring that their views were not in fact reasonable. Or we may have to make contestable analogies to deal with situations and contexts never considered or imagined. Insisting on a unitary *and* a thick account of original public meaning under these conditions is an invitation to anachronism, special pleading, and the worst sort of "law office history."

In contrast, a thin theory of original public meaning is better suited to deal with the problems of dissensus and differing understandings among the public (or publics), as well as the many kinds of questions that the adopters and the public never considered or even imagined. A thin theory works best because it deliberately focuses on those aspects of constitutional meaning that are most likely to be widely shared, while leaving the rest to considerations of constitutional construction.

But, you may object, doesn't the complexity of history affect even a thin account of original public meaning? Surely it does. But by scaling down our ambitions, we can have far greater hope that history will converge on a relatively small range of original public meanings. If we ask for more, by contrast, we are far more likely to encounter indeterminacy, disagreement, and questions that the public never thought of.

Thus, the division of labor between interpretation and construction is deliberate. Most debates about the legal relevance of history will turn out to be questions of constitutional construction because they touch on aspects of history that are likely to be—as professional historians remind us—the most complicated and complex. Far from excluding these complications from constitutional argument, the thin theory embraces what is rich and diverse as a resource for construction in the present.

2. Accepting the Past on Its Own Terms

A second advantage of the thin theory is that a broad zone of constitutional construction is better able to avoid anachronism and treat the past on its own terms. The generations that adopted the Constitution and its amendments were trying to grapple with their problems in their world, not our problems in our world. Their arguments about constitutional meaning and principle emerged in the context of assumptions that may be alien to our world.[59] Most lawyers and judges deal with the problem of anachronism by simply ignoring it; yet it greatly complicates how to apply adoption-era debates and concerns to the constitutional issues of our day.

Lawyers and judges tend to downplay the possibility of anachronism for two reasons. First, the basic orientation of legal argument is presentist. Lawyers and judges are interested in the past because they want to interpret and apply law in the present.[60]

Second, some degree of anachronism is unavoidable in legal argument. To see why, contrast the practice of legal argument with the views of intellectual historians determined to avoid anachronism—for example, the members of the Cambridge School represented by Quentin Skinner.[61] For these scholars, the goal of studying history and historical texts is to understand what historical actors were trying to do in the context of the political and cultural struggles of their own time, rather than as the articulation of general ideas that transcend their time and may be fruitfully employed in the future.[62]

By contrast, making law normally involves producing texts that will apply in a potentially unknowable future in very different contexts of judgment. And in interpreting and applying old law, lawyers draw precedents from and analogies with the past to argue about what to do in the present. Legal argument, in other words, demands that we use old texts and concepts across time, and it approaches these texts and concepts in terms of their potential relevance to the present. In this way, the standard practices of legal argument push in the opposite direction from the Cambridge School's approach. Legal argument always takes some parts of the past—texts, precedents, political ideas, and legal concepts—out of their original historical situation and attempts to apply them in the present.

Nevertheless, the fact that the orientation of legal argument is presentist does not mean that lawyers and judges should feel free to reason about old texts, precedents, and concepts free from their historical contexts. And the fact that the application of old law in new contexts always involves some degree of anachronism does not mean that anachronism is a positive virtue in legal interpretation.

Lawyers should always do their best to understand the past in its historical context before they try to draw normative lessons from it. That means understanding how the past is different from our time as well as how it is similar. Indeed, sometimes we cannot truly understand how the past is similar until we begin to recognize how it is different. And we cannot make useful analogies from the past until we understand its differences from the present. Analogy to the past and differentiation from the past must work together.

Thick theories of original meaning tend to exacerbate law's tendencies toward anachronism. First, lawyers in quest of original meaning tend to focus on specific legal materials—statutes, constitutional texts, and judicial precedents—divorced from the historical contexts that produced them. Second, lawyers tend to think that because these materials are legal, lawyers are better equipped and trained to understand and use these materials than anyone else—including, in particular, historians.

Lawyers also tend to assume that the legal meanings of speeches, pamphlets, statutes, and other legal texts are intelligible on their face to contemporary lawyers. Therefore, lawyers can simply insert them into contemporary legal opinions and briefs without asking messier questions about the deeper social and ideological assumptions that gave rise to them. Judges, in turn, tend to rely on what the parties (and amicus briefs) place before them. This does not guard against anachronism—to the contrary, it invites it.

Lawyers and judges often attempt to derive original meaning from laws existing at the time of adoption. They ask what particular practices were legally required, permitted, or forbidden without considering the social and technological contexts in which these laws and precedents were created. For example, in *New York State Rifle & Pistol Association, Inc. v. Bruen*, the Supreme Court identified the scope of the Second Amendment right to keep and bear arms with state laws existing at the time of the founding.[63] But it did not ask how these laws might have been influenced by the world in which they were adopted, including, for example, the lower population density of cities and towns, the presence or absence of organized law enforcement, the technological power and accuracy of weapons, the past's views about violence, personal honor, life expectancy, and so on.[64]

Finally, because lawyers and judges tend to read legal texts in isolation from the contexts that produced them, they tend to ignore significant jurisprudential differences between the world of the past and contemporary legal culture. Jonathan Gienapp has pointed out that lawyers at the founding believed that the text of the Constitution was embedded in a larger set of constitutional understandings that modern lawyers and judges do not share.[65]

Lawyers and judges also tend to assume that courts will employ the kind of strong judicial review that they are familiar with but that did not exist at the founding.[66] Similarly, lawyers arguing from Reconstruction history tend to forget that Congress assumed that it, and not the courts, would primarily define and protect the rights created by the Reconstruction Amendments.[67]

Finally, lawyers and judges also tend to assume that rights at the founding were strongly protected from state regulation in the same way that constitutional rights are today—for example, through contemporary doctrines of strict scrutiny. But the concept of strict scrutiny is a modern invention.[68] At the founding, many rights were thought of as natural rights that were instantiated in customary common-law doctrines; people often assumed that these liberties did not have fixed boundaries and could be regulated for the public good.[69]

A thin theory of original meaning coupled with a broad zone of constitutional construction is better equipped for dealing with a past that is very different from our own, contains multiple disagreements among adoption-era actors, and may feature ambiguity about which past practices exemplify fidelity to the Constitution and which are mistakes, violations, or exceptions. The inherent indeterminacy of translating the adopters' concerns into our world is a genuine problem if we must view history as imposing binding obligations on the present. But that problem of translation is greatly lessened—and in fact, may become a positive virtue—when we confront it in the context of constitutional construction.[70]

When we engage in constitutional construction, we are not trying to recover a definitive order from the distant past. Rather, we are looking to the past for lessons and for guidance about how to implement the Constitution in the present. Recognizing that we are engaged in construction is a more honest way of being tutored by the past.

Making historical arguments actually involves multiple steps, each of which involves some degree of normative and interpretive judgment. First, lawyers must decide what features of the past are salient and relevant to the question before them. Second, they must assess how the past is similar to our world and how it is different. Third, to the extent that the past is different, they must draw analogies; the construction of these analogies depends on normative judgments that explain and justify why features of the past and present should be considered similar or different. Fourth, lawyers must draw normative lessons from the history and from the analogies they construct. Fifth, and finally, they must apply these normative lessons to present-day circumstances, which, in turn, may require drawing further analogies and further assessments of similarity and difference.

Normative judgment, imagination, and creativity are involved in each stage of this process. Much of historical dispute in law concerns how to make the proper analogies to the past and which normative lessons to draw from the past. These are creative endeavors. That is why these historical arguments properly belong in the construction zone.

I do not think that responsible historical argument is impossible, that it is too difficult for lawyers to accomplish, or that the experience of the founders, framers, and adopters should be irrelevant to us today. My point, rather, is that we should understand what lawyers' uses of history actually involve—the construction of constitutional norms in the present rather than a humble surrender to the past. Recourse to the past is not a way of avoiding disputes about values—it is a way of engaging in these disputes in the present. Fighting over a shared history is how people argue about the commitments of their Constitution and the nature of their country.

In general, legal arguments about history do not come in two and only two flavors—either they are good and faithful history or they are bad and misused history. There can always be clear mistakes, to be sure—people might misidentify or misquote sources, ignore highly salient evidence, and so on. But not all historical disputes in law can be reduced to the presence or absence of clear mistakes. Sometimes, perhaps usually, they reflect disputes about present-day visions and values.

When lawyers look to adoption-era practices to determine original meaning, they often assume that these practices faithfully exemplify constitutional norms. But we cannot read the meaning of the Constitution off of the brute facts of practice, because some of these practices might be violations of the Constitution, mistakes, or exceptional cases. So we must also make a normative judgment about which parts of past practice are consistent with the Constitution and which are mistaken or exceptional.

The history of congressional delegations of policy decisions and rule-making in the early years of the republic might show that there was no principle against nondelegation at the founding.[71] Or it might show that early Congresses sometimes violated the separation of powers. The passage of the 1798 Sedition Act might show that the First Amendment does not protect seditious libel and criticism of government.[72] Or it might show that the Federalist Congress that passed it overreached.[73] Proclamations of thanksgiving and prayer by presidents and Congress in the early republic—and subsidies to pay for clergy and churches for the benefit of Native American tribes—might show that government endorsements of religion and government subsidies of religion do not violate the Establishment Clause.[74] Or they might show that politicians do not always act in accordance with their principles.[75] What lawyers and judges make of early practice—what constitutes the appropriate example and what constitutes the violation or the exception—often depends on interpretive judgments about history's lessons and normative judgments about what the Constitution should mean in practice.[76]

More generally, we cannot draw lessons from the past without bringing our own present-day perspective to it—what Hans Georg Gadamer famously called our "horizon of understanding."[77] That horizon of understanding includes our cultural memory, our experiences, and our values, including our political values. What people regard as a good analogy or a bad analogy, what they regard as an anachronistic use of history or a permissible use of history, what they deem an unduly selective or an appropriately stylized account of history, is informed by their values and by their understanding of the present and the problems they face in the present. In this respect, lawyers and judges are no different from anyone else.

Moreover, because each generation confronts the past from its own horizon, future generations may see different similarities and differences, make different analogies, and draw different lessons than we do today. So the lessons we draw today from history are probably not permanent lessons. That admonition applies to conservative originalism too. The originalism of 1950 is not the originalism of 1980, which is not the originalism of 2010 and will not be the originalism of 2050 either. The conceit of originalism is that it offers stability and permanence in a changing world. In fact, originalism is a moving target, the product of each generation's interaction with the historical record of the past.

3. Taking Sides in Constitutional Disputes

If the legitimacy of constitutional decision depends on uncovering and applying the Constitution's original meaning, then uncovering a multiplicity of original public meanings is usually a problem. And simply asserting that a legal position held only by one group of adopters is the original meaning of the Constitution is question-begging. But if most contested questions of constitutional law fall in the zone of constitutional construction, the problem disappears, or is at least greatly diminished. That is because in constitutional construction, we are not in search of diktats from the past; rather, we are interested in what history might have to teach us, and how to use that knowledge to persuade other people about the best way to go forward in the present.

In constitutional construction, we may be more willing—and better able—to take sides in disagreements among constitutional participants in the past, and to say that some constructions were better than others, and more faithful to the Constitution rightly understood. Therefore, we are permitted, even encouraged, to favor some opinions over others—even minority opinions in their day—and render judgments on the past. We can say forthrightly that we prefer Hamilton's reading of the spending power to Madison's, or vice versa. We may prefer the views of the free Black people of Ohio about the privileges and immunities of citizenship to those of their white-supremacist neighbors, or Susan B. Anthony's reading of the Reconstruction Amendments to those of the men who prosecuted her for trying to cast a ballot.[78]

We need not pretend that there was always a single correct answer to these questions—our job is to choose the best answer for us in our own time. The project of constitutional construction is different from the project of ascertaining original meaning. Constitutional construction understands the past as a dialectical tradition of readings and counterreadings that might help us understand how to continue the constitutional enterprise in the present. Constitutional construction views the past as a resource that we draw on in the present to forge a narrative connection between ourselves and our political traditions as we now understand them.

Take the contentious question of the original public meaning of the Fourteenth Amendment. Opponents of originalism, hoping to land a knockout blow, often like to assert that originalists cannot explain *Brown v. Board of Education* and *Loving v. Virginia*.[79] Originalists have responded that the framers and ratifiers of the Fourteenth

Amendment actually sought to ban segregated public schools and outlaw restrictions on interracial marriage or, in the alternative, that regardless of the framers' and ratifiers' purposes or intentions, the original legal meaning of the Fourteenth Amendment generates these results.[80]

Whether either *Brown* or *Loving* is required by original public meaning (or original legal meaning) turns out to be quite complicated and difficult to answer conclusively. There is evidence that some Republicans did believe that the Fourteenth Amendment required racially integrated public schools, and some believed that it protected a right to racial intermarriage.[81] But many more people who participated in the ratification process disagreed; both positions were deeply unpopular among white people in the 1860s. Had supporters made clear that the original public meaning—or the original legal meaning—of the Fourteenth Amendment required integrated public schools and recognition of racial intermarriage, it is very unlikely that the amendment would have been adopted.[82] It is also difficult to prove that most lawyers in 1868 thought that the amendment would have these legal meanings. (And the idea of asking, in the wake of a bloody Civil War with deep partisan divides and disagreements about race, what an ideal observer of no particular politics or party would have thought about legal meaning seems particularly clueless.)

A lot depends on who has the burden of proof in the face of uncertainty and what kinds of inferences we are willing to make from an incomplete historical record.[83] Depending on how we define what we are looking for—the original intention of congressional Republicans in drafting the amendment, the original understanding of the adopters in the various states, the original meaning of the amendment to the general public, or the original legal meaning to well-trained lawyers in 1868—the kinds of evidence that count as relevant, and the kinds of inferences we may reasonably draw from this evidence, we will get different answers.[84]

Part of the difficulty arises from the way that conservative originalists have framed the question. They would like to show that the results in *Brown* and *Loving* were *always* the law, and not just products of the Second Reconstruction in the twentieth century. They want to insist that these results were part of the original public meaning of the Fourteenth Amendment despite what most white people actually thought in 1868. Nonoriginalist critics insist that originalists cannot meet this standard.

But suppose we change the inquiry. Suppose the question is whether *Brown* and *Loving* are good *constructions* of the Fourteenth Amendment's original public meaning. Then the answer is easy, at least in today's world. Not only are they good constructions, but I have argued that they are the best constructions.[85]

Once we understand the question as one of constitutional construction, all the evidence that originalists have mustered to explain *Brown* and *Loving* is both useful and powerful. It shows us that, from the outset, there were supporters of the amendment who read it in a broadly egalitarian way. Perhaps they were not a majority, but they were hardly insignificant. That fact is especially important: for if there was no consensus in favor of integrated schools and a right to racial intermarriage, there was also no consensus against these results either.

When we develop our doctrines of the Fourteenth Amendment today, we can and should be proud to point for authority to these early, far-sighted Republicans and to their belief in racial equality. We should be happy to argue that these people correctly understood the Constitution and that most of their contemporaries, who insisted on a more limited construction, did not. When we do this, however, we follow the example of these early Republicans not because we are *required* to by original public meaning but because we *choose* to, given our present-day understanding of what is most faithful to the Constitution and its purposes. We honor them because we think that they were right.

4. Recognizing Multiple Sources of Legitimacy

This difference in framing the problem is quite important. It recognizes that the past takes on new meaning to us as we proceed through history and that what we want from history changes as our political circumstances change. The reason why contemporary originalists want to show that *Brown* and *Loving* were always part of original meaning is the intervening history of the civil rights revolution, which transformed Americans' understanding of constitutional equality and

constitutional justice. As a result, today the legitimacy of constitutional theories depends on whether they can explain *Brown* and *Loving* and not the other way around.

An earlier generation of conservative originalists, like Alfred Avins
and Raoul Berger, thought that *Brown* and *Loving* were wrongly
decided.[86] They did not assume that *Brown* and *Loving* must have
always been correct and that *Plessy v. Ferguson* was "wrong the day it
was decided."[87] But later generations of originalists did—because the
world they lived in had changed and the conditions of political and
constitutional legitimacy had changed. And so originalism's agendas
changed with them.

By the 1980s, it became increasingly important to reconcile
originalism with *Brown* if not *Loving*. The Second Reconstruction
and the civil rights revolution had worked a significant change in the
grounds of constitutional legitimacy for liberals and conservatives
alike. This led many originalists, led notably by Robert Bork and
Michael McConnell, to rethink older assumptions about whether
Brown could be explained on originalist grounds.[88] The fact that the
vast majority of originalists moved in this direction strongly suggests that the framework model of constitutions, with its multiple
sources of democratic legitimacy, is the best account of how the
American Constitution actually works.

One should not assume that later originalist scholars were being
disingenuous in attempting to prove that *Brown* was an originalist
result. Originalist scholars, like all other scholars, hope to improve
on the work of their predecessors and to correct the mistakes of
previous generations. My point, however, is that what constitutes
"improvement" in originalist argument—and indeed, legal argument
generally—is not altogether independent of changes in politics and
public opinion. Whether they admit it to themselves or not, originalist lawyers and judges are part of the processes of living constitutionalism just like everyone else.

In this chapter, I have argued that original meaning is not something that originalists simply find in the past. Rather, it is a theoretical construction crafted by lawyers in order to do the work of
constitutional interpretation. There is no single way to generate original meaning from the materials of the past. What we do produce
depends in part on what we think constitutions are for and how they

are supposed to work. It also depends on the practical needs of people in the present who are in search of a legal meaning that they can employ in legal argument.

I have also argued that a thin theory of original public meaning, coupled with a division of labor between interpretation and construction, is the best approach to constitutional interpretation. Of course, even a thin theory has its limitations. On some questions, the original semantic meaning may be irreducibly ambiguous, or there may be no single original public meaning that we can treat as binding today.[89] In those cases, the best we can do is move directly to constitutional construction. We should accept this lesson with grace and humility. And we should remember—with openness and even with delight—that the past always contains the ability to surprise us, and reveal that what we thought was natural and obvious is far more complicated and interesting than we had ever imagined.

CHAPTER NINE

Making Originalist Arguments

A. Adoption History and the Forms of Argument

Originalist arguments fall into two types. Some concern the content of the basic framework—the original semantic meaning of the Constitution's words and phrases and the legal meaning of generally recognized terms of art. But, as we have seen, the basic framework does not provide answers to most contested constitutional questions. So most originalist arguments are really arguments of constitutional construction.

Not all arguments from adoption history count as "originalist." Critical uses of history may treat members of the founding generation as negative examples. Originalist arguments are usually obedient uses of history. They argue that the founders, framers, or adopters have theoretical or practical authority for us today and that we should follow their views or emulate their practices.[1] When originalist arguments use the past as a negative precedent, it is usually to highlight what the founders, framers, or adopters opposed.

When people engage in constitutional construction, they use the standard forms of legal argument. Originalist arguments are no different. For each modality of argument, there is a corresponding kind of originalist argument, which asserts that the founders, framers, or adopters have *special insight* or that the events leading up to or contemporaneous with adoption have a *special status*.

149

1. Arguments from *text*. To understand the meaning of the text, the scope of the concepts it uses, and the application of these concepts, we should look to the views, writings, and actions of the founders, framers, and adopters, to contemporaneous uses of language, and to contemporaneous state constitutions and laws.

2. Arguments about constitutional *structure*. To understand how the constitutional system as a whole should operate and how the various parts of the system should interact with each other, we should look to the views, writings, and actions of the founders, framers, and adopters and to contemporaneous state constitutions and laws.

3. Arguments from constitutional *purpose*. To understand the point or purpose of the Constitution—or particular clauses and phrases in the Constitution—we should look to the views, writings, and actions of the founders, framers, and adopters.

4. Arguments from *consequences*. To understand the consequences of a proposed interpretation, we should look to the views, writings, and actions of the founders, framers, and adopters and examples from history with which the founders, framers, and adopters would have been familiar.

5. Arguments from *judicial precedent*. To understand and implement the Constitution's provisions, we should look to judicial decisions that are contemporaneous with or previous to the adoption of the Constitution (or its subsequent amendments)—whether from the United States, from the individual states, or from pre-1787 Great Britain—with which the founders, framers, and adopters would have been familiar.

6. Arguments from *political convention*. We should interpret the Constitution in light of political conventions that have their roots in practices known to the founders, framers, and adopters or that developed shortly following the adoption of the Constitution or of the particular amendments we are interpreting.

7. Arguments from the people's *customs* and lived experience. We should interpret the Constitution consistent with mores and social customs that date back to the founding or to particular amendments to the Constitution.

8. Arguments from *natural law or natural rights*. We should interpret the Constitution consistent with the founders', framers', and adopters' acceptance and use of natural law and natural rights.

Text	Structure	Purpose	Consequences	Judicial Precedent	Political Settlement/ Convention	Custom	Natural Law	Ethos	Tradition	Honored Authority

Founders, framers, and adopters have special insight
or special status with respect to each form of argument

Figure 9.1. The use of adoption history in constitutional construction

9. Arguments from *national ethos*. We should interpret the Constitution consistent with the values of the founders, framers, and adopters, because these values are central to the character of our nation and to its political culture and institutions.

10. Arguments from *political tradition*. We should interpret the Constitution consistent with the experiences, values, and examples of the founders, framers, and adopters (including contemporaneous federal and state laws and practices), and we should draw lessons about the meaning of our constitutional commitments from their actions, successes, failures, struggles, and experiences.

11. Arguments from *honored authority*. We should interpret the Constitution consistent with the values, beliefs, and examples of the founders, framers, and adopters; they are honored authorities whose views are valuable to us today because of who they were and the role they played in the formation of the country's political institutions.

Note once again that there is no separate modality of historical argument; instead adoption history is available to support each style of justification. Although people tend to think of originalist arguments as an undifferentiated whole, or at most as concerned with "text, history, and structure," originalist arguments come in many different kinds, and they make many different kinds of claims about the past.

What makes originalist arguments persuasive when people engage in constitutional construction? Why should interpreters accept originalist arguments over other arguments? For many conservative originalists, this question will seem beside the point. According to the originalist model of authority, the best originalist arguments simply state the law that we must follow. To be sure, originalists may disagree about which historical account is best. But once we stipulate to the best account of original meaning, understanding, or intention, there is no choice about whether we must accept it or not. One does not need to be persuaded vis-à-vis other alternatives.

But since most originalist arguments actually occur in the construction zone, this approach will not work. We have to decide how best to implement the Constitution given the particular interpretive problem before us and the entire history of previous constructions, some of which may have occurred decades, if not centuries, after the founding. The initial construction of the Constitution's text may or may not be the best construction. Hence the question: What makes originalist arguments persuasive in constitutional construction?

There is one obvious answer, but it does not capture most of the cases. Where a question has not been litigated much—or at all—there may be no significant body of doctrine and/or previous constructions to work with. Two examples are the meaning of "natural born citizen" as a qualification for the presidency and the rules governing presidential impeachments. Lacking a rich history of previous judicial constructions, interpreters will probably want to start from the beginning. They will closely examine the initial constructions of the text and then ask how we might apply these ideas in the present. It is no accident that in these kinds of cases, everyone—whether originalist or nonoriginalist—looks to adoption history.

In most other cases, however, there *is* a significant body of previous constructions. Suppose that these constructions are consistent with the initial ones when the Constitution was adopted or amended. Then appealing to these original constructions is just another way of arguing from precedent or convention. After all, if there is an unbroken line of precedent or practice dating back to the founding (or to the adoption of an amendment), ordinarily one should follow that unbroken line of precedent or practice.

The more interesting case is when there is a significant body of previous constructions, and they vary from the initial constructions. In these cases, people make originalist arguments because they want to discard later constructions and start over again, or because they want to modify later constructions in light of the earlier ones. In these situations, what makes appeals to the founders, framers, and adopters persuasive?

An originalist argument might be persuasive because it is persuasive independent of the fact that it is originalist. It might offer the best account of constitutional structure, for example. But an important reason why originalist arguments are persuasive in American legal culture is that the founders, framers, and adopters have special ethical authority. By "ethical authority," I mean that the founding generation powerfully represents the ethos of the nation and its political traditions, not that the founding generation was especially moral or ethical. Therefore, if we want to be true to the nation's character, traditions, and values, we should follow the example of these honored authorities.

Arguments from ethos, tradition, and honored authority have special persuasive power to the extent that we identify our values with those of the founders, framers, and adopters.

In some areas of the law, people strongly identify with the values of the founders, framers, and adopters—at least as they understand or imagine them. So when advocates can successfully portray their position as just doing what the founders wanted, assumed, or expected, their arguments take on an extra heft.

In other areas of the law, including many technical questions, people may just want an answer to difficult legal problems, and so it is fairly easy for them to identify with the views of the founders, framers, and adopters as they understand or imagine them. In these areas of the law, the pull of ethos, tradition, and honored authority can be especially persuasive.

But when people find the founders', framers', or adopters' values alien, hostile, or irrelevant, the founders, framers, and adopters lose their ethical authority. Then originalist arguments seem much less persuasive. That is why when people learn that the founders believed that prosecutions for blasphemy were consistent with freedom of speech, or that states could deny married women the right to own property, they generally do not find these arguments persuasive interpretations of the Constitution. The ethical authority of the founders is dissolved. Even in seemingly technical areas of the law, people may resist identification with founding- or adoption-era solutions if they think these solutions will have bad consequences for contemporary policy questions. (Or conversely, they will interpret the history differently to avoid these consequences.)

America is a large and diverse country with many different groups of people who remember the past in different ways and often disagree about the country's values. Americans both admire *and* criticize the people who adopted the U.S. Constitution. For this reason, we cannot assume that the ethical authority of the founders, framers, and adopters will remain constant for each and every contested question. For some Americans, the founders (or some relevant group of them) will have ethical authority on a particular issue, while for other Americans, the founders will exemplify outmoded or unjust values that the country must transcend. For some Americans, on some issues, the founders remain culture heroes, and so they may find originalist arguments persuasive. But for other Americans, the founders are irrelevant or even antiheroes, and on many questions, they will find originalist arguments singularly unpersuasive.

The framers' ethical authority also may be less important in two other situations.

The first situation is when people use adoption history deconstructively—to rebut other people's originalist arguments and show that the historical record is more complicated. When people rebut originalist arguments with counterarguments about adoption history, they may believe that the founders, framers, or adopters have special ethical authority, but they do not have to. Their goal is to show that even if one accepts the founders' authority, the petitioner's interpretation is incorrect, and the historical evidence is either inconclusive or points in the opposite direction.

The second example concerns the interpretation of state constitutions. As explained in chapter 5, originalism in the United States is deeply tied to narratives of national identity. State constitutional framers and adopters normally do not receive the same degree of reverence as the nation's Founding Fathers and generally do not possess very much ethical authority. That is especially so because state constitutions are of varying ages and are constantly being amended.

B. Persuasiveness and Ethos

To understand the role that ethical authority plays in originalist argument, the best place to start is with the last three modalities—arguments from ethos, tradition, and honored authority. These arguments appeal directly to the founders' ethical authority. Even though the nation's political traditions have constantly evolved, Americans generally view the founding generation as marking the beginning of American political traditions, and therefore the founding serves as a potent symbol of these traditions. (Colonial history is imagined as leading up to or culminating in the founding.) The founders are also among the most hallowed symbols of American values and American national character. Finally, the founders are among the most salient and the most honored authorities in American political memory, although, as noted earlier, they are not equally honored on every question.

Note that I have just spoken of "founders" rather than of constitutional adopters generally. The authority of arguments from ethos, tradition, and honored authority is a function of how Americans constitute their cultural memory. At present, the founding generation—and particular individuals within that generation—enjoy special authority in American cultural memory, while later generations, even when they adopt important amendments to the Constitution, have less. The framers and adopters of the Twenty-Second Amendment, for example, are mostly forgotten today. Even the framers of the Reconstruction Amendments—including John Bingham, Thaddeus Stevens, Lyman Trumbull, William P. Fessenden, Charles Sumner, and Jacob Howard—have remarkably little ethical authority given the importance of these amendments and are known today mostly to specialists. The reason has nothing to do with the comparative importance of their respective contributions to the Constitution. Rather, it is due to the cultural memory of Reconstruction.[2] Downplaying the importance of Reconstruction to America's constitutional culture helped assuage tensions between Northern and Southern whites after the Civil War.[3] For many years, historians in the Dunning School, and those they influenced, treated this crucial period of political reform as mistaken and corrupt.[4] Only Abraham Lincoln, who was assassinated before the drafting and adoption of the Fourteenth and Fifteenth Amendments, is widely regarded as a culture hero today. All this may change, of course: Americans may come to venerate the Reconstruction founders as much as they venerate the founding generation. But that will happen because of larger changes in American political culture.

The founders have disproportionate power over American political imaginations because of Americans' constitutive myth, which I described in chapter 6: Through an act of revolution, the American people brought themselves into being and created a state and a Constitution under which they still live. In American cultural memory, the founding—which actually spanned several decades—appears as a single magical period of time. Because Americans imagine the creation of their state, their national identity, and their Constitution as roughly simultaneous, they imbue the founding generation (which they identify correctly or incorrectly with the revolutionary generation) with enormous symbolic power. This is what I have called the "ethical trifecta": Americans think of the same group of people as responsible for creating the American state, the American nation, and the American Constitution; and certain founders who had key roles in the process, like Washington, Jefferson, Franklin, Madison, Adams, and Hamilton, have taken on the status of culture heroes. We return to them—and to the founding generation as a whole—again and again for wisdom and example.

Even people who severely criticize the founders for their views on slavery or their treatment of women and Native Americans may quote the founders about the Constitution and its proper interpretation. That is because the context of judgment is different—for example, when people are discussing presidential impeachment rather than racial equality. As the context changes, cultural heroes may become antiheroes, and vice versa. Using the past contextually and selectively is a characteristic feature of ethical argument.

C. How Ethos, Tradition, and Honored Authority Interact with Other Modalities of Argument

Examine the other eight modalities of originalist argument, and you will discover that ethical authority matters there as well. Take, as an example, arguments about the original meaning of the text. The linguistic uses of the founders, framers, and adopters are perfectly good evidence of original meaning, but any competent speaker of the English language during the same period should be an equally good authority.[5] Some arguments from original meaning do look to dictionary definitions, contemporaneous newspaper accounts, correspondence, and corpus linguistics.[6] Nevertheless, as Jamal Greene has pointed out, lawyers and judges often quote texts from the founders or framers—like *The Federalist*—as evidence of original public meaning. They do so not because the founders were more competent speakers of the English language but because of their ethical authority and their special status in the American political tradition.[7]

Next, consider arguments from structure and purpose. Arguments from structure and purpose need not be arguments from original meaning, original intention, or original understanding.[8] Nevertheless, most American lawyers—and, indeed, most Americans—accept that members of the founding generation have special insight into the Constitution's point or purpose, and special insight into how its various parts were designed and should function together. That is so even if intervening events have rendered some of the founders' assumptions outmoded.

In fact, many arguments about the Constitution's "original meaning" that quote the founders, framers, or adopters are really arguments about their purposes, intentions, or expectations, or about their views on constitutional structure. This type of argument is very familiar in thick accounts of original meaning, and it rests, either explicitly or implicitly, on the ethical authority of the founders, framers, or adopters and their centrality to the American political tradition.[9]

What about the other modalities—arguments from consequences, judicial precedent, interbranch convention, social custom, and natural law? Even here, originalist arguments usually rely implicitly on ethical authority.

The founders, framers, and adopters are unlikely to have special insight into the consequences of constitutional interpretations in a future they could know nothing about. But interpreters may nevertheless claim that these honored authorities have special wisdom that is relevant to today's world. People describe the founders' judgments of political cause and effect in general terms so that they apply to us today. Or they cherry-pick those predictions or causal judgments that turned out roughly correct while ignoring those that have turned out to be wildly inaccurate or irrelevant. Consider, for example, Madison's statement in Federalist No. 47 that "[t]he accumulation of all powers legislative, executive and judiciary in the same hands, whether of one, a few or many, and whether hereditary, self appointed, or elective, may justly be pronounced the very definition of tyranny."[10] A lawyer might quote this passage to criticize government surveillance practices or a particular development in the administrative state, even though the passage speaks in general terms and Madison would not have comprehended the situation—much less the modern administrative and national security state—in his 1788 essay. By treating statements by various founders as general principles, we can take them out of their historical contexts and apply them to contemporary situations. Many people have made similar arguments about how the concentration of power leads to tyranny. What gives this argument special force is that Madison made it: that is, the argument trades on Madison's ethical authority.

In making originalist arguments, lawyers sometimes cite old judicial precedents (including English precedents) prior to or contemporaneous with the founding. These precedents help us understand the legal background at the time of adoption. But these legal precedents are relevant because the founders, framers, and adopters either rejected them or incorporated them by reference in their understanding of the Constitution. The same is true of arguments that look to contemporaneous state constitutions and state legislation. These sources are important because they offer evidence of what the founders, framers, and adopters believed the Constitution meant. So, like originalist arguments from text, purpose, and structure, these arguments gain additional force from the ethical authority of the founders, framers, or adopters.

What about interbranch conventions? Many of these conventions began after the founding; others may have begun contemporaneously but evolved significantly later on. Nevertheless, interbranch conventions may have special persuasive authority if we can show that they are roughly contemporaneous with the adoption of the Constitution. If the founders reached a political settlement early on, that is a reason not to disturb it. Their views stand for the entire tradition of practice, and we invoke their understandings because of their distinctive status as honored authorities. For example, to this day, people still argue about the proper interpretation of the "Decision of 1789" and whether it gave the president power to remove executive officers at will.[11]

Equally important, people often point to the founders' views in order to argue for a *change* in current interbranch conventions and a *return* to original understandings. For example, advocates of congressional war powers do not like the expansion of executive power in the twentieth century. Therefore, they may argue that we should return to the views of the founders, who believed Congress should play a larger role.[12] (We could also classify these arguments as structural.) These arguments employ the ethical authority of the founders to call for a return to past arrangements. Invoking the founders allows people to justify breaking with settled practice in the name of a deeper continuity. And like all appeals to ethical authority, this one is selective. People who quote the founders to argue that Congress should have more of a say in the conduct of war may not want to adopt the framers' views on race, federalism, or sex equality.[13]

Finally, people may invoke the founders, framers, and adopters to argue about natural law or natural rights. It is likely that philosophers like Aristotle, Thomas Aquinas, John Locke, or Immanuel Kant had greater expertise. But the fact that various founders, framers, and adopters spoke in terms of natural law and natural rights gives these arguments special force in American constitutional argument.[14] This persuasive force comes not from the founders' philosophical expertise but from their status as honored authorities in the American political tradition.

D. The Hybrid Nature of "Originalist" Arguments

There is a recurrent pattern in our march through the modalities. Many originalist arguments are *hybrids*. Formally, they may be arguments from purpose, structure, consequences, and so on; but they also rely on the ethical authority of the founders, framers, or adopters and their special status in the American political tradition. These arguments appeal explicitly or implicitly to ethos, tradition, or honored authority in the service of other modes of argument, like text, structure, purpose, or consequences (figure 9.2).

The rhetorical advantage of hybrid arguments is obvious: an ar-

Founders, framers, and adopters have special insight
or special status with respect to each form of argument

Text	Structure	Purpose	Consequences	Judicial Precedent	Political Settlement/ Convention	Custom	Natural Law	Ethos	Tradition	Honored Authority
Plus appeal to ethos, tradition, or honored authority	Plus appeal to ethos, tradition, or honored authority	Plus appeal to ethos, tradition, or honored authority	Plus appeal to ethos, tradition, or honored authority	Plus appeal to ethos, tradition, or honored authority	Plus appeal to ethos, tradition, or honored authority	Plus appeal to ethos, tradition, or honored authority	Plus appeal to ethos, tradition, or honored authority			

Figure 9.2. Originalist argument in constitutional construction

gument about constitutional text, purpose, structure, or consequences becomes more powerful if a famous framer also made it or if one can associate it with the founders in general. Conversely, one way of critiquing an opponent's arguments is by associating them with opponents of the Constitution, with other cultural antiheroes, or with a now discredited or anticanonical opinion like *Dred Scott v. Sandford* or *Plessy v. Ferguson*.[15]

The distinctive role of ethos, tradition, and honored authority in originalist argument explains why originalist arguments are so commonplace in American constitutional culture and why both originalists and nonoriginalists make appeals to adoption history. Regardless of their theoretical disagreements, both originalists and nonoriginalists have a stake in American political traditions, and both recognize the normative importance and rhetorical force of those traditions among lawyers, judges, citizens, and government officials in the United States.

Why are originalist arguments so often hybrids? The reason, it turns out, is connected to the reasons why American judges employ originalism selectively and opportunistically. The *hybridity* of originalism and the *selectivity* of originalism are two sides of the same coin, as I shall now explain.

E. Why Americans Are Cafeteria Originalists

Earlier I noted that Americans are cafeteria originalists—they pick and choose when to make originalist appeals and when to allow themselves to be bound by their founders. In American constitutional culture, originalist arguments are not mandatory; they are defeasible. In disputes over constitutional construction, lawyers do not always offer originalist arguments, and judges do not always use or accept them. Conservative original meaning originalists who argue that fidelity to original meaning offers the only correct interpretation of the Constitution nevertheless often leaven their theory by making room for nonoriginalist precedents and for evolving traditions.[16]

These accommodations make particular sense if originalist arguments are themselves appeals to tradition and ethos. Where appeals to past traditions are normatively attractive to judges, they make originalist arguments; where they are not, judges ignore them.

For example, regardless of the founders', framers', or adopters' views, few lawyers today would bother to argue that paper money, Social Security, the Americans with Disabilities Act, or the Fair Labor Standards Act are unconstitutional; that states may prevent Black and white people from marrying; or that states may take away women's rights to make contracts and own property upon marriage. If lawyers did offer these arguments, most judges would quickly dismiss them.

To be sure, originalist scholars may come up with explanations for why all of these problems are illusory. Originalist scholars are nothing if not ingenious and persistent. But the point is that they do so because they understand that failing to do so would be an embarrassment for the theory. That is to say, originalists seek to show that paper money is constitutional not because there is significant doubt about this question but to shore up originalist theory itself.

If originalist analyses generated binding legal obligations rather than resources for constitutional construction, lawyers would always cite them as their most powerful legal arguments, and judges would never ignore them. But that is not how American lawyers and judges operate. As we saw in the case of *Parents Involved* (discussed in chapter 4), none of the justices—including the two originalists, Justices Thomas and Scalia—focused on the views of the Reconstruction framers to resolve the issues in the case. Instead, they focused on the ethical authority of *Brown*, the early civil rights movement, and the NAACP's campaign to overturn *Plessy v. Ferguson*.

On the other hand, these practices make particular sense if originalist arguments in constitutional construction are implicit appeals to national ethos, political tradition, and honored authority. Then it is entirely reasonable that these arguments would not be mandatory but would be defeasible. Contemporary Americans will accept appeals to the values of the founders, framers, or adopters to the extent that they can identify these values with their own values and their own sense of what is lasting and valuable about American traditions.[17] Traditions, however, change over time, and elements and norms that once were central may later become peripheral or even repudiated. If contemporary Americans no longer identify their values or their understanding of America's political traditions with the views of the founders, framers, or adopters, they will not regard the latter as possessing ethical authority or the authority of tradition; therefore, they will not treat originalist arguments as having special force.

When we find commonality between the values of the founders, framers, or adopters and our own values, it is much easier to accept their will as representing our will, and to believe that they and we are the same We the People who adopted the Constitution and its amendments.[18] That is why arguments from original understandings and intentions are most powerful in the years immediately following the adoption of an amendment. It is much easier to identify with recent adopters and view them as representing or speaking for all citizens in the present.[19]

As time passes, however, these connections become attenuated, because norms change, conceptions of what is reasonable and unreasonable evolve, and political traditions mutate, discarding some elements while accumulating others. Although founders, framers, and adopters may retain their status as honored authorities, we will invoke them only selectively, in certain contexts, or in abstract or general ways.

Constitutional scholars have often argued that lawyers' ability to characterize original intentions and understandings at higher and lower levels of generality presents a problem for originalism, because it makes originalist argument indeterminate and thereby undermines its ability to constrain wayward judges.[20] But suppose that we view originalist arguments—at least those in the construction zone—as appeals to tradition and ethos. Then what seemed like a bug now looks like a feature. People often invoke traditions and make claims about national character by selectively describing the past at varying levels of generality. Because traditions contain multiple and conflicting elements, there is often more than one way to characterize them and draw normative lessons from them.[21] People's claims about tradition are likely to differ (1) because past practices are complex and not uniform, (2) because the meaning and lessons of tradition are often best described through generalization (and there is often more than one way to do this), and (3) because traditions evolve by discarding or rejecting previous elements of tradition and absorbing new ones. Traditions, in short, are always breaking away from parts of themselves, glomming onto what is new, and then redescribing the changes as always having been part of the tradition, correctly understood.[22]

People in a democracy disagree with each other about values, about the content and force of political traditions, and about the meaning and importance of historical events. This means that not only will people invoke the founders, framers, and adopters selectively, but they will also disagree about when and how it is appropriate to do so. Some people will reject the authority of the founders, framers, and adopters in particular constitutional contexts—like gay rights or the scope of federal power—while others will find their views very important indeed. People will quote different framers for different propositions. They will see different things in adoption history. And they will reinterpret the views of the framers differently in light of contemporary concerns. This does not make originalist arguments useless or irrelevant in constitutional construction. Rather, it helps us understand what they really are: resources for understanding and arguing about our common future rather than decrees from the past.

F. The Gap between Originalist Practice and Originalist Theory

Finally, the role of ethos, tradition, and honored authority in originalist argument also explains the remarkable mismatch between contemporary academic theories of originalism and the actual practice of originalist argument by lawyers, judges, and the general public. The way that Americans—including most American lawyers and

judges—make originalist arguments is heavily infused with appeals
to ethos, tradition, and honored authority. These arguments usually
ignore the distinction between interpretation and construction and
casually run together claims about the original meaning of the Constitution with appeals to tradition and the ethical authority of the
past.

Jamal Greene has pointed out a curious feature of contemporary
constitutional theory. Today, most originalists are original public
meaning originalists. They argue that what is binding on later generations is what the words of the text would have meant to the general public. As Greene notes, originalists converged on this theory
because of theoretical difficulties with earlier forms of originalism
that looked to the intentions of the framers and the understandings
of the ratifiers.[23]

However, if the relevant question is what the text meant to a
member of the lay public, contemporary dictionaries, newspapers,
and private correspondence should be just as authoritative as the
statements of framers and ratifiers.[24] (This is the focus of much corpus linguistics work today.) Moreover, the use of a particular word
or phrase by an opponent of the Constitution should be just as authoritative as usage by a proponent.[25] Yet this does not appear to
match the practice of American constitutional lawyers and judges.
Citations to *The Federalist* and to Madison's notes of the Philadelphia Convention are among the most frequently cited forms of adoption history; Greene has shown that they have become even more
widely cited in the period in which originalist scholars moved to theories of original public meaning.[26]

Moreover, *The Federalist* and Madison's notes are not entirely
reliable sources of original meaning, original intention, or original
understandings.[27] They may not reflect a consensus either of the
ratifiers or of the general public. Indeed, in some respects, they may
not even represent Madison's, Hamilton's, or Jay's own views.[28] The
essays in *The Federalist* were propaganda pieces directed at the New
York ratifying convention. It is not clear that they had much influence on the outcome of that convention.[29] It is even less clear that
they had much influence on the other state ratifying conventions.[30]
As Ray Raphael has explained, "Publius's first five essays were reprinted in an average of eight papers outside of New York State, but

after that out-of-state publication fell off dramatically."[31] In fact, "[a]fter *The Federalist No. 16*, no essays were printed in more than one paper out of state."[32] And "following *The Federalist No. 23*, the remaining sixty-two essays never made it across New York's borders at all, except for an excerpt from *The Federalist No. 38* in the *Freeman's Oracle*, published in Exeter, New Hampshire."[33] Although reprints of speeches and essays about the Constitution "were customary at the time, . . . Publius's last seventy essays stand as anomalies, the *least* likely pieces to have appeared in more than one state."[34]

In addition to publication in newspapers, a collection of the essays in *The Federalist* was printed in two volumes, the first (containing numbers one through thirty-six) appearing in March 1788 and the second in May 1788.[35] But it is very unlikely that the two-volume set influenced the state ratifying conventions. The "initial printing of this now-famous work was only 500 copies, and 'several hundred' of these were still unsold in the fall of 1788, after the Constitution had been ratified."[36] Moreover, the first volume was not published until six states had already ratified.[37]

Madison's notes on the Constitutional Convention also have weaknesses as evidence of public understanding—let alone public consensus—at the time of adoption. They were not made public until many years after the ratification of the Constitution and therefore could not have influenced the public debate leading up to ratification.[38] They are also quite brief and leave out most of what actually transpired at the convention.[39] And Mary Sarah Bilder famously showed that Madison altered his notes in the decades following the Philadelphia Convention.[40]

To be sure, some original meaning originalists with the courage of their convictions might argue that these texts should receive no special treatment and that lawyers and judges should stick to dictionaries and similar sources of information. But for the most part, their suggestions have fallen on deaf ears. Lawyers and judges continue to cite *The Federalist*, Madison's notes, the ratification debates, letters from and between famous framers, and so on.[41]

What explains this curious state of affairs? As Greene points out, the best explanation is that lawyers and judges are simply using these materials differently than contemporary originalist theories of original public meaning prescribe.[42] Appeals to *The Federalist* and to Madison's notes do a special kind of work in legal argument. Although these arguments seem to appeal to original intentions or original meaning, they are actually forms of ethical argument. In the typology offered earlier, they are hybrid arguments that appeal in part to national ethos, political tradition, and honored authority.

The Federalist and Madison's notes are authoritative for American lawyers and judges not because they are reliably representative of the thought of the adopters as a whole or because they are especially good sources of the original public meaning of words and phrases appearing in the Constitution. They are authoritative because of their revered status in the American political tradition. They are part of America's political scripture. Accordingly, lawyers and judges quote them like scripture to establish key principles and ideas in the American political tradition.

What is true of *The Federalist* and Madison's notes also extends to other familiar sources of adoption history: the ratification debates in the state conventions and letters and public statements written by key framers like Madison and Jefferson. (Jefferson, of course, was off in France during the debate over the Constitution.) Each of these sources has its own drawbacks and limitations in demonstrating a consensus about intentions, understandings, or meanings. But that has not stopped American lawyers and judges, who continue to cite and invoke them with reverence.

Recently, the Supreme Court has been explicitly merging arguments from tradition with arguments from original meaning. Examples are the Court's Establishment Clause cases and its most recent Second Amendment case, *New York State Rifle & Pistol Association, Inc. v. Bruen*.[43] These cases look to traditions of federal and state practice (including early statutes and executive actions) to expound the Constitution's original meaning. The familiar mantra of text, history, and structure has given way to a new slogan of "text, history, and tradition."[44]

Considered solely from the standpoint of academic theories of originalism, the merger of original public meaning and tradition is a bit puzzling. That is because original public meaning and traditions of practice are not identical. Original meaning originalists ask what the meaning or understanding of a word or phrase was at the time of adoption. But a focus on tradition is different; instead of looking at meanings or understandings, it looks at the continuity of practices over long periods of time.[45] Unlike original meanings, traditions do not have to begin at any particular point in time, and they may change over time. For example, if a right was not recognized at the founding but there is a long tradition of protecting it that developed in the 1880s, there would not be an originalist argument for the right, but there would be an argument from tradition.

In the hands of the current Court, the use of tradition in specific areas like the Second Amendment and the Establishment Clause seems to be a way of equating original meaning with what the Court believes the founding generation understood or expected. That is, it is yet another strategy for producing relatively thick accounts of original public meaning that rely on original expected applications. And it has all the problems that thick accounts generally have.

But equating original public meaning with tradition or using tradition as a proxy for original public meaning has additional problems. When we use tradition as evidence of original meaning, it is not enough to show that a practice existed. One must also show that people self-consciously understood the practice—which might be quite different in diverse times, contexts, and places—to be part of the meaning of the text that they adopted. In the case of firearm regulation or abortion practices—to take two recent examples—this may be very difficult to do. There is no guarantee that the founders, framers, and adopters—much less the general public—were actually aware of all of the law in the various states (and colonies before the Revolution) or the history of English law dating back to the thirteenth century and earlier. Unlike today's originalist advocates, the founding generation lacked easy access to legal decisions and statutes in all these various jurisdictions. Comprehensive collections of legal sources may not have been widely available in eighteenth- and nineteenth-century America; there certainly were no online compendiums of current and historical sources as there are today. So when today's lawyers and judges rummage through ancient statutes and reports of practice in England and the various states to construct a single, unitary legal tradition, the result may not be what the public or the adopters actually understood. What we may have is not the original meaning as understood by the public but rather an invented tradition produced in the present and projected onto the past.

It is possible that the current Court's merger of originalism and tradition is simply opportunistic—majorities will employ it in some cases and then revert to different kinds of arguments in other cases, just as they do with originalist arguments more generally. Or the merger could simply be a function of the current coalition of justices that makes up the Court's conservative majority.

In another sense, however, the Court's recent merger of originalism and tradition is entirely predictable, for the reasons I have described in this chapter. All that the current Court is doing is making more explicit the fact that originalist arguments are hybrids—a hybridity that has always been present.

There is nothing wrong with hybrid appeals to originalism and tradition as one form of persuasive argument among others, as long as we recognize them for what they are, and understand the nature of the claims being made. In constitutional construction, originalist arguments may appropriately invoke the authority of ethos and tradition. They may call on the memory of honored authorities and argue that we should emulate their principles, ideals, and practices. These kinds of arguments are part of American constitutional culture. Both originalists and nonoriginalists can make them and do make them.

But we should not confuse the use of these arguments in specific cases with a plausible general approach to constitutional interpretation. Above all, we should not confuse these claims with binding orders from the past. When we do so, we give originalist arguments an authority they do not really deserve. Correctly understood, however, originalist arguments can still have legitimate persuasive power. Like other uses of history, they exemplify how Americans use the common resources of the past to argue about the meaning of the present and the appropriate direction of the future—the subject of the next chapter.

CHAPTER TEN

Originalist Arguments
for Everyone

ONSERVATIVE (I.E., THICK) VERSIONS of original meaning originalism seek to discover the initial legal construction of the words and phrases in the Constitution and then, by creative extension, apply them to contemporary problems. One cannot avoid this creativity because the initial legal constructions were developed in a different world with different assumptions and different problems. One must draw analogies and make extrapolations to apply them to today's problems in today's world.[1] There is nothing wrong with creative extension, if we recognize it for what it is. It is part of the lawyer's trade. The task of thick versions of originalism, however, is to disguise this creativity and analogical extension so that it appears that if we want to be faithful to the law—as opposed to being lawless—we really have no choice but to follow the past's commands.

But this is appearance, not reality. Originalists with thick conceptions of original meaning shift to thinner, more abstract conceptions when necessary, all the while denying that their methods have changed. They make allowances for contemporary values, constructions, and understandings that would be too embarrassing, difficult, or delegitimating to disavow, either by creatively updating their readings of historical materials or by selectively adhering to precedent.

Successive generations of originalists have taken different positions, finding new things in history that allow them to keep up with changing mores and political assumptions.

A. Conservative Originalism as Living Constitutionalism

Taken together, the tools and devices of conservative originalism are a conservative version of living constitutionalism.[2] They produce a Constitution-in-practice that is adapted to the problems of the present as conservatives understand them. Although the conceit of this approach is its forswearing of value-oriented jurisprudence and its selfless submission to the law, it is actually a way of creatively engaging with the law in ever-changing circumstances to promote and defend constitutional and political values that conservative lawyers and judges cherish. This approach is anything but rigid and uncompromising. It is flexible and adaptable, even if it bends in directions that liberals often do not like. Although it aspires to legality and methodological rigor, it is neither neutral nor apolitical. It is a form of legal creativity that meshes with the constitutional politics of the present.

Living constitutionalism promises to keep the Constitution in touch with contemporary values. And that is precisely what conservative originalism does. It keeps the Constitution in touch with contemporary conservative values, infusing constitutional law "with the outlook of an insurgent political movement."[3] Moreover, as the values and concerns of conservatives have changed over the course of half a century, so too have the kinds of arguments that conservative originalists have made about the Constitution. For example, Raoul Berger thought *Brown v. Board of Education* was wrongly decided; Robert Bork read the First Amendment narrowly to exclude commercial speech; Antonin Scalia crippled the Free Exercise Clause.[4] Today's originalists depart from all three positions.

As the conservative movement has changed its mind about various issues, successive generations of conservative originalists have also changed their views about what the Constitution has always required. In some cases, conservative originalists have made their peace with liberal precedents and given them conservative reinterpretations

(*Brown*, First Amendment doctrine); in other cases, they have pushed to dismantle existing precedents further than earlier conservatives had sought to go.

What has made conservative originalism successful as an approach to constitutional interpretation over the course of half a century is not that it provides a single coherent, apolitical method uniformly followed. As we have seen, there are many versions of originalism, and originalist judges, like everyone else, are cafeteria originalists, who pick and choose how and when to apply originalist insights. Rather, what has made conservative originalism successful is that it has successfully connected conservative legal argument to a changing conservative political culture.[5] Even as the views of conservatives evolved, and even after conservatives gained control of the federal judiciary, conservative originalism has offered itself as a way to critique misguided judges and appeal to an original, unchanging Constitution.

Conservative originalism has also been successful because it connects constitutional argument to a compelling historical narrative about modernity.[6] It argues for constitutional restoration of an imagined past that was once faithful to the Constitution in a way that the contaminated, decadent, unfree present is not. The language of restoration allows legal conservatives to make arguments from original meaning *and* arguments from tradition, even though in academic theory, arguments from long-standing traditions are distinct from arguments about the original meaning of the constitutional text at a particular point in time.

Equipped with arguments from original meaning and tradition, conservative jurists are able to show why the Constitution does not protect—or positively forbids—liberal and progressive innovations, while simultaneously protecting and furthering conservative values and policies. In this way, conservative originalism connects legal argument to a conservative vision of the world and a conservative politics of restoration. And it allows conservatives to identify their conservative values with respect for the Constitution and the rule of law.

All of this has produced a conservative version of living constitutionalism that eschews the label but does all the work that living constitutionalism is supposed to do: it keeps the Constitution in line with the changing views of conservatives confronting a changing society.[7]

In chapter 5, I argued that living constitutionalism and originalism were twins separated at birth, mirror-image interpretive approaches designed to deal with modernity and change that have their roots in American political and legal culture. I do not claim that there is no difference between these approaches or that these approaches produce the same results. Rather, I am claiming that originalism and living constitutionalism are both methods of creative adaptation to modernity using history.

The distinction between interpretation and construction makes these similarities easier to comprehend. Most arguments from adoption history fall within the zone of constitutional construction. They are usually also implicit or explicit appeals to national ethos, political tradition, and honored authority. And they employ a set of flexible tools for interpreting and using history under the sign of fidelity to the past.

B. Why Nonoriginalists Should Make Originalist Arguments

Because originalist argument is a way of adapting to change and calling for reform, there is no particular reason why nonoriginalists should refrain from making arguments from adoption history. To be sure, some nonoriginalists may shy away from making these arguments because they fear that this will be seen as an implicit confession that conservative originalism is the correct way to interpret the Constitution. If nonoriginalists make originalist arguments, this will only serve to legitimize conservative arguments they oppose.

But the distinction between interpretation and construction shows why these fears are misplaced. When people build out the Constitution-in-practice, they can and should use every available tool of argument and persuasion. Adoption history and arguments from ethos, tradition, and honored authority are among those tools; indeed, in American legal culture, they are often quite powerful tools. Originalist argument is a characteristic rhetorical feature of the processes of living constitutionalism; if so, those who call themselves "living constitutionalists" should certainly make use of it. Arguments from adoption history and invocations of American culture heroes do not belong to any sect or party. Appeals to the founders, framers, and adopters occurred long before the rise of modern originalism, and they will no doubt continue to be offered long after the current configuration of political argument and academic theory has passed into oblivion.

Thus, even people who actively oppose originalism as a comprehensive theory of interpretation should have no qualms about making originalist arguments. In fact, they should make them regularly, for at least three different reasons.

First, as a practical matter, and for the foreseeable future, the American judiciary is likely to be filled with many originalists. Both scholars and advocates should make originalist arguments to persuade these judges to the extent they can and, at the very least, shape how they understand both history and the law.

Second, even if they do not manage to persuade originalist judges, scholars and advocates should make arguments about adoption history to critique how these judges use history.[8] Scholars and advocates can show that history points in a different direction (an obedient and critical use of history). Or they can attempt to show that history does not yield a clear lesson and that one cannot employ history as judges do without creative extension and controversial choices of value (a deconstructive use of history).

The third reason, however, is perhaps the most important. Quite apart from the demands of litigation, scholars, advocates, and political actors should regularly make originalist arguments because these arguments draw on the normative power of the nation's cultural memory. Originalist arguments are only a special case of arguments from cultural memory, of course. There is far more to history than adoption history, and historical claims may be critical of the founders, framers, and adopters. As I argue throughout this book, constitutional interpreters should mine all of history, not just the history of adoption, and they should engage in critical and deconstructive accounts of the past, not just obedient accounts.

According to this view, one does not make originalist arguments simply because one's opponents might make them in a brief. Rather, one makes them because of the role that cultural memory plays in establishing legitimacy and authority. Invoking the past and telling stories about its meaning is important to any version of a living constitutionalism that seeks to connect the Constitution to the political values of the present.

A living tradition of constitutionalism needs the resources of tradition and cultural memory to work with. These do not have to be impediments to change. They are also the wellsprings of change and justifications for change. They provide important intellectual tools for people within a living tradition to understand the challenges of the present and to argue with their fellow citizens about the proper direction of the constitutional project in the future.[9]

Those who are not originalists also have a stake in the constitution of America's political traditions and in its conceptions of national ethos. They have a stake in the stories Americans tell themselves about their origins and achievements and in how Americans understand the meaning and direction of their history. They have a stake in who is considered an honored authority and why they are honored. They have a stake, in short, in the construction of the nation's cultural memory.

Conservative originalism has succeeded not because it is apolitical or methodologically coherent. It has succeeded because it constructs memory and gives voice. Conservative originalism has given people a way to connect their vision of the world to the authority of the Constitution, and to articulate their political objections in terms of fidelity to the Constitution. Conservative originalism does not separate constitutional law from constitutional politics. It allows constitutional law to speak constitutional politics. And it helps the Constitution keep up with the changing values and mores of conservatives.

If liberals and progressives wish to contest this version of living constitutionalism with a successful living constitutionalism of their own, they must find a way to articulate their vision of social life and connect that vision to the Constitution.[10] Appeals to history and collective memory give people a way to make that connection and claim legal authority for their political vision. Appeals to history and collective memory give people a way to do more than argue for sensible policies. They allow people to speak in the name of the Constitution itself.

C. Restoration and Redemption

There is one important difference, however, between the way that conservative originalists and liberal living constitutionalists will likely marshal the resources of history. The standard trope of conservative originalists, as we have seen, has been constitutional restoration. Now living constitutionalists may also argue for a restoration of rights, conventions, and arrangements wrongly discarded or abused by an out-of-touch judiciary. But they will probably also employ history in a different key: through arguments for constitutional redemption.[11]

The tropes of restoration and redemption employ history differently. Restoration seeks a return to the values and practices of an age that has been lost. Redemption seeks to fulfill promises made in the past.[12]

The concept of redemption does not assume that the world was once better and that we have fallen away from it. Quite the contrary, it assumes that the world of the past, like that of the present, has often fallen short of our ideals. The present world is compromised and constructed by the injustices and deficiencies of the past, whose consequences still live with us today. The present, like the past, is broken, and one reason why it is broken is because of what came before. The point of a redemptive constitutionalism is that we can nevertheless strive to realize ideals that were only imperfectly articulated and realized in the past. We can do our best to make good on the promises of the past in the present. We can do our part to repair a broken world in our own time.

Restoration sees the present as a falling away from the past. Redemption sees the past and the present as fallen and hopes to repair the future. So its use of history is not simply obedient; it is also critical. History contains both the ideals and the failings of the past, the cumulative weight of past injustices, and the moral example of people who named those injustices and fought against them.

Political redemption is never final, not only because our efforts at repair are always imperfect and limited by the world into which we were born, but also because each generation faces new challenges to surmount, and because each generation produces ever new ways that people can be unjust to each other.

What redemption requires at different points in history may be different as we confront new problems, old problems in new contexts, and the cumulative wreckage of past injustices, mistakes, and failures of nerve. Even so, the quest for political redemption requires us to remember the past every bit as much as the quest for restoration does. And originalist arguments can serve both the politics of restoration and the politics of redemption.

Staking a claim to the past is not alien to the idea of a living Constitution; it is how a living Constitution operates. Living constitutionalists score no theoretical points for refusing to engage in originalist styles of argument. All that one achieves is to limit the ability to draw on powerful symbols of ethos, tradition, and honored authority. And this is no small cost, because what is often at stake in debates over constitutional interpretation is whose version of history will shape political and legal discussion and whose memory of the past will be heard.

Tradition and cultural memory are not fixed. They are shaped by how people choose to argue, articulate, persuade, and remember. They are shaped by how people actively invest in memory and encourage others to remember. We the People of the United States are no fixed thing. The "We" is contested and constantly changing. As the "We" changes, so too does the memory of the past.

Through politics and through interventions in culture, different people, groups, and institutions can move in and out of the pantheon of honored authorities, can gain or recede in salience and prominence, and can take on different meanings and associations. Even if the past does not change, the memory of the past certainly does. Refusing to claim the past for oneself means accepting other people's versions. Those who will not deign to speak in the name of tradition and cultural memory will have tradition and cultural memory deployed against them.

PART IV

Constitutional Memories

CHAPTER ELEVEN

The Power of Memory
and Erasure

THROUGHOUT THIS BOOK, I have noted the importance of collective memory to the ways that lawyers use history to argue about the Constitution. This chapter and the next two try to explain why this is so. I begin with a general explanation of the normative and ideological power of collective memory, and then I turn to the uses of memory in constitutional interpretation.

Memory concerns what people remember about the past and how they remember it. Memory is not the same as an accurate record of events.[1] The memory of the American Civil War, for example, may be different from what actually happened in the Civil War.

Collective memory is a set of stories, icons, symbols, and events that help constitute members of a social group as a group and that help constitute the group's identity and its sense of shared values.[2] Collective memory shapes group members' understanding of their past and how they reason about the present in light of the past. In this way, collective memory grounds and shapes people's practical reasoning in politics, in policy debates, and in their relationships with others.[3]

Collective memory is a distinctively social phenomenon.[4] It is different from the sum of individual memories about the group or the nation. Some individuals may know things about the past that other people do not, but they live together in societies with shared memories and symbols of the past and shared associations and meanings about people and events from the past.[5] A great deal of what people know about the past comes from the memory and recounting of others, so that memory becomes a sort of shared resource.[6] Even *how* people remember is shaped by the cultures in which they live.[7] Moreover, people not only have their own sense of the past and its meaning but they also have a sense of what other people in their group believe about the past. Thus, people recognize that they and others have *shared* memories, symbols, and narratives.[8]

Collective memory is embodied in the stories people tell each other about the past and in the cultural references and allusions they make in everyday speech.[9] It is preserved and propagated socially in everyday expressions, in political rhetoric, in religion, in popular culture, in memes, in museums, in schoolbooks, in historical scholarship, in legal opinions, and so on.[10] Collective memory is also embodied in the central or sacred texts of a culture, like the Declaration of Independence or the Bible, in works of art, in architecture, in monuments, and in rituals.[11] Thus, rather than simply being a collection of individual memories, the collective memory of the past is embedded in social life, institutions, and artifacts.[12] The more often a historical event, person, or epoch is referred to or institutionalized in texts, art, monuments, and rituals, and the more often people draw on it and tell stories about it, the more likely it is to become part of the group's collective memory even if people do not remember all the details or even get them wrong.[13]

The fact that members of a group share collective memory does not require that everyone in the group remembers the same things or remembers them in the same way.[14] For example, Americans have very different memories of the American Civil War and why it was fought. Indeed, features of a group's collective memory are often simultaneously shared *and* contested.[15] These contests often reflect or correspond to present-day differences and struggles within the group. Memories of a group's past, in other words, may be contested *because* they are shared and constitutive.

Shared memory is less about historical accuracy and more about a common set of cultural resources for making claims in the present. The civil rights activist Rosa Parks is now a part of the collective memory of the United States.[16] But that does not mean that everyone in the United States knows who Rosa Parks is or what she did. Some people may know little about her other than her name, and their views about her may be quite hazy and ill informed. When people are arguing a point or defending themselves from potential criticism, they may invoke Rosa Parks or the meme that she refused to give up her seat and move to the back of a bus, and they may do so in creative and even tendentious ways.

In short, people continually use collective memory as a rhetorical resource for reasoning with others. People reinterpret or appropriate elements of the past and the meaning of the past to persuade others about what is happening in society and what we should or should not do. This rhetorical use of memory is especially important and powerful in legal argument.

Subcultures and subcommunities, such as the African American community or the American Jewish community, can have a different collective memory about events, stories, and persons, one that is connected to their experiences and constitutive of their distinctive identities. These memories may overlap with the historical memories of other groups but may also be at odds with them.[17]

Moreover, specific professional or institutional communities, such as the community of lawyers or academics, may have different and more detailed shared memories and stories than those held in the general public. The collective memory of American lawyers is shaped by their legal education and by the opinions, briefs, and legal writings that they encounter. Important cases like *Lochner v. New York* or *McCulloch v. Maryland* will have meanings and resonances for American lawyers that will mostly be lost on the general public.[18] For professions and academic disciplines, what is collectively remembered is often closely connected to what is canonical.

Thus, collective memory refers to a very complex social phenomenon: the distribution of partly similar and partly different shared beliefs about the past by different people and groups in society, and the way those beliefs are preserved, contested, and altered through rhetoric, social interaction, art, institutions, and rituals.[19]

A. The Normative Power of Memory

Memory is important to politics and to law because of its normative power. Memory has normative power because it helps constitute the identity, values, and reasoning assumptions of a group and its members.[20] A group's collective memory helps explain who members of the group are, what things mean, and how things got to be the way they are.[21] A group's collective memory includes the group's past achievements and failures, stories about its previous struggles, triumphs, and defeats, and the injustices or humiliations the group suffered or righted along the way.[22]

In this way, memory undergirds common sense and practical judgment. It tells members of the group who they are and what they stand for, what they regard as just and unjust, what they value and do not value.[23]

People understand themselves through the stories they tell about themselves, and they understand the groups and nations to which they belong through stories about the emergence and history of their group or nation.[24] Through these stories about how things came to be (and what these stories make salient or forget), people get a sense of how society should be ordered, what needs to preserved and defended, and whether and how society needs to change.

Memory shapes understanding because it offers narratives that a group's members can use to understand current events. These stories give people a sense of how social and political life works, how things came to be the way they are, and how events are likely to unfold. Memory also provides examples to reason with and argue with, to judge situations and persons with, and to compare and contrast with the present.

What people think happened in the past shapes their views about the present and future. If you think that Reconstruction was a period of political corruption in which Black people were thrust unprepared into citizenship and unscrupulous Northern carpetbaggers invaded and took advantage of a defeated South, you will have a different view about race relations and federalism than if you believe that Reconstruction was a crucial period of reform, constitutional renewal, and Black empowerment that was tragically undermined by white Southern resistance and terrorist violence.[25] If you think that Franklin Roosevelt's court-packing plan was a failure that was rejected by politicians of both parties and that undermined his domestic agenda for the rest of his presidency, you will have a different view of court expansion today than if you believe that Roosevelt's plan failed only because of the sudden death of the Senate majority leader and that Roosevelt actually achieved his most important goals.[26] If you believe that the Senate filibuster has always existed, you will have a different view about reforming or abolishing it than if you believe that the Senate's voting and debate rules have changed repeatedly throughout the country's history and that current practices imposing a sixty-vote requirement for most legislation are a relatively recent innovation.[27]

Thus, memory does not merely recollect or describe. It also grounds practical judgment and imposes a normative order on the world. Memory has normative power because it structures common sense.

First, what we remember (and do not remember) offers a sense of what is normal, natural, traditional, or to be expected and, conversely, what is abnormal, unusual, deviant, or unexpected.[28] Memory helps generate the sense that certain features of a situation are representative or expected, while others appear extraordinary or unusual; memory helps identify certain features as salient while placing others in the background.

Second, memory of what is normal serves as a template for norms, both descriptive and normative.[29] As a descriptive matter, memory of how things happened is a template for comparing or contrasting what will happen this time. As a normative matter, memory shapes political and moral authority because it shapes what we regard as natural, normal, or appropriate. "It has always been this way" or "it has never been this way," "this is the way it happened before" or "this has never happened" are not merely descriptions of events. They are also rhetorically powerful normative arguments.

Third, memory provides an origin story for us and for other groups and persons that we interact with. It provides a template and a ready set of expectations for our interactions with others on which we can improvise.[30]

Fourth, narrative memory tells us what our current situation is and therefore what, if anything, we should do about it. In this way, memory can either rationalize or condemn existing social relations.[31]

Fifth, the narratives in collective memory provide historical and social scripts for social analysis and social interaction. People fit current social relations into examples of existing stories, using the latter to understand how to behave in the present. A group's stories create scripts—the story of the Boston Tea Party, the story of Prohibition, the story of the Vietnam War—that suggest how things happened and how they are likely to happen in the present. Historical scripts are normatively powerful because they suggest how people are likely to behave and how they should behave.[32] These scripts also have normative power because they are bound up with associations and judgments of success and failure, wisdom and folly, good and evil, justice and injustice.

Sixth, memory gives a trajectory to events.[33] It tells us that we are in decline or at a stage of upward progress. It tells us whether the arc of history bends toward justice or disappointment. It offers a list of things left undone, promises to be fulfilled, wrongs to be righted, or injuries to be revenged.

Seventh, memory shapes whom and what we identify with and whom and what we dis-identify with, whom we root for in a conflict and whom we oppose. It offers examples of endeavors that succeeded (World War II) and those that failed (Prohibition). Memory offers associations of good and bad characteristics to events, things, and persons. By telling stories, people assign praise and blame and diagnose justice and injustice. Stories about the past allow people to express grievance and excuse. They give people examples of heroes and villains (and of ambiguous characters in between), just actions and unjust actions, triumphs and disasters, things to be done, and things never to do again.[34] For example, from the memory of the civil rights movement, Americans get Rosa Parks and Martin Luther King Jr. as paradigmatic heroes, segregated water fountains and police turning firehoses on civil rights demonstrators as paradigmatic injuries, and so on.

B. Remembering and Forgetting: The Power of Erasure

Memory involves selective remembering and forgetting.[35] One cannot remember everything, and remembering too many things may undermine a coherent narrative.[36] So, in memory, some features of the past receive emphasis, and others recede into the background or are not mentioned at all. In other words, memory is an economy of what is remembered (or misremembered) and what is not remembered or forgotten. Therefore, whenever we speak about memory, we must also speak about erasure.

What is remembered may be normatively powerful, but erasure may be even more powerful.[37] Like what is remembered, erasure has both descriptive and normative effects. If memory offers accounts of past injury, failure to remember erases the recognition of injury; it erases both the assignment of blame and the recognition of credit and praise. If memory tells us a story of how things came to be, erasure occludes origins, disguises causes, hides defeats, and falsifies achievements. If the memory of the past tells us that current arrangements are the result of previous injustices that people contested and resisted, erasure of the past makes the present appear legitimate and the result of consent and free choice.

Whatever is erased from memory loses its power to shape meaning. Forgotten injustices lead people to assume that the present is more or less justified. The power of tradition, or of what has always been done, depends on people not remembering that things have been done differently in the past or that past practices were contested and diverse. The belief that things have always been this way depends on people not remembering the conflicts and struggles that resulted in the status quo.

Erasure amplifies the moral meaning of what is remembered, while evaporating the moral meaning of what is erased. If we did not remember the civil rights movement, its moral authority—and its ability to shape our views of paradigmatic cases of justice and injustice—would disappear.

That is why erasure—what is not remembered—is as important to the normative significance of the present as remembering. To gain legitimacy or moral authority, therefore, it is important to have control over memory.[38] Hence, fights over memory are never-ending, because what is at stake in remembering the past is the moral high ground of the present. The meaning of the past is the terrain on which battles over the present are fought.

C. Memory Entrepreneurs

Although some elements of a group's memory are long lasting, other parts change over time. In fact, what people remember about their past is always changing as one generation succeeds another. The transformation and transvaluation of memory is not merely a passive process. Memory and historical narratives are always in motion through education of the next generation and through public contestation, assertions, and representations made in institutions such as journalism, religion, politics, and art.

Changes in how we remember things often result from the efforts of people and institutions that want people to remember the past differently or remember different things. These people and institutions are memory entrepreneurs.[39] Just as norm entrepreneurs attempt to change people's norms, memory entrepreneurs try to change memory and narratives of the past.[40] And since memory has normative power, these two tasks are often closely linked.

Because memory is an economy of remembering and forgetting, memory entrepreneurship attempts to alter this economy, offering a different mixture of what we remember and what we forget in order to produce an altered set of meanings and inferences about the normal and the unusual, the natural and the constructed, the legitimate and the illegitimate, the just and the unjust. Memory entrepreneurship attempts to restructure identity, obligation, and common sense through selective emphasis and de-emphasis, remembering and forgetting.[41]

Uncovering old history and publicizing it is an example of memory entrepreneurship. So too is telling the story of the past differently, reframing origin stories, placing familiar historical figures in different lights, recasting honored authorities as deeply flawed or familiar villains as newly sympathetic characters, and recovering and promoting forgotten people, movements, and claims. Just as the origin stories of literary characters and comic book heroes and villains are revised from time to time, so too are narratives of a group's history and the cultural associations of the figures, movements, and communities within them. One need only witness the continual rise and fall—and the continuing historical transformations—of the reputations of founders like Thomas Jefferson and Alexander Hamilton over the course of American history.[42]

To be sure, this reshaping of the past and characters from the past can be propagandistic and in the service of state power. Politicians may bury inconvenient events and offer fabricated accounts designed to avoid recognition of injustices and place their party and themselves in the best possible light. There is a saying attributed to Milovan Diljas, the former Yugoslavian revolutionary (and later critic of communism), that "the hardest thing about being a Communist is trying to predict the past."[43] History had been constantly revised by the communist regime's propagandists to fit the party's current needs.

But much memory entrepreneurship is less morally troubling. Indeed, it is an almost inevitable feature of political and social life. Retelling the story of the past and reconfiguring its meaning for the present is a familiar feature of our lives.[44] One reason for this is that the past continually looks different to us as we move into the future.[45] Historical episodes, some remembered, some forgotten, become newly relevant and salient as our situation changes.[46] The pandemic of 2020 caused people to pay attention to and reinterpret the history of previous pandemics and public health emergencies, for example.[47] And each generation, if it learns of the past at all, must learn of it from where that generation sits in time and experience.

Not only is memory entrepreneurship ubiquitous; it is difficult to imagine the work of the historical profession without it. Accuracy is surely important to historians, but so too are fresh perspectives that help us understand lost worlds. A historian who revealed nothing new that was not in previous historical accounts, who made no fresh discoveries of persons, places, and events, who offered no new perspectives on the past or new ways of telling familiar narratives would likely be regarded as undistinguished or routine. Historians are honored not only for remembering but also for remembering differently, in ways that can successfully resonate with, enlighten, and persuade their audiences. Memory entrepreneurship is not alien to their professional norms; it is part of them.

Memory entrepreneurship is also a key feature of politics and legal change.[48] As social and political movements seek to gain legitimacy and influence, these movements turn to history to retell and reconfigure familiar stories about the past, and to offer new stories about people who have been forgotten, marginalized, or previously condemned.[49] Lawyers on opposite sides of a dispute have reasons to shape memory differently because of the normative conclusions they want decision-makers to reach. Although both lawyers and historians can be memory entrepreneurs, how they attempt to retell the story of the past is shaped by their different professional norms, leading to familiar conflicts and tensions between them.[50]

D. Memory Wars, Mobilization, and Status Conflicts

Just as we can speak of memory entrepreneurs, we can speak of *memory wars*—struggles over how to remember the past, which parts of the past to emphasize and which parts to de-emphasize and even forget.[51] Eastern European countries have fought memory wars about who is responsible for atrocities in World War II, and countries have passed memory laws to try to control what people remember about the past.[52] In the United States, politicians have sought to pass laws limiting what children can be taught about race, slavery, and other "divisive" subjects.[53]

Perhaps the most common occasion for struggles over memory is in political and legal disputes. "Disputes about forging a common future," Reva Siegel explains, "are . . . expressed as claims about a shared past."[54] People struggle over what to do in the present by making claims about what happened in the past and what it means. When people fight over what they should do in the future, they often fight about what happened in the past. This means that political and social conflicts are also often conflicts over memory, and memory itself becomes an important terrain of struggle.

When social movements seek to persuade others to adopt reforms, they often attempt to remind people about past injustices and their current effects.[55] But in order to persuade people outside the movement that the movement's claims are just, they also often invoke shared features of a common political culture that have normative authority.[56] In the antebellum era, free Black people invoked the Declaration of Independence's claim that "all men are created equal" to argue for their civil rights.[57] The Seneca Falls Declaration of 1848 arguing for women's rights is also modeled on the text of the Declaration.[58]

It does not matter that the historical purpose of the Declaration was not to secure sex equality, undermine slavery, or give Black people equal rights, but to justify a revolt of white colonists—many of whom owned slaves—against the British Empire.[59] Nor does it matter that many, if not most, of the Declaration's signers would have opposed claims of race and sex equality. What mattered was that, by the early nineteenth century, the Declaration had become an honored object of collective memory in the United States that could be mobilized to claim that equality—however imperfectly realized at the founding—was always at the heart of American values and commitments.

Disputes over memory may also form part of larger conflicts over social status as an existing status order is changing. Conflicts over status are struggles over who is more (or equally) important, moral, worthy of respect, central to the nation's identity, or exemplary of its values, virtues, and character.[60] Societies such as the United States have multiple status hierarchies of race, ethnicity, religion, immigrant status, sex, sexual orientation, and so on. As status relations change, some group members who fear losing their comparatively higher status may resist these changes, often bitterly, and sometimes even violently. They may resist because—in the short run at least—changes in status relations tend to be zero-sum: any gain in status for a formerly subordinate group is felt as a comparative loss of status for higher-status groups.[61]

One way that people resist changes in status relations is through assertions about memory and attempts to control what is remembered and forgotten about the past. For example, during the establishment of Jim Crow, and again during the civil rights revolution, white Southerners reasserted their status through monuments and histories that celebrated the Confederacy as Southern heritage.[62] Today, as white people slowly approach a numerical minority in American society, racially conservative white people fight over school curricula and whether students will be taught "divisive subjects," which include materials (history books, novels, and other forms of art) that call attention to the role of slavery, Jim Crow, and racism in American history.[63] Although these materials were previously part of school curricula, they have become newly controversial because the politics of race has changed in the United States in the past decade and a half.[64]

Emphasizing the deeds, arguments, and even existence of people and of communities with comparatively lower status symbolically raises the status of groups that identify with them today. An apparent change in status occurs because members of these groups—and their voices, arguments, and accomplishments—now appear to matter more to the history of the country.[65]

Increased attention to the accomplishments of women and racial minorities in historical accounts may feel like a status injury to groups that previously dominated the canon of historical memory. Thus, racially conservative white people may object to increasing attention to nonwhite people and the concerns of nonwhite people in history and memory.[66] That is because attention—and even attention in memory—is a scarce commodity. Moreover, attention is linked to status, and status, in turn, is linked to cultural and political power. Those who are remembered, and by proxy, those who identify with them today, gain higher status because they gain a larger share of attention.[67] A similar, although not identical, effect occurs when minority groups gain a greater share of attention in movies, television shows, or advertisements. The shift of attention toward minority characters alters cultural meanings and social status by redefining what is normal, expected, and natural in social life. The balance of who is seen and heard, and therefore whose concerns are salient, reshapes, however subtly, who counts in social life.

The controversy over the 1619 Project, which argued that the country's origins cannot be separated from its maintenance of chattel slavery, and the related debate over the extent to which the Constitution actually accommodated or protected slavery, are fights about memory with obvious connections to contemporary anxieties about who Americans really are and the values America holds today.[68] These controversies arose following the election of the nation's first Black president, Barack Obama, which sensitized many white people to questions of race and their own racial identity, and the election of a racist demagogue, Donald Trump, immediately following the Obama presidency.[69] President Trump's creation of a "1776 Project" to rebut the 1619 Project is an unsubtle example of a fight over memory.[70] It is a dispute about the American story and how America became the country it is today.[71] Similarly, historical arguments about whether the Constitution was really pro- or antislavery reflect contemporary concerns about the nature of the country and the story of how our present world came to be. These debates are exercises in memory entrepreneurship that struggle over what America means, what is good and bad about it, what needs to be preserved and honored, and what needs to be denounced and changed.

CHAPTER TWELVE

Constitutional Memory and Constitutional Interpretation

W HEN PEOPLE MAKE ARGUMENTS about the proper interpretation of the Constitution, they call on features of the past to gain authority for their arguments (or to undermine the authority of their opponents' arguments). Following Reva Siegel, we might call the invocation of memory in constitutional argument the use of constitutional memory.[1] Constitutional memory shapes and organizes people's views about what the law means and why people have authority, what is normal and what is abnormal, usual or unusual, and what arguments about the Constitution are plausible and implausible.

In constitutional disputes, different parties often invoke different accounts of memory. They attempt to reshape memory through persuasive narratives and redescriptions. They emphasize certain aspects of the past while leaving out others, offer new examples and historical research, and recharacterize existing stories, people, events, and understandings to support their arguments. Lawyers and judges continually invoke and construct memory, and judicial decisions both rely on constitutional memory and produce constitutional memory.[2] Thus, constitutional interpreters, including lawyers and judges, are often memory entrepreneurs. And, as we will see shortly, many uses of constitutional memory involve significant forms of erasure.[3]

The legitimacy of public and private power is at stake in these dueling claims. Constitutional interpreters use memory to bestow authority on their arguments, invoking the kinds of memory that they hope will buttress their claims.[4] Meanwhile, their opponents attempt to deconstruct and complicate these claims of memory, offering counternarratives and counterexamples.

Lawyers draw on both what they know as citizens and what they know as members of a legal profession educated in the law. Therefore, the constitutional memory of lawyers and judges may be different and, in some ways, more specialized than the constitutional memory of the public as a whole because the constitutional canon is different for lawyers and judges than it is for ordinary citizens, who have not studied the history of the American Constitution and its development.[5]

Supreme Court opinions construct the professional memory of constitutional lawyers and judges.[6] These opinions, in turn, are tutored by lawyers making arguments, by amicus briefs that provide historical quotes, events, and contexts, and by law review articles and legal scholarship that other lawyers read, quote, and cite. Judicial opinions both depend on and amplify conceptions of constitutional memory, and therefore they both depend on and amplify the ideological effects of what is remembered and what is forgotten.[7]

A. The Canon and Constitutional Memory

Constitutional memory has deep connections to the constitutional canon. Sanford Levinson and I argue that the constitutional canon consists not only of key decisions, statutes, and conventions, but also widely shared constitutional narratives.[8] To a large extent, learning American constitutional law also involves learning a set of stories about American constitutional development and especially the work of the Supreme Court. In other words, education in constitutional law is education in constitutional memory. It follows that disagreements about constitutional interpretation, and even over constitutional theory, are often fights over what counts as canonical. These fights are not only about which decisions and opinions are or should be viewed as canonical, but also about which stories and memories of the creation and development of the Constitution are or should be canonical. Fights over constitutional interpretation, in other words, are often fights over constitutional memory.

Take, for example, the constitutional memory associated with *Lochner v. New York*, a 1905 decision that struck down a maximum hour law for bakers.[9] For many years, *Lochner* was regarded as a central example of the anticanon—that is, famous decisions that exemplify how not to interpret the Constitution.[10] *Lochner's* anticanonical status is embedded in a canonical narrative about the lessons of the constitutional struggle over the New Deal. *Lochner* symbolizes the Old Court and its jurisprudence that was overthrown in the "constitutional revolution of 1937" and the New Deal settlement.[11] But in the past thirty years, *Lochner's* anticanonical status has begun to change. These days many legal intellectuals—primarily conservatives and libertarians—argue that the case is not so wrong or perhaps is even correctly decided.[12] This shift in *Lochner's* anticanonical status reflects the increasing power and influence of the conservative legal movement.[13] But it is also connected to a dispute over memory, as conservative intellectuals have attempted to retell the story of the Progressive era and the New Deal in a much less flattering light.[14] In other words, canons change as memory changes, and vice versa.

Changing generational attitudes about judicial review also reflect changing understandings of constitutional memory.[15] Liberals and conservatives have changed their minds about strong judicial review not once but twice between the beginning of the twentieth century and the present.[16] These changes in attitude correspond to changes in constitutional memory that reflect the different perspectives of succeeding generations.[17]

For example, consider the generational transformations in the constitutional memory of liberals and progressives. Progressives who came of age during the first decades of the twentieth century were generally hostile to judicial review.[18] In the stories they told about the Constitution, judges were out of touch with the needs of society and mostly served the interests of big business. These views were shaped by memories of *Lochner v. New York*; *Hammer v. Dagenhart*, which struck down a federal ban on child labor; the *Pollock* decision, which struck down the federal income tax; and the use of labor injunctions to stifle and destroy unions.[19] Liberals who came of age in the middle of the century had a very different understanding of judicial review because their constitutional memories were shaped by *Brown v. Board of Education* and the civil rights revolution.[20] Finally, progressives who came of age in the last years of the twentieth century and the first decades of the twenty-first are increasingly skeptical of judicial review; their memories have been shaped by many years of conservative dominance on the Supreme Court and decisions like *Citizens United v. FEC* and *Shelby County v. Holder*, which progressives believe have weakened democracy.[21]

B. Memory, Erasure, and the Legitimation of Authority

Disputes about constitutional memory are disputes about which voices, which experiences, and which history should count in how we interpret and construct the Constitution. We can restate this point in terms of three related questions.

First, which history and whose experiences will be emphasized or deemed relevant to the meaning of the Constitution today, and which history and whose experiences will be forgotten or deemed irrelevant?

Second, which claims about the Constitution and its adoption, amendment, or interpretation will be heard today, and which will be de-emphasized or ignored?

Third, which people and which groups count as "constitutional meaning makers"—that is, as people whose opinions and experience should matter to how people interpret the Constitution today?

The American constitutional tradition is a dialectical tradition of arguments and responses to those arguments. Different accounts of constitutional memory highlight some persons and their arguments, while leaving other persons and their arguments out of view.[22] If arguments are forgotten or not even considered, they vanish from the tradition. They are lost to memory, so that we do not even consider them in thinking about our current situation and how the Constitution applies to it. At best, we must reinvent these arguments without knowing that others once had similar views and advocated for them. Therefore, if you want power over the interpretation and construction of the Constitution and over which pathways of constitutional development appear possible or even thinkable, it is useful to gain control over constitutional memory.

Every approach to constitutional interpretation is also implicitly an account of constitutional memory. And because memory involves both what we remember and what we forget, different theories and practices of constitutional interpretation pose different problems of erasure.

We often judge rival approaches to interpretation in terms of how they legitimate judicial review. But if legitimacy is our concern, we must pay careful attention to the kind of constitutional memory each method presumes or fosters.

The scope of constitutional memory matters to legitimacy because many features of constitutional legitimacy depend, whether directly or indirectly, on implicit notions of societal consensus, majority opinion, and the consent of the governed. But if the consensus is not real, if the majority is artificially constructed, and if the consent of the governed is not genuine, this may undermine assumptions about legitimacy.

Suppose that the practices of constitutional interpretation have an unduly constricted account of constitutional memory, selectively describe past events, or severely limit the class of relevant constitutional meaning makers. Then these practices will create the false appearance of majority opinion, of a consensus of values, and of consent to existing social and political arrangements, some of which may be very unjust. As Reva Siegel explains, when constitutional memory is constricted in this way, it "can legitimate authority by generating the appearance of consent to contested status relations and by destroying the vernacular of resistance."[23]

Therefore, one way to think about the pros and cons of different theories of constitutional interpretation is in terms of the forms of memory *and* erasure they encourage or produce. What a theory discards or forgets is as important as what it encourages us to remember, because what is erased from memory can have no claim on authority or legitimacy.

C. Doctrine and Memory

Consider three familiar approaches to constitutional interpretation: one that focuses on doctrine and past judicial decisions, one that focuses on original meaning, and one that focuses on tradition.

If the central method of constitutional interpretation is doctrinal, then the key articulators of constitutional meaning and the key speakers of the constitutional tradition are current and former Supreme Court justices, a group that is very select and demographically and culturally very narrow. Put another way, in doctrinal argument, no one else's interpretation of the Constitution is remembered unless that person or group happened to influence the arguments of some current or former justice.

To be sure, the justices sometimes cite dissenting opinions—especially their own. They may also cite dissenting opinions that have since won out or even become canonical, like the dissents of Justice Oliver Wendell Holmes Jr. and Justice Louis Brandeis in free speech cases.[24] But this very example shows how much doctrinal argument tends to narrow the scope of constitutional memory. Holmes and Brandeis had important things to say about why freedom of speech is important. But they did not write in a vacuum. Before Holmes and Brandeis—and indeed contemporaneous with them—is a huge collection of arguments about freedom of speech by Americans who were not Supreme Court justices.[25] These include arguments by free Black people and white abolitionists before the Civil War, suffragists, advocates of reproductive rights in the early years of the twentieth century, and especially labor union activists.[26] For example, the Industrial Workers of the World (Wobblies), like other radical labor groups, pushed for the right to collectively bargain during the early 1900s and drew widespread attention in a series of "free speech fights," which used direct action and civil disobedience to secure the right to speak on the public streets.[27] These groups, and many others beside them, had different accounts of why free speech is important and the interests it protects that did not penetrate into the arguments of Holmes and Brandeis.[28] They are not part of the constitutional memory that doctrinal argument invokes. (Indeed, during the 2010s, the Roberts Court used the First Amendment to undermine labor unions.)[29]

D. Originalism and Memory

Next, consider originalist arguments. As we have seen in this book, originalist arguments come in many forms. In what follows, I will focus on the most widely used versions of original public meaning originalism employed by conservative lawyers today. But the points I make about memory can easily be applied to other varieties of conservative originalism.

Originalism is more than a theory of constitutional interpretation. It is also a theory of constitutional memory, because it has a distinctive view about who matters in the creation of constitutional meaning. It has its own economy of remembering and forgetting and its own combination of emphasis and erasure.

For most conservative originalists, the relevant constitutional meaning makers are the people who framed the constitutional text or who participated in the debates over its adoption. In order to understand the public meaning of the words they chose and the concepts they employed, however, one may also look to anyone whose arguments might have influenced the framers and adopters. One may also look to the events that led to or were roughly contemporaneous with the production of the Constitution's text. So, for example, if the framers and adopters relied on Blackstone, English law, the memory of the Glorious Revolution, or the language of contemporary state constitutions in choosing particular constitutional language, one should also pay attention to these sources and events because they contributed to the public constitutional meanings produced by the framers and adopters.

Thus, originalism is both a theory of constitutional meaning and a theory of constitutional memory because it tells us which kinds of memory matter to constitutional interpretation. Originalism tells us what we should remember and what we need not remember in order to interpret and apply the U.S. Constitution faithfully.

The originalism employed by the conservative legal movement almost inevitably involves a significant amount of forgetting. That is because conservative originalists want the Constitution's original meaning to resolve as many legal questions as possible. Ideally, conservative originalists want the study of the original meaning to converge on a relatively limited set of possible answers that, in turn, will resolve most important constitutional controversies.

In contrast, my own theory of living originalism does not assume that original meaning can resolve most constitutional controversies; it has a broad zone for constitutional construction in which

many different kinds of history might be relevant. Hence, living originalism demands a far more expansive conception of constitutional
memory and a far broader view about who might count as a maker
of constitutional meanings.

Because conservative originalists maintain that original meaning can usually decide most contested constitutional questions, their
originalist arguments tend to focus on the views of a small number
of key founders, framers, and adopters, as well as the law of the states
at the time of adoption and English law before the American Revolution. With respect to the Reconstruction Amendments, originalist
arguments care about the people who debated, drafted, and ratified
these amendments, as well as any antebellum or contemporaneous
law that sheds light on the legal meaning of the words the framers
and adopters chose. These people, sources, and events are the central focus of originalist constitutional memory. Conversely, those
persons who did not participate in the framing and adoption of the
Constitution, including those who could not have participated, like
women and enslaved people, are not constitutional meaning makers.
To interpret the Constitution correctly, it is not especially important
to remember their distinctive views or experiences, except, of course,
to the extent that these views or experiences contributed to the legal
meanings and understandings of those who framed and adopted the
Constitution.[30]

Thus, originalist argument creates authority through a selective
remembering—foregrounding some people, positions, and events
and not others. Conservative originalism is a practice of erasure,
because it finds large portions of the American experience (and the
American population) irrelevant to the Constitution's original public meaning.

This remembering and forgetting are opposite sides of the same
coin. On the one hand, originalist methodology focuses our attention on a relatively small set of historical persons, events, and legal
texts. On the other hand, it downplays or effaces the constitutional
views and experiences of other persons and events in American history. Although these persons, and their opinions and experiences,
may be quite relevant to American *political* memory, originalists might
concede, they are not relevant to *constitutional* memory, which is the
memory we need to interpret the Constitution correctly.

Accordingly, conservative originalists encourage their own distinctive form of memory entrepreneurship. Originalist lawyers vie
with each other to discover ever new information about the founding era and subsequent periods of constitutional adoption in order
to reshape constitutional memory and make persuasive arguments.
Just as originalism promotes a certain type of constitutional memory, it also constructs a particular type of constitutional tradition, in
which originalist inquiry is central while other aspects of history recede. Conservative originalism is a form of memory entrepreneurship
that promotes its own economy of remembering and forgetting.

Originalism's conception of constitutional memory, in turn, re-
inforces its claims to authority as the sole correct method of constitutional interpretation.[31] Because only some events and persons
matter to constitutional meaning, constitutional interpretation should
focus on them and not on other persons or events. Hence, the kind
of history worth studying is the kind of history that originalists
study, because it is the kind of history that properly generates legal
authority.

It is naive, therefore, to think of originalism as merely a theory
about the meanings of words. Originalism is also a construction of
constitutional memory and of the constitutional tradition. It is an
account of whose voices matter and whose may be forgotten, an account that, in turn, buttresses the authority of its particular vision of
constitutional interpretation.

E. Tradition and Memory

Finally, consider how arguments from tradition shape constitutional
memory. Traditions may involve arguments, practices, customs, or
laws.

As a preliminary matter, let me distinguish between two different ideas of tradition. The first is a *dialectical* tradition. The second is
a *unitary* tradition.

By a dialectical tradition, I mean the collection of different views
that people have expressed, different practices they have engaged in,
and different laws they have enacted or interpreted over the course
of the history of a country, nation, people, or group.[32] A dialectical
tradition may have common themes, but it is full of disagreements

and features multiple perspectives and approaches. It resists closure and finality and is always in a process of becoming. The Talmud is an example of a dialectical tradition; it includes multiple voices and many disagreements that appear next to each other on which later readers can draw. (Of course, the Talmud is not comprehensive. It offers a skewed picture of the Jewish tradition, because it also excludes many dissident views as heretical.)

There is also a dialectical tradition of arguments, practices, customs, and laws relevant to the U.S. Constitution produced by many different people, from many different groups, of high and low status, and from all walks of life. This dialectical tradition also has common themes, and it does not include every conceivable view about the Constitution. Nevertheless, it too offers a rich source of competing ideas and examples that later participants can draw on.

When lawyers and judges make arguments from tradition, by contrast, they are seeking a unitary tradition. A unitary tradition is a single viewpoint or continuous course of conduct, whether imagined or real, that stretches in a relatively unbroken line from the distant past to the present.

Lawyers and judges often prefer a unitary tradition to a dialectical tradition because they want tradition to have normative authority in present-day argument. For lawyers and judges, tradition has normative authority because it announces how things have always been done or asserts viewpoints that have long been held. At the very least, invoking a unitary tradition presupposes a dominant viewpoint or practice with only minor deviations that either do not matter or are normatively dispreferred.

Thus, arguments from tradition are not simply an interpretive method. They also involve memory work. People hypothesize unitary traditions and assert as a social fact that this is how things have always been done and therefore how they should be done. To have normative force, these arguments must tell the story of the past as one of relatively unbroken continuity and consensus. Hence, these arguments will downplay or disguise the existence of rupture, revolution, dissent, lack of consensus, or countertradition. Arguments from tradition may obscure or omit the fact that dominant practices and understandings developed without real consent, as the by-product of domination, or through the subordination of groups too weak or diffuse to resist.

Because claims of tradition offer an official story of the past, they may suppress the history of resistance and nonconforming practices by people and communities with less prestige, authority, and status.

To be sure, precisely because arguments from tradition portray memory selectively, critics of these arguments will offer alternative accounts of memory. They will attempt to combat the erasure by trying to get people to remember things differently.[33] First, one can draw different normative lessons from a tradition by describing it more abstractly or more narrowly. Second, one can show that the tradition is not unitary and does not reflect a single dominant view or practice that is continuous through history. Third, one can demonstrate that the tradition is an invented tradition that was concocted by later authors. Fourth, one can explain why elements of the tradition are not honorable, are morally compromised, are unjust, or have become oppressive.

Two recent Supreme Court cases exemplify the use of tradition in constitutional interpretation. They show how when lawyers and judges argue about tradition, they employ a combination of memory and erasure to bestow legitimacy on their arguments.

Dobbs v. Jackson Women's Health Organization overruled *Roe v. Wade* and *Planned Parenthood of Southeastern Pennsylvania v. Casey* and held that there was no federal constitutional right to abortion.[34] *New York State Rifle & Pistol Association, Inc. v. Bruen* built on earlier decisions in *District of Columbia v. Heller* and *McDonald v. City of Chicago*.[35] It held that the Second Amendment protected "an individual's right to carry a handgun for self-defense outside the home."[36] It struck down a New York law that required people to show a special need for self-protection if they sought a license to carry a concealed firearm. Although *Dobbs* and *Bruen* make many different kinds of arguments, they primarily rely on arguments about tradition.

1. Dobbs *and the Creation of a Worthy Tradition*

In *Dobbs,* Justice Alito invokes a doctrinal test, taken from *Washington v. Glucksberg,* to decide whether the Constitution protects fundamental rights under the Due Process Clause of the Fourteenth Amendment.[37] The test is whether a right is "deeply rooted in our Nation's history and traditions."[38] This test requires courts to tell a story about what the nation's tradition is. Alito reaches back to thirteenth-century England to argue that abortion after quickening (roughly sixteen to twenty weeks into a pregnancy) was a crime under the common law; therefore, there was no tradition of protecting it.[39]

Alito's historical account immediately faces a problem. Before quickening, the common law did not consider abortion a crime, and that might suggest that there actually was a common-law tradition of not interfering with women's decision to have an abortion before quickening.[40]

Alito solves this difficulty in two ways. First, Alito points to Hale and Blackstone's view that those who attempted a prequickening abortion that resulted in a woman's death could be punished.[41] But the purpose of this doctrine seems to be protecting the life of pregnant women rather than protecting unborn life prior to quickening. After all, if the woman was not harmed, there was no crime.

Second, Alito argues that beginning in the decades before the Civil War and through the middle of the nineteenth century, there was a successful campaign to criminalize abortion throughout pregnancy.[42] This second claim sounds like an originalist argument, because it appears to make the meaning of the Due Process Clause turn on what the people who adopted the Fourteenth Amendment intended or expected. But if one tried to apply this kind of argument more generally, it would undermine a great deal of contemporary constitutional law. So instead Alito presents the history primarily as an argument for why there was no deeply rooted tradition of protecting women's right to abortion.[43] He argues that there was no support for a right to abortion until the latter part of the twentieth century.[44]

To use tradition as a source of legitimacy, however, the relevant tradition of recognition (or nonrecognition) must be worthy of respect, or at the very least not unworthy. An important reason why we look to traditional practices, and why these practices have normative authority for us, is that we think that tradition reflects the accumulated wisdom of many generations. Therefore, if there was a tradition of protecting a right, past generations must have thought it important to protect, and so should we. Conversely, if there is no tradition of protecting a particular right, past generations must not have thought it especially important to protect, and so we need not protect it either. In both cases, we defer to the judgments of the past.

But suppose that past practices developed because of morally unjust or unworthy reasons.[45] For example, suppose that the law did not protect a certain activity—or even criminalized it—in order to buttress slavery or Jim Crow. Then it is not clear why the judgment of the past is worth deferring to today.

This is where the concept of memory comes in. First, a tradition is not the past. It is a story about the past—a story about what people did and why they did it that has normative lessons for the present. But human conduct is diverse and occurs in many different times and places. Therefore, invoking a unitary tradition means condensing a complicated history of human activity and presenting the past as featuring a more or less unitary set of practices and meanings. One must shape the diverse and conflicting elements of the past into something that can have normative authority for us today.

Second, memory and erasure are important to the construction of tradition because they affect how much we actually remember about the past. If we describe a tradition only in general or abstract terms, or if we know nothing about its origins, it has the presumption of moral authority. But as soon as we begin to remember distasteful facts about how and why past practices developed and continued over time, the moral authority of the past threatens to evaporate.

The mid-nineteenth-century campaign in the states to criminalize prequickening abortions did not arise merely from a desire to protect innocent life.[46] It arose for many different reasons. Sensational stories about seduced women dying from botched abortions led to calls to outlaw the procedure.[47] Male doctors wanted to wrest control of childbirth from (female) midwives.[48] Nativists such as Dr. Horatio Robinson Storer, who spearheaded the campaign to criminalize abortion, were concerned that the country would soon be overrun with Catholic immigrants who had more children than white Protestants and that Protestant women were shirking their duties to become mothers—duties for which they were "physiologically constituted" and "destined by nature."[49]

Alito mentions some of these facts in passing but dismisses them.[50] He argues that "[t]his Court has long disfavored arguments based on alleged legislative motives" and that "it is quite a leap" to assume that traditions of regulation developed for prejudicial or unjust reasons.[51] "Are we to believe," he exclaims, "that the hundreds of lawmakers whose votes were needed to enact these laws were motivated by hostility to Catholics and women?"[52] One might compare Alito's shock at the possibility of pervasive anti-Catholic and anti-immigrant prejudice in the nineteenth century with his extensive discussion of it in his concurrence in *Espinoza v. Montana Department of Revenue*, where he invokes this history to justify striking down laws banning state aid to parochial schools.[53] In that case, Alito recognized that the historical background could undermine respect for a tradition of practice.

In any case, there is a deeper problem in Alito's construction of tradition.[54] The historical periods he describes—going back to the thirteenth century—were not periods in which women enjoyed very much liberty or equality. Quite the contrary, regulations of abortion were part of more general features of law and social practices that kept women subservient, denied them equal opportunities, and regulated their sexuality and autonomy. In nineteenth-century America, women had very few rights. Under the common-law coverture rules, married women could not own property, make contracts in their name, or sue in court.[55] Married women were subject to their husbands' physical discipline and had no recourse if their husbands raped them.[56] Women could not vote or hold office; and this was justified on the theory that men adequately represented their interests.[57] So the same tradition that denied women control over their reproductive lives was part of a larger tradition of male dominance.[58] Alito's failure to reckon with the deep connections between the history of abortion regulation and the subordination of women generally is an example of how judges engage in historical erasure when they construct a constitutional tradition.

A doctrinal test that asks whether a right is deeply rooted in our nation's traditions invites this kind of erasure, because it treats tradition as presumptively legitimate and not reflecting a history of subordination or mistreatment of any relevant group. But in the case of abortion, as in the case of sexual freedom generally, this erasure matters greatly. When applied to questions of women's sexual freedom and sex equality, the *Glucksberg* test of constitutional liberty grounds the inquiry in deeply unjust and inequitable practices. Thus, a good reason why women's reproductive rights are unlikely to be deeply rooted in our nation's traditions is that traditionally the United States was committed to keeping women from having very many rights. Conversely, it is no accident that reproductive justice claims start to get taken seriously as soon as women start to win a broad range of equal rights in American society. When women mobilized for equal rights in the 1970s, among their key demands were access to contraception and abortion.[59] The *Glucksberg* approach is designed to overlook all of this history.

2. Bruen *and the Lawyerly Creation of Memory*

Justice Thomas's approach in *Bruen* is perhaps even more overt in its techniques of constructing historical memory. Thomas argues that the people have a presumptive right to bear arms for their self-defense; therefore, government can only regulate this conduct if doing so is "consistent with this Nation's historical tradition of firearm regulation."[60] Thus, Thomas makes the test of consistency with original meaning turn on how we construct tradition. He does not specify whether courts should measure this tradition as of 1791 (when the Second Amendment was adopted) or 1868 (when the Fourteenth Amendment, which applies the Second Amendment to the states, was adopted).[61] Rather, his opinion runs the two periods together, assuming that they constitute a single unbroken tradition.[62] He argues that there was no tradition "of broadly prohibiting the public carry of commonly used firearms for self-defense . . . [or of] limiting public carry only to those law-abiding citizens who demonstrate a special need for self-defense."[63] Therefore, New York's licensing statute (which actually dated back over a century to 1911) was not consistent with the nation's historical tradition of firearm regulation and was therefore unconstitutional.[64]

Arguments from tradition are stories we tell each other about what the past must have been like based on our normative values in the present. But, as noted earlier, human behavior over a wide range of places and times may not fit neatly into a simple cohesive narrative that confirms and vindicates these values. So, judges must fashion a narrative that is selective—one that overlooks or excludes certain features of the past as not really counting or as exceptions. In other words, they must tell a story that massages the past so that it fits what the judge believes the tradition was and always should have been.

And this is precisely what Thomas does with the history of gun regulation that does not fit his views about the Second Amendment. He invents a tradition that conforms to his judicial philosophy. As the historians who contributed to amicus briefs pointed out, there is considerable evidence of regulation of carriage of weapons in England, in the colonial period, in the early republic, and especially in the years surrounding Reconstruction.[65] But Thomas, relying on a different set of amici, bobs and weaves to avoid or recharacterize this evidence, so that he can produce a story in which regulation of carriage in public was rare or exceptional.[66] This practice of beating history into shape, so that it provides a coherent and unitary story that, in turn, allows him to draw a clear and satisfactory legal conclusion, is memory work.

Justice Thomas acknowledges that contemporary legislatures responding to contemporary problems may pass laws that may not be identical to those existing at the time of adoption.[67] Therefore, judges will sometimes have to reason by analogy to decide "whether modern and historical regulations impose a comparable burden on the right of armed self-defense and whether that burden is comparably justified."[68] What is "comparable" and "comparably justified," of course, may look different to a person generally skeptical of gun regulation and a person who believes guns pose a significant threat to public safety. It will also depend on how we construct the relevant memory of the past.

Bruen is a celebration of the lawyerly construction of memory in the face of history. Justice Stephen Breyer's dissent complains that judges are not professionally trained as historians and are not well suited to the task of historical research: "Legal experts typically have little experience answering contested historical questions or applying those answers to resolve contemporary problems."[69] Justice Thomas agrees, but in his view, it does not matter.[70] His explanation is remarkably candid. Judges and justices do not have to be professionally trained historians to make historical judgments about tradition and original meaning, because they can rely on the briefs submitted by the parties and amici. As Thomas explains, "'[i]n our adversarial system of adjudication, we follow the principle of party presentation.' . . . Courts are thus entitled to decide a case based on the historical record compiled by the parties."[71]

Thomas argues that judges can rely on the parties and amici to construct the relevant historical memory that will constitute the constitutional tradition that, in turn, will determine the scope of permissible regulation under the Second Amendment. This system is far superior, Thomas explains, to having judges engage in scrutiny rules that weigh the contemporary costs and benefits of gun regulation: "[R]eliance on history to inform the meaning of constitutional text— especially text meant to codify a *pre-existing* right—is, in our view, more legitimate, and more administrable, than asking judges to 'make difficult empirical judgments' about 'the costs and benefits of firearms restrictions,' especially given their 'lack [of] expertise' in the field."[72]

Thomas's reliance on advocates to tutor him on history, however, is not significantly more legitimate or objective. There is no guarantee that counsel and amici will not read history selectively—and even occasionally tendentiously—to push the normative views they would like to prevail. After all, lawyers make arguments before courts in order to win cases for their clients and the causes they represent. Contemporary academic historians work under professional norms that restrain them far more than legal advocates; but they, too, are required to explain their research under the strictures of legal brief writing for an audience that eschews complication and seeks easily citable answers.

Because judges can simply look to the briefs for historical information, they are also free to choose which parties and which amici they trust and write the history accordingly. In *Bruen* itself, Thomas accepted the version of history offered by the parties and amici who supported gun rights, many of whom were associated with the conservative legal movement. These were the sources he trusted most. Conversely, Thomas mostly rejected the version of history offered by the parties and amici arguing for regulation, many of whom represented movements, academics, and legal networks he trusts less.[73]

Precisely because judges are not historians, the question of whom they trust to provide accounts of history is especially important to how they construct constitutional memory. One of the most significant contributions of the conservative legal movement has been the production of amicus briefs and research aimed at informing and influencing judges who are part of the same movement and who are connected to conservative legal and policy networks.[74] It is hardly surprising that judges like Justice Thomas are more likely to trust historical claims made by other members of the conservative legal movement. Hence, they will be more likely to construct constitutional memory in ways that advance conservative legal claims.[75]

Judges' reliance on parties and amici for historical research, and their ability to pick and choose the sources they most trust, mean that judges have considerable leeway to construct a version of historical memory that buttresses their ideological and philosophical priors. And because judges produce precedents that later courts must work with and follow, their work imposes and solidifies a particular version of historical memory in law, even if that history is incorrect.[76] Justice Thomas insisted that it was better to ground constitutional doctrine in historical research than in traditional rules of judicial scrutiny, because judges are ill equipped to balance real-world costs and benefits.[77] But Thomas's conception of how judges should engage in historical research does not produce a greater degree of constraint, much less a greater degree of objectivity. And by allowing judges to retreat into a historical memory that they themselves partly create, Thomas absolves judges from reckoning with the real-world consequences of their constitutional doctrines.

CHAPTER THIRTEEN

Expanding Constitutional
Memory

A. The Loss of Constitutional Memory
Impoverishes Constitutional Meaning

So far, I have described how doctrinal arguments, originalist arguments, and arguments from tradition determine which voices, histories, and experiences matter in interpreting the Constitution. This
selectivity is important because of its consequences for legal authority. If we tell the story of the formation of the Constitution and its
amendments with white men as the central actors, then the American constitutional tradition belongs to them. It is due to their
achievements that women and racial minorities have rights. In other
words, women and racial minorities have constitutional rights because white men allowed them to have them. These rights then appear as acts of magnanimity or beneficence on the part of the white
men who adopted the Constitution rather than the result of a struggle for democracy in which dominant groups only surrendered power
because of a protracted struggle, a struggle that, in fact, is not finished to this day.[1]

Once we pay attention to it, the erasure of the role of women
and minorities in creating constitutional rights is particularly striking. As Reva Siegel notes, American lawyers today reason about the

meaning of the Fourteenth and Nineteenth Amendments innocent of
the role of women in transforming the constitutional order. "Women
seeking to vote faced deep and entrenched resistance in contests beginning before the Civil War, spanning several constitutional amendments and countless state and local laws and ordinances, and continuing into the late twentieth century," Siegel explains.[2] "Yet despite this
intergenerational struggle, no Supreme Court opinion has named—
much less quoted—the leaders of women's quest for political voice in
our constitutional order, except Justice Stevens's passing mention of
Susan B. Anthony in his flag-burning dissent."[3] In particular, "[t]here
is no mention in the United States Reports of Elizabeth Cady Stanton, Sarah Grimké, Sarah Parker Remond, Lucretia Mott, Lucy
Stone, Sojourner Truth, Frances Ellen Watkins Harper, Mary Church
Terrell, Alice Paul, Crystal Eastman, Florence Kelley, Ida B. Wells,
or Mary McLeod Bethune."[4] Although "[m]en's personal letters and
post-ratification reflections are regularly quoted," the justices do not
quote the works of the key players who fought for women's civil and
political equality.[5] "The erasure is so fundamental it passes without
notice."[6]

Why does this erasure matter? If you want to know what a constitutional provision should mean in practice and how we might apply
its principles today, it might be good to consult the views of those
who fought for its adoption over many decades. A constitutional
memory composed only of the opinions of men who supported (or
acceded to) woman suffrage is quite different from the constitutional memory of the women who sought to be included as part of
We the People. For men, the question was whether women would
gain the formal right to vote. But for the suffragists themselves, the
issues ran far deeper.

For the women who fought for the right to vote, the point of
suffrage rights was to democratize the family and alter unequal relations of political, economic, and sexual power between men and
women.[7] This meant ending the rule of men in the family. It meant
ending women's relegation to an inferior status in civil society because of their sex-assigned roles within the family.[8]

At the founding, and at common law, men were the governors of
their households.[9] They were assumed to virtually represent the interests of the women who lived under their governance, just as we

think that parents represent the interests of their minor children today.[10] Women had no voice in political governance, and they were subordinate in civil society because of their assigned place in the family under the rule of men.[11]

If women became full participants in democratic governance, this also meant that they had to be liberated from forms of domination of family life. This required not only women's economic independence and the redistribution of power within the family but also women's ability to control their sexual and reproductive lives. Democratization of political power meant democratization of the family.[12]

The erasure of women's arguments about the Constitution is also the erasure of the wide range of issues and concerns that motivated the struggle for woman suffrage.[13] These concerns involved far more than the mere demand for a formal grant of the right to vote, which is how constitutional doctrine has understood the Nineteenth Amendment—if doctrine pays it any attention at all.[14]

The loss of this constitutional memory impoverishes constitutional meaning. Because women lacked the right to vote, or the right to serve in Congress or in the state legislatures that adopted the Fourteenth and Nineteenth Amendments, their views are not part of the memory that informs the interpretation of the Constitution.[15] Yet if we recover what has been erased from constitutional memory, we discover buried constitutional treasure: an argument that for America to truly be a democracy, family life must also be democratized; an argument for the reorganization of work and economic life that does not depend or build on the traditional gender roles of the family; and an argument for voluntary motherhood and reproductive freedom.[16]

B. Who Makes Constitutional Meaning?

One might object to this argument in the following way: It does not matter that the views of groups shut out of constitution-making (or those of post-adoption social movements) are not part of constitutional memory. If these groups played no part in the framing and adoption of the Constitution, their views have no relevance to the production of the Constitution's legal meaning. The argument that constitutional memory is impoverished assumes that those who were excluded from framing and adoption—or who lived later on—should somehow count as makers of constitutional meaning. But this assumption is unjustified.

This objection shows that what is at stake in the construction of constitutional memory is which historical figures and movements may serve as makers of constitutional meaning for the present. It is therefore worth responding to this objection in some detail.

As a preliminary matter, it is important to emphasize that actual practice does not justify such a narrow conception of constitutional memory. Lawyers and judges do not restrict constitutional memory to the words, acts, and deeds of constitutional framers and adopters. They invoke many different kinds of constitutional memory outside of adoption history, and they treat as honored authorities people who were not framers and adopters or who lived many years later. In particular, even self-described originalist judges often ignore the founding when it is convenient, focusing instead on later events and precedents.[17] Indeed, lawyers and judges, including originalist lawyers and judges, have no consistent practices about which kinds of constitutional memory count or which people or groups count as relevant makers of constitutional meaning.[18] Rather, they invoke whatever memories of the past they think will make their arguments persuasive to their intended audiences.[19] The actual practices of lawyers and judges suggest that the class of constitutional meaning makers is far larger than the framers and adopters of the Constitution and its amendments, just as the class of constitutional meaning-making events is far greater than the events that led up to the Constitution's framing and adoption.[20]

Lawyers and judges regularly invoke the memory of events that happened long after the adoption of the Constitution or particular amendments. These might include the memory of wars, international conflicts like the Cold War, natural disasters, political and social movements, and economic, technological, and social transformations. They also invoke the memory of past injustices like religious or racial discrimination or acts of censorship. They point to the spirit of past judicial decisions that have become canonical and to the memory of other decisions that have been rejected and are now invoked primarily as negative examples.[21] The memory of all of these events clearly has constitutional meaning for lawyers and judges. It shapes how they believe the Constitution should be interpreted and applied today. Moreover, lawyers and judges use arguments from memory of these events to persuade other people about how the Constitution should be interpreted and applied.

Thus, when lawyers and judges argue about constitutional equality, they invoke the memory of Jim Crow, *Plessy v. Ferguson*, the civil rights movement and *Brown v. Board of Education*, the *Korematsu* case and the Japanese internment.[22] When they argue about religious liberty, they invoke the memory of nineteenth-century Protestant oppression of Catholics.[23] When they discuss freedom of speech, they invoke the canonical dissents of Justices Holmes and Brandeis.[24] When they warn about the dangers of substantive due process, they invoke memories of cases like *Dred Scott v. Sandford* and *Lochner v. New York*.[25] None of these are invocations of the memory of the founding or of the words and deeds of the founders.

Arguments from tradition, which are a staple of constitutional argument, are arguments from memory but not necessarily about adoption history. Sometimes the tradition developed later on or, as with claims of traditional morality, is not connected to the founding at all.[26]

Arguments from tradition or from traditional practice purport to describe the history of political or social practices, often in a highly abbreviated fashion. Although some legal scholars might reject appeals to "bottom-up" social history as irrelevant to constitutional argument, arguments from tradition *are* arguments from social history. They are simply a highly stylized form of social history that dispenses with most of the messy details. If arguments from tradition are relevant to constitutional meaning, then so too should be the experiences and opinions of those dissenters and countertraditions that have been effaced and disregarded by gauzy and overbroad claims of our country's unbroken moral and political traditions.

In making arguments about what is traditional and canonical or about what is honored and dishonored in American history, lawyers and judges also invoke the memory of figures who were not framers and adopters. Justice Clarence Thomas, an originalist, has invoked the memory of Frederick Douglass in his opinions, even though Douglass, as a Black man, could not, because of the *Dred Scott* decision, become a citizen—much less a framer or adopter of the Fourteenth Amendment.[27] Nevertheless, Thomas treats Douglass as an authority whose views matter to the proper interpretation of the Constitution. Similarly, in debates over race and affirmative action, the justices invoke the memory of civil rights advocates in America's fraught racial history.[28] But if Frederick Douglass is a constitutional meaning maker, it is not clear why Elizabeth Cady Stanton is not. And if Martin Luther King Jr. and Robert Carter (who was part of the NAACP's challenge against segregated schools) are constitutional meaning makers, it is not clear why Black people before the Civil War, the suffragists, or the Wobblies are not. People who discuss social history or social movements are not the only ones engaged in memory entrepreneurship. Originalist lawyers and judges are engaged in it too.

C. Constitutional Memory and a Usable Past

Who counts as a relevant maker of constitutional meaning is not settled, therefore, by who had official authority to adopt the Constitution or its subsequent amendments. Rather, it is the question of whom constitutional interpreters in the present—including citizens, lawyers, and judges—find relevant to the interpretation and application of the Constitution. Frederick Douglass is a constitutional meaning maker for Justice Thomas because he thinks Douglass deserves to be, and he believes that Douglass's positive reputation will resonate with others that Thomas wishes to persuade.

Put another way, the question of who counts as a constitutional meaning maker is the question of how we construct a usable past and, in particular, which figures from the past are usable for us today. Historical figures become relevant makers of constitutional meaning because people in the present believe that these figures can tutor us about the best interpretation of the Constitution—because of their experiences, wisdom, or vision. Even if people were not powerful officeholders in their own day, or advocated positions rejected by a then-existing majority, their constitutional vision might still speak to us in the present.

This expansion of constitutional memory does not mean that everyone's views are equally valuable. The whole point of a usable past is its selectivity.[29] Some figures are useful to remember because we think that they were wrong, misguided, or evil. Even figures whose views seem loathsome to us today might still instruct us as negative examples.

Conversely, many figures and social movements that we celebrate today were not uniformly heroic. For example, "beginning in the late 1860s, some white woman suffragists turned to racist and nativist arguments in support of their cause."[30] Instead of papering over their faults, we should be willing to recognize and learn from their compromises and limitations.

Although retelling stories about the framers and adopters is part of a usable past for American constitutional law, it is far too narrow a use of history. In fact, Van Wyck Brooks's original conception of a usable past did not focus on the most celebrated figures in American history.[31] Rather, he argued that in order for Americans to create a usable past, they should remember figures who had been forgotten and discarded by history, the "limbo of the non-elect."[32] These were people whose genius had been stifled or limited by the society around them and therefore had been lost to memory. American culture, Brooks argued, would not be renewed by rehashing tales of canonical authors and works but rather by recovering and remembering those left out of the canon who had been unfairly disregarded by the dominant culture and taking inspiration from their values and their vision.[33] In like fashion, there may be sources of constitutional renewal in the experiences, voices, and views of those who were legally excluded from constitution-making but who expressed their views through dissent, protest, and petition. If this is true of the free speech tradition in the United States, how much more might it be true with respect to other parts of the Constitution?

Brooks's point is that a usable past is not simply given by history, nor is it determined by current conceptions of who is canonical, essential, or important. Rather, a usable past is creatively uncovered, retold, and reinterpreted by people in the present who need to solve problems in their own time. People who invoke memory in their political and social disputes decide whom it is useful to remember, and thus who counts as a maker of constitutional meanings.

To be sure, what makes a past usable for creating an American culture, which was Brooks's concern, may be different from the kind of constitutional memory that is useful for interpreting and apply-

ing the U.S. Constitution in today's world. The forms of memory—
and the people and events remembered—may be different.

Accordingly, I now turn to reasons that are distinctive to legal
theory and legal argument. Why should the opinions and concerns
of those who have been left out of formal constitution-making be
part of what my colleague Akhil Amar has called America's "constitutional conversation," and, conversely, why does their erasure in constitutional memory create a problem of constitutional legitimacy?[34]

As a shorthand, I will call this the question of why we should
expand constitutional memory, and I will offer four central reasons:

(1) Many people formally left out of constitution-making actually participated in and shaped the agendas of lawmaking through
dissent and petition.

(2) Nonadoption history is an integral part of constitutional
construction.

(3) People left out of formal constitution-making may nevertheless edify and tutor people in the present about how best to implement the Constitution in today's world.

(4) The Constitution's contemporary legitimacy depends on the
claim that it is "our law"—that we are the same transhistorical "We
the People" who created it. But the people who created it excluded
and oppressed the ancestors of many of the people who now live
under it. Expanding constitutional memory allows members of historically subordinated or excluded groups to recognize the Constitution as also belonging to them and to make claims for its eventual
redemption.

D. Participation

First, even people who were formally excluded from framing and
adoption often played an important role in setting agendas and shaping public debates.[35] That is one reason why Justice Thomas regularly invokes Frederick Douglass in his dissents. Especially in the
period before the Civil War, petitions directed to government officials were a crucial means for people who did not have the right to
vote or hold office to draw attention to their issues and concerns.[36]
Petitions by women and free Black people, and special conventions

that produced these petitions, were important parts of the constitutional culture of the antebellum period.[37]

Even beyond the practice of petitioning, women and free Black people continuously protested and agitated for recognition of their rights.[38] Because these people were active in the politics of their time and because of their influence on the agendas of constitutional politics, they can justly be considered makers of constitutional meaning, and their work should be part of constitutional memory.

E. Construction

Second, the opinions and experiences of people shut out of formal adoption—as well as those who came afterward—may be especially important in constitutional construction. The Constitution's language is not self-applying. It contains rules, standards, and principles whose scope and application must be applied in ever-changing circumstances.[39] Constitutional construction is the task of applying the Constitution's often vague and general language in our own time through creating, developing, or implementing doctrines, practices, and conventions.[40] All forms of history, including post-ratification history, are important to constitutional construction.

When we engage in constitutional construction, therefore, we may look to the ideas, experiences, struggles, concerns, and opinions of people who were shut out of the formal ability to frame and adopt the Constitution. We can look to the ideas of people whose views were unpopular or minority positions in their own day but whose understanding of the proper application of the Constitution turned out to be far wiser than the dominant opinions of their time. We can also learn from constitutional claims made by people and movements after adoption—such as the civil rights movement—whose examples and accomplishments have become part of our constitutional traditions.

In constitutional construction, many different people, and not just framers and adopters, can contribute to the making of constitutional meaning. They are makers of constitutional meaning because they offered constructions of the Constitution that we can use today. This is true even if their proposed constructions were not accepted or were even ignored in their own time. What matters is whether they can serve as positive or negative examples for us today.[41]

F. Edification

Third, the expansion of constitutional memory can tutor the present. The expansion of constitutional memory can do more than merely complicate history.[42] It can also provide additional sources of authority.[43]

The memory of groups excluded from constitution-making can serve as a negative precedent. The memory of these groups and their struggles stands "as a record of past wrongs that the nation strives to remedy and against which the nation defines itself."[44] The memory of past injustices can also illuminate similar or analogous injustices in our own day. It shines a light on injuries, dangers, and temptations that we must remedy, prevent, or forestall. By understanding how people in these movements understood, diagnosed, and criticized injustices in their world, we are better able to critique our existing arrangements and perceive how elements or the effects of these past wrongs are still with us in contemporary life.[45]

In addition, constitutional interpreters can also incorporate this history as a positive precedent. We can remember figures and movements from the past "who model constitutional virtues."[46] The history of previous struggles for constitutional rights can highlight key figures and movements that embody important constitutional values and whose commitments we should recognize and strive to redeem in our own time. We can look to their experience and wisdom just as Americans look to the wisdom and experience of famous framers and famous historical figures like Abraham Lincoln or Martin Luther King Jr. The memory of these figures and groups can be a source of forgotten constitutional claims and arguments that have renewed salience today. In this sense, quoting wisdom from Washington or Hamilton is no different from quoting the petition of a convention of free Black people before the Civil War or a speech by Susan B. Anthony or Sojourner Truth.[47]

Once we expand constitutional memory beyond the relatively small group of framers and ratifiers, we may get a different account of what past generations thought the Constitution should mean, the injustices they fought against, and the problems they believed the Constitution should address. For example, when we exclude the memory of women and minorities from our constitutional conversation, we miss out on why the Constitution and proposed amendments were important to them, what they wanted these texts to do, and what features they found wanting. The relatively small group of white men who framed and adopted these provisions understood these issues only as refracted through their own limited experiences.

Consider, for example, the Thirteenth Amendment, which ended "slavery [and] involuntary servitude," and gave Congress the power to eradicate the "badges and incidents of slavery."[48] If one wants to know what slavery actually consists in, how slavery limits human freedom, enables arbitrary power, and injures the spirit, the best source of this information would be the slaves themselves and the conventions of free Black people before the Civil War.

To understand what freedom is, one might want to understand what slavery was. To understand what citizenship is, one might want to listen to the views of those denied it.[49] The testimony of slaves and the conventions of free Blacks petitioning for redress of grievances might inform the construction of all three Reconstruction Amendments. The experience of Black citizens whose rights to vote were slowly strangled and snuffed out by decades of Jim Crow politics might be useful testimony for the construction of the Fifteenth Amendment. As Kate Masur notes in her book *Until Justice Be Done*, it was free Black people, many of whom had escaped from slavery, who placed the question of Black civil and political equality on the agenda of antebellum politics.[50] Their concerns were often quite different from those of the white abolitionists with whom they allied, especially because the latter often supported decolonization rather than full equality.[51]

A key element of chattel slavery was sexual domination.[52] Black women lacked control over their reproductive lives.[53] Slaves were forced to bear children for the benefit of those who owned them.[54] Enslaved women's lack of control over how and when they became pregnant—often at the direction or at the hands of their masters— was a central attribute of their slavery.[55]

Another important feature of slavery was the precariousness of family relationships.[56] Slaves could not officially marry and had no rights to their children.[57] Slave owners could keep enslaved people from forming families, from living as families, and from raising their own children.[58] Couples, parents, and children lived in perpetual fear of separation, because slave masters could separate and sell enslaved people at will.[59]

Black and white abolitionists decried the outrages of separated families, the destruction of parental relationships, and the forced pregnancies of enslaved women.[60] "[M]embers of the Thirty-eighth Congress debating the Thirteenth Amendment repeatedly acknowledged the fundamental and inalienable character of rights of family,"[61] Peggy Cooper Davis has shown, and "anti-slavery members of Congress repeatedly acknowledged that freedom required restoration of rights of family. In debates over the Reconstruction Amendments and related legislation, speaker after speaker denounced slavery's abrogation of family rights."[62]

Nevertheless, despite the valuable work of scholars detailing this history, the constitutional memory of the Reconstruction Amendments does not emphasize these features of slavery. It does not reflect the perspectives of enslaved women, and it does not recognize that, for women, denials of sexual autonomy and reproductive freedom were among the greatest harms of slavery.[63] And for this reason, the rights of marriage, family formation, child rearing, and control over sexual reproduction do not appear as central to the original meaning of the Thirteenth and Fourteenth Amendments, and the denial of these rights does not appear as part of the paradigmatic harms that these amendments sought to prevent.[64]

Instead, in the standard account, the framers and adopters of the Thirteenth and Fourteenth Amendments sought to protect the rights of property ownership, the freedom to make contracts, rights to sue and give testimony in the courts, and equality of treatment in the civil and criminal justice systems.[65]

Yet the men who framed and adopted the Civil Rights Act of 1866 and the Thirteenth and Fourteenth Amendments thought of the rights of marriage and family formation as part of what we now think of as purely economic rights of contract and property.[66] The right to marry, as a special case of contractual freedom, was understood to be an aspect of civil liberty, and "[m]ainstream nineteenth-century legal theory understood a man's right to control and protect his wife and children as a property right."[67]

To be sure, the framers and adopters of the amendments, all white men, thought of these rights primarily in terms of men's interests. Therefore, it is probably not surprising that they did not devote much attention to women's rights to control their own sexuality or women's freedom from involuntary pregnancy. After all, the framers and adopters of the Reconstruction Amendments sought to maintain their own control over the sexual freedom of their wives and daughters.[68] But enslaved and free women well understood the importance of these rights, even if they were shut out of formal political participation.[69]

All of these ideas, although long known to specialists, have mostly been lost to constitutional memory. One likely reason is the New Deal settlement, which divided economic and property rights from all other civil liberties and frowned on judicial protection of rights it considered outside the constitutional text. But the very failure to see these rights as implicated by the textual prohibition on slavery and the textual guarantee of the privileges or immunities of citizenship is due to the production of memory.

Because of the way that constitutional memory has been constructed (and erased), the protection of sexual and reproductive freedoms and the rights of marriage and family formation usually do not appear among the purposes behind the Reconstruction Amendments.[70] In the way the story is usually told, these rights seem to be foreign to the original meaning of the Constitution—illicit additions from the twentieth century and the sexual revolution.[71] Moreover, because of the constitutional memory of the New Deal, rights of marriage, sexual freedom, and family formation are classified as dubious examples of substantive due process. These rights are often treated with suspicion because they seem to have no basis in the text and therefore commit the same sin as *Lochner v. New York*—a case that, in constitutional memory, exemplifies how courts should not interpret the Constitution.[72]

But suppose that we expand constitutional memory to include the concerns of the people for whom the Reconstruction Amendments were actually created—both enslaved women and enslaved men. Suppose we were to ask what they valued about freedom and what denials of liberty they suffered. Then these rights of sexual freedom, marriage, and family formation no longer seem peripheral. They seem obvious and central.[73]

Or take the case of women—of all races—who fought for civil and political equality in the social movement for woman suffrage that lasted eight decades. The experiences and concerns of these women were often quite different from those of the men who adopted the Fourteenth and Nineteenth Amendments.[74] For the suffragists, the quest for the vote was also the quest for the democratization of the family.[75] Its goal was to end the multiple techniques by which men dominated women economically and sexually as well as politically. When they argued about the vote, they also argued about the structure of the family and about the idea that women should not be dependent on men either politically or economically.[76]

These arguments were lost to history because the men who wrote and ratified the Constitution neither understood them nor made them.[77] But nineteenth-century women both understood and named the connections between economic dependence, sexual domination, and political subordination. These arguments are important because they show that women were arguing for reproductive freedom and for full equality in the family and in civil society not only during the 1970s but even as the Reconstruction Amendments were debated.[78]

It is hardly surprising that the men who adopted the Fourteenth and Nineteenth Amendments did not think much about these things. Consequently, the many decades of women's civil rights activism and the arguments that suffragists made about the injustices built into family and civil society have all but vanished from our constitutional memory. But when we expand constitutional memory to include the concerns, arguments, and diagnoses of the women who sought rights for themselves, we get a much richer picture, and a deeper and more sophisticated account of what sex equality is and what it requires.

In the task of constitutional construction, we are not limited to the original expected applications of the white men who framed and adopted the Reconstruction Amendments. We may, and should, consider why the people who fought for their freedoms held freedom so dear and the kinds of oppressions and evils they sought to escape.

It is true enough that we always hear advice from the past filtered through our present-day preoccupations. So, it is not surprising that we may only see these connections following the sexual revolution and social movements for marriage equality. But that is how the reclamation of the past works. The past has things to teach us when we are ready to learn them.

G. Making the Constitution "Our Law"

Finally, if constitutional memory is conceived too narrowly, it can undermine the Constitution's present-day legitimacy. In *Living Originalism*, I argued that the legitimacy of the American Constitution depends on its success as basic law, as higher law, and as our law.[79] The Constitution operates as basic law when it "provides a viable framework for governance that allocates powers and responsibilities."[80] The Constitution operates as higher law when it "serves as a source of aspiration, a reflection of values that stand above our ordinary legal practices and hold them to account."[81]

But the Constitution must also succeed as *our law*—a constitution that Americans view "as our achievement and the product of our efforts as a people, which involves a collective identification with those who came before us and with those who will come after us."[82] The Constitution's present-day legitimacy depends, in part, on the fact that the people who live under it regard it as *their* Constitution.[83] They must be able to see it as something that *they*, as part of We the American People, created through an act of popular sovereignty.

Our ability to view the Constitution as "our law" requires accepting "a constitutional story—a constitutive narrative through which people imagine themselves as a people, with shared memories, goals, aspirations, values, duties, and ambitions."[84] This constitutional story "constructs a collective subject with a collective destiny that engages in collective activities."[85] It "binds together people living in different times and different places as a single people."[86] It "allows us to see the hopes, desires, actions, ambitions, and achievements of people who lived long ago as our hopes, desires, actions, ambitions, and achievements."[87]

The success of this story depends on constitutional memory. The story is only believable if Americans think that they are part of the same "We the People" who adopted the Constitution and its amendments.[88] But if contemporary Americans see the Constitution as an alien imposition by other people, especially those who are long dead, it becomes difficult to sustain the belief that the Constitution belongs to them and is the work of their hands.

The problem is that many Americans belong to groups that the framers and the adopters of the Constitution deliberately excluded from participation in drafting and ratifying the Constitution. And these groups were not only excluded from framing and ratification; they were also repeatedly subordinated and oppressed and, in some cases, enslaved and murdered. These groups were kept outside the body of Americans who had the right to "ordain and establish" the Constitution and govern the country.[89]

This is yet another version of originalism's race and gender problem.[90] The problem is why contemporary members of formerly excluded groups—women, racial minorities, and Indigenous peoples—should see themselves as part of the We the People who adopted the Constitution. As Annette Gordon-Reed explains, this "is the problem of asking current-day Americans whose ancestors were excluded from power, and indeed who were under the power of (and in some cases actually mistreated and enslaved by) these men—women, enslaved people, and Indigenous people—to see these men and their actions as the prime informers of our civic virtue."[91]

It is no answer to say that the Reconstruction Amendments and the Nineteenth Amendment cured these problems.[92] The exclusion of women and minorities from the full rights of citizenship continued despite these amendments and was even rationalized through them.[93] In addition, these amendments did next to nothing for Native Americans, most of whom were only granted citizenship by statute in 1924.[94] They did nothing for Chinese immigrants, who were long excluded from citizenship, or for the people of Puerto Rico and other American possessions, whose territories were deemed "unincorporated" and not fully subject to constitutional guarantees.[95]

Moreover, these amendments do not really cure the problem of how to understand the Constitution as ordained and established by We the People, because these amendments too were framed and adopted by a relatively small group of white men. If these men are the makers of constitutional meaning, then the story these amendments convey is that the inclusion of other people is a gift from these men—the work of *their* hands—and not the achievement of those who were later brought into the circle of governance.

Because, as we have seen, what lives in memory shapes who has authority, the originalist account of framers and founders—who not only sat atop but also enforced a system of racial and sexual hierarchy—is also the story of who has authority to proclaim the Constitution's meaning for us today. And according to this story of America's origins, only a small segment of powerful, privileged white men pronounced what the Constitution meant and therefore what it still means. To understand the Constitution's meaning, we must delve into *their* ideas and opinions and obsessively concern ourselves with *their* public speeches and private correspondence. The rest of America lives in the shade of their authority.

This version of the past is deeply corrosive of the belief in a trans-historical We the People who can bestow legitimacy on the Constitution today. It asks for a heroic deference by women and minorities. And this fact helps explain why many women and minorities have found so little to like in the originalist project.[96] The problem is not simply that most originalists are political conservatives or that originalist conclusions often conflict with the judgments of many women and minorities.[97] All of this may change over time, and in any case, the country's most prominent originalist, Justice Clarence Thomas, is a Black man.[98] Rather, the deeper problem is the originalist conception of who counts as a constitutional meaning maker and who matters in interpreting the American Constitution. The problem, in short, is one of constitutional memory.

It is no answer to say that the framers and adopters made the law that we live under today, that they acted in the name of We the People of the United States, and therefore that their views count, and not the views of others who, however unfortunately, had no voice. This is an argument from popular sovereignty; but the argument begs the question of whether that We the People is still the same people who live under the Constitution today. For the law to be our law, we must be able to identify with it as ours. Thus, some women and minorities might object as follows: What does the story of the framers and adopters have to say to me? People like me did not count in that world. People like me had no voice. Their values, their experiences, and their strivings are legally irrelevant, flushed down the memory hole. Why should I identify with the oppressors?

That is why the expansion of memory to include constitutional claims by women and minority groups—and the work of post-adoption social movements—is important to the Constitution's contemporary legitimacy. The expansion of memory is crucial to the plausibility of the belief in a transhistorical We the People, and the allied claim that the Constitution we have today is the work of all of our hands, not just the hands of a favored few. As constitutional memory expands, and our constitutional conversation becomes larger and richer, more people can view it as *their* conversation about *their* Constitution. Gordon-Reed makes a similar point about the rise of social history by American historians: "What historians who have abandoned traditional narratives of the founding in favor of writing about more obscure people and communities have been trying to do is to write such people into the national narrative."[99] They "are saying, 'These people, too, were a part of the Founding,' for the express purpose of creating an 'us' coherent enough, and inclusive enough, for all segments of society to feel connected to it."[100] The expansion of constitutional memory does not by itself guarantee the redemption of the Constitution. It only assists in that larger task.[101]

The American constitutional tradition is not a unitary tradition. It is a dialectical tradition with many participants from many different perspectives, often in serious disagreement.[102] Some parts of this tradition will seem edifying and inspiring to us; others will seem abhorrent or unwise. But the expansion of constitutional memory does not require us to honor all parts of our tradition equally. Quite the contrary, as we have seen, the past is full of both negative and positive precedents, and this means that we will bestow praise and blame, honor and dishonor on events and people as we try to persuade our fellow citizens. The point of expanding constitutional memory, rather, is to unlock the storehouse of the past for present-day use and to make more of our past a usable past.

PART V

Lawyers and Historians

CHAPTER FOURTEEN

Historians Meet the Modalities

T HE QUARREL BETWEEN LAWYERS and historians about
the proper use of history in constitutional law is an old
one. It predates the rise of conservative originalism in
the 1970s and 1980s. For example, the term "law office
history"—now regularly employed to criticize lawyers who engage
in historical arguments that are opportunistic, anachronistic, and
unsophisticated—was employed by the legal historian Alfred Kelly
in 1965.[1]

Kelly's target was not today's movement conservatives. He criticized the Supreme Court's practices throughout the nineteenth century.[2] Kelly especially objected to the work of liberal justices in the
1940s, 1950s, and 1960s, who, he argued, had misused the history of
the founding to overturn older, politically conservative precedents.[3]
The justices, Kelly complained, had anachronistically invoked history "as a precedent-breaking instrument, by which the Court could
purport to return to the aboriginal meaning of the Constitution. It
was thus able to declare that in breaking with precedent it was really
maintaining constitutional continuity."[4] What historians object to
today—lawyers sanctimoniously using the authority of the founding
to enact their contemporary policy preferences—was not a modern
innovation, Kelly explained. It had been the Supreme Court's standard operating procedure.

The quarrel, however, is not simply one between lawyers on the one side and historians on the other. Lawyers (including legal academics) are often much more sharply critical of each other's historical arguments than are professional historians.[5] Many law professors have been trained as historians, and some hold doctorates in history. Perhaps more important, lawyers may be especially sharply critical of how other lawyers use history because they are trying to win arguments within law and legal theory. (The often heated debates over the meaning of the Second Amendment are a prime example.)[6] The adversary culture of legal argument encourages portraying opposing arguments as incomplete, mistaken, anachronistic, or wrongheaded. So lawyers find themselves on all sides of debates about how lawyers should (and should not) use history in constitutional interpretation.

Even to speak of "lawyers" as a group neglects the fact that there are many kinds of lawyers. Some are judges deciding cases. Some are advocates before courts, legislatures, and administrative agencies. Some are legal academics writing learned studies that argue for the best interpretation of constitutional provisions. And some are legal academics who study history much as professional historians do, focusing not on which interpretation of the law is correct but on how law and society developed in the way they did.

The opposition between "lawyers" and "historians" runs together two distinctions. The first opposition concerns *professional training* and *professional culture*. Lawyers are educated to be lawyers and have law degrees. They are trained in an adversary culture, and they are taught to assert and dispute claims about legal authority, to enter into and win arguments about what the law is or should be. They think about history and use history in ways that reflect this adversarial culture of authority claiming.[7] Historians are trained differently. Their central task is not winning legal arguments and establishing or demolishing legal authority. They are interested in the past for many reasons other than present-day legal debates.[8] Historians are taught to relish and respect ambiguity, the complexity and multivocality of the past, and the inevitability of multiple interpretations. They are trained to recognize that the past is a different world and that the concerns and understandings of people living in the past were often very different from the concerns and understandings of people living in the present.[9] To be sure, this first distinction between lawyers and historians—in professional training and professional culture—is neither clear-cut nor universal, because many law professors (and some practicing lawyers) have been trained as historians and hold history PhDs.

The second, and more important, distinction concerns *rhetorical aims* and *rhetorical structure*. This is not a distinction between those people who have law degrees, practice law, sit on the bench, or teach in law schools and those who do not. It is a distinction that concerns how one makes an argument and what one is trying to achieve in making that argument. On the one side are those I will call "legal advocates"—most but not all of whom are trained as lawyers. This group includes judges, lawyers, and citizens: anyone who wants to make—or wants to win—an argument about the proper legal interpretation of the Constitution. On the other side are those I will call "scholar-historians"—who may include people in or out of the academy, including the legal academy. This group includes those who study history for reasons other than winning legal arguments or establishing the correct interpretation of the law.

The difference between these groups does not consist in the fact that one group makes arguments and the other does not. (Historians can be very argumentative when they want to be!) The difference is not that one group just focuses on the facts and the other has normative values. Historians' work may be strongly normative, in their interpretations, in the presuppositions they bring to their work, in their choice of subject matter, or in all three. And the difference is not that one group's work is aimed at influencing contemporary politics and public policy and the other eschews any ambition for influence or consequences. Historians, like legal advocates, may be very much in the world. Their histories may reflect present-day concerns. Their choice of subject matter, their treatment of that subject matter, and the conclusions they draw may be designed to comment critically on the present.[10]

Rather, the key difference between the categories of lawyer-advocates and scholar-historians is that lawyer-advocates make arguments that are *legally prescriptive* as well as normative. Their work *prescribes* the correct interpretation of law. It asserts what the law is or, when the law is unsettled, unclear, or in need of reform, what the best interpretation of the law should be. This way of arguing does not simply assert what is moral or immoral, prudent or imprudent, true or false. Rather, it claims legal authority, or it offers facts and arguments to support such claims of authority.[11]

Lawyers learn to argue for and against legal interpretations, to claim legal authority for their positions and to undermine the claims of legal authority of those they disagree with. They try to reduce uncertainty into certainty and turn complication into persuasive argument. Lawyers believe that their audiences want clear-cut answers, and so they provide them.

The tensions between the work of lawyer-advocates and scholar-historians are at their greatest precisely when lawyer-advocates are most adversarial and most prescriptive, when they are most determined to establish clear legal authority for their arguments and undermine or explode the claims of authority made by their opponents.[12] Historians have noted this tension repeatedly when they write or join amicus briefs in high-profile cases, for example, concerning abortion and gun rights.[13]

In the legal academy, this assertion of legal authority may be several steps removed. Legal academics may renounce any interest in prescriptive arguments about legal authority. They may insist that they are not telling courts how to decide cases. But if courts are interested in a particular ground of decision—for example, the original meaning of the Constitution—this, and not that, is the correct answer to the question.[14] In this way, a legal academic, disclaiming all normative ambitions, may focus intensively on uncovering the original meaning of a particular constitutional provision, with the implication that if courts want to be faithful to the original meaning, they should see it the same way.

In the quest for authority, lawyers do not merely condense and simplify. They also *extend* legal authority from the past. They seek to infer, from an incomplete historical record reflecting a different historical context, how the past would bear on present-day problems. They complete arguments that may have never been completed; they draw inferences and apply insights that may never have been drawn or applied by people living in the past. This act of extension in pursuit of authority is always creative.[15]

Because they focus on cases, statutes, and other legal materials, professionally trained lawyers may not pay very much attention to what professionally trained historians think about the topics on which they expound. As Michael Rappaport puts it succinctly, "[T]he originalist is not looking for 'what the past tells us about a matter.' The originalist is looking for the original meaning."[16]

But when historians do criticize lawyers, lawyers may tend to react defensively. In a blog post titled "Challenging the Priesthood of Professional Historians," the law professor Randy Barnett argued that historians' criticisms of originalism were often misguided: "[S]ome [historians] apparently believe that they, and they alone, can recover the meaning of a law enacted in the Eighteenth Century when they would not be able to understand the meaning of a law enacted in the Twenty-First. That's either hubris or chutzpah."[17] Reviewing Jack Rakove's Pulitzer Prize–winning book *Original Meanings*, Saikrishna Prakash complained that "Rakove's primary problem is that he approaches the law as a historian. . . . Rakove recounts events in the time-honored tradition of the historian less concerned about the meaning of legal text and more concerned with ideas."[18] Confronted by historians' critiques, lawyers may argue that historians do not understand what they are doing and emphasize that historians and lawyers are engaged in different projects.[19]

Lawyers attempt to escape the gaze and condemnation of historians through two standard stories that explain the differences between what lawyers and historians do. The first is the story of *legal science*—by which I do not mean experimental science but an organized body of thought and methods characteristic of a learned profession. The second is the story of a *usable past*. Each explanation seeks to turn the tables on historians, arguing that they lack something necessary to interpret the Constitution correctly.

The first story portrays lawyers as experts in legal science—a body of knowledge and a rigorous set of methods and practices that is known and practiced only by professionally trained lawyers with legal degrees. Historians are uneducated laypersons, unskilled in the special techniques of legal reasoning—the professional knowledge available only to the possessors of the JD degree—and ignorant of the artificial reason of the law. "[S]ome historians," Randy Barnett explains, "seem to think they can investigate the meaning of legal terms and concepts in the past without any legal training. For this it helps to be a lawyer. True, some of the best legal historians do have legal training, but not all who opine on the 'meaning' of the Constitution do."[20]

The second story portrays lawyers as practical people who must solve contemporary problems of great importance. Because of these worldly and professional obligations, lawyers need a usable past.[21] "The search for a useable past," Cass Sunstein argues, "is a defining feature of the constitutional lawyer's approach to constitutional history."[22] Lawyers, Alexander Bickel explained, "are guided in our search of the past by our own aspirations and evolving principles, . . . principles that we can adopt or adapt, or ideals and aspirations that speak with contemporary relevance."[23] But historians, because of their own professional norms and obligations, have a different approach. So they fail to understand what lawyers need in order to do their jobs; and this makes their criticisms unhelpful. In this story, historians are antiquarians: academics ensconced in the ivory towers of the humanities. Perversely, historians see it as their mission to make the past alien, convoluted, complicated, and of no practical use to anyone.[24]

These two rhetorical strategies push in opposite directions. The story of lawyers as legal scientists portrays lawyers as gatekeepers of an elite specialized knowledge misunderstood by and inaccessible to the general public, while the story of the need for a usable past portrays lawyers as practical problem solvers who, unlike historians, are very much in the world. But what unites the two stories is their emphasis on the distinctive professional identity of lawyers. Because (non-JD) historians do not face the professional imperatives of lawyers and lack their professional training, historians' objections are either naive or misguided.

Both of these stories are misleading. First, they paint a false picture of how the work of historians is relevant to legal argument. Second, by emphasizing lawyers' professional differences from historians, they disguise disagreements *within* the class of lawyers and legal advocates about how to use (and how not to use) history. When lawyers try to fend off historians, often what they are actually doing is engaging in long-running disputes with other lawyers who disagree with their interpretive theories, their methods, and their conclusions.

We need a better account of the relationship between legal argument and historical scholarship, an account that shows how legal advocates and historians actually join issue in debates about the Constitution.

If you have followed the argument of this book up to now, you know that there is a fairly straightforward way to explain what is going on—the modalities of constitutional argument. The modalities mediate and filter the past through rhetorical forms, and they are also the lenses through which lawyers see and discover history. If we want to understand the disputes between lawyers and historians, or between legal advocates and scholar-historians, there is no better place to look than the structure of legal rhetoric, because the structure of legal rhetoric reflects the structure of legal reasoning.

Once we examine the quarrel between lawyers and historians through the lens of the modalities, many issues become clear—why self-confident lawyers ignore historians or find them irrelevant, why they nevertheless cannot escape the critical gaze of historians, and why they cannot do without historians' history, however much they may abuse or mangle it.

How do scholar-historians fit into the rhetorical structures I have described in this book? This assumes, of course, that they *want* to participate. They might resist being drawn into forms of rhetoric at cross-purposes with their scholarly enterprise.[25] But many historians now author amicus briefs and serve as expert witnesses in constitutional controversies.[26] So we can ask how they might intervene in lawyers' forms of argument.

First, historians can use the standard forms of constitutional argument just as well as lawyers can. They can also make arguments from text, structure, purpose, consequences, custom, convention, tradition, ethos, honored authority, and so on. Most of the standard modalities of constitutional argument do not require any special professional training. A central motivation behind Bobbitt's original model of modalities, after all, was that lawyers and ordinary citizens alike could practice constitutional interpretation.[27] The modality of argument that seems to benefit most from specialized legal training is precedential argument: the ability to employ and manipulate legal precedents—for example, creating narrow and broad versions, distinguishing and connecting bodies of case law, and developing new doctrinal distinctions.[28] The ability to cite and employ canons of statutory construction might be a second, related skill. However, the majority of historical inquiry in law does not depend on these special skills. (And, of course, historians who are also lawyers have received this training.)

Second, with respect to some of the modalities of legal argument—arguments from custom, tradition, ethos, and honored authority or arguments from consequences that depend on historical evidence and historical examples—we might expect that historians would be *better* than nonhistorian lawyers in using and deploying historical sources. That is especially the case for those periods of history and those parts of the world with which most lawyers are unfamiliar. But it is equally true of periods of intense lawyerly concern, such as the history of Great Britain in the seventeenth and eighteenth centuries, the founding, the Civil War, and Reconstruction. Historians may also be far more competent at the history of political and social movements (both successful and unsuccessful) that have shaped the American political tradition.

Third, as noted earlier, lawyers use history both to construct authority and to undermine and poke holes in other lawyers' uses of history. They use history both constructively and deconstructively. Historians can certainly marshal the kinds of evidence needed to support the standard forms of legal argument, perhaps better than many lawyers can. But historians can also offer the kinds of counterevidence, counternarratives, and complications that are useful in rebutting these arguments. In fact, historians are likely to be even better at these tasks than most lawyers are.[29] After all, historians are professionally rewarded for discovering new forms of counterevidence, offering interesting counternarratives, and noting historical complications. They are rewarded for undermining previous historians' takes and producing ever new perspectives on the past.

Fourth, in constitutional law, lawyers not only disagree about history but also disagree about theories of legal interpretation—including the many varieties of originalism. Legal dispute occurs *both* at the level of historical inquiry and at the level of the interpretive theories that connect history to legal norms. Lawyers are hardly agreed on a single set of interpretive theories, and judges may switch their theoretical assumptions from case to case.

Because lawyers disagree about theory as much as about history, historians might play yet another role in legal disputes. They can offer examples from history (and from historiography) to critique the plausibility or practicality of some of these interpretive theories. They can explain why certain kinds of interpretive theories are anachronistic or unlikely to be successful on their own terms.[30] They can offer reasons and evidence to show why certain theories of legal interpretation ask questions of history that the historical record cannot reliably answer.[31] They can show that certain historical sources that lawyers rely on have a different meaning or importance than lawyers think they do or are not as reliable as lawyers imagine them to be.[32] Here again, historians are as likely to be as good as (or better than) lawyers at this particular critical task.

Posing the issues in this way has a certain partiality: it asks whether historians can play effectively on lawyers' turf. Historians might well wonder why this is the proper inquiry. After all, the door between the two professions swings both ways. Certainly one could ask with equal merit whether lawyers can do the kind of archival research, ask the kinds of research questions, and offer the kinds of answers and analyses that professional historians would regard as competent.[33] Indeed, lawyers, who are often dogged investigators of facts, may be able to shed light on the historical record and correct the views of historians.[34] Nothing in what I say here denies the importance of these questions—or for that matter, the equal status and equal worth of the professional perspectives of lawyers and historians. But the focus of this book is the uses of history in constitutional interpretation and constitutional argument. That interpretation and those arguments are structured in the special topics of constitutional law. Therefore, I ask whether there is something special about the modalities of legal argument that justifies lawyers discounting the contributions of historians. The answer is no.

Viewed from the perspective of the modalities, it is easy to understand how historians join issue with lawyers on the legal interpretation of the Constitution. Professional differences aside, the topics of legal argument are common topics for all—not just lawyers and judges—that facilitate a common conversation.

CHAPTER FIFTEEN

The Special Skill and Knowledge of Lawyers

ERHAPS THE MOST COMMON way that lawyers try to deflect criticism from historians is to assert that historians are ignorant of the specialized craft of lawyerly reasoning. Professionally trained lawyers possess special techniques—known only to the professionally educated and accredited—that allow them to discern the *legal meaning* and the *legal consequences* of texts. Because non-legally-trained historians do not understand these techniques, their criticisms of lawyers' use of history are likely to miss the mark. In our day, this kind of complaint is most likely to come from conservative originalists, who often find themselves beset by historians who claim that originalist uses of history are narrow, parochial, and anachronistic.

Michael Rappaport offers a good example of this strategy. He argues that historians do not understand "the enterprise of interpretation as practiced by originalists."[1] "[T]he original public meaning approach asks what the meaning of a provision would have been to a reasonable and knowledgeable person at the time. Historians often do not understand or apply this correctly."[2] Because of this misunderstanding, "they often make statements that originalists would strongly disagree with, without any strong reasons backing them up—statements such as, because there was disagreement at the time of the

Constitution on a provision, that means there was no original meaning."[3] Because historians do not accede to or correctly apply originalist theories of interpretation, their historical objections are irrelevant. Rappaport has dubbed these irrelevant objections "history office law," a play on "law office history."[4]

What Rappaport sees as misunderstanding or an inability to use legal sources properly, however, could equally be described as a theoretical disagreement about the best way to interpret the Constitution. Rappaport's objection does not actually turn on whether historians possess or lack legal training. Rather, his argument depends on the assumption that historians should accept his theory of the Constitution's "original public meaning."

As I explained in chapter 8, "original public meaning" is a theoretical construction, a mediated account of the past that serves the purposes of law and legal theory. This theory of interpretation selects certain features of the past as relevant to legal inquiry and discards the rest. It takes those features of the past that it deems relevant and reconfigures them for purposes of a particular theory of law. Then, having selected and reconfigured the past, it dubs the result the "original public meaning" and declares it binding on everyone.

Lawyers—including originalist lawyers—do not assume that the past generally comes to us in the form of unambiguous and easily intelligible directives; often it does not. Rather, originalist theory treats the past as it does because of its theoretical commitments and the practical needs of the present.[5] History looks the way it does to originalist theory because of what originalism needs the past to be in order for it to serve the requirements of present-day law.[6] Originalism seeks to obey the past, but it can only do so if it reconfigures the past so that it can be followed. Originalism is a servant that needs a particular kind of master, and therefore goes about constructing one. The past that emerges from originalist inquiry is not simply a description of past events. It is an understanding refracted through theoretical choices, some of which may be plausible to other lawyers and some of which may be highly controversial.

Originalist theories are hardly unique in this respect. Rather, they exemplify how law and legal theory usually employ history. They do not simply report what happened at a special moment in time. Rather, they construct events—drawing together occurrences in disparate locations and collapsing and telescoping time frames—to draw conclusions about meanings and purposes. The "founding," for example, is not a magical moment in time. It occurs in many different places, over several decades. But originalist theories tend to treat the founding as a unified event producing meanings that are intelligible and tractable.

Originalist theories select elements from the historical record, leaving much of the messy details of history on the cutting-room floor. They reorganize and reconfigure the record of the past to produce the kind of knowledge that might be useful to the legal enterprise. They make the past useful to lawyers so that lawyers can employ it for present-day purposes. They beat the past into a shape that can serve present-day objects.[7]

Once again, we should not see this as a particular problem of originalism. All legal theories reconfigure history to theory in varying degrees. All legal theories beat the past into shape; they simply do it in different ways and for different ends. Theoretical commitments tell lawyers what facts are relevant and important and why they are relevant and important. These commitments shape what lawyers look for in the past and what they find there, what they obsessively focus on and what they casually discard.

Theories of original public meaning, in short, construct the past so that it can serve the needs and values of the present. However, there is nothing wrong with this as long as (1) people are candid about the nature of the enterprise, (2) they do not pretend that they are simply reporting facts free from theoretical framing and reconfiguration, and (3) they are candid about the values that their interpretive theory serves and are willing to defend those values openly.

Thus, the dispute is not over whether historians understand or misunderstand constitutional interpretation or constitutional law. Rather, it is a dispute over whether a particular theoretical construction— offered by a lawyer, judge, or legal scholar—is a good way to approach constitutional interpretation, or whether it is too artificial, too limited, or too blinkered.

Most historians probably do not accept Rappaport's views about the best way to interpret the Constitution. But most well-trained lawyers in the United States probably do not accept this theory either. Not all lawyers are originalists, and even among originalists, there are important theoretical disagreements about what original meaning is, how it is best demonstrated, and what legal force it should have.[8] Lawyers might make some of the same objections that historians would. That is hardly surprising; lawyers on either side of a controversy reach out for support from other disciplines all the time.

In short, the problem is not that historians do not understand the enterprise of originalist interpretation. It is that they do not agree with the underlying theory, and many other lawyers would probably agree with them.[9] Instead of a dispute between untutored historians and knowledgeable lawyers, we also have an intermural scrum among lawyers. Instead of a dispute between "law" and "history," we actually have a dispute *within* legal theory itself. It is a dispute over how law should select from, filter, and reconfigure the past so that law can use it for legal purposes.[10] With respect to that task, historians have something to say, not because they are experts in legal theory, but because they know something about what kinds of theoretical projects the historical record can plausibly support.

If lawyers would disagree with Rappaport about these matters, it is not clear that similar objections by historians may be dismissed as irrelevant. Put another way, it does not matter *who* raises the objection, as long as the objection is an appropriate one in the context of the forms of legal argument.[11]

To be sure, given historians' professional outlook and training, they may have particular reasons for objecting to a given theory of original meaning. Jack Rakove, for example, has strongly criticized the notion that we should equate original meaning with the hypothetical reasonable and informed person at the time of adoption. He points out that this is simply not a credible way to do history.[12] Inquiries into original meaning, he believes, should be based on sound practices of historical research; otherwise the account of original public meaning will be anachronistic and "nothing more nor less than a creature of the modern originalist jurist's imagination."[13]

Rakove's objections, however informed by his professional training, would also be perfectly sensible for any lawyer to make in rebutting arguments from text, structure, or purpose.[14] In legal argument, it is always appropriate to point out that one's opponents employ an implausible methodology, that their arguments misuse historical sources, that their theory of original meaning is question begging, or that their inferences about historical meaning are naive or anach-ronistic. It should not matter that these objections come from the mouth of a professionally trained historian, who, if anything, has even greater credibility in making them.

Rappaport might respond that lawyers who do not agree with his theory of original public meaning are also wrong. They have the wrong theory of interpretation, and therefore their historical objec-tions are equally irrelevant. But this means that his complaint is not really that historians lack some skill that lawyers possess or that his-torians cannot grasp the special forms of reasoning of professionally trained lawyers. Rather, his objection is that other people—including both professionally trained lawyers and historians—do not share his particular theory. Agreeing with a particular jurisprudential theory is not the same thing as possessing lawyerly skill.

Randy Barnett has pointed out that if one adopts the New Orig-inalism, much history is not especially necessary or even helpful to the task of interpretation.[15] That is because New Originalists are mostly concerned with the definitions of words and phrases, along with their use in legal context. "The fact that a legal text is old some-times makes the identification of meaning more difficult, but far from impossible in most cases. For one thing, the meaning of lan-guage hasn't changed that much."[16] Historians, Barnett suggests, are interested in "describing past events, . . . explaining why what hap-pened in the past happened, [and] why people did what they did; as a result, they are very concerned with identifying motives, or other causal influences."[17] These skills, he contends, are not particularly helpful in ascertaining the objective meaning of legal terms.[18]

Barnett's argument somewhat overstates the case. Historians are not simply or exclusively interested in motives and causal influences. They, too, care a great deal about how people used words and what they meant by those words.[19] More to the point, historians are also interested in how people used words as rhetorical weapons, and how different political, religious, or social groups used the same words in slightly different ways. Historians are interested in the rough and tumble of rhetorical combat. They are interested in the refusal of par-ticular combatants to employ key words and ideas in the same ways as their opponents (something that, I should point out, happens even today).

Moreover, historians, like lawyers, may be interested in how people deliberately used vague and equivocal language to win others over or deflect uncomfortable difficulties in their political positions. Historians care about such things because they recognize that the exercise of language and the exercise of social and cultural power are not fully distinct enterprises. The most important words and phrases of a particular time may have been a terrain of political combat in the eighteenth and nineteenth centuries, just as they are today. People wielded language as a weapon in politics then just as they do now.

In sum, both historians and lawyers may think that language works somewhat differently than Barnett describes. Therefore, they may disagree with his assumption that it is fairly easy to pin down a univocal original public meaning as to highly contested terms such as "executive power," "arms," or "commerce." Once again, this is not a dispute that can be resolved simply by noting that one is a lawyer and pointing to one's superior legal expertise. Rather, it is a dispute about theories—and practices—of interpretation to which many kinds of scholars might contribute.

In any case, even if we accept Barnett's central point—that much history is not needed to understand the standard meanings of words in common use—it only goes to the question of interpretation. It says nothing about construction. When we turn to constitutional construction, wide swaths of history—and the work of historians—become relevant and important. In an extensive argument for why historians' accounts—and intellectual history more generally—are irrelevant to the study of original public meaning, Lawrence Solum briefly mentions the possibility that this work might be relevant to constitutional construction.[20] But this concession seems to give away the game. Since most issues are resolved through construction, historians' accounts should be very important indeed.

William Baude and Stephen Sachs offer an ingenious way to sidestep this problem. They argue that law avoids most of the complications and uncertainties that professional historians find in the past because law uses history in only limited ways. The task of lawyers is to follow the law of the past, which continues as law until it is (lawfully) changed.[21] Deciding what the law of the past is draws on lawyers' legal training. Although "lawyers must often defer to historical expertise on the relevant questions," Baude and Sachs explain, those relevant questions are greatly circumscribed, so that "the legal inquiry is a refined subset of the historical inquiry."[22] In particular, law "looks to legal doctrines and instruments specifically, rather than to intellectual movements more generally."[23] The law "interprets these instruments in artificial ways, properly ignoring certain facts about their historical authors and audience. And when there is uncertainty, it also applies various evidentiary principles and default rules that can give us confidence about today's law, even when yesterday's history remains obscure."[24]

Because the focus of law is the application of old doctrines and old statutes, rather than the entire corpus of historical knowledge and intellectual history, the problem of applying old law in new factual settings is greatly reduced. Ordinary legal reasoning already involves the application of "old law to new facts."[25] This means that "originalism demands no more than ordinary lawyer's work."[26] For example, "[d]eciding whether a 'no vehicles in the park' ordinance forbids motorized wheelchairs differs only in degree from reviewing warrantless GPS searches under Founding-era trespass doctrines."[27] Lawyers employ standard techniques when they apply an ancient ordinance to new factual situations that were not imagined at the time of its adoption: "We would need to know the legal content of the ordinance when it was made, the sorts of considerations that validly guided its application at the time, and so on. These questions are the bread-and-butter of ordinary legal reasoning."[28] Thus, "[w]e do not know what James Madison thought about video games, but we do know how to apply general legal concepts to facts, even when the concepts are very old and the facts are very new."[29]

For the same reason, lawyers need not worry too much about historical indeterminacy. Lawyers have the situation well in hand— this is what they do for a living. There may be multiple answers, but some answers are likely to be better than others from a legal perspective. "[T]oday's lawyers are fully capable of rendering an opinion on which side of a Founding-era dispute had the better claim."[30] The reason is that these are "claims of legal interpretation, *as are their negations*; just as much the bread-and-butter of modern judges as 'no vehicles in the park.'"[31]

Baude and Sachs seek to insulate law from historians' methodological criticisms by arguing that no history gets in unless law says that it does. That is, Baude and Sachs argue for the methodological autonomy of law. Law, in this account, is a bit like a submarine that travels blissfully through the oceans of history and only lets water in on its own terms. Otherwise, the submarine would sink. Put another way, law that is fully permeable to historical inquiry is about as useful as a screen door on a submarine.

Baude and Sachs are correct that law uses history for its own ends. They are also correct that how lawyers think about history and employ history is refracted through standard forms of legal justification. Indeed, these are the central claims of this book. The difficulty is that lawyers use many different modalities of argument, far more than Baude and Sachs let on. These modalities of argument use history in ways that make it far more difficult to ignore historians' work and historians' objections. Because these modalities are part of legal argument, they continually invite history—and historical criticism—inside Baude and Sachs's carefully constructed scheme of legal reason.

Equally important, lawyers have incentives both to construct authority and to undermine the authority of their opponents through the use of history. Although Baude and Sachs claim that legal doctrines and legal methods tend to keep history out of legal argument, the incentives of legal argument work in precisely the opposite direction. It may well be that lawyers employ a truncated version of history to establish authority. But lawyers on the other side of a dispute may not let them get away with it. They will object to how history is being used *as part of their legal arguments*. Conversely, lawyers with novel claims will have incentives to bring new historical claims, new historical sources, and new methods of historical proof to lend authority. The recent emergence of corpus linguistics is an example of lawyers' perpetual quest for ever new ways to wield history to establish their claims and discomfit their opponents.[32] To the extent that historians' criticisms are useful to lawyers who want to criticize other lawyers or buttress their own work, Baude and Sachs will not be able to keep history or historians sealed off from law.

Baude and Sachs foreground only a few types of legal argument out of many. This follows from their theory of originalism, which asks whether today's legal decisions have a traceable pedigree to the law of the past and to the doctrines of the past.[33] Because of their distinctive theory of originalism, their paradigm case of legal argument

is *precedential* argument, which constructs doctrines from past decisions, reasons from case to case, and applies existing doctrines to
new facts. They also advert to textual arguments that apply familiar
canons of construction. These modalities of argument seem very
lawyerly and isolated from much of historical inquiry. Baude and
Sachs's emphasis on these modalities gives their argument much of
its rhetorical force.

But there are plenty more arguments in constitutional law than
are dreamt of in their philosophy. When we turn to arguments from
purpose, structure, consequences, convention, custom, ethos, tradition, and honored authority, it is hard to foreclose recourse to lots
and lots of history, and not just adoption history—all kinds of history
from different times and places. As soon as we focus on questions of
purpose or tradition or structure or consequences or custom, it becomes difficult to make a hard distinction between "legal doctrines
and instruments," on the one hand, and "intellectual movements,"
on the other.[34]

And even if we focus only on doctrinal argument, we cannot seal
off law from history. Doctrinal arguments can have lots of historical
tests embedded within them—for example, whether a group has
been subject to a long history of discrimination, whether a certain
right or interest is deeply rooted in our nation's history and traditions, or whether there is historical evidence of a purpose or effect
to promote religion.[35] When forming doctrines and applying precedents, lawyers do not seem to be able to resist gesturing to the past,
and as soon as they do, historical inquiry seeps in. Or to vary the
metaphor, the more that lawyers try to flee from history, the more
history catches up with them.

Take Baude and Sachs's own example: the status of warrantless
GPS searches under the Fourth Amendment.[36] In applying new
technologies to old understandings, it will not be sufficient to parse
"Founding-era trespass doctrines."[37] We will have to make analogies.
Making analogies will require inquiries into—among other things—
purpose, institutional history, structure, and consequences. Making
analogies will require what Lawrence Lessig has called "translation."[38]
It will require us to understand the world the framers operated in and
consider how best to realize their purposes in a very different historical context with different institutional structures and law-enforcement

practices. Or in the words of my fellow originalist Judge Robert Bork, we must attempt "to discern how the framers' values, defined in the context of the world they knew, apply to the world we know."[39] As we make these inquiries, we will not be able to avoid venturing outside of the history of doctrine or beyond the comfortable cocoon of common-law canons of construction. We will have to understand "the context of the world the [framers] knew," and that will invite the historians in. And even if we ourselves refuse to venture into broader historical inquiries, we will not be able to prevent the other lawyers we must argue with from venturing outside.

We can put the point more generally. Lawyers use history to make arguments through standard forms of interpretation. They use history to give their arguments authority—many different kinds of authority, in fact. Because lawyers use history to establish authority, they must allow arguments about history into legal disputes. And because they must allow arguments about history, they must allow those who study and interpret history—that is, historians—into these disputes as well. Chief Justice John Roberts once famously asserted that "history will be heard."[40] It would be quite odd—and perhaps even a bit hypocritical—to announce that history will be heard but not historians. It would be like saying that one is very serious about climate change but has no interest in hearing from any climate scientists.

All that may be so, Baude and Sachs might respond, but the way that lawyers use these various modalities cuts off a great deal of historical evidence and historical argument. Lawyers, unlike historians, are simply not interested in endlessly going down historical rabbit holes. Lawyers, unlike historians, are not interested in endless disputation. They seek closure and decision. They seek easily tractable questions that lawyers can answer on their own. And once lawyers have set up the questions in ways that lawyers believe they can answer—for example, What is the best legal analogy between a GPS system and a common-law trespass?—historians, and their annoying complications, can (very politely) be shown the door. It was lovely talking with you for a brief spell, dear historians, but your services are no longer needed. We've got this!

But of course, lawyers *are* interested in endlessly going down historical rabbit holes. And lawyers *are* interested in endless disputation.

This, too, is the "bread-and-butter" of ordinary legal practice.[41] Baude and Sachs are surely correct that, when lawyers argue, they are arguing about legal claims. They are also correct that lawyers believe that some legal claims are more plausible than others, and that judges make decisions about which arguments are more plausible all the time. But it does not follow that historical inquiry is limited in the way they suggest. Quite the contrary, precisely because lawyers have incentives to make whatever arguments they believe will persuasively construct legal authority, they also have incentives to make whatever arguments they believe will persuasively undermine the legal authority of their opponents. Thus, if lawyers use history to establish their authority, other lawyers will turn to history to dispute that authority. In response, the first group of lawyers will return to history to refute the arguments of the second group, the second group will return to history to rebut the arguments of the first group, a third group will intervene to say that the first two groups have completely misunderstood the history, and so on.

Some lawyers, it is true, may want to constrict historical inquiry and deny that historians have much to say to them. But other lawyers, hoping to rebut them, will happily bring the historians in. Historians do not even need to be invited—as I have argued previously, the modalities of argument are always available to them, as they are to all other citizens. Accordingly, we should not understand Baude and Sachs's arguments—or those of Rappaport and Barnett—as actually setting the ground rules for legal argument. Rather, they are particular moves *within* legal argument—moves designed to structure agendas and thereby make a particular set of theoretical claims and approaches seem more natural and plausible.

It is worth emphasizing this point. When a group of lawyers say that what historians do is not relevant to law or misses the point of legal argument, they are not simply drawing disciplinary boundaries between law and history. They are also attempting to set agendas, assert theoretical claims, and establish burdens of proof within legal argument. Lawyers and legal scholars who make these kinds of moves are not simply stiff-arming historians; they are also setting boundaries on how other lawyers should use history. By defining legal reason in this way, they seek to foreclose uses of history that might undermine their particular interpretive theories or might rebut arguments using those theories.

Attempts to fence out historians, in other words, are often intra-disciplinary rather than cross-disciplinary: lawyers who hope to fence out historians may also object to lawyers who would disagree with them about how to use history, or who would use history in different ways to rebut their claims to legal authority. Baude and Sachs's picture of legal reason portrays a rough consensus among lawyers about how to make arguments and what sources to draw on. It is a constricted set of considerations about which all (or almost all) well-trained lawyers agree. In fact, the historical tools available to lawyers—and disagreements about how to use history to persuade—are much broader than they let on.

Baude and Sachs hold out the hope that legal doctrines and canons of construction will limit disputation about history, that they will tell lawyers when to stop. They imagine that there is some constitutional law equivalent to a statute of frauds that will rule out of bounds large swaths of historical evidence. But—especially in constitutional law—it is quite the opposite, as anyone who has ever picked up an amicus brief or a (very long) law review article can tell you. Fights over constitutional doctrine do not hold off historical dispute; they encourage lawyers to find ever new ways to make their cases. They make historical dispute never-ending.

Law claims legal authority through legal arguments. But lawyers do not simply stop arguing. Even when things are settled—which they often are—lawyers will continue to find new ways to keep on arguing, and they will bring history to bear to help them argue in new ways. And each time that lawyers bring history to bear, they, or their opponents, or their opponents' opponents can and will enlist the work of historians. Historians cannot be kept out of legal argument because lawyers simply will not allow it. History is too valuable to law's claims to authority to banish historians.

It is precisely because lawyers' use of history is rhetorical—employed to persuade in conditions of uncertainty—that lawyers cannot really escape or seal off historical inquiry. And because lawyers cannot escape or seal off historical inquiry, they cannot escape or seal off those potential participants—historians—who are professionally devoted to knowing something about history. Lawyers cannot, as Baude and Sachs hope, limit historical inquiry, and stop the arguments from becoming ever more about history, or about new ways of proving (or disproving) what history shows (or does not show). Even if, as Baude and Sachs correctly state, law's interest in history is limited—indeed, *because* it is limited—it has a hydraulic effect. Lawyers want to establish authority, and other lawyers want to deny them that authority. This hunger for authority creates incentives to turn to history to construct and deconstruct authority, to find ever new ways to make historical claims and rebut them, to find ever new archives and methods (such as corpus linguistics) to demonstrate and to refute historical claims.

No doubt many historians will be horrified by what I have just said. History, they will point out, is not simply the plaything of adversarial legal argument. It is an inquiry into truth, even if the conditions of that truth are uncertain and contested. What I am describing is a perversion of the task of historical inquiry, a task transformed and corrupted by lawyers' desire to have the last word in an argument for authority—a last word that, I hasten to add, lawyers never really can have.

But the question on the table is not whether lawyers might misuse historical methods and the work of historians—I not only believe it, I have seen it done. Rather, the question is whether lawyers can find ways, internal to law, to keep historians from interrupting them and pointing out that their historical claims are anachronistic, naive, distorted, or simply wrong. The question is whether lawyers can successfully wield their professional identity and their professional norms to hold off historians' objections. The question is whether they can pound the table, announce that they are lawyers, and tell the historians to just shut up because, frankly, it's none of their business.

My point is that lawyers cannot successfully do this, and the reason they cannot do this is because of their very professional identity as lawyers and their own professional norms. The very features of professionalism that cause lawyers to distort history also open the door to history and historical criticism. As long as lawyers want to find ways of persuading others, and as long as they want to rebut the arguments of their fellow lawyers, they will find all sorts of history, and all sorts of historians, indispensable to their task. The relevance of history—and therefore historical dispute—is baked into the modalities of argument that lawyers unselfconsciously employ. This does not make lawyers good historians—it only makes them perpetually subject to historians' interventions.

Baude and Sachs, like Rappaport and Barnett, are simply the latest in a long line of defenders of law's methodological autonomy, the latest constructors of a Maginot line that hopes to let in only a controlled dose of history and keep the rest—and those pesky historians—out. The drawing of metes and bounds is not inappropriate by itself—it is part of what it means for a profession to be a profession. At the same time, for reasons internal to this particular profession, each attempt to simultaneously use history to establish legal authority *and* to exclude historical critiques from historians will fail. It will fail not because lawyers lack distinctive professional identities and professional training but *because of* their distinctive professional identities and their professional training. Because lawyers are lawyers, they will continually alternate between pushing away and embracing forms of expertise that might assist them in building up or chipping away at claims of legal authority. The problem is not that the historians won't shut up; it is that the lawyers won't shut up. Lawyers will always try to find new ways to establish the authority of their positions and undermine the authority of their competitors' claims. Lawyers, because they are lawyers, simply cannot help themselves.

CHAPTER SIXTEEN

Lawyers' Need for a Usable Past

T HE SECOND STANDARD WAY that lawyers attempt to deflect criticisms from historians is to argue that lawyers,
because they are practical people of the world, need a
usable past. As I noted earlier, the expression "a usable
past" was coined in a 1918 essay, "On Creating a Usable Past," by
the American literary critic Van Wyck Brooks.[1] Brooks was one of
the "Young Americans," who offered cultural criticisms of the United
States in the early twentieth century.[2] Many people have subsequently
spoken of a "usable past" without mentioning Brooks, while uncan-
nily replicating some of the themes of his essay. And of course, although Brooks coined the term "usable past," the idea that people
should deliberately use the memory of the past to inspire great work
in the present long precedes him. To give only one example, this is
one of the themes of Friedrich Nietzsche's famous 1874 essay "On
the Use and Abuse of History for the Present."[3]

Brooks's concern was not authority in constitutional interpretation but greatness in American letters. The problem, as Brooks saw
it, was how to create a national culture in the United States that
could inspire greatness in American writers and promote finer attitudes and better ideals. Unfortunately, Brooks believed, American
culture at the beginning of the twentieth century was a "travesty of
a civilization."[4] It was materialistic and stupid; it blindly worshiped

254

wealth and technological progress. Professors of literature and history in universities were of little use. They celebrated the great deeds of America's past, but only used this knowledge to shame young people rather than inspire them; moreover, academics were no less compromised by the technology-worship and materialism of the age.[5]

Brooks contrasted America with Europe. Europe, he believed, had a past that inspired and encouraged great art. (This assertion is somewhat ironic, of course, given the currents of artistic modernism then working their way through Europe.) Americans lacked a cultural memory that grounded their efforts, situated their art, and offered an artistic tradition to work with or against.

How could Americans use their past to enrich their culture? The answer, Brooks argued, was that Americans should invent the kind of past that they could use.[6] They should draw on elements of the past and reinterpret them into a worthy tradition that could inspire them: "The past is an inexhaustible storehouse of apt attitudes and adaptable ideals; it opens of itself at the touch of desire; it yields up, now this treasure, now that, to anyone who comes to it armed with a capacity for personal choices."[7]

In Brooks's account, a usable past is a selective history; it does not revel in needless complications or complexities. It does not require a comprehensive record of history. It wants just enough history to do its job—which is to inspire the present. Nor is a usable past a foreign country or an alien realm. Advocates of a usable past are not interested in the inherent pastness of the past but in its organic relationship to the present. A usable past is a past that is connected to us, not separated from us. A usable past is a past that we can understand and relate to, a past that is not hopelessly different from our own world. Above all, a usable past is a resource that people in the present can deploy selectively to support and inspire fellow citizens to great deeds and great works of art. Brooks uses the metaphor of a "storehouse" of objects that one might choose from, while leaving the others behind. The riches of this storehouse emerge from "desire" and "personal choice." It contains "apt" features that we can take with us to the present, and ideals that are "adaptable" to our needs. And above all, the storehouse is valuable *to us* because it can revitalize and motivate the present and spur great cultural achievements.

Brooks's fellow Young American Lewis Mumford emphasized that a usable past gave meaning to our endeavors by connecting us to the past. A culture needs continuity with the past to ground itself and give itself direction. Because America lacked a usable past, Mumford believed, it was prey to the social forces of the present, including social disconnection and unchecked materialism: "Establishing its own special relations with its past, each generation creates anew what lies behind it, as well as what looms in front; and instead of being victimized by those forces which are uppermost at the moment, it gains the ability to select the qualities which it values, and by exercising them it rectifies its own infirmities and weaknesses."[8]

A usable past is a form of cultural memory and tradition, and Brooks viewed cultural memory and tradition as constructed, either by accident or by design. Cultural memory is made up of what people in a society choose to remember about their past. Tradition is made up out of what they choose to honor. Brooks pointed out, for example, that other nations found plenty of things in the American experience to celebrate—and each nation found different things to admire because they saw things in America that resonated or contrasted with the cultural memory and traditions of their own countries.[9]

It followed, then, that Americans should create their own memories and traditions that could inspire them by mining the storehouse of the past to find what was useful for the present and to elevate it even if it had not previously been deemed important. To this end, Brooks argued against focusing on the relatively small number of celebrated American authors and acknowledged masterpieces of American literature.[10] Instead, to create a usable past, Americans should focus on the strivings of eccentrics and failures—now mostly forgotten—whose creativity and genius had been unfairly stunted by the national culture that surrounded them. Inspiration for great work in the future would come from rediscovering and elevating this "limbo of the non-elect."[11] American artists should select from the past according to their values and find their heroes, even among the forgotten and cast-off elements of history.

Some eighty years later, in 1995, the American legal scholar Cass Sunstein wrote a short essay in the *Columbia Law Review* titled "The Idea of a Useable Past."[12] His goal was to explain why constitutional lawyers could and should use history differently than professional historians. He offered virtually all of the standard arguments that lawyers make in their defense, and his article remains the best and most sustained argument for a "usable past" in the law review literature. Although Sunstein did not mention Brooks, his account has striking similarities to Brooks's.

Sunstein wrote to respond to criticisms—by both lawyers and historians—directed at the "republican revival" in American legal scholarship in the 1980s. Almost contemporaneous with the promotion of conservative originalism by the Reagan administration and the Federalist Society, liberal academics like Sunstein and Frank Michelman had begun to offer a left-liberal version of originalism, grounding a progressive constitutionalism in a distinctive account of the founding.[13] They drew on historical work by Bernard Bailyn, Gordon Wood, and J. G. A. Pocock, among others.[14]

Sunstein and Michelman argued that the true tradition of American constitutionalism was not exclusively Lockean liberal individualism, which generations of scholars had used to justify a focus on individual rights and interest-group pluralism. Rather, the founding generation was also steeped in the ideology of civic republicanism, which emphasized civic virtue, social connection, deliberative democracy, and the common good. By forgetting these traditions of civic republicanism, American legal scholars had cut themselves off from their own history and adopted a false narrative that legitimated a politics of selfishness and self-interest.

The republican revival, as it was called, generated rebuttals from historians and from legal scholars who specialized in founding-era history. Critics charged that neorepublicans were engaged in a more sophisticated version of the law-office history of conservative originalists. As Laura Kalman put it, the neorepublicans rummaged through the past "to find arguments for whatever vision of the social order they wished to promote. By mooring their vision in the Founding, law professors believed they could make a more powerful case for it. They could claim kinship with the Founders."[15]

To be sure, there were a few differences between the neorepublicans and conservative originalists. First, most professional historians, who were liberals themselves, tended to sympathize with the political project of the neorepublicans. Second, the neorepublicans drew on a wider range of sources and secondary literature than conservative originalists do, including the work of the most distinguished professional historians. "[T]he civic republicans," Mark Festa explained, "sought to invoke the authority not just of historical evidence itself, but also of the professional expertise of the historians who interpreted it."[16]

But these differences hardly absolved the liberal law professors in the eyes of professional historians. If anything, they made historians uneasy. It was one thing to see conservatives quoting Blackstone or *The Federalist* anachronistically and out of context. It was quite another to see the best historical scholarship deployed in this way.[17]

Historians like Gordon Wood and Joyce Appleby pointed out that neorepublicans could not find the historical pedigree they sought by appealing to the ideology of civic republicanism.[18] Linda Kerber noted that the civic republicanism of the founders was not easy to separate from militarism, patriarchy, and oligarchy, and that it was anachronistic to try to separate them.[19] Law professors, who are often the sternest critics of other law professors doing history, were more blunt. Mark Tushnet worried that the ideology of eighteenth-century civic republicanism "unravels once we attempt to disentangle the currently attractive strands from the currently unattractive ones."[20] H. Jefferson Powell argued that there was little connection between Sunstein's political ideals and "specific schools of thought in the founding era."[21] Barry Friedman argued that "[t]he very same problems that haunt originalism also haunt republicanism."[22] Martin Flaherty dubbed the republican revival "History Lite."[23]

In response, Sunstein defended his use of civic republicanism on the grounds that constitutional lawyers need a usable past, which he defined as "finding elements in history that can be brought fruitfully to bear on current problems."[24] In fact, Sunstein, argued, "[t]he search for a useable past is a defining feature of the constitutional lawyer's approach to constitutional history."[25]

Invoking Ronald Dworkin's idea of constructive interpretation, which tries to make the materials of the law "the best they can be," Sunstein asserted that "constitutional lawyers, unlike ordinary historians, should attempt *to make the best constructive sense out of historical events associated with the Constitution.*"[26] Consistent with the "fit" of historical facts, lawyers should "try to conceive of the materials in a way that makes political or moral sense, rather than nonsense, out of them to current generations."[27] Obviously this meant viewing history in the light of the present-day lawyer's moral and political judgments. "Everyone can see that the political or moral commitments of the constitutional lawyer are an omnipresent part of the constitutional lawyer's constitutional history." But this is not an embarrassment. "Political or moral commitments play a role because of the interpretive nature of the lawyer's enterprise, which involves showing how the history might be put to present use."[28]

Sunstein denied that there was anything illegitimate about "identify[ing] those features of the constitutional past" that a lawyer views as "especially suitable for present constitutional use."[29] "Constitutional law is based on ideas about authority, not just on ideas about the good or the right."[30] And "[t]he American constitutional culture gives special weight to the conventions of those who ratified constitutional provisions."[31]

Sunstein's model of a usable past was primarily concerned with adoption history. But not all of adoption history—much less all of American history—can form part of a usable past, Sunstein explained. "[M]uch in our constitutional history is bad and no longer useable."[32] For example, the founders accepted slavery; they had a "much narrower" conception of freedom of speech "than anyone would find reasonable today," and "the Framers' conception of equality would permit forms of discrimination that the Supreme Court would unanimously condemn" today.[33] Sunstein did not deny that these events happened. His point was that they were not useful to constitutional lawyers who sought to create a usable past: "Aspects of constitutional history that are of considerable importance to constitutional historians may not be so useful for constitutional lawyers."[34]

"[T]he constitutional lawyer, thinking about the future course of constitutional law, has a special project" that distinguishes the lawyer from the professional historian.[35] The professional historian is "subject to the discipline provided by the sources and by the interpretive conventions in the relevant communities of historians."[36] But "the constitutional lawyer is trying to contribute to the legal culture's repertoire of arguments and political/legal narratives that place a (stylized) past and present into a trajectory leading to a desired future."[37] Professional historians may have their eyes on the past, but constitutional lawyers have their eyes on the future. Constitutional lawyers want to forge a rhetorical connection between the admirable features of the founders' vision and the world they would like to bring into being. Because the founders are central to our constitutional heritage, they can encourage, authorize, and inspire our efforts in the present.

Two features make the past usable. First, the past "discipline[s] legal judgment." It bounds utopian speculation and connects legal argument to the American constitutional tradition. It requires lawyers to argue in terms of materials that have "at least some kind of democratic pedigree" because they were adopted by We the People.[38]

Second, and equally important, what makes the past usable is that it is normatively admirable by today's standards. Conversely, what is not normatively acceptable is not usable. As Sunstein put it, "much in our constitutional history is bad and no longer useable."[39] Again contrasting the interests of lawyers to those of historians, he explained, "Perhaps the historian wants to reveal the closest thing to a full picture of the past, or to stress the worst aspects of a culture's legal tradition," but "constitutional history as set out by the constitutional lawyer, as a participant in the constitutional culture, usually tries to put things in a favorable or appealing light without, however, distorting what can actually be found."[40]

Sunstein believed that the civic republican tradition offered an excellent example of how present-day lawyers could interpret the past constructively—that is, admirably—by abstracting away its normatively unacceptable features. The tradition of civic republicanism was built on social hierarchy. Male citizens could be devoted to the public good because they were heads of households. They were supported by women and (sometimes) slaves, who were regarded as properly subordinate to a community of equal male citizens. Civic duty was connected to obligations of militia service, including the willingness to fight and die for the republic; thus, the idea of civic virtue had overtones of militarism and manly virtue.

Sunstein was perfectly aware of all this but argued that it did not matter. The republican tradition, "in some of its incarnations," was "associated with unappealing and unusable ideas—exclusion of women, militarism, lack of respect for competing conceptions of the good, and more."[41] (Note, once again, that what makes these ideas "unusable" is that they are wrong by today's standards.) "But the commitment to deliberative democracy is not logically connected with those unappealing ideals; indeed, as an abstraction it is in considerable tension with them."[42] Abstracting away the unjust elements of a tradition is acceptable, Sunstein argued, and may even be necessary to render it usable to the present. "Constitutional lawyers who are interested in republicanism need not be embarrassed by its contingent historical connection with unjust practices."[43]

Despite the disciplinary differences between law and literature, Sunstein's account of a usable past is remarkably similar to Brooks's version in 1918. Americans need inspiration to achieve great things, whether in politics, law, or letters. To do that, they need a past that is useful for this purpose. Academic historians, with their eyes fixed on the past, and reined in by their professional norms, are often mired in antiquarian projects and can offer only limited assistance. Academic historians are far more likely to complicate than to elucidate, to depress and confuse their audiences than to inspire them to great things. American lawyers, like American literary critics, understand that the point of the past is to serve the future. Accordingly, they need to reach into the storehouse of history, construct inspiring narratives, and create a past worthy of instruction to the present. Just as Mumford believed that establishing connections with history could help us from being "victimized by those forces which are uppermost at the moment,"[44] Sunstein argued that retelling the story of civic republicanism could help constitutional lawyers combat the selfishness of 1980s politics. In this way, progressive lawyers could counter the neoliberal agenda of the Reagan years—itself defended in originalist terms—with a communitarian vision drawn from the founding.

In terms of the modalities of historical argument described in part 1 of this book, it is easy to see that Sunstein's version of a usable past is an appeal to ethos, tradition, and honored authority. His arguments about civic republicanism appeal to the same modalities of ethos, tradition, and honored authority as many conservative originalist arguments do—either implicitly or explicitly. That is why, I suspect, professional historians may have reacted in the way that they did.

Sunstein, however, was insistent that he was not countenancing bad history, much less advocating sloppiness: "[I]t is familiar to find a constitutional lawyer reading history at a very high level of abstraction ('the Framers were committed to freedom of speech') and concluding that some concrete outcome follows for us ('laws regulating obscenity are unconstitutional'). This use of history is not honorable."[45] The problem for Sunstein was that pointing to the level of abstraction did not really distinguish how he wanted to use history from the kind of historical arguments he did not respect. To create his version of a usable past, Sunstein also wanted to read history at a fairly high level of abstraction; and, as we have seen, he believed that one could abstract away the unpalatable parts of the civic republican tradition.

"The Framers," Sunstein explained, "were republicans. . . . [T]hey prized civic virtue and sought to promote deliberation in government—deliberation oriented toward right answers about the collective good."[46] Sunstein sought to apply these abstract propositions to modern First Amendment law and other doctrinal areas. His 1993 book *Democracy and the Problem of Free Speech*, for example, was premised on a "Madisonian" conception of free speech that purportedly reflected the founding-era ideals of deliberative democracy.[47] Reviewing Sunstein's book, I joked that "Sunstein's 'Madisonian' theory of the First Amendment is about as Madisonian as Madison, Wisconsin: It is a tribute to a great man and his achievements, but bears only a limited connection to his actual views."[48]

What distinguishes good from bad uses of history, however, is not the level of abstraction. It is whether we acknowledge or disguise our modality of argument. Bad uses of history mislead their audiences about the kinds of justification they actually employ. For example, they might assert that they are only concerned with discerning the historical facts of meaning, purpose, or intention when they are actually appealing to (and reconstructing) ethos and tradition, using the framers and the founding generation as culture heroes. Perhaps what Sunstein should have said was that while those who misused history refused to admit this, he would do so forthrightly. He was acting as what I call a "memory entrepreneur," seeking to construct inspiring narratives of the past to articulate a desirable conception of American values in the present.[49]

In hindsight, then, it would probably have been better for Sunstein to avoid making his First Amendment theory sound like conservative originalism, much less to assert that his theory of freedom of speech was Madison's theory or that it had "firm support" from founding-era history.[50] Instead, he might simply have emphasized that, like Justice Brandeis in *Whitney v. California*, he was making an argument about national ethos.[51] The American tradition of freedom of expression, understood in its best light and symbolized by Madison, the First Amendment's author, is a tradition that celebrates reason and deliberation to make democracy work. Put in terms of Sunstein's arguments about a useful past, he was "contribut[ing] to the legal culture's repertoire of arguments and political/legal narratives that place a (stylized) past and present into a trajectory leading to a desired future."[52] This might have robbed his arguments of the historical pedigree that originalist scholars sometimes like to claim for themselves. But it would have offered a more appropriate use of history.

Sunstein's account of a usable past is quite common among American constitutional lawyers, even if they have not always expressed their aims so coherently and candidly.[53] American lawyers are not interested in antiquarianism for its own sake. They want to draw lessons, advice, and directives from history. To this end, they seek a past that can justify interpretations of the Constitution in the present. They look for those features of the American constitutional tradition that, given their political and theoretical commitments, deserve to be continued and followed today. This is an example of what I earlier called an obedient use of history. We might call this model of a usable past the *model of admirable ancestors*. By the standards of this model, only some history is usable. The rest is not.

Understood as a justification for making arguments from ethos, tradition, and honored authority, the model of admirable ancestors is a perfectly legitimate use of history—legitimate, that is, if it does not try to conceal its nature to its audience. Nevertheless, as a general account of a usable past for constitutional argument, this model has very significant limitations.

First, the model of admirable ancestors is usually concerned with adoption history and especially the history of the founding. All other history of the nation, and indeed of the world, is, by implication, not usable for these purposes. Similarly, it is a history of persons and groups that successfully managed to change the text of the Constitution or to influence those who did. Thus, Locke and Blackstone are part of a usable past because the adopters read them and were influenced by them. The Anti-Federalists are part of a usable past because their objections to the proposed Constitution forced its advocates to modify their claims about how the Constitution would operate in practice and to support new amendments to the Constitution, some of which appeared in the Bill of Rights. Likewise, the views of nineteenth-century abolitionists are part of a usable past because their opposition to slavery eventually carried the day in the Reconstruction Amendments. In sum, this account of a usable past focuses on the history of those who won struggles for constitutional adoption—or influenced those who won—as opposed to those whose claims were ignored or crushed, or those who, like women before the adoption of the Nineteenth Amendment, were given no voice in governance.[54] (We might contrast this model of a usable past to that of Van Wyck Brooks, who sought to construct a tradition from those who lost so badly that they are not even remembered.) Selecting only the winners' perspectives discards a great deal of history as not usable.

Second, what makes the past usable in this model is that it is normatively admirable by today's standards—or at the very least acceptable and inoffensive. (More precisely, it is admirable in the eyes of the particular person making the historical argument.) Conversely, what is not normatively admirable or acceptable is not usable; therefore, it must be omitted, distinguished, or separated from the honorable and usable parts of history.

History is usable in this model because it teaches us something important about the past that we should follow in the present. We might follow it because it provides an authoritative construction of features of the Constitution, its purposes, text, and structure. Or we might follow it because it offers us models for appropriate behavior or principles for present-day law and politics. But in either case, a usable past gives us guidance about what to do today, through either instruction or inspiration. Thus, in terms of chapter 2's typology, the model of admirable ancestors is both an obedient and an authority-constructing use of history.

Nevertheless, this conception of a usable past throws away a great deal of history, and it discards many possible ways of using a complex tradition in the present.[55] History that shows that our constitutional traditions are not worthy, admirable, or inspiring is not usable. History that shows how application of past practices to present-day circumstances is inevitably anachronistic is not usable. History that complicates—that denies that we have inherited a coherent or unitary tradition—is not usable. Similarly, history that shows that there was not a clear, definitive answer to how the Constitution was understood at the time of adoption is not usable. Critical accounts of history, which show how our present traditions, values, and arrangements are inextricably bound up with past errors and injustices, are not usable. Historicist accounts, which show how features of the constitutional tradition—and our understanding of those features—have not been constant or enduring but have altered with changing times, are not usable.

The irony of this model of a usable past is that it renders so much history unusable.

It is a bit like a man who enters a huge room with a vast variety of fresh ingredients, meats, fruits, vegetables, condiments, and spices before him. He then proceeds to throw away almost everything in the room and make a grilled-cheese sandwich. He defends his wastefulness on the grounds that he is not a professional chef—he is a special kind of short-order cook. From his perspective, all of the other food in the room is simply unusable. And besides, he explains earnestly, the customers won't swallow anything else.

I myself have nothing against a really good grilled-cheese sandwich. But surely there is more nourishment to be found in history.

For history to be usable, it does not have to offer a clear command to the present. It does not have to be honorable or inspiring. The past is a motley arrangement of good and bad, just and unjust, often inextricably bound together. Negative precedents may be more valuable to us than hero worship. Knowing how the nation went wrong may be more useful than hearing yet again how splendidly our predecessors got things right. History may edify even if it does not inspire.

This point holds true even if we limit ourselves to arguments from ethos and tradition. In 1995, Sunstein hoped to abstract the tradition of civic republicanism from its unpalatable historical elements. These unjust elements, he thought, were merely "contingent."[56] But what if they were not? Suppose that the social hierarchy of the eighteenth century helped make civic republicanism possible? Then it would be partly constitutive of the tradition and not merely contingent. If we want to follow that tradition today, we may have to take the bitter with the sweet. Or we may have to change the tradition significantly, in which case we are not following it so much as transforming it.

Political traditions are entangled in complex social relations and historical contexts. Transporting these values from the past may bring other, less admirable features and complications along with them. If we assume that we can easily cleanse these traditions of their less troublesome elements, we may miss some of the most important lessons of the past for the present. Working within a tradition, no matter how hallowed, may involve moral compromises. There are no traditions without trade-offs.

Instead of trying to abstract away the problems of past traditions, it may be more appropriate to acknowledge their difficulties and complications. The past may be more usable if we do *not* treat our traditions as unequivocally admirable; it will simply be usable in a different way.[57] History has many uses besides imitation, obedience, or encouragement. It may edify, enlighten, or admonish us. We might use the past to make the present strange to us, thereby loosening us from our accustomed habits of thinking; this may help combat our constant tendency to accept the world before us as just and natural or, conversely, as incorrigible and impossible to reform.

History may reveal problems never solved and injustices never corrected whose consequences haunt us today. It may show the residue of ancient wrongs in a modern world. It may remind us not to paper over past difficulties with the banner of a glorious and unitary tradition. History might suggest alternatives to our present arrangements or offer warnings about disasters we should avoid. Instead of directing our course of action, it may clarify our choices. Instead of urging us to imitate our ancestors, it may remind us how much our actions must be our own responsibility.

To imagine a better model of a usable past for constitutional lawyers, begin with a different set of questions: What do lawyers want from the past, and what makes it useful to them? By this point in the book, the answer should be obvious. Lawyers want to use the past to help them make arguments that (1) successfully claim legal authority and (2) rebut claims to authority offered by their opponents.

It follows that a usable past might include any part of the past that might assist lawyers in the construction *or* the deconstruction of legal authority. The past is potentially usable whenever it assists lawyers in making or rebutting arguments according to the eleven modalities of constitutional argument. We might call this conception of a usable past *the model of multiple modalities*.

The model of admirable ancestors is only a special case of this model because it limits itself to certain arguments from ethos, tradition, and honored authority. The model of multiple modalities encompasses all of the history relevant to the model of admirable ancestors. But it includes far more history and values it for a much wider range of purposes.

To be sure, this account of a usable past is still selective. Not every part of the past is equally useful to the modalities of legal argument, even considered collectively. The model of multiple modalities is not a neutral or dispassionate inquiry into history, because of the close connections between usable history and theories of legal justification. Above all, this model of a usable past is shaped by lawyers' concerns. It is shaped by the needs of the legal profession—the need to create new arguments for new situations and to rebut the arguments of one's opponents. It differs from how other parts of the humanities and social sciences may think of the past; and historians may still criticize how lawyers use history for this reason.

Nevertheless, this conception of a usable past has definite advantages over the model of admirable ancestors.

First, it employs a far broader set of historical materials than adoption history. It ranges over the whole of American history and, indeed, the history of the world.

Second, it is not limited to appeals to ethos, tradition, and honored authority. History may be useful to assess consequences, to understand the structures of a well-functioning government, and to reckon with the meaning of events quite distant from the founding.

Third, this model does not require that history be admirable, uncomplicated, or univocal in order to be useful, especially when the advocate's task is criticism or rebuttal. It does not rule out complexity or shun a critical approach. It does not require that history be inspiring or that we must always place our traditions in their best light. And it does not assume that in searching for a usable past, we may excise what is unjust or uncomfortable, especially if we can learn from it.

Finally, the model of multiple modalities is a better account of a usable past because it better integrates the contributions of historians. It does not assume that professional historians cannot usefully critique lawyers' history because lawyers inhabit different professional roles and are engaged in different intellectual projects.

I have no quarrel with the notion of a usable past. But constitutional lawyers have not taken the idea seriously enough—or considered all of its ramifications. Even if we restrict ourselves to the lawyer's obsessive focus on constructing and deconstructing legal authority, there are many ways to use history, and many different kinds of history, from all times and places, that one might employ. Critical uses of history, which show the limits and failings of the past, may be every bit as useful as heroic accounts. Complicating uses of history, which reveal dissensus, ambiguity, and contingency, may be as important to understanding the present as stylized accounts that seek a single, univocal lesson or command.

If we want a usable past, we should not be wasteful. We should be willing to use as much of the past as possible and for as many purposes as we can. If we are economical with history and remember the multiple ways to employ and learn from it, it will provide us with all the riches we could desire.

Acknowledgments

I BEGAN THIS PROJECT in 2012, shortly after finishing *Living Originalism*, and the ideas have germinated for over a decade. Several chapters of this book are drawn from portions of previous articles, which have been extensively recombined, reedited, and rewritten. All appear with permission of the respective publishers and copyright holders. In chronological order, they are *The New Originalism and the Uses of History*, 82 Fordham L. Rev. 641 (2013); *Why Are Americans Originalist?*, *in* Law, Society and Community: Socio-Legal Essays in Honour of Roger Cotterrell (David Schiff and Richard Nobles eds., Ashgate Publishing 2014); *Constitutional Change and Interpretation in the United States: The Official and the Unofficial*, Jus Politicum, No. 14 (June 2015); *The Construction of Original Public Meaning*, 31 Const. Comment. 71 (2016); *Lawyers and Historians Argue about the Constitution*, 35 Const. Comment. 345 (2020); *Text, History and Tradition: Discussion Questions on* New York State Rifle and Pistol Association, Inc. v. Bruen, Balkinization (July 6, 2022), https://balkin.blogspot.com/2022/07/text-history-and-tradition-discussion.html [https://perma.cc/DS6N-DLS8]; *More on Text, History, and Tradition—Discussion Questions for* Dobbs, *Part One*, Balkinization (July 8, 2022), https://balkin.blogspot.com/2022/07/more-on-text-history-and-tradition.html [https://perma.cc/CWM8-AETA], and *Constitutional Memories*, 31 Wm. & Mary Bill Rts. J. 307 (2022).

During the COVID-19 pandemic, Sandy Levinson, Mark Graber, Steve Griffin, Jonathan Gienapp, and I began gathering on Friday afternoons on Zoom to discuss constitutional politics, history, and theory. I thank them all for their many conversations, for their comments on this book, and for their friendship and advice. Reva Siegel, another dear friend, has been my trusted interlocutor on constitutional theory and history since we both arrived at Yale in 1994. This book is deeply influenced by our many discussions.

Many friends and colleagues have commented on the various parts of this book as I developed its ideas over the years. In particular, I would like to thank Bruce Ackerman, Akhil Amar, Denis Baranger, Randy Barnett, Olivier Beaud, Josh Blackman, Philip Bobbitt, Saul Cornell, Quentin Épron, Dick Fallon, Jim Fleming, Jill Hasday, John McGinnis, Christina Mulligan, Robert Post, Mike Rappaport, Tim Scanlon, Scott Shapiro, Larry Solum, Seth Barrett Tillman, Alex Tsesis, and John Witt, as well as participants at the Harvard Law and Philosophy Colloquium.

My wife, Margret Wolfe, has been a steady source of support as I labored over these chapters over the course of many years. Nothing seems possible without her; everything seems possible with her love.

Notes

Chapter One. Arguing with History

1. Philip C. Bobbitt, Constitutional Fate: Theory of the Constitution 26 (1982); *see also* Philip C. Bobbitt, Constitutional Interpretation 13 (1991).
2. Richard H. Fallon Jr., *A Constructivist Coherence Theory of Constitutional Interpretation*, 100 Harv. L. Rev. 1189, 1244 (1987).
3. David E. Pozen and Adam M. Samaha, *Anti-Modalities*, 119 Mich. L. Rev. 729, 738 (2021) (noting the widespread adoption of the idea of modalities of constitutional argument); Jack M. Balkin, *Arguing about the Constitution: The Topics in Constitutional Interpretation*, 33 Const. Comm. 145, 179 (2018) ("Since Bobbitt coined the term in his 1982 book, *Constitutional Fate*, 'modalities' has caught on as the standard way to describe the basic forms of argument in constitutional law.")
4. Bobbitt, Constitutional Fate, *supra* note 1, at 26; *see also* Bobbitt, Constitutional Interpretation, *supra* note 1, at 13. Similarly, Richard Fallon's list of constitutional arguments refers to "[a]rguments of historical intent," which he identifies with "the intent of the framers." Fallon, *A Constructivist Coherence Theory, supra* note 2, at 1244, 1254 (1987). Both Bobbitt and Fallon wrote at a time when the focus of originalist theory was shifting from original intention and understanding to original meaning.
5. Alfred H. Kelly, *Clio and the Court: An Illicit Love Affair*, 1965 Sup. Ct. Rev. 119, 156. *See id.* at 157 ("The application of precedent, legal continuity, and balanced contemporary socio-political theory is almost certain to produce a more intelligent result than is the attempt to use a few scattered historical documents as though they possessed the qualities of Holy Writ. Most inquiry into the past illustrates dramatically the discontinuity of culture and social process rather than their continuity.").
6. Maurice Halbwachs, On Collective Memory 38 (Lewis A. Coser ed. & trans., 1992) (1925).

7. *See, e.g.*, Michael Schudson, *Journalism as a Vehicle of Non-Commemorative Cultural Memory, in* Journalism and Memory 85 (Barbie Zelizer and Keren Tenenboim-Weinblatt eds., 2014); Jane Greer and Laurie Grobman, *Introduction—Complicating Conversations: Public Memory Production and Composition and Rhetoric, in* Pedagogies of Public Memory: Teaching Writing and Rhetoric at Museums, Archives, and Memorials 4 (Jane Greer and Laurie Grobman eds., 2016).

8. Jan Assmann, *Collective Memory and Cultural Identity*, 65 New German Critique 125 (1995).

9. *Id.*

10. Reva B. Siegel, *The Politics of Constitutional Memory*, 20 Geo. J.L. & Pub. Pol'y 19, 19 (2022) (defining constitutional memory as a "form of collective memory: narratives that constitute a community as a community, accounts of experience that ground practical reason and create a group's sense of identity and justice and values as a people").

11. *Id.* at 23.

12. Jack M. Balkin, Living Originalism (2011).

Chapter Two. History and the Forms of Constitutional Argument

1. *See, e.g.*, Laura Kalman, The Strange Career of Legal Liberalism (1996); Patrick J. Charles, Historicism, Originalism, and the Constitution: The Use and Abuse of the Past in American Jurisprudence (2014); Hans W. Baade, *"Original Intent" in Historical Perspective: Some Critical Glosses*, 69 Tex. L. Rev. 1001 (1991); Randy E. Barnett, *The Relevance of the Framers' Intent*, 19 Harv. J.L. & Pub. Pol'y 403 (1996); Paul Brest, *The Misconceived Quest for the Original Understanding*, 60 B.U. L. Rev. 204 (1980); Michael C. Dorf, *A Nonoriginalist Perspective on the Lessons of History*, 19 Harv. J.L. & Pub. Pol'y 351 (1996); Michael C. Dorf, *Integrating Normative and Descriptive Constitutional Theory: The Case of Original Meaning*, 85 Geo. L.J. 1765 (1997); Christopher L. Eisgruber, *The Living Hand of the Past: History and Constitutional Justice*, 65 Fordham L. Rev. 1611 (1997); Paul Finkelman, *The Constitution and the Intentions of the Framers: The Limits of Historical Analysis*, 50 U. Pitt. L. Rev. 349 (1989); Martin S. Flaherty, *History "Lite" in Modern American Constitutionalism*, 95 Colum. L. Rev. 523 (1995); Martin S. Flaherty, *The Most Dangerous Branch*, 105 Yale L.J. 1725 (1996); Martin S. Flaherty, *The Practice of Faith*, 65 Fordham L. Rev. 1565 (1997); Mitchell Gordon, *Adjusting the Rear-View Mirror: Rethinking the Use of History in Supreme Court Jurisprudence*, 89 Marq. L. Rev. 475 (2006); Jamal Greene, *The Case for Original Intent*, 80 Geo. Wash. L. Rev. 1683 (2012); James H. Hutson, *The Creation of the Constitution: The Integrity of the Documentary Record*, 65 Tex. L. Rev. 1 (1986); Laura Kalman, *Border Patrol: Reflections on the Turn to History in Legal*

Scholarship, 66 Fordham L. Rev. 87 (1997); Alfred H. Kelly, *Clio and the Court: An Illicit Love Affair*, 1965 Sup. Ct. Rev. 119; Larry Kramer, *Fidelity to History—and through It*, 65 Fordham L. Rev. 1627 (1997); Larry D. Kramer, *When Lawyers Do History*, 72 Geo. Wash. L. Rev. 387 (2003); Lawrence Lessig, *Fidelity and Constraint*, 65 Fordham L. Rev. 1365 (1997); Charles A. Lofgren, *The Original Understanding of Original Intent?*, 5 Const. Comment. 77 (1988); David McGowan, *Ethos in Law and History: Alexander Hamilton, The Federalist, and the Supreme Court*, 85 Minn. L. Rev. 755 (2001); Buckner F. Melton Jr., *Clio at the Bar: A Guide to Historical Method for Legists and Jurists*, 83 Minn. L. Rev. 377 (1998); Robert Post & Reva Siegel, *Originalism as a Political Practice: The Right's Living Constitution*, 75 Fordham L. Rev. 545 (2006); H. Jefferson Powell, *Rules for Originalists*, 73 Va. L. Rev. 659 (1987); H. Jefferson Powell, *The Original Understanding of Original Intent*, 98 Harv. L. Rev. 885 (1985); Jack N. Rakove, *Fidelity through History (or to It)*, 65 Fordham L. Rev. 1587 (1997); John Phillip Reid, *Law and History*, 27 Loy. L.A. L. Rev. 193 (1993); Neil M. Richards, *Clio and the Court: A Reassessment of the Supreme Court's Uses of History*, 13 J.L. & Pol. 809 (1997); Cass R. Sunstein, *The Idea of a Useable Past*, 95 Colum. L. Rev. 601 (1995); Mark Tushnet, *Heller and the New Originalism*, 69 Ohio St. L.J. 609 (2008); Mark Tushnet, *Interdisciplinary Legal Scholarship: The Case of History-in-Law*, 71 Chi.-Kent L. Rev. 909, 918 (1996); Mark Tushnet, *The Concept of Tradition in Constitutional Historiography*, 29 Wm. & Mary L. Rev. 93 (1987); G. Edward White, *The Arrival of History in Constitutional Scholarship*, 88 Va. L. Rev. 485 (2002); William M. Wiecek, *Clio as Hostage: The United States Supreme Court and the Uses of History*, 24 Cal. W. L. Rev. 227 (1988); Paul Horwitz, *The Past, Tense: The History of Crisis—and the Crisis of History—in Constitutional Theory*, 61 Alb. L. Rev. 459 (1997) (reviewing Kalman, The Strange Career of Legal Liberalism, *supra*); Joshua Stein, Note, *Historians before the Bench: Friends of the Court, Foes of Originalism*, 25 Yale J.L. & Human. 359 (2013).

2. The Twenty-First Amendment repealed the Eighteenth Amendment. The Twenty-Seventh Amendment, although sent to the states in 1789 with the rest of the Bill of Rights, was not ratified until 1992. *See* Bruce Ackerman, *The Living Constitution*, 120 Harv. L. Rev. 1737, 1737–41, 1750 (2010) (observing that one can hardly understand the constitutional legacy of the twentieth century and the enormous changes it produced from studying the text of the amendments passed during that period).

3. Justice Antonin Scalia's opinion in *District of Columbia v. Heller*, 554 U.S. 570 (2008), looked to mid- and late nineteenth-century sources to determine the public meaning of the Second Amendment in 1791. *See id.* at 606–19. One can—and should—criticize Justice Scalia for his anachronistic use of historical sources, but it is still anachronism in the service

of adoption history. *See* Akhil Reed Amar, Heller, HLR, *and Holistic Legal Reasoning*, 122 Harv. L. Rev. 145, 173–74 (2008) (criticizing Justice Scalia's opinion for anachronism).

4. *See, e.g.*, Akhil Reed Amar, America's Unwritten Constitution: The Precedents and Principles We Live By (2012); Logan Beirne, Blood of Tyrants: George Washington & the Forging of the Presidency (2013); Steven G. Calabresi & Christopher S. Yoo, The Unitary Executive: Presidential Power from Washington to Bush (2008); Saikrishna Prakash, *A Two-Front War*, 93 Cornell L. Rev. 197, 212 (2007) ("Consider the Washington Administration, the most crucial administration because it was closest in time to the Constitution's creation and because its views best reflect the Constitution's original meaning."); Saikrishna B. Prakash & Michael D. Ramsey, *The Executive Power over Foreign Affairs*, 111 Yale L.J. 231, 295–96 (2001) (using examples from the Washington administration to explain the Constitution's original meaning).

5. *See* Stephen M. Griffin, Long Wars and the Constitution (2013).

6. *See* Jack M. Balkin, *A Night in the Topics: The Reason of Legal Rhetoric and the Rhetoric of Legal Reason*, *in* Law's Stories: Narrative and Rhetoric in the Law 211, 221 (Peter Brooks & Paul Gewirtz eds., 1996) ("The study of topics [*topoi*] is the study of the commonplaces that bind together a practice of reasoned argument. It is the study of a shared social practice of argumentation and thus the study of a shared form of social life. Legal topics are shared tools of understanding that characterize legal practice.").

7. *See* Philip C. Bobbitt, Constitutional Interpretation 13 (1991); Philip C. Bobbitt, Constitutional Fate: Theory of the Constitution 26 (1982).

8. Bobbitt, Constitutional Fate, *supra* note 7, at 7–8; Bobbitt, Constitutional Interpretation, *supra* note 7, at 12–13.

9. Bobbitt, Constitutional Fate, *supra* note 7, at 9; Bobbitt, Constitutional Interpretation, *supra* note 7, at 13.

10. Bobbitt, Constitutional Fate, *supra* note 7, at 9 (defining "[h]istorical arguments" as those that "depend on a determination of the original understanding of the constitutional provision to be construed"); Bobbitt, Constitutional Interpretation, *supra* note 7, at 13 ("A[] historical modality may be attributed to constitutional arguments that claim that the framers and ratifiers [of a constitutional provision] intended, or did not intend . . ."; "Historical, or 'originalist' approaches to construing the text . . . are distinctive in their reference back to what a particular provision is thought to have meant to its ratifiers."). *See also* Richard H. Fallon Jr., *A Constructivist Coherence Theory of Constitutional Interpretation*, 100 Harv. L. Rev. 1189, 1244, 1254 (1987) (including in his list of standard arguments "[a]rguments of historical intent," which concern "the intent of the framers").

11. Jack M. Balkin, *Arguing about the Constitution: The Topics in Constitutional Interpretation*, 33 Const. Comm. 183–84 (2018); Jack M. Balkin, *The New Originalism and the Uses of History*, 82 Fordham L. Rev. 641, 660 (2013).

12. One reason that my list is more extensive than either Bobbitt's or Fallon's is that their accounts do not crisply distinguish between different theories of justification. For example, Bobbitt's category of "precedential" argument lumps together appeals to judicial doctrine—which gain particular authority from rule of law values—with arguments from political settlements, interbranch conventions, social customs, and cultural traditions, which rest on different kinds of justifications. Fallon offers a category of arguments from "theory," which, as he recognizes, comprehends a wide array of different and potentially incompatible justifications. Fallon, *A Constructivist Coherence Theory*, *supra* note 9, at 1200–02 (describing different types of arguments from constitutional theory); *cf. id.* at 1204–09 (describing a wide range of different kinds of philosophical theories that might generate arguments from value).

13. That is, they are standard rhetorical *topoi* (topics) used for constitutional reasoning in our constitutional culture. Balkin, *Arguing about the Constitution*, *supra* note 10, at 152, 180–81. Bobbitt argues that the modalities of argument are "the ways in which legal propositions are characterized as true from a constitutional point of view." Bobbitt, Constitutional Interpretation, *supra* note 7, at 12. *See also* Philip Bobbitt, *Reflections Inspired by My Critics*, 72 Tex. L. Rev. 1869, 1881 (1994) ("[T]the modalities are the grammar of the law."). I prefer to restate Bobbitt's idea in terms of styles of justification. Each form of argument gives people reasons to accept beliefs about the Constitution-in-practice as true. A modality of argument—for example, an argument from structure or from purpose—offers a distinctive way of claiming that an interpretation is valid and correct. Different modalities of argument offer lawyers different ways to show why people should accept or be guided by their interpretations of the law.

    Bobbitt and Fallon do not distinguish between interpretation and construction. *See* Lawrence B. Solum, *Originalism and Constitutional Construction*, 82 Fordham L. Rev. 453, 481 (2013) (explaining that a pluralist model of multiple modalities "collapses the interpretation-construction distinction"). But I believe that the idea of modalities of argument makes the most sense as a theory about constitutional construction. In *Living Originalism*, for example, I described Bobbitt's list of modalities as a set of tools that lawyers use in constitutional construction. Balkin, Living Originalism 17, 46, 89, 129, 205, 256–57, 333, 341–42 (2011) (explaining that interpreters should use all of the traditional modalities of constitutional argument); Jack M. Balkin, *Nine Perspectives on Living Originalism*, 2012 U. Ill. L. Rev. 815, 824 ("[L]awyers can and should use all of the traditional resources of lawyers both in ascertaining original meaning and in creating constitutional constructions that implement original meaning."). Lawyers might use some of the same tools to resolve ambiguities about original meaning when linguistic evidence runs out. *See* Solum, *supra*, at 481 (arguing that all of the modalities are relevant to constitutional construction and that historical, textual, and structural modalities are also especially relevant to constitutional interpretation).

14.   The idea that argument is structured in rhetorical topics goes back to Aristotle. Aristotle, On Rhetoric: A Theory of Civic Discourse 44–46 (George A. Kennedy trans., 2d ed. 2007); Balkin, *A Night in the Topics*, *supra* note 6. The modalities are what Aristotle would have called "special topics" connected to a particular discipline or science. Balkin, *Arguing about the Constitution*, *supra* note 11, at 170, 181–82.

15.   *See* Richard H. Fallon Jr., *The Many and Varied Roles of History in Constitutional Adjudication*, 90 Notre Dame L. Rev. 1753 (2015).

16.   Bowen v. Gilliard, 483 U.S. 587, 602 (1987); City of Cleburne v. Cleburne Living Ctr., 473 U.S. 432, 440–41 (1985); Frontiero v. Richardson, 411 U.S. 677, 686 (1973) (plurality opinion).

17.   *See, e.g.*, United States v. Stevens, 559 U.S. 460 (2010) (test of tradition for exclusions from First Amendment coverage); Washington v. Glucksberg, 521 U.S. 702 (1997) (test of tradition in substantive due process).

18.   Fallon, *The Many and Varied Roles of History*, *supra* note 15.

19.   Encyclopedia of Rhetoric and Composition: Communication from Ancient Times to the Information Age 223 (Theresa Enos ed., 1996) ("[E]nthymeme generally refers to claims in arguments that are supported by probable premises assumed to be shared by the audience."). Laura Kalman has noted how lawyers use history as an enthymeme and has criticized the ways that this leads to unreflective practice: "The enthymeme here seems designed to confer authority and be dispositive— to foreclose choice and surrender authority to the past. In the context of contemporary constitutional law, it may be a move from rhetorical to logical syllogism, and perhaps from rhetoric to authoritarianism. It replaces interpreter with author in a vain attempt to invest authority in author, rather than in interpreter, and to bypass persuasion and interpretation." Laura Kalman, *Border Patrol*, *supra* note 1, at 114.

20.   *See* Robert W. Gordon, *The Past as Authority and Social Critic: Stabilizing and Destabilizing Functions of History in Legal Argument*, *in* Taming the Past: Essays on Law in History and History in Law 282–316 (2017) (describing lawyers' opposing uses of history); Robert W. Gordon, *The Struggle over the Past*, 44 Clev. St. L. Rev. 123, 125 (1996) ("The critical modes [of historical argument] are used to destroy, or anyway to question, the authority of the past."); *see also* Deborah A. Widiss, Note, *Re-viewing History: The Use of the Past as Negative Precedent in* United States v. Virginia, 108 Yale L.J. 237, 238 (1998) ("Abandoned past prac-

tices can be used to argue, through a process of negative inference, against analogous modern practices. Equally important, negative precedent acknowledges the injuries caused by past practices that now seem unacceptable."); *cf.* Kim Lane Scheppele, *Aspirational and Aversive Constitutionalism: The Case for Studying Cross-Constitutional Influence through Negative Models*, 1 Int'l J. Const. L. 296, 300 (2003) ("Aversive constitutionalism . . . is backward-looking, proceeding from a critique of where past (or other) institutions and principles went badly wrong and taking such critiques as the negative building blocks of a new constitutional order.").

Chapter Three. How Modality Shapes History

1. 343 U.S. 579 (1952).
2. *Id.* at 641 (Jackson, J., concurring); *id.*
3. *Id.* at 650; *id.* at 651.
4. *Id.* at 651–52.
5. *Id.* at 652.
6. *Id.* at 634.
7. *See, e.g.,* Jack M. Balkin & Sanford Levinson, *Constitutional Dictatorship: Its Dangers and Its Design*, 94 Minn. L. Rev. 1789, 1798, 1800–02, 1844, 1863, 1865 (2009) (drawing structural lessons from the design of the Roman dictatorship).
8. Washington v. Glucksberg, 521 U.S. 702 (1997).
9. 561 U.S. 742 (2010).
10. 554 U.S. 570 (2008); *id.* at 635.
11. McDonald v. City of Chicago, 561 U.S. at 813 (Thomas, J., concurring).
12. *Id.* at 826–38. In general, Justice Thomas describes himself as an original meaning originalist, but his account of original meaning is thick rather than thin, because he often treats original expected applications as part of original meaning. *See, e.g.,* Morse v. Frederick, 551 U.S. 393, 410–11 (2007) (Thomas, J., concurring) ("In my view, the history of public education suggests that the First Amendment, as originally understood, does not protect student speech in public schools."); McIntyre v. Ohio Elections Comm'n, 514 U.S. 334, 358–59 (1995) (Thomas, J., concurring) ("We should seek the original understanding when we interpret the Speech and Press Clauses, just as we do when we read the Religion Clauses of the First Amendment.").
13. *McDonald*, 561 U.S. at 770–78 (plurality opinion).
14. *Id.* at 767.
15. *Id.*
16. *Id.* (citing Duncan v. Louisiana, 391 U.S. 145, 149 (1968)); *id.* (quoting Washington v. Glucksberg, 521 U.S. 702, 721 (1997)).
17. *Id.* at 791.

18. *Id.* at 767–78.

19. *Id.* at 773 (noting that the thirty-ninth Congress's "efforts to safeguard the right to keep and bear arms demonstrate that the right was still recognized to be fundamental"); *id.* at 775 ("In debating the Fourteenth Amendment, the 39th Congress referred to the right to keep and bear arms as a fundamental right deserving of protection.").

20. As Randy Barnett shows, when Justice Alito briefly mentions the views of framers like John Bingham and Jacob Howard about the purposes of the Fourteenth Amendment, he states that they believed that the Fourteenth Amendment as a whole, rather than the Privileges or Immunities Clause, protected the right to bear arms. Randy E. Barnett, *The Gravitational Force of Originalism*, 82 Fordham L. Rev. 411, 427 (2013) (accusing the plurality of "bowdlerizing its sources to read that the right to bear arms was protected by the original meaning of the Fourteenth Amendment as a whole, rather than by the Privileges or Immunities Clause in particular"); *see also McDonald*, 561 U.S. at 3033 n.9.

21. *Cf.* Gerard N. Magliocca, *Why Did the Incorporation of the Bill of Rights Fail in the Late Nineteenth Century?*, 94 Minn. L. Rev. 102, 124 (2009) ("[E]nthusiasm for extending the substantive protections of the Bill of Rights to the states evaporated during the 1890s because of the sharp increase in agrarian radicalism and labor protests."); *see* David B. Kopel & Clayton Cramer, *State Court Standards of Review for the Right to Keep and Bear Arms*, 50 Santa Clara L. Rev. 1113, 1157 (2010) ("In the twentieth century, gun control ceased to be a peculiar Southern institution. Fear of labor unrest and massive waves of immigrants, as well as the emigration of Southern blacks, brought gun control north. Many gun control laws were upheld, and many others were not even constitutionally questioned." (footnote omitted)); *see, e.g.*, Reva B. Siegel, *Dead or Alive: Originalism as Popular Constitutionalism in* Heller, 122 Harv. L. Rev. 191, 207–12 (2008) (noting that the modern movement for gun rights began in the 1970s).

22. *McDonald*, 561 U.S. at 812 (Thomas, J., concurring) ("This Court's substantive due process framework fails to account for both the text of the Fourteenth Amendment and the history that led to its adoption."); Slaughter-House Cases, 83 U.S. (16 Wall.) 36 (1872); United States v. Cruikshank, 92 U.S. 542 (1875); *McDonald*, 561 U.S. at 808–13.

23. *McDonald*, 561 U.S. at 811 ("The notion that a constitutional provision that guarantees only 'process' before a person is deprived of life, liberty, or property could define the substance of those rights strains credulity for even the most casual user of words.").

24. *Id.* at 812.

25. *Id.* at 758 (plurality opinion).

26. *Id.*

Chapter Four. Arguments from National Ethos, Political Tradition, and Honored Authority

1. *See* Philip C. Bobbitt, Constitutional Interpretation 20 (1991) ("This form of argument denotes an appeal to those elements of the American cultural ethos that are reflected in the [U.S.] Constitution.").

2. *Id.*

3. *Id.*; *see also* Philip C. Bobbitt, Constitutional Fate: Theory of the Constitution 162 (1982) ("Ethical arguments arise from the ethos of limited government and the seam where powers end and rights begin.").

4. Philip Bobbitt, *Reflections Inspired by My Critics*, 72 Tex. L. Rev. 1869, 1937 (1994) ("I do not in fact think that the commitment to limited government is the only ethical commitment of the Constitution."). His original formula was probably influenced by the context in which *Constitutional Fate* was written: Bobbitt used ethical argument to demonstrate the right to abortion recognized in *Roe v. Wade*. *See* Bobbitt, Constitutional Fate, *supra* note 3, at 225–38 (arguing that the result in *Roe* follows from the ethical principle that a government of limited powers may not coerce intimate acts, which include carrying a child within one's body and giving birth).

5. Bobbitt, Constitutional Fate, *supra* note 3, at 144.

6. *See* Akhil Reed Amar, America's Constitution: A Biography 45–50, 106–10 (2005) (arguing that the Constitution and its enumerated powers flowed from geostrategic imperatives for a stronger centralized government with ample powers to protect liberty and security); Max M. Edling, A Revolution in Favor of Government: Origins of the U.S. Constitution and the Making of the American State (2003); Ray Raphael, Constitutional Myths: What We Get Wrong and How to Get It Right 114–23 (2013).

7. 142 S. Ct. 2228 (2022); *id.* at 2253–56.

8. *Id.* at 2276 ("[T]his Court is ill-equipped to assess 'generalized assertions about the national psyche.' . . . [O]ur cases . . . instead emphasize very concrete reliance interests, like those that develop in 'cases involving property and contract rights.'")

9. 274 U.S. 357 (1927).

10. *Id.* at 373–74 (Brandeis, J., concurring).

11. *Id.* at 375.

12. *Id.* at 377.

13. *Cf.* Poe v. Ullman, 367 U.S. 497, 542 (1961) (Harlan, J., dissenting) ("The balance of which I speak is the balance struck by this country, having regard to what history teaches are the traditions from which it developed as well as the traditions from which it broke. That tradition is a living thing.").

14. *See* James Morton Smith, Freedom's Fetters: The Alien and Sedition Laws and American Civil Liberties (1956) (describing the Federalist campaign for the Alien and Sedition Acts and their subsequent enforcement by Federalist judges).

15. *See* Whitney v. California, 274 U.S. 357, 375 n.2 (1927) (quoting Letter from Thomas Jefferson to Elijah Boardman (July 3, 1801), and Thomas Jefferson, First Inaugural Address (Mar. 4, 1801)).

16. *See, e.g.*, Michael P. Downey, Note, *The Jeffersonian Myth in Supreme Court Sedition Jurisprudence*, 76 Wash. U. L.Q. 683, 684 (1998) ("Jefferson's myth has enshrined him as a great advocate of individual liberties, but [in] reality [Jefferson] seems to have been a more pragmatic, and consequently a more repressive, figure" (footnote omitted).).

17. *Id.* at 696; Letter from Thomas Jefferson to Abigail Adams, Sept. 11, 1804, The Founders Online, https://founders.archives.gov/?q=abigail%20adams%20Author%3A%22Jefferson%2C%20Thomas%22%20Recipient%3A%22Adams%2C%20Abigail%22&s=1111311111&r=41 [https://perma.cc/RS8P-XVKW] ("[W]hile we deny that Congress have a right to controul the freedom of the press, we have ever asserted the right of the states, and their exclusive right, to do so.")

18. *See* Alfred H. Kelly, *Clio and the Court: An Illicit Love Affair*, 1965 Sup. Ct. Rev. 119, 131 n.50 (criticizing Justice Brandeis's opinion as "a prime example of history by a combination of essay, fiat, and revelation").

19. *See, e.g.*, Gitlow v. New York, 268 U.S. 652, 666–68 (1925) (rejecting First Amendment claims); Schenck v. United States, 249 U.S. 47, 52 (1919); Abrams v. United States, 250 U.S. 616, 628 (1919) (Holmes, J., dissenting). In *Whitney* itself, the Court upheld Charlotte Anita Whitney's conviction under California's Criminal Syndicalism Act for being a member of the Communist Labor Party. *Whitney*, 274 U.S. at 366–71. Despite Justice Brandeis's famous argument for free speech rights, his opinion actually concurred in upholding Whitney's criminal conviction because he believed that Whitney did not properly raise her federal constitutional objections in the lower courts. *Whitney*, 274 U.S. at 380 (Brandeis, J., concurring).

20. Jack M. Balkin, Constitutional Redemption: Political Faith in an Unjust World 44, 55–56 (2011) ("An appeal to the past [by social movements] . . . is a way of convincing others that we should be true to a larger set of common commitments to liberty, equality, and justice that we have compromised or forgotten.").

21. *Id.* at 44 ("Members of the political community [use narrative arguments] in order to make sense of current controversies and the proper direction of political/legal change."); Reva B. Siegel, *Text in Contest: Gender and the Constitution from a Social Movement Perspective*, 150 U. Pa. L. Rev. 297, 342–43 (2001) (arguing that history supplies both a sense of collective identity and "the field of collective experience through which we make

pragmatic judgments about how to realize constitutional commitments and values in practice").

22. *See* Balkin, Constitutional Redemption, *supra* note 20, at 25–32, 51–60 (explaining and defending the practice of narrative justification); Akhil Reed Amar, *The Supreme Court 1999 Term: Foreword: The Document and the Doctrine*, 114 Harv L. Rev. 26, 29 (2000) (arguing that done properly, textual argument requires understanding the meaning of key events in U.S. history and that "good historical narrative, in both a broad (epic-events) sense and a narrow (drafting/ratification) sense, should inform good textual analysis").

23. *Cf.* Gordon S. Wood, *No Thanks for the Memories*, N.Y. Rev. Books, Jan. 13, 2011, at 40, *available at* http://www.nybooks.com/articles/archives /2011/jan/13/no-thanks-memories/ [https://perma.cc/Z4WR-C8DU] (reviewing Jill Lepore, The Whites of Their Eyes: The Tea Party's Revolution and the Battle over American History (2010)) (explaining that social mobilizations like the Tea Party find it important to articulate the normative lessons of history, even if such groups inevitably understand history in simplified ways, and remarking that "[m]emory is as important to our society as the history written by academics").

24. Leonard Levy, Legacy of Suppression: Freedom of Speech and Press in Early American History (1960). Levy subsequently revised his views but retained his view that the framers did not intend to protect seditious libel under the First Amendment. Leonard W. Levy, Emergence of a Free Press (1985).

25. *See, e.g.*, David A. Anderson, *Levy vs. Levy*, 84 Mich. L. Rev. 777 (1986); David M. Rabban, *The Ahistorical Historian: Leonard Levy on Freedom of Expression in Early American History*, 37 Stan. L. Rev. 795 (1985); David Anderson, *The Origins of the Press Clause*, 30 UCLA L. Rev. 455 (1983).

26. 576 U.S. 644 (2015).

27. *Id.* at 671 ("If rights were defined by who exercised them in the past, then received practices could serve as their own continued justification and new groups could not invoke rights once denied. This Court has rejected that approach, both with respect to the right to marry and the rights of gays and lesbians.")

28. *Id.* at 665 ("[I]n assessing whether the force and rationale of its cases apply to same-sex couples, the Court must respect the basic reasons why the right to marry has been long protected. . . . [T]he reasons marriage is fundamental under the Constitution apply with equal force to same-sex couples.")

29. *Id.* at 664 ("The nature of injustice is that we may not always see it in our own times. The generations that wrote and ratified the Bill of Rights and the Fourteenth Amendment did not presume to know the extent of freedom in all of its dimensions, and so they entrusted to future generations a charter protecting the right of all persons to enjoy liberty as we learn its meaning.")

30. *Dobbs*, 142 S. Ct. at 2248–49.
31. *Id.* at 2252–54.
32. *See* Reva B. Siegel, *Memory Games:* Dobbs's *Originalism as Anti-Democratic Living Constitutionalism—and Some Pathways for Resistance*, 101 Tex. L. Rev. 1127, 1183, 1187–93 (2023) (explaining that despite the nineteenth-century crusade to criminalize abortion, grounded in nativist replacement arguments and anxiety about gender roles, the public continued to believe that quickening was the appropriate line for criminalization of abortion).
33. *See* Marc O. DeGirolami, *Traditionalism Rising*, J. Contemp. Legal Issues (forthcoming) (available on SSRN, https://papers.ssrn.com/sol3/papers .cfm?abstract_id=4205351) (arguing for a specific approach to tradition called "traditionalism," which does not involve abstract principles or common-law decision-making but rather looks for relatively concrete local practices widely adopted and existing for long periods of time); *id.* at *13 ("Traditionalism in *Dobbs* was fatal to the claim that the Constitution includes a right to abortion, and it seems plain after *Dobbs* that traditionalism will be the Court's methodological choice for discerning any new, substantive claims of "liberty" protected by due process.").
34. Siegel, *Memory Games, supra* note 32, at 56–67.
35. 142 S. Ct. 2111 (2022).
36. *Id.* at 2126, 2130, 2138.
37. *Id.* at 2118, 2132–33.
38. *Id.* at 2122; *id.* at 2169 (Breyer, J., dissenting)
39. *See* David Leeming, The Oxford Companion to World Mythology 88 (2005) (noting that often the culture hero "establishes the community's institutions and traditions").
40. Michael Dorf calls this style of argument "heroic originalism." Michael C. Dorf, *Integrating Normative and Descriptive Constitutional Theory: The Case of Original Meaning*, 85 Geo. L.J. 1765, 1803 (1997). The idea of honored authorities, however, applies beyond adoption history. *See id.* at 1811 ("If we appeal to the Framers because we believe that their unusual place in history as well as their wisdom make their views especially authoritative, should we not also consult the views of other historically well-situated, wise actors?").
41. *Cf.* Amos Tversky & Daniel Kahneman, *Judgment under Uncertainty: Heuristics and Biases*, *in* Judgment under Uncertainty: Heuristics and Biases 3, 4–14 (Daniel Kahneman et al. eds., 1982); Amos Tversky & Daniel Kahneman, *Availability: A Heuristic for Judging Frequency and Probability*, *in* Judgment under Uncertainty, *supra*, at 163–65 (noting heuristics that confuse salience with representativeness).
42. *See* Raphael, Constitutional Myths, *supra* note 6, at 94–101 (describing Madison's evolution from the Philadelphia Convention, in which he argued for the power of the federal government to veto all state legisla-

tion, to the Virginia Resolution of 1798, in which Madison argued for the power of state interposition).

43. *See* Akhil Reed Amar, America's Unwritten Constitution: The Precedents and Principles We Live By 313–14 (2012).

44. Balkin, Constitutional Redemption, *supra* note 20, at 17, 26, 31 (describing narrative justification's use of transgenerational "we" in constitutional argument).

45. Sacvan Bercovitch, The American Jeremiad 7 (1978) (contrasting the European jeremiad, with its "lament over the ways of the world" and the sins of the people, with the American jeremiad, which featured a call for action and renewal); Jack M. Balkin, *The Distribution of Political Faith*, 71 Md. L. Rev. 1144, 1152–54 (2012) (noting the use of the jeremiad in constitutional and political argument and identifying the argument of *Constitutional Redemption* with "the jeremiad of renewal"); Timothy P. O'Neill, *Constitutional Argument as Jeremiad*, 45 Val. U. L. Rev. 33, 40–41 (2010) (arguing that American "constitutional argument has absorbed th[e] structure of the American jeremiad").

46. Balkin, Constitutional Redemption, *supra* note 20, at 53–60 (describing processes of selective identification and disidentification in constitutional narratives and arguments).

47. *Id.* at 59 ("The stories through which we understand ourselves as part of We the People create a narrative economy of who 'we' are in the story and who 'they' are, who we are rooting for and who we are rooting against, who had wisdom and justice on their side and who made mistakes (or worse).").

48. Vasan Kesavan & Michael Stokes Paulsen, *The Interpretive Force of the Constitution's Secret Drafting History*, 91 Geo. L.J. 1113, 1152 (2003) ("The Federalists won, whereas the Anti-Federalists did not.").

49. Lochner v. New York, 198 U.S. 45 (1905); Dred Scott v. Sandford, 60 U.S. (19 How.) 393 (1856); Plessy v. Ferguson, 163 U.S. 537 (1896); Korematsu v. United States, 323 U.S. 214 (1944).

50. *See, e.g.,* Balkin, Constitutional Redemption, *supra* note 20, at 188 (describing use of canonical and anticanonical cases to bestow and withhold authority); John Hart Ely, *The Wages of Crying Wolf: A Comment on* Roe v. Wade, 82 Yale L.J. 920, 939–40, 944 (1973) (coining the term "Lochnering" and comparing *Roe* to *Lochner*).

51. 347 U.S. 483 (1954).

52. 551 U.S. 701 (2007) (plurality opinion).

53. *See* Mark Tushnet, Parents Involved *and the Struggle for Historical Memory*, 91 Ind. L.J. 493, 494 (2016); Reva B. Siegel, Heller *& Originalism's Dead Hand—In Theory and Practice*, 56 UCLA L. Rev. 1399, 1422–24 (2009). In fact, the only reference to the Reconstruction Amendments came from the dissenting opinion by Justice Stephen Breyer. *Parents Involved*, 551 U.S. at 829 (Breyer, J., dissenting) ("[A] well-established legal view of the Fourteenth Amendment . . . understands the basic objective

of those who wrote the Equal Protection Clause as forbidding practices that lead to racial exclusion. The Amendment sought to bring into American society as full members those whom the Nation had previously held in slavery.").

54. Even the way that the issue is phrased by the plurality and the dissent reflects contrasting interpretations of *Brown*. The plurality, understanding *Brown* as about colorblindness, sees the issue as "whether a public school that had not operated legally segregated schools or has been found to be unitary may choose to classify students by race and rely upon that classification in making school assignments." *Parents Involved*, 551 U.S. at 711. The dissent, by contrast, explains, "These cases consider the longstanding efforts of two local school boards to integrate their public schools . . . [and] to bring about the kind of racially integrated education that *Brown v. Board of Education* . . . long ago promised—efforts that this Court has repeatedly required, permitted, and encouraged local authorities to undertake." *Id.* at 803 (Breyer, J., dissenting).

55. *Id.* at 746 (plurality opinion) ("[W]hen it comes to using race to assign children to schools, history will be heard."); *id.* at 747 (quoting the argument of attorney Robert Carter in *Brown* that "[w]e have one fundamental contention, . . . that no State has any authority under the equal-protection clause of the Fourteenth Amendment to use race as a factor in affording educational opportunities among its citizens"); *id.* ("Before *Brown*, schoolchildren were told where they could and could not go to school based on the color of their skin. The school districts in these cases have not carried the heavy burden of demonstrating that we should allow this once again—even for very different reasons.").

56. *Id.* at 772 (Thomas, J., concurring) ("[M]y view was the rallying cry for the lawyers who litigated *Brown*."); *id.* at 778 ("What was wrong in 1954 cannot be right today.").

57. *Id.* at 773–79 (comparing the dissent to *Plessy* and noting "similarities between the dissent's arguments and the segregationists' arguments"); *id.* at 778 n.27 ("The segregationists in *Brown* [also] argued that their racial classifications were benign, not invidious."); *id.* ("It is the height of arrogance for Members of this Court to assert blindly that their motives are better than others.").

58. *Id.* at 867 (Breyer, J., dissenting) ("The lesson of history . . . is not that efforts to continue racial segregation are constitutionally indistinguishable from efforts to achieve racial integration. Indeed, it is a cruel distortion of history to compare Topeka, Kansas, in the 1950's to Louisville and Seattle in the modern day."); *id.* at 799 (Stevens, J., dissenting) ("The Chief Justice rewrites the history of one of this Court's most important decisions."); *id.* at 803 ("The Court has changed significantly since it decided *School Comm[ittee] of Boston [v. Board of Education*, 389 U.S. 572 (1968)] in 1968. It was then more faithful to *Brown* and more respectful

of our precedent than it is today. It is my firm conviction that no Member of the Court that I joined in 1975 would have agreed with today's decision.").

59. *See* Christopher W. Schmidt, Brown *and the Colorblind Constitution*, 94 Cornell L. Rev. 203 (2008) (discussing the controversy over the uses of *Brown* in *Parents Involved* and the ways that colorblindness was invoked in the *Brown* litigation). See also the contrasting accounts of constitutional memory in Students For Fair Admissions, Inc. v. President and Fellows of Harvard College, 143 S. Ct. 2141 (2023), which held race-conscious affirmative action programs unconstitutional. In *SFFA*, Justice Thomas finally made an unconvincing attempt to demonstrate that the framers and ratifiers of the Fourteenth Amendment sought a colorblind Constitution, and that the original meaning of the Fourteenth Amendment in 1868 required colorblindness, despite abundant historical evidence to the contrary.

60. *Compare Parents Involved*, 551 U.S. at 746–47 (plurality opinion) (declaring that *Brown* is about prohibiting differential treatment of students because of their race), *and id.* at 772 (Thomas, J., concurring) (arguing that *Brown* supports the view of a colorblind Constitution), *with id.* at 803, 804 (Breyer, J., dissenting) (arguing that *Brown* is about the achievement of an integrated society and "set[ting] the Nation on a path toward public school integration"). Justice Kennedy's concurrence also argues that *Brown* reflects a national commitment to an integrated society. *See id.* at 797 (Kennedy, J., concurring in part and concurring in the judgment) ("This Nation has a moral and ethical obligation to fulfill its historic commitment to creating an integrated society that ensures equal opportunity for all of its children.").

61. *Cf.* Joshua Stein, Note, *Historians before the Bench: Friends of the Court, Foes of Originalism*, 25 Yale J.L. & Human. 359, 380–82 (2013) (arguing that a primary task of historians should be to destabilize and complicate historical narratives used to support normative conclusions).

62. Coral Ridge Ministries Media, Inc. v. Southern Poverty Law Center, 142 S. Ct. 2453 (2022) (Thomas, J., dissenting from denial of certiorari); Berisha v. Lawson, 141 S. Ct. 2424 (2021) (Thomas, J., dissenting from denial of certiorari); McKee v. Cosby, 139 S. Ct. 675 (2019) (Thomas, J., concurring in denial of certiorari); *see also* Berisha v. Lawson, 141 S. Ct. 2425 (Gorsuch, J., dissenting from denial of certiorari).

63. See the discussion in chapter 12.

Chapter Five. Twins Separated at Birth

1. Oral argument transcript, Schwarzenegger v. Entertainment Merchants Association, No. 08-1448, Nov. 2, 2010, at 17, http://www.supremecourt.gov/oral_arguments/argument_transcripts/08-1448.pdf [https://perma.cc/WLB7-QCR6].

2. Thomas B. Colby & Peter J. Smith, *Living Originalism*, 59 Duke L.J. 239, 244 (2009) (noting "profound internal disagreement" within originalism, which has become "a smorgasbord of distinct constitutional theories that share little in common except a misleading reliance on a single label").

3. Ray Raphael, Constitutional Myths: What We Get Wrong and How to Get It Right (2013); Max M. Edling, A Revolution in Favor of Government: Origins of the U.S. Constitution and the Making of the American State (2008); Akhil Reed Amar, America's Constitution: A Biography (2005).

4. *See* Lawrence B. Solum, *Originalism versus Living Constitutionalism: The Conceptual Structure of the Great Debate*, 113 Nw. U. L. Rev. 1243, 1291 (2019) (noting "the conceptual mismatch between academic and judicial originalism").

5. Lawrence B. Solum, *Originalism and Constitutional Construction*, 82 Fordham L. Rev. 453, 459 (2013).

6. As Justice Scalia explained in *District of Columbia v. Heller*, 554 U.S. 570, 576–77 (2008), "In interpreting this text, we are guided by the principle that '[t]he Constitution was written to be understood by the voters; its words and phrases were used in their normal and ordinary as distinguished from technical meaning.' . . . Normal meaning may of course include an idiomatic meaning, but it excludes secret or technical meanings that would not have been known to ordinary citizens in the founding generation."

7. John O. McGinnis & Michael B. Rappaport, *The Constitution and the Language of the Law*, 59 Wm. & Mary L. Rev. 1321, 1327–28 (2018) ("[T]he language of the law often provides a more precise answer when ordinary language would not provide a clear one. . . . [M]uch of the best modern originalist scholarship is inconsistent with an ordinary language reading of the Constitution.").

8. Thomas B. Colby, Originalism and Structural Argument, 113 Nw. U. L. Rev. 1297 (2019).

9. Kevin Tobia, *The Corpus and the Courts*, U. Chi. L. Rev. Online 1 (2021); Thomas R. Lee & Stephen C. Mouritsen, *The Corpus and the Critics*, 88 U. Chi. L. Rev. (2021); James C. Phillips, Daniel M. Ortner & Thomas R. Lee, *Corpus Linguistics & Original Public Meaning: A New Tool to Make Originalism More Empirical*, 126 Yale L.J. F. 21, 24–27 (2016).

10. *See* Kevin P. Tobia, *Testing Ordinary Meaning*, 134 Harv. L. Rev. 726, 791 (2020) ("Verdicts from dictionaries were more strongly correlated with a term's extensivist uses than its prototypical ones. And verdicts from legal corpus linguistics were more strongly correlated with a term's prototypical uses than its extensivist ones."); *id.* at 794 ("Because legal corpus linguistics reflects the pragmatics of language *use*, there are a number of uses that are entirely consistent with ordinary meaning that nevertheless *should not* appear frequently in the corpus.") (emphasis in original);

Shlomo Klapper, *(Mis)judging Ordinary Meaning? Corpus Linguistics, the Frequency Fallacy, and the Extension-Abstraction Distinction in "Ordinary Meaning" Textualism*, 8 Br. J. Am. Leg. Studies 327, 361 (2019) ("if one is an epistemological skeptic, and believes that there is no way to recreate what Chomsky calls 'competence' from 'performance,' given that ordinary meaning is 'competence' (i.e. what a native speaker would comfortably use to describe a set of facts), then, indeed, this approach falls prey to the frequency fallacy, since every reliance on frequency is ipso facto a fallacy."); Lawrence M. Solan, *Can Corpus Linguistics Help Make Originalism Scientific?*, 126 Yale L.J. F. 57, 61 (2016) ("Assume that the corpus reveals that the phrase 'bear arms' was more often than not used in military contexts, but was not restricted to military contexts. What then? Should the interpreter prefer the phrase's narrower, ordinary meaning and limit the Second Amendment's protections to the military context? Should the interpreter prefer the phrase's broader meaning and extend Second Amendment protections to the home? The corpus does not help resolve this interpretive dilemma."). *See also* Stanley Fish, *The Interpretive Poverty of Data*, Balkinization (Mar. 2, 2018), https://balkin.blogspot .com/2018/03/the-interpretive-poverty-of-data.html [https://perma.cc /DZ93-3ZE8] ("Once you detach patterns from the intentional context in which they have significance, you can't get the significance back."); Ethan J. Herenstein, *The Faulty Frequency Hypothesis: Difficulties in Operationalizing Ordinary Meaning through Corpus Linguistics*, 70 Stan. L. Rev. Online 112, 117 (2017) ("[A] word might be invoked more frequently in one sense than another for reasons that have little to do with the common understanding of that word. More specifically, the frequency with which a word carries a particular meaning will, at least partly, reflect the prevalence or newsworthiness of the underlying phenomenon that it denotes.").

11.   Josh Jones, *Comment: The "Weaponization" of Corpus Linguistics: Testing Heller's Linguistic Claims*, 34 BYU J. Pub. L. 135, 136 (2020); Neal Goldfarb, *Corpora and the Second Amendment*, Lawnlinguistics, https://lawn linguistics.com/corpora-and-the-second-amendment/ [https://perma.cc /M32T-B63G] (last updated Aug. 8, 2018) (listing all Goldfarb's blog posts on the subject); Josh Blackman & James C. Phillips, *Corpus Linguistics and the Second Amendment*, Harv. L. Rev. Blog (Aug. 7, 2018), https://blog.harvardlawreview.org/corpus-linguistics-and-the-second -amendment/ [https://perma.cc/D6L9-FARZ]; Allison L. LaCroix, *Historical Semantics and the Meaning of the Second Amendment*, Panorama (Aug. 3, 2018), http://thepanorama.shear.org/2018/08/03/historical-semantics -and-the-meaning-of-the-second-amendment/ [https://perma.cc/LA4M -HVMA]; Dennis Baron, *Antonin Scalia Was Wrong about the Meaning of "Bear Arms,"* Wash. Post (May 21, 2018), https://www.washingtonpost .com/opinions/antonin-scalia-was-wrong-about-the-meaning-of-bear

-arms/2018/05/21/9243ac66-5d11-11e8-b2b8-08a538d9dbd6_story
.html [https://perma.cc/VBU5-ZVNP].

12. William Baude & Stephen E. Sachs, *Grounding Originalism*, 113 Nw. U. L. Rev. 1455, 1457 (2019); Stephen E. Sachs, *Originalism as a Theory of Legal Change*, 38 Harv. J.L. & Pub. Pol'y 817, 838 (2015); William Baude, *Is Originalism Our Law?*, 115 Colum. L. Rev. 2349 (2015).

13. Sachs, *Originalism as a Theory of Legal Change*, *supra* note 12, at 858–64.

14. *Id.* at 838, 851, 874, 881.

15. Stephen E. Sachs, *Originalism without Text*, 127 Yale L.J. 156 (2017).

16. Sachs, *Originalism as a Theory of Legal Change*, *supra* note 12, at 855 ("The range of potentially lawful changes since the Founding may be even broader than most originalists are used to. . . . [T]he rules of change— and the sorts of lawful changes that have been made—depend on history, not constitutional theory, and could upend some conventional views of originalism.").

17. Cass R. Sunstein, *Originalism*, 93 Notre Dame L. Rev. 1671, 1672 (2018) (arguing that originalism makes the most sense when "there is nowhere else to turn with respect to interpretation of the constitutional text, in the sense that other legally relevant materials are absent," and the answers it gives are "good enough, and it is far from clear that judges or other interpreters can improve on it").

18. *See, e.g.*, Tull v. United States, 481 U.S. 412, 417–18 (1987) (explaining that in deciding whether the Seventh Amendment jury trial right applies, "First, we compare the statutory action to 18th-century actions brought in the courts of England prior to the merger of the courts of law and equity. Second, we examine the remedy sought and determine whether it is legal or equitable in nature.").

19. Sanford Levinson, *The Limited Relevance of Originalism in the Actual Performance of Legal Roles*, 19 Harv. J.L. Pub. Pol'y 495 (1996). On the challenges for originalism in the lower courts, *see* Ryan C. Williams, *Lower Court Originalism*, 45 Harv. J.L. Pub. Pol'y 257 (2022); Josh Blackman, *Originalism and Stare Decisis in the Lower Courts*, 13 NYU J.L. & Liberty 44 (2019).

20. *See, e.g.*, *Tull*, 481 U.S. at 417–18.

21. On the Warren Court's uses of originalism, *see* Frank B. Cross, The Failed Promise of Originalism 136–43 (2013); Frank B. Cross, *Originalism— The Forgotten Years*, 28 Const. Comm. 37 (2012); Alfred H. Kelly, *Clio and the Court: An Illicit Love Affair*, 1965 Sup. Ct. Rev. 119.

22. *E.g.*, Frederick Douglass, *What to the Slave Is the Fourth of July? An Address Delivered in Rochester, New York, on 5 July 1852*, *in* 2 The Frederick Douglass Papers 359 (J. Blassingame ed., 1985).

23. *See* Reva B. Siegel, *Text in Contest: Gender and the Constitution from a Social Movement Perspective*, 150 U. Pa. L. Rev. 297, 337 (2001) ("As they constructed constitutional arguments to contest the justice of women's

disfranchisement, suffragists repeatedly invoked the memory of the American Revolution.").

24. Philip S. Gorski & Samuel L. Perry, The Flag and the Cross: White Christian Nationalism and the Threat to American Democracy 83–84 (2022); Philip Gorski, American Covenant: A History of Civil Religion from the Puritans to the Present 203 (2019); Steven K. Green, Inventing a Christian America: The Myth of the Religious Founding 215 (2017).

25. Jack M. Balkin, Living Originalism 277 (2011).

26. *Id.* at 278.

27. *See, e.g.,* Obergefell v. Hodges, 576 U.S. 644, 671 (2015) ("[R]ights come not from ancient sources alone. They rise, too, from a better informed understanding of how constitutional imperatives define a liberty that remains urgent in our own era."); Harper v. Virginia Bd. of Elections, 383 U.S. 663, 669 (1966) ("In determining what lines are unconstitutionally discriminatory, we have never been confined to historic notions of equality, any more than we have restricted due process to a fixed catalogue of what was at a given time deemed to be the limits of fundamental rights. . . . Notions of what constitutes equal treatment for purposes of the Equal Protection Clause do change."); Brown v. Board of Education, 347 U.S. 483, 492 (1954) ("In approaching this problem, we cannot turn the clock back to 1868 when the Amendment was adopted, or even to 1896 when *Plessy v. Ferguson* was written.").

28. Solum, *Originalism versus Living Constitutionalism, supra* note 4, at 1271–76 (listing a variety of different versions of living constitutionalism, including moral readings, constitutional pluralism, representation reinforcement, and common-law constitutionalism).

29. Michael Kammen, A Machine That Would Go of Itself: The Constitution in American Culture 17, 62 (1986). For a critique of this widely accepted view, *see* Note, *Organic and Mechanical Metaphors in Late Eighteenth-Century American Political Thought,* 110 Harv. L. Rev. 1832 (1997).

30. Jonathan Gienapp, The Second Creation: Fixing the American Constitution in the Founding Era 34 (2018) ("The British constitution was fixed and constant, yet because it was inherently customary and discoverable through usage and acquiescence, it was perpetually changing."); McCulloch v. Maryland, 17 U.S. (4 Wheat.) 316, 415 (1819) ("This provision is made in a constitution, intended to endure for ages to come, and consequently, to be adapted to the various *crises* of human affairs.").

31. Woodrow Wilson, Constitutional Government in the United States 56–57 (1908) ("[G]overnment is not a machine, but a living thing. It falls, not under the theory of the universe, but under the theory of organic life. It is accountable to Darwin, not to Newton."); Howard Gillman, *The Collapse of Constitutional Originalism and the Rise of the Notion of the "Living Constitution" in the Course of American State-Building,* 11 Stud. Am. Pol. Dev. 191, 192–93 (1997); Morton J. Horwitz, *The Supreme Court*

1992 Term—Foreword: The Constitution of Change Legal Fundamentality without Fundamentalism, 107 Harv. L. Rev. 30, 51–56 (1993).

32. Zachary Elkins, Tom Ginsburg & James Melton, The Endurance of National Constitutions 129 (2009).

33. The Federalist 49 (Madison) (arguing against regularly creating new constitutions because "frequent appeals would, in a great measure, deprive the government of that veneration which time bestows on every thing, and without which perhaps the wisest and freest governments would not possess the requisite stability").

34. Sanford Levinson & Jack M. Balkin, Democracy and Dysfunction (2019); Sanford Levinson, Framed: America's 51 Constitutions and the Crisis of Governance (2012).

35. Jack M. Balkin, The Cycles of Constitutional Time (2020); Jack M. Balkin *How to Do Constitutional Theory While Your House Burns Down*, 101 B.U. L. Rev. 1723 (2021) .

36. *See* Balkin, The Cycles of Constitutional Time, *supra* note 35.

37. *See* Levinson & Balkin, Democracy and Dysfunction, *supra* note 34.

38. Sanford Levinson & J. M. Balkin, *Law, Music, and Other Performing Arts*, 139 U. Pa. L. Rev. 1597, 1629–39 (1991).

39. *Id.* at 1637–40.

40. *E.g.*, Randy E. Barnett, Restoring the Lost Constitution: The Presumption of Liberty (rev. ed. 2014); Myron Magnet, Clarence Thomas and the Lost Constitution (2019); *see* Jamal Greene, *Fourteenth Amendment Originalism*, 71 Md. L. Rev. 978, 998 (2012) (noting the connection between originalism and narratives of restoration).

41. *See* Erwin Chemerinsky, Worse than Nothing: The Dangerous Fallacy of Originalism 139 (2022) ("[O]riginalists often abandon the method when it fails to give them the results they want."); Eric J. Segall, Originalism as Faith 147–55 (2018) (arguing that the Supreme Court's originalists selectively invoke or ignore originalism to match their ideological priors and policy preferences).

42. *See* Jeremy M. Christiansen, *Originalism: The Primary Canon of State Constitutional Interpretation*, 15 Geo. J.L. & Pub. Pol'y 341 (2017) (collecting cases).

43. *See* Jeffrey S. Sutton, 51 Imperfect Solutions: States and the Making of American Constitutional Law 20, 174–76 (2018); Clint Bolick, *Principles of State Constitutional Interpretation*, 53 Ariz. St. L.J. 771, 782 (2021) (noting the practice and arguing against it); Christiansen, *Originalism*, *supra* note 42, at 360–62.

44. *See, e.g.*, Bolick, *Principles of State Constitutional Interpretation*, *supra* note 43, at 787–89.

45. Levinson, Framed, *supra* note 34.

46. Ethan Hutt, Daniel Klasik & Aaron Tang, *How Do Judges Decide School Finance Cases?*, 97 Wash. U. L. Rev. 1047 (2020) (concluding that state

courts are generally not using thick versions of originalism in school finance cases, although what they do might be consistent with thin versions, like the New Originalism, which are consistent with living constitutionalism); Christiansen, *Originalism, supra* note 42, at 359–60 (noting the rise of living constitutionalism in state courts in the twentieth century). *See also* Baude, *Is Originalism Our Law?, supra* note 12, at 2400 ("If positivist originalism is correct, then the answer will turn on each state's political and legal culture. . . . [P]erhaps originalism is the duty of judges in Michigan, and not in Connecticut.").

47.   Emily Zackin, Looking for Rights in All the Wrong Places: Why State Constitutions Contain America's Positive Rights (2013); Sutton, 51 Imperfect Solutions, *supra* note 43 (celebrating the role of state courts in innovation).

48.   Douglas NeJaime, *Winning through Losing*, 96 Iowa L. Rev. 941, 990–98 (2011) (describing the role that state courts played in advancing gay rights claims).

49.   *See* Jeremy Kirk, *Constitutional Implications (II): Doctrines of Equality and Democracy*, 25 Melbourne U. L. Rev. 24, 27 (2001). *See also* Jeffrey Goldsworthy, *The Case for Originalism, in* The Challenge of Originalism: Theories of Constitutional Interpretation 42 (Grant Huscroft & Bradley W. Miller eds., 2011); and Jeffrey Goldsworthy, *Originalism in Constitutional Interpretation*, 25 Fed. L. Rev. 1, 38–39 (1997); Kim Lane Scheppele, *Jack Balkin Is an American*, 25 Yale J.L. & Human. 23, 23 (2013) ("Inquiring this closely into a constitution's original meaning is done almost nowhere else in the world, with some lonely holdouts at the High Court of Australia. Instead, purposive interpretation—or one of its close variants—leaves originalism in the dust in many other advanced constitutional systems."); Lael K. Weis, *What Comparativism Tells Us about Originalism*, 11 Int. J. Con. L. 842 (2013).

50.   Yvonne Tew, *Originalism at Home and Abroad*, 52 Colum. J. Transnat'l L. 780 (2014); Weis, *What Comparativism Tells Us about Originalism, supra* note 49; Goldsworthy, *Originalism in Constitutional Interpretation, supra* note 49.

51.   William Baude argues that the central question is the political and legal culture of a nation or a state, so it would not be surprising that countries with different histories are not originalist. *See* Baude, *Is Originalism Our Law?, supra* note 12, at 2402–03 ("As with state constitutions, grounding originalism in positive law allows originalists to acknowledge some foreign practices as nonoriginalist without having to argue that they are conceptually incoherent or lead to the supposedly bad consequences of nonoriginalism. Indeed, a positivist originalist might say that when in Rome one ought to do as Romans do.").

52.   Jud Mathews & Alec Stone Sweet, *All Things in Proportion—American Rights Review and the Problem of Balancing*, 60 Emory L. J. 797 (2011).

53. Scheppele, *Jack Balkin Is an American*, *supra* note 49, at 24.
54. Michel Rosenfeld, *Constitutional Adjudication in Europe and the United States: Paradoxes and Contrasts*, 2 Int'l J. Const. L., 633, 656 n.83 (2004).
55. Jamal Greene, *On the Origins of Originalism*, 88 Tex. L. Rev. 1, 20–38 (2009).
56. Edwards v. Attorney-General for Canada, [1930] A.C. 124, 136 (P.C.) (appeal taken from Can.) (U.K.) (*The Persons Case*).
57. Peter W. Hogg, *Canada: From Privy Council to Supreme Court*, *in* Interpreting Constitutions: A Comparative Study 55, 83 (Jeffrey Goldsworthy ed., 2006).
58. Colin Feasby, *The New Approach to Charter Interpretation*, SSRN (Apr. 19, 2022), https://papers.ssrn.com/sol3/papers.cfm?abstract_id=4037702; Léonid Sirota, *Purposivism, Textualism, and Originalism in Recent Cases on Charter Interpretation*, 47 Queen's L.J. 78 (2021); The Honourable Bradley W. Miller, *Constitutional Supremacy and Judicial Reasoning*, 45 Queen's L.J. 353 (2020); Jeff Goldsworthy & Grant Huscroft, *Originalism in Canada and Australia: Why the Difference?*, *in* Canada in the World: Comparative Perspectives on the Canadian Constitution 183 (Richard Albert & David R. Cameron eds., 2018); Léonid Sirota & Benjamin Oliphant, *Originalist Reasoning in Canadian Constitutional Jurisprudence*, 50 UBC L. Rev. 505 (2017); Bradley W. Miller, *Origin Myth: The Persons Case, the Living Tree, and the New Originalism*, *in* The Challenge of Originalism: Essays in Constitutional Theory (Grant Huscroft & Bradley W. Miller eds., 2011); Grant Huscroft, *The Trouble with Living Tree Interpretation*, 25 U. Queensland L.J. 3 (2006).
59. *See* Rafi Reznik, *The Rise of American Conservatism in Israel*, 8 Penn St. J.L. & Int'l Aff. 383 (2020) (arguing that the influence of the U.S. conservative movement has led to the adoption of "purposive originalism" within the Israeli Supreme Court).

Chapter Six. Why Are Americans Originalist?

1. The locus classicus for this well-known idea is Baron de Montesquieu, Charles-Louis de Secondat, The Spirit of the Laws (1748) (Thomas Nugent trans., 1949).
2. Aziz Rana, The Two Faces of American Freedom (2010).
3. Articles of Confederation of 1781, art. XIII.
4. David Fontana, *Comparative Originalism*, 88 Tex. L. Rev. See Also 189, 190 (2010).
5. On the role of political revolutions in shaping constitutional culture and development, *see* Bruce Ackerman, Revolutionary Constitutions: Charismatic Leadership and the Rule of Law (2019).
6. Akhil Reed Amar, The Words That Made Us: America's Constitutional Conversation, 1760–1840, at 97–98, 105–06, 110–11 (2021).

7. The Founders Online, http://founders.archives.gov/.

8. *See* David Leeming, The Oxford Companion to World Mythology 88 (2005) (noting that often the culture hero "establishes the community's institutions and traditions").

9. Hence, as with Adam and Eve, people may accuse the founders of committing America's original sin. *See, e.g.*, Barack Obama, Address at the National Constitution Center in Philadelphia: "A More Perfect Union" (Mar. 18, 2008), *in* The American Presidency Project (J. Woolley and G. Peters eds.), https://www.presidency.ucsb.edu/documents/address -the-national-constitution-center-philadelphia-more-perfect-union [https://perma.cc/P5CF-A8AW] ("The document [the framers] produced was . . . ultimately unfinished. It was stained by this nation's original sin of slavery, a question that divided the colonies and brought the convention to a stalemate until the founders chose to allow the slave trade to continue for at least twenty more years, and to leave any final resolution to future generations.").

10. Ozan O. Varol, *The Origins and Limits of Originalism: A Comparative Study* 44 Vand. J. Transnat'l L. 1239, 1246 (2011).

11. Sacvan Bercovitch, American Jeremiad 141 (1978).

12. Jack M. Balkin, Constitutional Redemption: Political Faith in an Unjust World (2011); Sanford Levinson, Constitutional Faith (rev. ed. 2012).

13. Sir Lewis Namier, Conflicts: Studies in Contemporary History 70 (1942).

14. Simon J. Gilhooley, The Antebellum Origins of the Modern Constitution: Slavery and the Spirit of the American Founding (2020).

15. *See, e.g., id.* (in the antebellum era); Jonathan Gienapp, The Second Creation: Fixing the American Constitution in the Founding Era (2018) (in the early republic); David Sehat, The Jefferson Rule: How the Founding Fathers Became Infallible and Our Politics Inflexible (2016) (by the Jeffersonian Republicans); Jonathan O'Neill, Originalism in Law and Politics: A Constitutional History (2005) (in the nineteenth century); Jack N. Rakove, Original Meanings: Politics and Ideas in the Making of the Constitution (1996) (in the debates over the Jay Treaty).

16. *See* Sanford Levinson & J. M. Balkin, *Law, Music, and Other Performing Arts*, 139 U. Pa. L. Rev. 1597, 1629–39 (1991).

17. Karl Marx & Friedrich Engels, Manifesto of the Communist Party, *in* The Marx-Engels Reader 469 (Robert C. Tucker ed., 2d ed. 1978).

18. Franklin D. Roosevelt, Fireside Chat Discussing the Plan for Reorganization of the Federal Judiciary, March 9, 1937, *in* The American Presidency Project, *supra* note 9, http://www.presidency.ucsb.edu/ws/index .php?pid=15381 [https://perma.cc/NQ3S-6RRN].

19. *Id.*

20. *Id.*

21. *Id.*

22. Franklin D. Roosevelt, Address on Constitution Day, Washington, D.C.,

September 17th, 1937, *in* The American Presidency Project, *supra* note 9, http://www.presidency.ucsb.edu/ws/index.php?pid=15459 [https://perma .cc/8TLE-PBT4]; The Constitution of the United States Was a Layman's Document, Not a Lawyer's Contract (Sept. 17, 1937), *in* 6 The Public Papers and Addresses of Franklin D. Roosevelt 359, 367 (S. I. Rosenman ed., Macmillan 1941).

23.   The Constitution of the United States Was a Layman's Contract, at 367.

24.   Paul Brest, *The Misconceived Quest for the Original Understanding*, 60 B.U. L. Rev. 204, 204 (1980).

25.   *See* Frank B. Cross, The Failed Promise of Originalism 92–96 (2013) (describing the use of adoption history in the Warren Court school prayer, reapportionment, and criminal procedure opinions); Alfred H. Kelly, *Clio and the Court: An Illicit Love Affair*, 1965 Sup. Ct. Rev. 119 (listing as examples Establishment Clause, reapportionment, and criminal procedure cases).

26.   Kelly, *Clio and the Court, supra* note 25; *id.* at 122.

27.   *Id.* at 125–26.

28.   *Id.* at 131.

29.   Frank B. Cross, *Originalism—The Forgotten Years*, 28 Const. Comment. 37 (2012); Cross, The Failed Promise of Originalism, *supra* note 25, at 136–43.

30.   Robert H. Bork, The Tempting of America 351–52 (1990) ("[J]udges must always be guided by the original understanding of the Constitution's provisions. Once adherence to the original understanding is weakened or abandoned, a judge . . . can reach any result."); Robert H. Bork, *Original Intent: The Only Legitimate Basis for Constitutional Decision Making*, 26 Judges J. 13 (1987); Edwin Meese III, U.S. Att'y Gen., Address before the American Bar Association (July 9, 1985), *in* The Great Debate: Interpreting Our Written Constitution 1, 9 (Paul G. Cassell ed., 1986) (arguing that constitutional jurisprudence "should be a Jurisprudence of Original Intention"); Edwin Meese III, U.S. Att'y Gen., Address before the D.C. Chapter of the Federalist Society Lawyers Division (Nov. 15, 1985), *in* Office of Legal Policy, U.S. Dep't of Justice, Original Meaning Jurisprudence: A Sourcebook 91, 95, 96, 98 (1987) (arguing for a "jurisprudence of original intention"); Edwin Meese III, *Construing the Constitution*, 19 U.C. Davis L. Rev. 22, 25–26, 30 (1985) (same); Edwin Meese III, *The Supreme Court of the United States: Bulwark of a Limited Constitution*, 27 S. Tex. L. Rev. 455, 465–66 (1986) ("It has been and will continue to be the policy of this administration to press for a jurisprudence of original intention.").

31.   Robert Post & Reva Siegel, *Originalism as a Political Practice: The Right's Living Constitution*, 75 Fordham L. Rev. 545 (2006).

32.   O'Neill, Originalism in Law and Politics, *supra* note 15, at 133–41; Post & Siegel, *Originalism as a Political Practice, supra* note 31; Keith E.

Whittington, *The New Originalism*, 2 Geo. J.L. & Pub. Pol'y 599, 601–04 (2004).

33. Whittington, *The New Originalism*, *supra* note 32, at 601–02.

34. Jack M. Balkin, *Why Liberals and Conservatives Flipped on Judicial Restraint: Judicial Review in the Cycles of Constitutional Time*, 98 Tex. L. Rev. 215, 253–55 (2019); Whittington, *The New Originalism*, *supra* note 32, at 601–04 ("As conservatives found themselves in the majority, conservative constitutional theory—and perhaps originalism—needed to develop a governing philosophy appropriate to guide majority opinions, not just to fill dissents.").

35. Clark M. Neily III, Terms of Engagement: How Our Courts Should Enforce the Constitution's Promise of Limited Government 129–30 (2013); Clark Neily, *Judicial Engagement Means No More Make-Believe Judging*, 19 Geo. Mason L. Rev. 1053, 1053 (2012); Ilya Shapiro, *Against Judicial Restraint*, Nat'l Affairs, Fall 2016, at 113, 117, 125, https://www.nationalaffairs.com/publications/detail/against-judicial-restraint [https://perma.cc/LCE3-YQ3E]; Inst. for Just., *Supreme Court at a Crossroads: Judicial Engagement vs. Judicial Restraint: What Should Conservatives Prefer?*, http://ij.org/event/supreme-court-crossroads-judicial-engagement-vs-judicial-restraint-conservatives-prefer/ [https://perma.cc/F6VX-QPGQ]; Mark Tushnet, *From Judicial Restraint to Judicial Engagement: A Short Intellectual History*, 19 George Mason L. Rev. 1043 (2012).

36. Post & Siegel, *Originalism as Political Practice*, *supra* note 31.

37. Levinson, Constitutional Faith, *supra* note 12.

Chapter Seven. Living Originalism

1. Jack M. Balkin, Living Originalism (2011).

2. Lawrence B. Solum, *Originalism and Constitutional Construction*, 82 Fordham L. Rev. 453, 455–58 (2013) (explaining that the distinction between interpretation and construction is characteristic of the New Originalism).

3. Balkin, Living Originalism, *supra* note 1, at 36–37, 45; Jack M. Balkin, *Must We Be Faithful to Original Meaning?*, 7 Jerusalem Rev. Legal Stud. 57, 61 (2013).

4. Balkin, Living Originalism, *supra* note 1, at 27, 282.

5. *Id.* at 5.

6. *Id.* at 3.

7. Jack M. Balkin, *Constitutional Interpretation and Change in the United States: The Official and the Unofficial*, 14 Jus Politicum 1, 3 (2015), http://juspoliticum.com/uploads/5709f15cf28c4-jp14_balkin.pdf ("the constitution is always unfinished and . . . you can't step into the same constitution twice").

8. For example, the New Originalist Randy Barnett and his coauthor Evan

Bernick argue that in constitutional construction, we must attempt to further the Constitution's spirit and purpose. Randy E. Barnett and Evan Bernick, *The Letter and the Spirit: A Unified Theory of Originalism*, 107 Geo. L.J. 1, 3 (2018) ("[O]riginalism must be committed to the Constitution's original spirit as well—the functions, purposes, goals, or aims implicit in its individual clauses and structural design.").

9. *See* Jack M. Balkin, *Arguing about the Constitution: The Topics in Constitutional Interpretation*, 33 Const. Comm. 145, 229, 238–42 (2018); Richard H. Fallon Jr., *A Constructivist Coherence Theory of Constitutional Interpretation*, 100 Harv. L. Rev. 1189, 1192–93 (1987); *cf.* Cass R. Sunstein, How to Interpret the Constitution (2023) (arguing for reflective equilibrium among fixed points and theories of constitutional interpretation).

10. Balkin, *Arguing about the Constitution, supra* note 9, at 242–44. Thus, I do not agree with Philip Bobbitt's view that different modalities are incommensurable and that the only way to decide constitutional issues when the modalities conflict is by resort to individual conscience. First, the modalities are not incommensurable. The boundaries between different kinds of arguments are not fixed, and different kinds of arguments may overlap to some degree. People's judgments about which argument in each modality is best are affected by their judgments about which arguments in other modalities are best, and vice versa. Second, the modalities are tools for thinking; people think through the modalities rather than outside them. Third, the idea of resort to individual conscience is misleading because people decide what the Constitution means through processes of mutual social influence; the modalities are among the ways people reason with and influence each other. Constitutional thinking is social thinking.

11. Solum, *Originalism and Constitutional Construction, supra* note 2, at 456.

12. Balkin, *Must We Be Faithful to Original Meaning?, supra* note 3, at 77.

13. Balkin, Living Originalism, *supra* note 1, at 13. Thus, "writings" in the Progress Clause "refers to more than written marks on a page but also includes printing and (probably) sculpture, motion pictures, and other media of artistic and scientific communication." *Id.* Similarly, "speech" in the First Amendment refers to more than speaking. It also refers to writing and other forms of expression. *Id.* When the Constitution speaks about slavery in the infamous three-fifths clause of Article I, section 2, and the Fugitive Slave Clause of Article IV, section 2, it uses another literary trope—euphemism. It speaks of "other Persons" and "Person[s] held to Service or Labor."

14. *Id.*

15. *Id.*; Lawrence B. Solum, *Originalist Methodology*, 84 U. Chi. L. Rev. 269, 271 (2017); Solum, *Originalism and Constitutional Construction, supra* note 2, at 456.

16. Solum, *Originalism and Constitutional Construction, supra* note 2, at 458, 469–72 (defining the "construction zone" as the domain in which constitutional norms are underdetermined by the original public meaning).

17. Balkin, Living Originalism, *supra* note 1, at 224; Ward Farnsworth, *Women under Reconstruction: The Congressional Understanding,* 94 Nw. U. L. Rev. 1229, 1230 (2000) ("The [Fourteenth] Amendment was understood not to disturb the prevailing regime of state laws imposing very substantial legal disabilities on women, particularly married women.").

18. *See* Balkin, Living Originalism, *supra* note 1, at 7 ("Thus, the original expected application includes not only specific results, but also the way that the adopting generation would have expected the relevant constitutional principles to be articulated and applied.").

19. *Id.* at 6–7.

20. *See* Balkin, Living Originalism, *supra* note 1, at 23, 25, 277–80.

21. Robert H. Bork, *Original Intent: The Only Legitimate Basis for Constitutional Decision Making,* 26 Judges J. 13 (1987).

22. *Id.*

23. *See, e.g.,* Antonin Scalia & Bryan A. Garner, Reading Law: The Interpretation of Legal Texts 13–15 (2012) ("[T]he supposed distinction between *interpretation* and *construction* has never reflected the courts' actual usage."); John O. McGinnis & Michael B. Rappaport, *Original Methods Originalism: A New Theory of Interpretation and the Case against Construction,* 103 Nw. U. L. Rev. 751, 773 (2009) (rejecting the distinction between interpretation and construction and arguing that using original methods resolves almost every controversy). For a rebuttal to Scalia and Garner's historical claim, *see* Solum, *Originalism and Constitutional Construction, supra* note 2, at 483–88.

24. *See* Balkin, Living Originalism, *supra* note 1, at 7; Balkin, *Must We Be Faithful to Original Meaning?, supra* note 3, at 70.

25. *See* Balkin, Living Originalism, *supra* note 1, at 6–12. This distinction is not original with me; it has been made, in different versions, by many scholars. *E.g.,* Kermit Roosevelt III, The Myth of Judicial Activism: Making Sense of Supreme Court Decisions (2006); Ronald Dworkin, *Comment, in* A Matter of Interpretation: Federal Courts and the Law 115, 116, 119 (Amy Gutmann ed., 1997); Randy Barnett, Restoring the Lost Constitution: The Presumption of Liberty (2004); Christopher R. Green, *Originalism and the Sense-Reference Distinction,* 50 St. Louis U. L.J. 555 (2006); Randy E. Barnett, *An Originalism for Nonoriginalists,* 45 Loy. L. Rev. 611 (1999); Mark D. Greenberg & Harry Litman, *The Meaning of Original Meaning,* 86 Geo. L.J. 569 (1998); Jeffrey Goldsworthy, *Originalism in Constitutional Interpretation,* 1 Fed. L. Rev. 1 (1997).

26. *E.g.,* Morse v. Frederick, 551 U.S. 393, 410–11 (2007) (Thomas, J. concurring) (conflating original meaning with original understanding); Antonin Scalia, *Response, in* A Matter of Interpretation, *supra* note 25, at 140

(equating the original meaning of "cruel and unusual punishments" with those considered cruel and unusual at the founding); James C. Phillips & John C. Yoo, *You're Fired: The Original Meaning of Presidential Impeachment*, 94 S. Cal. L. Rev. 1191, 1193 (2021) (conflating original meaning with original understanding); Nelson Lund, *Living Originalism: The Magical Mystery Tour*, 3 Tex. A&M L. Rev. 31, 34–35 (2015) ("Genuine originalism, however, requires that the purpose of the provision *as it was originally understood* should constrain its application. If the enactors meant to leave specific laws or practices unaffected, a contradictory purpose may not be imputed to vague or ambiguous texts."); *see also* Thomas R. Lee and James C. Phillips, *Data-Driven Originalism*, 167 U. Pa. L. Rev. 261, 276 (2019) (explaining that in Justice Thomas's arguments about the original meaning of the Commerce Clause, "Justice Thomas seems to be resorting to evidence of original expected applications rather than original communicative content"); Thomas B. Colby, *The Sacrifice of the New Originalism*, 99 Geo. L.J. 713, 729 (2011) (explaining that original expectations originalism "has also been employed as a form of original meaning jurisprudence—as an attempt to follow the original public meaning of the constitutional provision, with the gloss that the original expectations are dispositive evidence of how the original meaning applies to particular circumstances").

27. *Nomination of Judge Antonin Scalia: Hearings before the Senate Committee on the Judiciary*, 99th Cong. (1986), reprinted in 13 The Supreme Court of the United States: Hearings and Reports on Successful and Unsuccessful Nominations of Supreme Court Justices by the Senate Judiciary Committee, 1916–1987, at 89, 142 (Roy M. Mersky and J. Myron Jacobstein eds., W. S. Hein 1989) (testimony of Antonin Scalia on Aug. 5, 1986); *see also* Caleb Nelson, *Originalism and Interpretive Conventions*, 70 U. Chi. L. Rev. 519, 558 (2003) ("[O]ur views of 'original meaning' and 'original intention' will tend to converge in practice even if the two concepts remain distinct in theory.").

28. *E.g.*, William Baude, *Is Originalism Our Law?*, 115 Colum. L. Rev. 2349, 2356–57 (2015); Keith E. Whittington, *Originalism: A Critical Introduction*, 82 Fordham L. Rev. 375, 382–85 (2013); Steven G. Calabresi & Julia T. Rickert, *Originalism and Sex Discrimination*, 90 Tex. L. Rev. 1, 3 (2011); Christopher R. Green, *Originalism and the Sense-Reference Distinction*, 50 St. Louis U. L.J. 555 (2006); Michael W. McConnell, *The Importance of Humility in Judicial Review: A Comment on Ronald Dworkin's "Moral Reading" of the Constitution*, 65 Fordham L. Rev. 1269, 1280–81, 1284 (1997). *Cf.* Bostock v. Clayton County, 140 S. Ct. 1731, 1750–54 (2020) (opinion of Gorsuch, J.) (arguing that original meaning, and not original expected applications, controls in statutory interpretation).

29. *E.g.*, John O. McGinnis & Michael Rappaport, *Original Interpretive Principles as the Core of Originalism*, 24 Const. Comment. 371, 378 (2007)

("[W]hile the original meaning may not be defined by the expected applications, these applications will often be some of the best evidence of what that meaning is."); Steven G. Calabresi & Saikrishna B. Prakash, *The President's Power to Execute the Laws*, 104 Yale L.J. 541, 556 (1994) ("[T]he constitutional text, read alone, can give only incomplete answers as to the original understanding. The originalist inquiry, then, has usually been pushed back from purely textual arguments to arguments based on evidence from the Constitution's enactment and postenactment history.").

30. The Supreme Court's major attempt to justify commercial speech protection on originalist grounds appears in *44 Liquormart, Inc. v. Rhode Island*, 517 U.S. 484, 495–96 (1996):

> Even in colonial days, the public relied on "commercial speech" for vital information about the market. Early newspapers displayed advertisements for goods and services on their front pages, and town criers called out prices in public squares. See J. Wood, The Story of Advertising 21, 45–69, 85 (1958); J. Smith, Printers and Press Freedom 49 (1988). Indeed, commercial messages played such a central role in public life prior to the founding that Benjamin Franklin authored his early defense of a free press in support of his decision to print, of all things, an advertisement for voyages to Barbados. Franklin, An Apology for Printers, June 10, 1731, reprinted in 2 Writings of Benjamin Franklin 172 (1907).

See also id. at 522 (Thomas, J., concurring in part) ("I do not see a philosophical or historical basis for asserting that 'commercial' speech is of 'lower value' than 'noncommercial' speech.").

31. *Id. See also* Lorillard Tobacco Co. v. Reilly, 533 U.S. 525, 575 (2001) (Thomas, J., concurring in part) ("I doubt whether it is even possible to draw a coherent distinction between commercial and noncommercial speech."); Daniel E. Troy, *Advertising: Not "Low Value" Speech*, 16 Yale J. on Reg. 85, 107–08 (1999) ("Franklin's defense of his handbill and the attacks on the Stamp Acts indicate a willingness, particularly on the part of printer-revolutionaries, to defend advertising with the same ardor, and employ the same arguments, that they mustered in fighting off other attacks on the freedom of the press. . . . [C]ommercial speech was inseparable from the very idea of a free American press. Advertising not only provided the revenues for colonial newspapers, but contained substantive commercial information that was at least as eagerly valued as news by many readers.").

32. *See* Troy, *Advertising, supra* note 31, at 111–12 (arguing that from the founding through the antebellum period, regulations on advertising were limited to restrictions on illegal products and services); *see* United States

v. Caronia, 703 F.3d 149 (2d Cir. 2012) (employing modern commercial speech doctrine to hold that defendant's promotion of off-label drug use was protected by the First Amendment).

33. Jud Campbell, *Natural Rights and the First Amendment*, 127 Yale L.J. 246 (2017).

34. *Id.* at 310 ("[S]tate governments routinely and uncontroversially restricted plenty of speech that did not directly violate the rights of others. Evidence from the late 1780s and early 1790s provides no indication that the First Amendment adopted a different understanding of expressive freedom.").

35. For example, state restrictions on political speech were underenforced during the Revolutionary period, but this by itself does not tell us which kinds of laws banning sedition were unconstitutional—a matter of considerable debate between Federalists and Jeffersonians in the 1790s. There *is* a good argument that the 1798 Sedition Act was unconstitutional, but it is a structural argument about popular sovereignty and representative democracy, not an argument from colonial underenforcement.

36. Larry D. Kramer, *When Lawyers Do History*, 72 Geo. Wash. L. Rev. 387, 400 (2003).

37. *Id.* at 407.

38. *E.g.*, Erwin Chemerinsky, Worse than Nothing: The Dangerous Fallacy of Originalism (2022); Eric J. Segall, Originalism as Faith (2018); James E. Fleming, Fidelity to Our Imperfect Constitution: For Moral Readings and against Originalisms (2015); Cass R. Sunstein, Radicals in Robes: Why Extreme Right Wing Courts Are Wrong for America (2005); Richard H. Fallon Jr., *The Chimerical Concept of Original Public Meaning*, 107 Va. L. Rev. 1421 (2021); Thomas B. Colby & Peter J. Smith, *Living Originalism*, 59 Duke L.J. 239 (2009); Mitchell N. Berman, *Originalism Is Bunk*, 84 N.Y.U. L. Rev. 1 (2009); Larry D. Kramer, *Two (More) Problems with Originalism*, 31 Harv. J.L. & Pub. Pol'y 907 (2008).

39. *E.g.*, John O. McGinnis & Michael B. Rappaport, *Reconciling Originalism and Precedent*, 103 Nw. U. L. Rev. 803, 836–37 (2009) ("Precedent should be respected when overruling it would result in enormous costs."); Scalia, *Response, supra* note 26, at 139–40 (arguing for retaining nonoriginalist precedents as a "pragmatic exception" in the interests of stability); Antonin Scalia, *Originalism: The Lesser Evil*, 57 U. Cin. L. Rev. 849, 861 (1989) ("[A]lmost every originalist would adulterate it with the doctrine of stare decisis.").

40. Scalia, *Response, supra* note 26, at 139 ("The whole function of the doctrine" of stare decisis "is to make us say that what is false under proper analysis must nonetheless be held true, all in the interests of stability.").

41. Balkin, Living Originalism, *supra* note 1, at 8–11.

42. Some originalists allow the practical meaning of some parts of the Constitution to change as a result of long-standing traditions, customs, and

political conventions. *See, e.g.*, Michael W. McConnell, *Textualism and the Dead Hand of the Past*, 66 Geo. Wash. L. Rev. 1127, 1128 (1998) (arguing for originalism tempered by tradition and judicial restraint). They also treat these parts of the Constitution as raising questions of constitutional construction because they are interested in the meaning and practical application of tradition, custom, and convention. *See generally id.*

43.   Balkin, Living Originalism, *supra* note 1, at 9.

44.   Calvin Terbeek, *"Clocks Must Always Be Turned Back"*: Brown v. Board of Education *and the Racial Origins of Constitutional Originalism*, 115 Am. Pol. Sci. Rev. 821 (2021).

45.   *See* Robert H. Bork, The Tempting of America: The Political Seduction of the Law 81–82 (1990); Michael W. McConnell, *Originalism and the Desegregation Decisions*, 81 Va. L. Rev. 947 (1995); Michael W. McConnell, *The Originalist Justification for* Brown: *A Reply to Professor Klarman*, 81 Va. L. Rev. 1937 (1995).

46.   Bolling v. Sharpe, 397 U.S. 497 (1954). *See* Bork, The Tempting of America, *supra* note 45, at 83 ("*Bolling*, then, was a clear rewriting of the Constitution by the Warren Court. *Bolling*, however much one likes the result, was a substantive due process decision in the same vein as *Dred Scott* and *Lochner*."); Michael W. McConnell, *Opinion Concurring in the Judgment, in* What *Brown v. Board of Education* Should Have Said: The Nation's Top Legal Experts Rewrite America's Landmark Civil Rights Opinion 165–68 (Jack M. Balkin ed., 2001) (explaining that *Bolling* cannot be squared with the Constitution's original meaning but that the District of Columbia school board was not authorized to segregate the public schools). Loving v. Virginia, 388 U.S. 1 (1967). *See* Michael J. Klarman, Brown, *Originalism, and Constitutional Theory: A Response to Professor McConnell*, 81 Va. L. Rev. 1881, 1919–20 (1995) (arguing that "McConnell's originalist interpretation of the Fourteenth Amendment would apparently permit the state to draw racial distinctions in all areas of life not qualifying as civil rights" as understood in 1868, which would allow bans on interracial marriage, restrictions on jury service, and segregated public accommodations like public golf courses and swimming pools); William E. Nelson, The Fourteenth Amendment: From Political Principle to Judicial Doctrine 152 (1988) ("Most early cases . . . held that the Fourteenth Amendment had no effect on state miscegenation legislation, reasoning that state law operated on both races alike by prohibiting both from marrying outside their own race."). In the debates over the 1866 Civil Rights Act, which guaranteed equal civil rights for whites and Blacks, supporters gave assurances that equality of civil rights would not affect state bans on interracial marriage. *See, e.g.*, Cong. Globe, 39th Cong., 1st Sess. 505 (Jan. 30, 1866) (statement of Sen. Fessenden) (arguing that there was no discrimination because the position of whites and Blacks was symmetrical); *id.* at 322 (Jan. 19, 1866) (same).

47. *See* David R. Upham, *Interracial Marriage and the Original Understanding of the Privileges or Immunities Clause*, 42 Hastings Con. L. Rev. Q. 213 (2015) (arguing that *Loving v. Virginia* follows from the original meaning of the Privileges or Immunities Clause of the Fourteenth Amendment); Ryan C. Williams, *Originalism and the Other Desegregation Decision*, 99 Va. L. Rev. 493 (2013) (arguing that the result in *Bolling* might follow from the Fourteenth Amendment's Citizenship Clause). If this is a proposal for a subsequent *construction* of the Fourteenth Amendment, it is an excellent one. I have argued for *Bolling* on the same grounds. Balkin, Living Originalism, *supra* note 1, at 433 n.150; Jack M. Balkin, *Judgment of the Court, in* What *Brown v. Board of Education* Should Have Said, *supra* note 46, at 87. But subsequent constructions are not part of original meaning, and even under a thick account of original meaning, Williams does not show that the result in *Bolling* was part of the initial legal construction of the Citizenship Clause. Williams, *supra*, at 600 ("[T]he mere existence of an analogous constitutional ban on federal discrimination does not answer the question of whether *Bolling* was correctly decided. Among other things, a comprehensive originalist defense of *Bolling* would require proof that public education fell within the class of interests to which the citizen-equality principle would have been understood to extend and that racial segregation in public schools should be understood to deny equality in a constitutionally relevant way.").

48. Steven G. Calabresi and Hannah M. Begley, *Originalism and Same-Sex Marriage*, 70 U. Mia. L. Rev. 648 (2016); Steven G. Calabresi & Julia T. Rickert, *Originalism and Sex Discrimination*, 90 Tex. L. Rev. 1 (2011).

49. 303 Creative, LLC v. Elenis, 143 S. Ct. 2298 (2023) (holding application of public accommodations law unconstitutional as to website designer); Janus v. Am. Fed'n of States, Cty., and Mun. Emps., Council 31, 138 S. Ct. 2448 (2018) (striking down mandatory dues to public-sector unions on freedom of association grounds); Ariz. Free Enter. Club's Freedom Club PAC v. Bennett, 564 U.S. 721 (2011) (striking down subsidies in state campaign finance law); Sorrell v. IMS Health Inc., 564 U.S. 552, 557 (2011) (striking down data privacy regulation on commercial speech grounds); Citizens United v. FEC, 558 U.S. 310 (2010) (striking down restrictions on corporate expenditures in elections); Boy Scouts of America et al. v. Dale, 530 U.S. 640 (2000) (holding application of public accommodations law unconstitutional on freedom of association grounds); 44 Liquormart, Inc. v. Rhode Island, 517 U.S. 484 (1996) (striking down restrictions on advertising liquor prices on commercial speech grounds).

50. *See* Campbell, *Natural Rights and the First Amendment, supra* note 33.

51. *See, e.g.*, Robert H. Bork, *The Constitution, Original Intent, and Economic Rights*, 23 San Diego L. Rev. 823, 823 (1986) ("I wish to demonstrate that original intent is the only legitimate basis for constitutional decisionmaking."); Scalia, *Originalism: The Lesser Evil, supra* note 39, at 854 ("The

principal theoretical defect of nonoriginalism . . . is its incompatibility with
the very principle that legitimizes judicial review of constitutionality.").

52. Solum, *Originalism and Constitutional Construction, supra* note 2, at 459–
62 (describing the "Fixation Thesis" and "Constraint Principle," which
(almost) all forms of originalism share). For an exception, *see* Stephen E.
Sachs, *Originalism without Text*, 127 Yale L.J. 156 (2017).

53. Justice Scalia has argued that this approach helps to constrain judges.
Scalia, *Originalism: The Lesser Evil, supra* note 39, at 863–64 (noting that
"the main danger in judicial interpretation of the Constitution . . . is
that the judges will mistake their own predilections for the law" and that
"[o]riginalism . . . establishes a historical criterion that is conceptually
quite separate from the preferences of the judge himself"). But many
contemporary originalists do not emphasize judicial restraint as the primary justification for originalism. *See, e.g.,* Keith E. Whittington, *The
New Originalism*, 2 Geo. J.L. & Pub. Pol'y 599, 608 (2004) ("The new
originalism is less likely to emphasize a primary commitment to judicial
restraint . . . [and features] less emphasis on the capacity of originalism
to limit the discretion of the judge.").

54. For examples of this kind of argument, *see* Balkin, Living Originalism,
supra note 1, at 55; Balkin, *Must We Be Faithful to Original Meaning?, supra*
note 3, at 59; Randy E. Barnett, *The Gravitational Force of Originalism*, 82
Fordham L. Rev. 411, 412 (2013) ("The New Originalism stands for the
proposition that the meaning of a written constitution should remain
the same until it's properly changed.").

55. *See* Balkin, *Must We Be Faithful to Original Meaning?, supra* note 3, at 60,
66 (arguing that fidelity to original meaning assumes that Americans
want to stick with the plan adopted in 1787 as subsequently amended
through Article V).

56. For example, Jamal Greene has argued that originalist argument is a
species of ethical argument. *See* Jamal Greene, *On the Origins of Originalism*, 88 Tex. L. Rev. 1, 64, 82–88 (2009); Jamal Greene, *The Case for
Original Intent*, 80 Geo. Wash. L. Rev. 1683, 1697 (2012). *See also* David
McGowan, *Ethos in Law and History: Alexander Hamilton,* The Federalist,
and the Supreme Court, 85 Minn. L. Rev. 755, 757–59, 825–35 (2001)
(arguing that regardless of theoretical commitments, the actual practices
of original meaning jurisprudence are often appeals to ethos); Robert
Post, *Theories of Constitutional Interpretation*, 30 Representations 13, 29
(1990) (explaining that the claim that the framers speak for present generations "is neither more nor less than a characterization of the national
ethos"); Richard Primus, *The Functions of Ethical Originalism*, 88 Tex. L.
Rev. See Also 79, 80 (2009) ("[T]he deeper power of originalist argument sounds in the romance of national identity."). Michael Dorf has
argued that originalist argument appeals either to political traditions
(which he calls "ancestral originalism") or to honored authorities (which

he calls "heroic originalism"). Michael C. Dorf, *Integrating Normative and Descriptive Constitutional Theory: The Case of Original Meaning*, 85 Geo. L.J. 1765, 1770, 1800–05 (1997).

57. *See* Greene, *The Case for Original Intent, supra* note 56, at 1697; McGowan, *Ethos in Law and History, supra* note 56, at 835–40.

58. *See* Post, *Theories of Constitutional Interpretation, supra* note 56, at 29; Primus, *The Functions of Ethical Originalism, supra* note 56, at 80.

59. *See, e.g.,* Seth Barrett Tillman, *The Two Discourses: How Non-Originalists Popularize Originalism and What That Means,* The New Reform Club (Mar. 28, 2016), https://reformclub.blogspot.com/2016/03/the-two-discourses -how-non-originalists.html [https://perma.cc/K7UN-C35V].

60. David Strauss is the major exception, but even he argues that because the text serves as a convenient focal point, one should not discard clear rules in the text without very good reasons. *See* David Strauss, The Living Constitution 104–06 (2010).

Chapter Eight. Why It's Better to Be Thin

1. *Compare* Scott Soames, *Originalism and Legitimacy*, 18 Geo. J.L. & Pub. Pol'y 241, 247 (2020) ("I extend a well-understood model of linguistic communication among individuals to linguistic communication between collective speakers and collective audiences.") *with* Lawrence B. Solum, *Communicative Content and Legal Content*, 89 Notre Dame L. Rev. 479, 501–02 (2013) ("The framers and ratifiers of the United States Constitution faced a communicative context that created distinctive constraints on successful communication."). For a critique, *see* Richard H. Fallon Jr., *The Chimerical Concept of Original Public Meaning*, 107 Va. L. Rev. 1421 (2021).

2. The classic legal realist version of this point in tort law is Leon Green, *The Casual Relation Issue in Negligence Law*, 60 Mich. L. Rev. 543 (1962). The Model Penal Code, which sought to clarify the concept of mens rea in criminal law, described four different kinds of intent that legislatures could choose to make material elements of a crime. Model Penal Code § 2.02(2) (1962).

3. *See* Andrei Marmor, *Meaning and Belief in Constitutional Interpretation*, 82 Fordham L. Rev. 577, 593–95 (2013) (arguing that questions of moral and political theory drive our conclusions about how language functions in constitutions).

4. *See, e.g.,* Randy E. Barnett, *The Gravitational Force of Originalism*, 82 Fordham L. Rev. 411, 417 (2013) ("We are searching for an empirical fact: what information would these words on the page have conveyed to the reasonable speaker of English in the relevant audience at the time of enactment?"); *id.* ("[H]aving stressed that the original public meaning is an empirically objective fact, I now acknowledge that the New Originalism does *also* make a *normative claim*, and it is this: the original meaning

of the text provides the law that legal decisionmakers are bound by or *ought* to follow.").

5. *See, e.g.*, Randy E. Barnett, *The Original Meaning of the Commerce Clause*, 68 U. Chi. L. Rev. 101, 105 (2001) ("'[O]riginal meaning' refers to the meaning a reasonable speaker of English would have attached to the words, phrases, sentences, etc. at the time the particular provision was adopted."); Michael Stokes Paulsen, *The Text, the Whole Text, and Nothing but the Text, So Help Me God: Un-Writing Amar's Unwritten Constitution*, 81 U. Chi. L. Rev. 1385, 1440 (2014) ("[T]he true, original public meaning of the language employed . . . [is] the objective meaning the words would have had, in historical, linguistic, and political context, to a reasonable, informed speaker and reader of the English language at the time that they were adopted."). For a critique, *see* Ilya Somin, *Originalism and Political Ignorance*, 97 Minn. L. Rev. 625 (2012) (pointing out that actual people, both at the time of the founding and in the present, are unlikely to know much about the kinds of facts that originalists assume they do).

6. *See, e.g.*, Gary Lawson, *Delegation and Original Meaning*, 88 Va. L. Rev. 327, 398 (2002). Lawson argues,

> Originalist analysis, at least as practiced by most contemporary originalists, is not a search for concrete historical understandings held by specific persons. Rather, it is a hypothetical inquiry that asks how a fully informed public audience, knowing all that there is to know about the Constitution and the surrounding world, would understand a particular provision. Actual historical understandings are, of course, relevant to that inquiry, but they do not conclude or define the inquiry—nor are they even necessarily the best available evidence. Enactments of early Congresses are particularly suspect because members of Congress, even those who participated in the drafting and ratification of the Constitution, are not disinterested observers. They are political actors, responding to political as well as legal influences, who are eminently capable of making mistakes about the meaning of the Constitution.

See also Vasan Kesavan & Michael Stokes Paulsen, *The Interpretive Force of the Constitution's Secret Drafting History*, 91 Geo. L.J. 1113, 1145 n.113 (2003) ("[T]he hypothetical audience should be 'in possession of all relevant information about the Constitution and the world around it.'").

7. Gary Lawson & Guy Seidman, *Originalism as a Legal Enterprise*, 23 Const. Comment. 47, 48 (2006).

8. John O. McGinnis & Michael B. Rappaport, *The Constitution and the Language of the Law*, 59 Wm. & Mary L. Rev. 1321, 1325 (2018).

9. *See* John O. McGinnis & Michael Rappaport, Originalism and the Good Constitution 118 (2013).

10. *Id.* at 126.

11. District of Columbia v. Heller, 554 U.S. 570, 576–77 (2008).

12. McGinnis & Rappaport, Originalism and the Good Constitution, *supra* note 9, at 128–29.

13. John O. McGinnis & Michael B. Rappaport, *The Power of Interpretation: Minimizing the Construction Zone*, 96 Notre Dame L. Rev. 919, 923, 938 (2021). *See also* John O. McGinnis & Michael Rappaport, *Jack Balkin on Original Methods Originalism: A Response*, Balkinization (Nov. 14, 2018), https://balkin.blogspot.com/2018/11/jack-balkin-on-original-methods.html [https://perma.cc/76Y3-EA3P] ("But we have never claimed that there was such a general consensus. And, in fact, we have disclaimed relying on that consensus. In short: *original methods works both interpretively and normatively whether or not there was a consensus on interpretive methods.*").

14. McGinnis & Rappaport, *The Power of Interpretation*, *supra* note 13, at 938; *see also* McGinnis & Rappaport, *Jack Balkin on Original Methods Originalism*, *supra* note 13 ("Even if the support for two opposing interpretive rules were relatively equal, [people at the time of adoption] would choose the rule that had greater support—what we call the 51/49 rule—a rule we have previously applied to resolve ambiguities in the text.").

15. McGinnis & Rappaport, *The Power of Interpretation*, *supra* note 13, at 923; *id.* at 942.

16. *Id. See also id.* at 924 ("The more we know about a constitutional provision, particularly through its legal meaning and context, the less likely it is to appear indeterminate.").

17. *Id.* at 945 (arguing that many examples of vagueness are actually ambiguities); *id.* at 946 ("[E]ven if a term is vague in ordinary language, it may not be so in legal language. . . . Or the legal interpretive rules may provide a nonvague understanding of the term."); *id.* at 947 ("[W]e believe that many provisions that others consider to be vague are not actually vague.").

18. McGinnis & Rappaport, Originalism and the Good Constitution, *supra* note 9, at 117–18 (arguing that original methods originalism is a positive theory of what the Constitution means regardless of whether this is normatively desirable).

19. As they note, "Our normative and positive theories converge because they are linked by an insistence that both positive meaning and the normatively desirable interpretation are generated by the interpretive rules obtaining at the time the Constitution was enacted." *Id.*

20. McGinnis & Rappaport, Originalism and the Good Constitution, *supra* note 9, at 19.

21. *Id.* at 33, 81–85. To be sure, this assumes that the Constitution *was* ratified by a supermajority of "We the People." In 1787, women (among others) could not vote, and African Americans were held in slavery. The Fourteenth Amendment poses other problems: it was proposed by Con-

gress only after Southern representatives and senators were excluded so that Northern Republicans could secure a two-thirds majority for an amendment. Southern states were not readmitted to the Union until they agreed to ratify the proposed amendment. McGinnis and Rappaport, however, maintain that the passage of the Fourteenth Amendment was a lawful and appropriate supermajority decision. *Id.* at 70–71. They further argue that the Reconstruction Amendments and the Nineteenth Amendment cured any potential problems for their theory. These amendments, they contend, provide the Constitution with all of the provisions that African Americans and women would have obtained if they had participated fully in the ratification of the Constitution in 1789. *Id.* at 107–08, 111–12.

22. *Id.* at 85.
23. *Id.* at 149.
24. *Id.* This echoes Justice Scalia's assertion in *District of Columbia v. Heller*, 554 U.S. 570, 604–05 (2008), that there is no reason to believe "that different people of the founding period had vastly different conceptions of the right to keep and bear arms. That simply does not comport with our longstanding view that the Bill of Rights codified venerable, widely understood liberties."
25. McGinnis & Rappaport, Originalism and the Good Constitution, *supra* note 9, at 149.
26. *See id.* at 118 (arguing that "the Constitution will produce the beneficial effects" of supermajoritarian rules "only if it is given its original meaning" and that this "suggests that the document should be interpreted using the original interpretive rules"); *id.* at 150–51 ("[J]udicial discretion to resolve matters of construction is less likely to produce good results than the supermajoritarian constitution-making process.").
27. Jack M. Balkin, Living Originalism 353–56 & n.18 (2011); Jack Balkin, *Nine Perspectives on Living Originalism*, 2012 U. Ill. L. Rev. 815, 827–28 (2012).
28. *See* Saul Cornell, *The People's Constitution vs. The Lawyers' Constitution: Popular Constitutionalism and the Original Debate over Originalism*, 23 Yale J.L. & Human. 295, 304 (2011); Larry D. Kramer, The People Themselves: Popular Constitutionalism and Judicial Review 6–7 (2004). *See also* Christina Mulligan, Michael Douma, Hans Lind & Brian Quinn, *Founding Era Translations of the Constitution*, 31 Const. Comm. 1, 52 (2016) (explaining that the presence of multiple translations of the Constitution "suggests that at least some members of the educated, founding-era public might not have always recognized each of the legal or specialized terms in the Constitution" and might have "failed . . . to defer to a lawyer's interpretation").
29. *E.g.*, Martin Jordan Minot, *The Irrelevance of Blackstone: Rethinking the Eighteenth-Century Importance of the* Commentaries, 104 Va. L. Rev. 1359,

1375–80 (2018) (noting that legal education at the time of the founding was often informal, practical, and spotty); *id.* at 1382 (noting that much of founding-era legal education involved self-directed reading and note-taking and that a "mix of Coke, various secondary treatises, and English reporters was fairly standard fare for the eighteenth-century law student, subject to the availability of law books for study").

30. *See* Farah Peterson, *Expounding the Constitution*, 130 Yale L.J. 2, 2–3 (2020); Larry Kramer, *Two (More) Problems with Originalism*, 31 Harv. J.L. & Pub. Pol'y 907, 912–13 (2008); Caleb Nelson, *Originalism and Interpretive Conventions*, 70 U. Chi. L. Rev. 519, 555–56, 561, 571–73 (2003).

31. *See* Joseph M. Lynch, Negotiating the Constitution: The Earliest Debates over Original Intent 6 (1999) (noting that in the early Congresses, disputes over policy produced continual interpretive disagreements, with no consistency in interpretive methods); Ray Raphael, Constitutional Myths: What We Get Wrong and How to Get It Right 156–58 (2013) (listing interpretive controversies in the first decade of the new Constitution).

32. McGinnis & Rappaport, Originalism and the Good Constitution, *supra* note 9, at 149; *see also* Balkin, *Nine Perspectives on Living Originalism*, *supra* note 27, at 835–38 (arguing that fundamental disputes about the meaning of the First Amendment during the debate over the Sedition Act cast doubt on McGinnis and Rappaport's assumptions).

33. McGinnis & Rappaport, *The Power of Interpretation*, *supra* note 13, at 942–43.

34. McGinnis & Rappaport, Originalism and the Good Constitution, *supra* note 9, at 149.

35. McGinnis & Rappaport, *Jack Balkin on Original Methods Originalism*, *supra* note 13 ("If there was uncertainty about what the meaning was or the interpretive rules that would be applied to it, then that would probably reduce the net benefits of the document they were evaluating. Ultimately, the ratification conventions would have to decide whether the expected net benefits of the document outweighed the uncertainty that they had about its meaning.").

36. *See, e.g.*, Saikrishna B. Prakash, *Unoriginalism's Law without Meaning*, 15 Const. Comment. 529, 539–40 (1998); Randy E. Barnett, *Challenging the Priesthood of Professional Historians*, The Volokh Conspiracy (Mar. 28, 2017, 11:51 AM), https://www.washingtonpost.com/news/volokh-conspiracy /wp/2017/03/28/challenging-the-priesthood-of-professional-historians/ [https://perma.cc/X7W4-EEC2]; Mike Rappaport, *Historians and Originalists*, The Originalism Blog (Aug. 21, 2013), http://originalismblog .typepad.com/the-originalism-blog/2013/08/historians-and-originalists mike-rappaport.html [https://perma.cc/SLK3-HVZP].

37. *See* Balkin, Living Originalism, *supra* note 27, at 21–22.

38. *Id.* at 21–25; *see* Jack M. Balkin, *The Framework Model and Constitutional*

Interpretation, in Philosophical Foundations of Constitutional Law 241–43 (David Dyzenhaus & Malcom Thorburn eds., 2016).

39. Balkin, *The Framework Model and Constitutional Interpretation, supra* note 38, at 243; *see also* Sanford Levinson & Jack M. Balkin, *Constitutional Crises,* 157 U. Pa. L. Rev. 707, 714 (2009).

40. For a discussion of how constitutional construction promotes democratic legitimacy over the long run, *see* Balkin, Living Originalism, *supra* note 27, at 54–55, 113–15; and chapters 13 and 14, *infra.*

41. McGinnis & Rappaport, Originalism and the Good Constitution, *supra* note 9, at 15, 139–40 (rejecting the interpretation-construction distinction); John O. McGinnis & Michael B. Rappaport, *Original Methods Originalism: A New Theory of Interpretation and the Case against Construction,* 103 Nw. U.L. Rev. 751 (2009).

42. McGinnis & Rappaport, *The Power of Interpretation, supra* note 13, at 958 ("[W]e believe that the construction zone under the Constitution is likely to be of minor significance. While the construction zone may not be empty, it is likely to have a relatively small size and not to have a central role to play in the implementation of the Constitution. Cases in the construction zone will not often arise and when they do arise will not involve fundamental questions.").

43. *See* Balkin, *The Framework Model and Constitutional Interpretation, supra* note 38, at 4.

44. Jack M. Balkin, *Must We Be Faithful to Original Meaning?,* 7 Jerusalem Rev. Legal Stud. 57, 71 (2013) (arguing that the thin theory follows from the framework model of constitutions); *id.* at 77–80 (arguing that the thin theory is necessary for democratic legitimation over time); *see also* Andrei Marmor, *Meaning and Belief in Constitutional Interpretation,* 82 Fordham L. Rev. 577, 593–96 (2013) (explaining that how we should interpret constitutions depends on what we think constitutions are and what they are for). *Cf.* John Danaher, *The Normativity of Linguistic Originalism: A Speech Act Analysis,* 34 Law & Phil. 397, 428–31 (2015) (arguing that even the most basic assumptions about constitutional interpretation depend on normative views about the nature of constitutional speech acts).

45. The argument in this section is adapted from Balkin, *Must We Be Faithful to Original Meaning?, supra* note 44, at 77–80.

46. Balkin, Living Originalism, *supra* note 27, at 69–73, 81, 98, 112–15, 134–37.

47. *See* Bruce Ackerman, *The Living Constitution,* 120 Harv. L. Rev. 1737, 1737–41, 1750 (2010).

48. Akhil Reed Amar, America's Constitution 7, 17–18, 308 (2005) (noting that the rules for adoption by state conventions were inclusive by eighteenth century standards). *But see* Michael J. Klarman, The Framers' Coup: The Making of the United States Constitution (2016) (arguing

that the ratification process was skewed and manipulated to favor wealthy elites).

49. To give only a few examples: The 1787 Constitution was designed to make redistributive legislation difficult to pass. It protected the institution of slavery in various ways. It offered no protection for women. Its division of power between the federal government and the states not only limited redistribution but helped to protect slavery from federal interference and helped lock in the power of ruling elites in state governments.

50. Jed Rubenfeld, Revolution by Judiciary: The Structure of American Constitutional Law (2005); Jed Rubenfeld, Freedom and Time: A Theory of Constitutional Self-Government (2001).

51. Sanford Levinson, Constitutional Faith (2d ed. 2012); Jack M. Balkin, Constitutional Redemption: Political Faith in an Unjust World (2011).

52. *See* Heidi Kitrosser, *Interpretive Modesty*, 104 Geo. L.J. 459, 495 (2016) (arguing for a thin account of original meaning on these grounds).

53. *See* Jack N. Rakove, *Joe the Ploughman Reads the Constitution, or, the Poverty of Public Meaning Originalism*, 48 San Diego L. Rev. 575, 586 (2011); *see also* Saul Cornell, *Conflict, Consensus & Constitutional Meaning: The Enduring Legacy of Charles Beard*, 29 Const. Comment. 383, 405 (2014) ("Given the contentious nature of Founding era legal culture it seems unreasonable to assume that one can identify a single set of assumptions and practices from which to construct an ideal reasonable reader who could serve as model for how to understand the Constitution in 1788.").

54. Rakove, *Joe the Ploughman Reads the Constitution, supra* note 53, at 593.

55. Cornell, *Conflict, Consensus & Constitutional Meaning, supra* note 53, at 405.

56. *See* Rakove, *Joe the Ploughman Reads the Constitution, supra* note 53, at 581–82 (describing the multiplicity of sources that influenced debates over the framing).

57. Think only, for example, about the vehement disagreements about the meaning of "an Exchange established by the State under section 1311 of the Patient Protection and Affordable Care Act," 26 U.S.C. § 36B(b) (2) (A) (2012), which led to the litigation in *King v. Burwell*, 576 U.S. 473 (2015). The Affordable Care Act had been passed only five years previously, and yet people held diametrically opposed views about how to interpret the statute's language. Indeed, some participants in the debate, like Justice Antonin Scalia, insisted that if their view was not vindicated, "[w]ords no longer have meaning." *See id.* at 500 (Scalia, J., dissenting).

58. *See* Rakove, *Joe the Ploughman Reads the Constitution, supra* note 53, at 588 ("It is one thing, after all, to suppose that words fraught with political content retain a relatively fixed meaning in quiet times, but it is quite another to apply that assumption to a period like the late 1780s or the Revolutionary era more generally."); *id.* at 593 ("The adopters of the Con-

stitution inhabited a world that was actively concerned with . . . the instability of linguistic meanings, and . . . arguments about the definitions of key words and concepts were themselves central elements of political debate."); *see also* Cornell, *Conflict, Consensus & Constitutional Meaning*, *supra* note 53, at 405.

59. *See, e.g.*, Bernard Bailyn, Sometimes an Art: Nine Essays on History 22 (2015) ("The past is a different world. . . . [A]ll historical study is the search for past contexts."); Jonathan Gienapp, *Historicism and Holism: Failures of Originalist Translation*, 84 Fordham L. Rev. 935, 942 (2015) ("[T]he first key to understanding the American Founding is appreciating that it is a foreign world.").

60. Of course, historians are often also interested in using history for the present, but their professional values also cause them to be especially concerned with understanding the past on its own terms. James Kloppenberg argues that historians in the tradition of "pragmatic hermeneutics" have "[y]ok[ed] archival research to their understanding that history is written in the present and for the present." James T. Kloppenberg, *Thinking Historically: A Manifesto of Pragmatic Hermeneutics*, 9 Modern Intellectual History 201, 201 (2012). "[T]hese writers shared a commitment to producing history that, no matter how precisely it follows the evidence, inevitably reflects the concerns of the moment. They aimed to reconstruct the past with as much accuracy as possible and to address the needs and aspirations of their contemporary cultures as they understood them." *Id.*

61. *See, e.g.*, Quentin Skinner, *Meaning and Understanding in the History of Ideas, in* Meaning and Context: Quentin Skinner and His Critics 29 (James Tully & Quentin Skinner eds., 1988). *See also* Saul Cornell, *Meaning and Understanding in the History of Constitutional Ideas: The Intellectual History Alternative to Originalism*, 82 Fordham L. Rev. 721, 728 (2013) ("The current model of intellectual history, what [James] Kloppenberg calls pragmatic hermeneutics, also acknowledges an important debt to the work of the Cambridge School's approach to the history of political thought.").

62. Skinner, *Meaning and Understanding in the History of Ideas, supra* note 61, at 48 ("[N]o agent can eventually be said to have meant or done something which he could never be brought to accept as a correct description of what he had meant or done."); *id.* at 65 ("Any statement . . . is inescapably the embodiment of a particular intention, on a particular occasion, addressed to the solution of a particular problem, and thus specific to its situation in a way that it can only be naïve to try to transcend.").

63. 142 S. Ct. 2111 (2022).

64. On the problems of translating the framers' world into ours, *see* Mark V. Tushnet, *Following the Rules Laid Down: A Critique of Interpretivism and Neutral Principles*, 96 Harv. L. Rev. 781, 798–804 (1983); Paul Brest, *The*

Misconceived Quest for Original Understanding, 60 B.U. L. Rev. 204, 220–22 (1980).

65. Jonathan Gienapp, *Written Constitutionalism, Past and Present*, 39 Law & Hist. Rev. 321 (2021); Jonathan Gienapp, The Second Creation: Fixing the American Constitution in the Founding Era (2018).

66. *See, e.g.*, Larry D. Kramer, The People Themselves: Popular Constitutionalism and Judicial Review (2004) (arguing that judicial review at the founding was infrequently exercised and mostly deferential); William Michael Treanor, *Judicial Review before* Marbury, 58 Stan. L. Rev. 455 (2005) (arguing that federal judicial review was mostly deferential except for certain state laws and laws that affected the judiciary and juries).

67. Mark A. Graber, The Forgotten Fourteenth Amendment: Punish Treason, Reward Loyalty xxxiii (2023).

68. *See* Richard H. Fallon Jr., *Strict Judicial Scrutiny*, 54 UCLA L. Rev. 1267, 1270 (2007) ("[T]he modern strict scrutiny test is of relatively recent origin, having developed only in the 1960s."); Stephen A. Siegel, *The Origin of the Compelling State Interest Test and Strict Scrutiny*, 48 Am. J. Legal Hist. 355, 361 (2006) (tracing the different elements of strict scrutiny—narrow tailoring, burden shifting, and compelling state interest test—to their origins in the twentieth century).

69. Jud Campbell, *Natural Rights and the First Amendment*, 127 Yale L.J. 246, 259 (2017) ("As a general matter, natural rights did not impose fixed limitations on governmental authority. Rather, Founding Era constitutionalism allowed for restrictions of natural liberty to promote the public good—generally defined as the good of the society as a whole."); *id.* at 291 ("[C]ustomary positive law helped reveal the proper scope of natural liberty.").

70. *See* Lawrence Lessig, *Fidelity in Translation*, 71 Tex. L. Rev. 1165, 1179 (1993). I have argued that Lessig's theory of translation is best understood as a theory of constitutional construction. *See* Jack M. Balkin, *Translating the Constitution*, 118 Mich. L. Rev. 977 (2020) (reviewing Lawrence Lessig, Fidelity and Constraint: How the Supreme Court Has Read the American Constitution (2019)).

71. *See, e.g.*, Julian Davis Mortenson & Nicholas Bagley, *Delegation at the Founding*, 121 Colum. L. Rev. 277 (2021); Nicholas R. Parrillo, *A Critical Assessment of the Originalist Case against Administrative Regulatory Power: New Evidence from the Federal Tax on Private Real Estate in the 1790s*, 130 Yale L.J. 1288 (2021); Christine Chabot, *The Lost History of Delegation at the Founding*, 56 Ga. L. Rev. 81 (2021).

72. *See* Leonard Levy, Legacy of Suppression (1960).

73. *See* Akhil Reed Amar, The Words That Made Us: America's Constitutional Conversation, 1760–1840, at 442–44, 672–73 (2021); James Morton Smith, Freedom's Fetters: The Alien and Sedition Laws and American Civil Liberties (1956).

74. Wallace v. Jaffree, 432 U.S. 38, 103–04 (1985).

75. *See* Lee v. Weisman, 505 U.S. 577, 616 & n.3; 623 & n.5 (Souter, J. concurring).

76. A recent example is Justice Thomas's and Justice Breyer's dueling histories of gun regulation in *New York State Rifle & Pistol Association, Inc. v. Bruen*, 142 S. Ct. 2111 (2022).

77. Hans-Georg Gadamer, Truth and Method 313 (2d ed. 1989). Gadamer maintained that one could engage in a spirit of openness to the past that brings our own perspectives to understanding it, an example of what he called the "fusion" of horizons. *Id.* at 317, 406, 415.

78. *See* Kate Masur, Until Justice Be Done: America's First Civil Rights Movement, from the Revolution to Reconstruction (2021); 2 History of Women Suffrage 642–44, 687–89 (Elizabeth Cady Stanton, Susan B. Anthony, and Mathilda J. Gage eds., 1881, repr. 1970).

79. Loving v. Virginia, 388 U.S. 1 (1967); Brown v. Board of Education, 347 U.S. 483 (1954). For nonoriginalist criticisms, *see, e.g.*, Michael J. Klarman, Brown, *Originalism, and Constitutional Theory: A Response to Professor McConnell*, 81 Va. L. Rev. 1881 (1995).

80. For an originalist defense of *Brown, see* Michael W. McConnell, *Originalism and the Desegregation Decisions*, 81 Va. L. Rev. 947 (1995); Michael W. McConnell, *The Originalist Justification for* Brown: *A Reply to Professor Klarman*, 81 Va. L. Rev. 1937 (1995). For an originalist defense of *Loving, see* David R. Upham, *Interracial Marriage and the Original Understanding of the Privileges or Immunities Clause*, 42 Hastings Const. L. Q. 213 (2015).

81. On congressional Republicans' attitudes concerning desegregation of public schools, *see* McConnell, *Originalism and the Desegregation Decisions, supra* note 80; on the views of Republicans about interracial marriage, *see* Peter Wallenstein, Tell the Court I Love My Wife: Race, Marriage, and Law—An American History (2002); Upham, *Interracial Marriage and the Original Understanding of the Privileges or Immunities Clause, supra* note 80.

82. *See* Upham, *Interracial Marriage, supra* note 80, at 244 ("[T]here is abundant evidence of nearly universal distaste for, and even disapprobation of, interracial marriage."); McConnell, *The Originalist Justification for* Brown, *supra* note 80, at 1938–39 (noting that integrated schooling was deeply unpopular at the time the Fourteenth Amendment was ratified but that the amendment was pushed through "with little regard for public opinion"); *see also* Klarman, Brown, *Originalism, and Constitutional Theory, supra* note 79, at 1885–94; Michael J. Klarman, From Jim Crow to Civil Rights: The Supreme Court and the Struggle for Racial Equality 25–26, 146 (2004) ("[T]he original understanding of the Fourteenth Amendment plainly permitted school segregation.").

83. For a good example of the problems, see the exchange between Michael McConnell and Michael Klarman in response to McConnell's original

article. McConnell, *The Originalist Justification for* Brown, *supra* note 80; Klarman, Brown, *Originalism, and Constitutional Theory, supra* note 79.

84. To give only one example, McConnell focuses on debates in Congress between 1870 and 1875 over what became the 1875 Civil Rights Act. He argues that we can use the views of these members of Congress as a proxy for original public meaning (or original legal meaning). By the time these debates were held, however, there had been considerable turnover from the 39th Congress (elected in 1864), so we do not know what a majority—much less a supermajority—of the 39th Congress actually believed. Political incentives had also changed significantly in the years after 1866, when the 39th Congress sent the amendment to the states. After the ratification of the Fifteenth Amendment in 1870, Black people had become an important constituency of the Republican Party, especially in the South. Congressional Republicans had reasons to read an already adopted amendment more broadly in ways that they would never have publicly acknowledged or accepted in 1866 when the amendment was under consideration in the states. On the other hand, as the 1870s wore on, the public tired of Reconstruction. For a discussion of the conflicting inferences one can draw from the evidence, *see* McConnell, *The Originalist Justification for* Brown, *supra* note 80, at 1944–47; Klarman, Brown, *Originalism, and Constitutional Theory, supra* note 79, at 1903–11.

85. Balkin, Living Originalism, *supra* note 27, at 231; *see also* Randy E. Barnett & Evan D. Bernick, The Original Meaning of the Fourteenth Amendment: Its Letter and Spirit 29–30 (2021) (arguing that *Brown* is a faithful construction of the Privileges and Immunities Clause of the Fourteenth Amendment).

86. *See* Calvin TerBeek, *"Clocks Must Always Be Turned Back":* Brown v. Board of Education *and the Racial Origins of Constitutional Originalism*, 115 Am. Pol. Sci. Rev. 821 (2021) (showing that the Republican Party's attraction to originalism grew directly out of political resistance to *Brown v. Board of Education* by conservative governing elites, intellectuals, and activists in the 1950s and 1960s); Alfred Avins, *De Facto and De Jure School Segregation: Some Reflected Light on the Fourteenth Amendment from the Civil Rights Act of 1875*, 38 Miss. L.J. 179 (1967); Raoul Berger, Government by Judiciary: The Transformation of the Fourteenth Amendment 117–33, 245 (1977); *see generally* Earl Maltz, *Originalism and the Desegregation Decisions—A Response to Professor McConnell*, 13 Const. Comm. 223 (1996).

87. *See* Jack M. Balkin, Constitutional Redemption: Political Faith in an Unjust World 174 (2011) (quoting Planned Parenthood of Se. Pa. v. Casey, 505 U.S. 833, 863 (1992) (joint opinion of Kennedy, O'Connor, and Souter, JJ.)).

88. *See, e.g.*, Robert H. Bork, The Tempting of America: The Political Seduction of the Law 81–83 (1990); McConnell, *Originalism and the Desegregation Decisions, supra* note 80.

89. *See* Christina Mulligan, Michael Douma, Hans Lind & Brian Quinn, *Founding Era Translations of the Constitution*, 31 Const. Comm. 1, 4 (2016) (noting that Dutch and German translations of the Constitution circulated among non-English-speaking citizens during adoption, so that some parts of the text would have different public meanings even under a thin conception); Heidi Kitrosser, *Interpretive Modesty*, 104 Geo. L.J. 459, 482 (2016) ("[W]here no common core meaning exists, . . . it is preferable to . . . identify the range of plausible original meanings in the interpretation zone, while choosing between those meanings in the construction zone.").

Chapter Nine. Making Originalist Arguments

1. Generally speaking, theoretical authorities give us reasons to believe something, while practical authorities give us reasons to do things. Joseph Raz, Between Authority and Interpretation: On the Theory of Law and Practical Reason (2009); Joseph Raz, The Authority of Law: Essays on Law and Morality (1979). The originalist theory of authority treats framers and adopters as possessing both theoretical authority about the meaning of the Constitution and practical authority about how we should apply it.

2. *See, e.g.*, Michael Kent Curtis, *John A. Bingham and the Story of American Liberty: The Lost Cause Meets the "Lost Clause,"* 36 Akron L. Rev. 617, 620 (2003) ("[F]or years our national story largely ignored our second group of framers who gave the nation the new birth of freedom in the post–Civil War amendments."); Tom Donnelly, *Our Forgotten Founders: Reconstruction, Public Education, and Constitutional Heroism*, 58 Clev. St. L. Rev. 115 (2010) (noting lack of attention to Reconstruction-era founders in public education).

3. *See* David W. Blight, Race and Reunion: The Civil War in American Memory 2 (2009) (describing the "story of how the forces of reconciliation overwhelmed the emancipationist vision in the national culture, how the inexorable drive for reunion both used and trumped race"); Pamela Brandwein, Reconstructing Reconstruction: The Supreme Court and the Production of Historical Truth 61–68 (1999) (noting how Supreme Court opinions since the Civil War have portrayed Reconstruction and downplayed its egalitarian and transformative aspects); Robert Meister, *Forgiving and Forgetting: Lincoln and the Politics of National Recovery, in* Human Rights in Political Transitions: Gettysburg to Bosnia 135, 163–64 (Carla Hesse & Robert Post eds., 1999); Norman W. Spaulding, *Constitution as Countermonument: Federalism, Reconstruction, and the Problem of Collective Memory*, 103 Colum. L. Rev. 1992, 2033 (2003) ("Respect for state sovereignty (and the twin theory that the War was fundamentally about preserving the Union) thus became a powerful, publicly acceptable,

and legally authoritative framework for expressing the rather perverse desire to abandon the principles of equality implicated in the War for the sake of reconciliation with southern whites.").

4. *See* Donnelly, *Our Forgotten Founders, supra* note 2, at 142–43 (describing the Dunning School's influence).

5. If the issue is generally recognized legal terms of art, the opinions of any well-trained lawyer or judge of the period should be equally good.

6. *See, e.g.*, Baze v. Rees, 553 U.S. 35, 97 (2008) (Thomas, J., concurring) (consulting a dictionary as to the meaning of the word "cruel" in the Cruel and Unusual Punishments Clause); Randy E. Barnett, *New Evidence of the Original Meaning of the Commerce Clause*, 55 Ark. L. Rev. 847, 856–65 (2003) (examining every use of the term "commerce" in the *Pennsylvania Gazette* that appeared from 1728 to 1800).

7. Jamal Greene, *The Case for Original Intent*, 80 Geo. Wash. L. Rev. 1683, 1697 (2012). Akhil Amar's well-known defense of textualism is largely about the text's relationship to ethos, tradition, and honored authority. Amar emphasizes the text's wisdom, its connection to epic narratives of American history, its role as a common cultural focal point, and its singular ability to bind the diverse people of the United States together as one nation. *See* Akhil Reed Amar, *The Supreme Court 1999 Term: Foreword: The Document and the Doctrine*, 114 Harv L. Rev. 26, 29–30 (2000) (emphasizing that the text must be understood against epic narratives and great events); *id.* at 43–45 (emphasizing the comparative wisdom of the text); *id.* at 47 ("[I]n the Constitution itself, we can all find a common vocabulary for our common deliberations, and a shared narrative thread. . . . [T]he Constitution is and should be our national bedtime story.").

8. *See* Jack M. Balkin, Living Originalism 142 (2011) ("Structural principles do not have to have been intended by anyone in particular; indeed, they may only become apparent over time as we watch how the various elements of the constitutional system interact with each other."); *id.* at 262 ("[S]tructural principles might emerge from the constitutional system that no single person or generation intended. . . . We must look to other generations as well as the founding generation to understand how constitutional structures should work (and how they might fail to work).").

9. *See, e.g.*, Morse v. Frederick, 551 U.S. 393, 410–11 (2007) (Thomas, J., concurring) (arguing that children have no First Amendment rights independent of their parents).

10. The Federalist No. 47, at 293 (James Madison) (Gary Wills ed., 2003).

11. *See, e.g.*, Seila Law LLC v. Consumer Financial Protection Bureau, 140 S. Ct. 2183 (2020); Michael W. McConnell, The President Who Would Not Be King: Executive Power under The Constitution (2020); Jonathan Gienapp, The Second Creation: Fixing the American Constitution in the Founding Era (2018); Jane Manners & Lev Menand, *The Three*

Permissions: Presidential Removal and the Statutory Limits of Agency Independence, 121 Colum. L. Rev. 1 (2021); Jed Handelsman Shugerman, *Presidential Removal: The Marbury Problem and the Madison Solutions,* 89 Fordham L. Rev. 2085 (2021); Daniel D. Birk, *Interrogating the Historical Basis for a Unitary Executive,* 73 Stan. L. Rev. 175 (2021); Christine Kexel Chabot, *Is the Federal Reserve Constitutional? An Originalist Argument for Independent Agencies,* 96 Notre Dame. L. Rev. 1, 3–4 (2020); Julian Davis Mortenson, *The Executive Power Clause,* 168 U. Pa. L. Rev. 1269 (2020); Julian Davis Mortenson, *Article II Vests the Executive Power, Not the Royal Prerogative,* 119 Colum. L. Rev. 1169 (2019).

12. *See, e.g.,* Louis Fisher, Presidential War Power (1995); John Hart Ely, War and Responsibility: Constitutional Lessons of Vietnam and Its Aftermath 3–10, 139–52 (1993); Harold Hongju Koh, The National Security Constitution: Sharing Power after the Iran-Contra Affair 74–77 (1990); Alexander M. Bickel, *Congress, the President and the Power to Wage War,* 48 Chi.-Kent L. Rev. 131 (1971).

13. Similar points apply to arguments from custom. Current customs may have begun long after the founders or may have evolved significantly since their day. People might argue for a return to or a restoration of the (imagined) mores of the founding generation, despite intervening changes in society. This is not an argument for following long-standing custom; it is an argument for *reform* or *revision* of long-standing custom based on the ethical authority of the founders. Thus, it is better described as an argument from ethos or honored authority.

14. Moreover, to the extent that people identify a timeless common law with the natural rights of Englishmen, the common law at the time of the founding becomes a proxy for natural rights. *See* John Phillip Reid, *Law and History,* 27 Loy. L.A. L. Rev. 193, 211–12 (1993) (discussing the theory of the "ancient constitution" identified with Magna Carta).

15. *See* Jack M. Balkin, *"Wrong the Day It Was Decided": Lochner and Constitutional Historicism,* 85 B.U. L. Rev. 677, 681 (2005) ("Anti-canonical cases serve as examples of how the Constitution should not be interpreted and how judges should not behave."); J. M. Balkin & Sanford Levinson, *The Canons of Constitutional Law,* 111 Harv. L. Rev. 963, 1018–19 (1998) (explaining that the anticanon consists of "cases that any theory worth its salt must show are wrongly decided" and that help normalize belief about law); Jamal Greene, *The Anticanon,* 125 Harv. L. Rev. 379, 384 (2011) (explaining that anticanonical cases are a device of ethical argument because they "symbolize a set of generalized ethical propositions that we [as a nation] have collectively renounced"); Richard A. Primus, *Canon, Anti-canon, and Judicial Dissent,* 48 Duke L.J. 243, 245 (1998) (explaining that the anticanon consists of "the set of texts that are important but normatively disapproved").

16. *See, e.g.,* Thomas W. Merrill, *Originalism, Stare Decisis and the Promotion*

of Judicial Restraint, 22 Const. Comment. 271, 273 (2005) (arguing for "a strong theory of precedent in constitutional law" even when it might conflict with originalism because "it would promote judicial restraint"); Henry Paul Monaghan, *Supremacy Clause Textualism*, 110 Colum. L. Rev. 731, 794 (2010) ("Unless we are prepared to condemn our existing constitutional practice as illegitimate, the propriety of other modes of argument besides originalism, particularly those based upon precedent, must be acknowledged."); Antonin Scalia, *Originalism: The Lesser Evil*, 57 U. Cin. L. Rev. 849, 861 (1989) ("[A]lmost every originalist would adulterate [the theory] with the doctrine of stare decisis."); Antonin Scalia, *Response, in* A Matter of Interpretation: Federal Courts and the Law 129, 139–40 (Amy Guttman ed., 1997) (defending use of nonoriginalist precedents as a "pragmatic exception" in the interests of stability); *cf.* Michael W. McConnell, *The Importance of Humility in Judicial Review: A Comment on Ronald Dworkin's "Moral Reading" of the Constitution*, 65 Fordham L. Rev. 1269, 1292 (1997) (noting the roles of text, original understanding, the presumption of constitutionality, tradition, and precedent as appropriate constraints on judicial decision-making that produce humility). Other originalists, by contrast, argue that original meaning should generally control. *See, e.g.*, Akhil Reed Amar, Heller, HLR, *and Holistic Legal Reasoning*, 122 Harv. L. Rev. 145, 157–62 (2008) (arguing that "a proper consideration, consistent with the Constitution's general structure of coordinate branches, should not treat the Supreme Court's past constitutional errors as categorically different from the past constitutional errors of other branches"; nevertheless, liberty-expanding precedents that are incorrect when decided should survive when there has been popular ratification); Gary Lawson, *The Constitutional Case against Precedent*, 17 Harv. J.L. & Pub. Pol'y 23, 24 (1994) ("[T]he practice of following precedent is not merely nonobligatory or a bad idea; it is affirmatively inconsistent with the federal Constitution."); Michael Stokes Paulsen, *The Intrinsically Corrupting Influence of Precedent*, 22 Const. Comment. 289, 291 (2005) ("*Stare decisis* not only impairs or corrupts proper constitutional interpretation. [It] is *unconstitutional*, precisely to the extent that it yields deviations from the correct interpretation of the Constitution!").

17. *See* Robert Post, *Theories of Constitutional Interpretation*, 30 Representations 13, 29 (1990) ("[H]istorical interpretation seemingly presents itself as a self-denying submission to the identity of past ratifiers, . . . [yet] that identity is authoritative only insofar as we can be persuaded to adopt it as our own.").

18. *Id.* (arguing that "the authority of historical interpretation will in significant measure depend" on our present "identification, [or] a community of interest, with the framers or ratifiers" so that "'[t]heir' consent . . . is 'our' consent; they spoke 'for' us").

19. *Id.* at 28–29, 40 n.77; *see also* Richard A. Primus, *When Should Original Meanings Matter?*, 107 Mich. L. Rev. 165, 209 (2008) (arguing that recent amendments should be construed according to original understandings out of "respect for democratic decisionmaking").

20. *See, e.g.,* David A. Strauss, *Can Originalism Be Saved?*, 92 B.U. L. Rev. 1161, 1163 (2012) ("If we are allowed to change the level of generality at which we characterize the original understandings, then originalism can justify anything."); Laurence H. Tribe & Michael C. Dorf, *Levels of Generality in the Definition of Rights*, 57 U. Chi. L. Rev. 1057, 1063 (1990) ("Whose intent matters and at what level of generality? No judge can answer this question without reference to a value-laden, extra-textual political theory.").

21. *See, e.g.,* Michael H. v. Gerald D., 491 U.S. 110, 127 n.6 (1989) (Scalia, J.) (noting that traditions can be described at various levels of generality and arguing that judges must "adopt the most specific tradition as the point of reference" in order to avoid "arbitrary decisionmaking"); J. M. Balkin, *Tradition, Betrayal, and the Politics of Deconstruction*, 11 Cardozo L. Rev. 1613, 1615 (1990) (noting that traditions can be characterized multiply, are constantly in the process of change, and may feature tensions or even inconsistencies when viewed at different levels of generality); Tribe & Dorf, *Levels of Generality in the Definition of Rights, supra* note 20, at 1059 (criticizing Scalia's test and arguing that "judges trained in the method of the common law can generalize from prior cases without merely imposing their own values").

22. *See* Balkin, *Tradition, Betrayal, and the Politics of Deconstruction, supra* note 21, at 1615.

23. *See* Paul Brest, *The Misconceived Quest for the Original Understanding*, 60 B.U. L. Rev. 204, 213–17 (1980) (noting difficulties that the framers themselves did not recognize intentionalism as a valid form of argument, that there may not be an original intention or understanding on a wide range of certain questions, that intentions and understandings may have differed among the relevant adopters, that intentions and understandings may be indeterminate, or that they cannot be made determinate "unless those intentions are understood at a level of generality too high to give practical guidance"); Greene, *The Case for Original Intent, supra* note 7, at 1687–88 (citing Randy E. Barnett, *An Originalism for Nonoriginalists*, 45 Loy. L. Rev. 611, 611–12, 620 (1999)); H. Jefferson Powell, *The Original Understanding of Original Intent*, 98 Harv. L. Rev. 885, 886–88 (1985); *see also* Hans W. Baade, *"Original Intent" in Historical Perspective: Some Critical Glosses*, 69 Tex. L. Rev. 1001 (1991) (noting that general acceptance of arguments from intention appear well after the founding period); Caleb Nelson, *Originalism and Interpretive Conventions*, 70 U. Chi. L. Rev. 519, 585–86 (2003) (noting that a theory of original understanding "has trouble handling disagreements among the ratifiers about the

meaning of the Constitution. . . . [I]t is hard enough to identify consensus interpretations within a single state's convention. The difficulties are only magnified when one tries to identify consensus interpretations across different states" that ratified at different times in the debate).

24. *See* David McGowan, *Ethos in Law and History: Alexander Hamilton,* The Federalist, *and the Supreme Court,* 85 Minn. L. Rev. 755, 757 (2001) ("On the public-meaning theory, *The Federalist* is no more than a topical equivalent of Samuel Johnson's dictionary or any other usage guide, and the theory cannot distinguish the writings of Hamilton and Madison from those of any literate hack of the day."). Vasan Kesavan and Michael Stokes Paulsen agree. Vasan Kesavan & Michael Stokes Paulsen, *The Interpretive Force of the Constitution's Secret Drafting History,* 91 Geo. L.J. 1113, 1156–57 (2003) ("We should read *The Federalist* because those essays show the meaning of the words of the Constitution, in context, to ordinary readers, speakers, and writers of the English language, reading a document of this type, at the time adopted."). Nevertheless, Kesavan and Paulsen go on to explain why familiar sources like *The Federalist,* the state ratifying conventions, and Madison's notes should nevertheless have greater authority than the correspondence of ordinary citizens. They are, among other things, "an excellent topical concordance" of words and phrases in the Constitution. *Id.* at 1147–48. In addition, they provide "second-best sources of original public meaning," which nevertheless are "not *constitutive* of meaning, and hence binding determinations of meaning in their own right." *Id.* at 1148–49.

25. *See* Greene, *The Case for Original Intent, supra* note 7, at 1693 ("As evidence of the objective public meaning of the Necessary and Proper Clause, it is not obvious why [the Anti-Federalist] Brutus's view—that it gives Congress 'virtually unlimited power'—is any less reliable than Hamilton's or Madison's."); *id.* at 1694 (arguing that if proponents of the Constitution are cited more often than opponents, "it is not because opponents are somehow less knowledgeable about the contemporary meaning of words or have less access to prevailing public wisdom").

26. *See id.* at 1691. Greene relies on studies in Pamela C. Corley, Robert M. Howard & David C. Nixon, *The Supreme Court and Opinion Content: The Use of* The Federalist Papers, 58 Pol. Res. Q. 329, 330 (2005); Melvyn R. Durchslag, *The Supreme Court and* The Federalist Papers*: Is There Less Here than Meets the Eye?,* 14 Wm. & Mary Bill Rts. J. 243, 295, 297 (2005); Ira C. Lupu, *Time, the Supreme Court, and* The Federalist, 66 Geo. Wash. L. Rev. 1324, 1328 (1998); and Louis J. Sirico Jr., *The Supreme Court and the Constitutional Convention,* 27 J.L. & Pol. 63, 70–71 (2011).

27. *See* Greene, *The Case for Original Intent, supra* note 7, at 1694–95 (listing various problems with these sources).

28. *See* Ray Raphael, Constitutional Myths: What We Get Wrong and How

to Get It Right 114–23 (2013) (noting that Alexander Hamilton's essays probably did not reflect his own views on a number of subjects). Madison, who had strongly opposed the compromise that gave the small states equal votes in the Senate, was nevertheless required to defend it in *The Federalist No. 62*. Madison had wanted a stronger national government than the convention ultimately produced, and he had repeatedly pushed for a national power to veto all state legislation. He even expressed to Jefferson his fears that the new government might fail without the powers he sought for it. Raphael, *supra*, at 84–90; Letter from James Madison to Thomas Jefferson, Oct. 24, 1787, *in* 1 The Founders' Constitution, ch. 17, document 22 (Philip B. Kurland & Ralph Lerner eds., 2000), *available at* http://press-pubs.uchicago.edu/founders/documents /v1ch17s22.html [https://perma.cc/4XLZ-HG25]. Nevertheless, in public, Madison lauded the careful balance of federal and state powers in the new Constitution and emphasized the states' retention of sovereignty in *The Federalist No. 39* and *The Federalist No. 45*. Raphael, *supra*, at 89–91.

29. *See* Raphael, Constitutional Myths, *supra* note 28, at 112 (noting that by the time New York voted, New Hampshire and Virginia had already ratified). Moreover, "[f]ollowing *The Federalist No. 21*, only one of the remaining sixty-four essays appeared in any of the state's papers north of the city." *Id.* at 275 n.23; *see also* John P. Kaminski, *New York: The Reluctant Pillar*, *in* The Reluctant Pillar: New York and the Adoption of the Federal Constitution 71–72 (Stephen L. Schechter ed., 1985) ("Despite the significant place *The Federalist* has assumed in American political thought, its impact on New York's reception of the Constitution was negligible.").

30. *See* Jack N. Rakove, *Fidelity through History (or to It)*, 65 Fordham L. Rev. 1587, 1597 (1997) ("*The Federalist* exercised much less influence over the debates of 1787–88 than did James Wilson's published speeches to a Federalist crowd at the Pennsylvania statehouse and at the Harrisburg ratifying convention.").

31. Raphael, Constitutional Myths, *supra* note 28, at 111.

32. *Id.*

33. *Id.*

34. *Id.*

35. *Id.* at 106.

36. *Id.*

37. Kesavan & Paulsen, *The Interpretive Force of the Constitution's Secret Drafting History*, *supra* note 24, at 1153.

38. *See* James H. Hutson, *The Creation of the Constitution: The Integrity of the Documentary Record*, 65 Tex. L. Rev. 1, 24 (1986) ("At [Madison's] death in 1836, the notes passed to his widow who sold them to the federal government, which commissioned their publication in 1840.").

39. *See id.* at 34 ("If read aloud, Madison's notes for any particular day consume only a few minutes, suggesting that he may have recorded only a small part of each day's proceedings.").

40. Mary Sarah Bilder, Madison's Hand: Revising the Constitutional Convention (2015).

41. *See* Greene, *The Case for Original Intent, supra* note 7, at 1702 ("[O]riginal intent as such, invoked for its inherent authority value, has been a significant part of constitutional practice since the beginning of the republic and remains significant today."); Richard S. Kay, *Original Intention and Public Meaning in Constitutional Interpretation,* 103 Nw. U. L. Rev. 703, 704 (2009) ("The idea that judicial interpretation of the Constitution should be governed by the real subjective intentions of the human beings who established it as governing law was, for a long time, so natural as to require no name.").

42. Greene, *The Case for Original Intent, supra* note 7, at 1696–97 (noting that originalist arguments "are authoritative not because they specify the semantic meaning of a text, but because they reflect a set of values that are offered by proponents as uniquely or especially constitutive of American identity"); McGowan, *Ethos in Law and History, supra* note 24, at 757–59, 825–35 (noting that in practice, original meaning arguments appeal to ethos); Post, *Theories of Constitutional Interpretation, supra* note 17, at 29 (historical appeals to framers are "a characterization of the national ethos"); *cf.* Michael C. Dorf, *Integrating Normative and Descriptive Constitutional Theory: The Case of Original Meaning,* 85 Geo. L.J. 1765, 1770, 1800–05 (1997) (describing and approving of "ancestral" and "heroic" uses of originalism in constitutional argument).

43. Kennedy v. Bremerton School District, 142 S. Ct. 2407 (2022); American Legion v. American Humanist Association, 139 S. Ct. 2067 (2019); Town of Greece v. Galloway, 572 U.S. 565 (2014); New York State Rifle & Pistol Assn., Inc. v. Bruen, 142 S. Ct. 2111 (2022).

44. *New York State Rifle & Pistol Assn.,* 142 S. Ct. at 2161 (Kavanaugh, J., concurring).

45. This paragraph and the next two are adapted from Jack M. Balkin, *Text, History and Tradition: Discussion Questions on* New York State Rifle and Pistol Association, Inc. v. Bruen, Balkinization (July 6, 2022), https://balkin.blogspot.com/2022/07/text-history-and-tradition-discussion.html [https://perma.cc/DS6N-DLS8].

Chapter Ten. Originalist Arguments for Everyone

1. Larry D. Kramer, *When Lawyers Do History,* 72 Geo. Wash. L. Rev. 387, 407 (2003) ("[T]he originalist interpretive method unavoidably involves a creative act by the modern interpreter—that of completing an argument that may have been unfinished when the Constitution was adopted."). As

Robert Bork put it, "It is the task of the judge in this generation to discern how the framers' values, defined in the context of the world they knew, apply to the world we know." Robert H. Bork, The Tempting of America 167–68 (1990) (quoting Ollman v. Evans, 750 F.2d 970, 995 (D.C. Cir. 1984) (*en banc*) (Bork, J., concurring), cert. denied, 471 U.S. 1127 (1984)).

2. *See* Robert Post & Reva Siegel, *Originalism as a Political Practice: The Right's Living Constitution*, 75 Fordham L. Rev. 545, 565, 569 (2006).

3. *Id.* at 569.

4. Raoul Berger, Government by Judiciary: The Transformation of the Fourteenth Amendment (1977); Robert H. Bork, *Neutral Principles and Some First Amendment Problems*, 47 Ind. L.J. 1, 28 (1971) (arguing that the First Amendment protects only political speech and "does not cover scientific, educational, commercial or literary expressions as such"). By the 1990s, after many conservatives had changed their minds and supported First Amendment protections for commercial speech, so too did Bork. *See* Jonathan H. Adler, *Robert Bork and Commercial Speech*, 10 J.L. Econ. & Pol'y (2013–14) (offering a number of possible different reasons for Bork's shift); Employment Division, Department of Human Resources of Oregon v. Smith, 494 U.S. 872 (1990) (majority opinion of Scalia, J.).

5. Post & Siegel, *Originalism as a Political Practice*, supra note 2, at 570 ("[T]he real lifeblood of originalism has been its organization as a political practice, which forges a living connection between the Constitution and contemporary conservative ideals.").

6. *See id.* at 572 ("Originalism is so powerfully appealing because conservatives have succeeded in fusing contemporary political concerns with authoritative constitutional narrative . . . driven by a politics of restoration, which encourages citizens to protect traditional forms of life they fear are threatened . . . by modern mores and by a Court that has (mis)construed the Constitution to require social change.").

7. *Id.* at 571–72.

8. Joshua Stein, Note, *Historians before the Bench: Friends of the Court, Foes of Originalism*, 25 Yale J.L. & Human. 359 (2013).

9. Jack M. Balkin, *Must We Be Faithful to Original Meaning?*, 7 Jerusalem Rev. Legal Stud. 57, 85 (2013) (comparing constitutional change to the oral tradition in Jewish law and explaining that "[a] living tradition needs memory and resources to work with, even if it changes over time").

10. *See* Post & Siegel, *Originalism as a Political Practice*, *supra* note 2, at 574 ("To counter originalism, progressives need more than a logical critique. They need—as they have had at different junctures in our nation's history—a vision of collective life able to generate constitutional claims of equal motive and authority, whether those claims sound in the register of restoration or redemption.").

11. *See* Jamal Greene, *Fourteenth Amendment Originalism*, 71 Md. L. Rev. 978, 998 (2012) ("Those who affiliate with originalism tend to emphasize restorative narratives; those who affiliate with living constitutionalism tend to emphasize redemptive narratives.").

12. Jack M. Balkin, Constitutional Redemption: Political Faith in an Unjust World 5 (2011).

Chapter Eleven. The Power of Memory and Erasure

1. Eviatar Zerubavel, Time Maps: Collective Memory and the Shape of the Past 2 (2003) ("[N]ot everything that happens is preserved in our memory, as many past events are actually cast into oblivion. Even what we conventionally consider 'history' . . . is not a truly comprehensive record of everything that ever happened, but only a small part of it that we have come to preserve as public memory.").

2. Chris Weedon & Glenn Jordan, *Collective Memory: Theory and Politics*, 22 Soc. Semiotics 143 (2012) ("Collective memory and the institutions and practices that support it help to create, sustain and reproduce the 'imagined communities' with which individuals identify and that give them a sense of history, place and belonging.") (citing Benedict Anderson, Imagined Communities: Reflections on the Origin and Spread of Nationalism (rev. ed. 2006)).

3. *See* Reva B. Siegel, *The Politics of Constitutional Memory*, 20 Geo. J.L. & Pub. Pol'y 19, 21 (2022) (defining constitutional memory as a "form of collective memory forged through constitutional interpretation"); *id.* ("The Constitution's interpreters are continuously producing constitutional memory . . . as they tell stories about the nation's past experience to clarify the meaning of the nation's commitments, to guide practical reason, and to help express the nation's identity and values.").

4. Maurice Halbwachs, On Collective Memory 38 (Lewis A. Coser ed. & trans., Univ. of Chi. Press 1992) (1925).

5. Zerubavel, Time Maps, *supra* note 1, at 2–4; *see also* Ernest Renan, *What Is a Nation?*, *in* What Is a Nation? and Other Political Writings 247, 261 (2018) ("A nation is a soul, a spiritual principle. Two things that, in truth, are but one constitute this soul, this spiritual principle. . . . One is the possession in common of a rich legacy of memories; the other is present consent, the desire to live together, the will to perpetuate the value of the heritage that one has received in an undivided form.").

6. Halbwachs, On Collective Memory, *supra* note 4, at 38.

7. Zerubavel, Time Maps, *supra* note 1, at 4 ("The difference between what Americans and Indians tend to recall from wedding ceremonies, for example, is a product of their having been socialized into different *mnemonic traditions* involving altogether different mental filters commonly shared by their respective mnemonic communities.").

8. *Id.*
9. Jan Assmann, *Collective Memory and Cultural Identity*, 65 New German Critique, 126–27 (1995). Assmann calls these forms of collective memory "communicative memory," which he distinguishes from cultural memory.
10. *Id.*
11. *Id.* at 128–30. Assmann calls these forms of collective memory "cultural memory," while others use the terms "collective memory" and "cultural memory" more or less interchangeably.
12. *See generally* Pierre Nora, *Conflicts and Divisions, in* 1 Realms of Memory: The Construction of the French Past (Arthur Goldhammer trans., 1996) (theorizing the locations of memory in various material and nonmaterial sites and practices).
13. *See, e.g.*, Sanford Levinson, Written in Stone: Public Monuments in Changing Societies (rev. ed. 2018) (explaining how commemorative monuments are employed to shape collective memory); Yael Zerubavel, Recovered Roots: Collective Memory and the Making of Israeli National Tradition 5–6 (1995) (explaining that commemoration is "central to our understanding of the dynamics of memory change"); Paul Connerton, How Societies Remember (1989) (emphasizing the role of commemoration and performance in constructing social memory).
14. Zerubavel, Time Maps, *supra* note 1, at 2.
15. *See, e.g.*, Barbie Zelizer, *Reading the Past against the Grain: The Shape of Memory Studies*, 12 Critical Stud. Mass Comm. 214, 214 (1995) ("By definition, collective memory . . . presumes activities of sharing, discussion, negotiation, and, often, contestation."); *see also* Jeffrey K. Olick & Joyce Robbins, *Social Memory Studies: From "Collective Memory" to the Historical Sociology of Mnemonic Practices* 24 Ann. Rev. Soc. 105, 126–28 (1998) (reviewing the literature on the social contestation of memory); Levinson, Written in Stone, *supra* note 13 (describing how public monuments become the occasion for continuing controversies in political and social life).
16. *See* Barry Schwartz, *Collective Forgetting and the Symbolic Power of Oneness: The Strange Apotheosis of Rosa Parks*, 72 Soc. Psychol. Q. 123, 123 (2009) (explaining how, through processes of commemoration that produce collective memory, Rosa Parks became remembered as the singular example of the courage of civil rights protesters).
17. *See, e.g.*, Zerubavel, Recovered Roots, *supra* note 13, at 11 ("Counter-memory challenges . . . hegemony by offering a divergent commemorative narrative representing the views of marginalized individuals or groups within the society."); Katherine M. Franke, *The Uses of History in Struggles for Racial Justice: Colonizing the Past and Managing Memory*, 47 UCLA L. Rev. 1673, 1679 (2000) ("For most racial and ethnic groups in the United States, the memory of 'their' treatment in the past is relevant to

the present insofar as it plays a fundamental role in the constitution of present group identity."); Olick & Robbins, *Social Memory Studies, supra* note 15, at 126–27 (discussing countermemories).

18. Lochner v. New York, 198 U.S. 45 (1905); McCulloch v. Maryland, 17 U.S. 316 (1819).

19. *See* Zerubavel, Recovered Roots, *supra* note 13, at 5; Assmann, *Collective Memory and Cultural Identity, supra* note 9, at 130.

20. Eviatar Zerubavel, *Social Memories: Steps to a Sociology of the Past*, 19 Qualitative Soc. 283, 290 (1996).

21. *Id.* ("[S]*ociobiographical memory* . . . accounts for the sense of pride, pain, or shame we sometimes experience with regard to events that had happened to groups and communities to which we belong long before we joined them.").

22. *See* Renan, What Is a Nation?, *supra* note 5, at 261 ("Where national memories are concerned, grief is of more value than triumphs, for it imposes duties, it requires a common effort. A nation is therefore a vast solidarity, constituted by the sentiment of the sacrifices one has made and of those one is yet prepared to make.").

23. *Cf.* Zerubavel, Time Maps, *supra* note 1, at 3 ("[A]cquiring a group's memories and thereby identifying with its collective past is part of the process of acquiring any social identity, and familiarizing members with that past is a major part of communities' efforts to assimilate them.").

24. J. M. Balkin, Cultural Software: A Theory of Ideology 203–05 (1998) (discussing the functions of group narratives); Michael Schudson, *Dynamics of Distortion in Collective Memory, in* Memory Distortion: How Minds, Brains, and Societies Reconstruct the Past 355 (Daniel L. Schacter ed., 1995) ("To pass on a version of the past, the past must be encapsulated into some sort of cultural form, and generally this is a narrative, a story . . . with a protagonist and obstacles in his or her way and efforts to overcome them.").

25. *See* W. E. B. Dubois, Black Reconstruction in America, 1860–1880 (1935); Eric Foner, Reconstruction: America's Unfinished Revolution, 1863–1877 (1988).

26. *Court Packing as History and Memory: Testimony Before the Presidential Commission on the Supreme Court of the United States* 1–3, 21–22 (June 30, 2021) (statement of Laura Kalman, Distinguished Research Professor, U.C. Santa Barbara), https://www.whitehouse.gov/wp-content/uploads/2021/06/Kalman-06.25.2021.pdf [https://perma.cc/6LT4-Z54K].

27. *See* Tara Subramaniam, *Fact-Checking Manchin's Claim the Senate Filibuster Has Not Been Changed in 232 Years*, CNN (Jan. 13, 2022, 4:40 PM), https://www.cnn.com/2022/01/13/politics/manchin-filibuster-fact-check/index.html [https://perma.cc/EA78-D9FH].

28. Balkin, Cultural Software, *supra* note 24, at 191–93, 210.

29. *Id.*

30. *Id.* at 208, 210–12.
31. *Id.* at 210–11.
32. *Id.* at 212–15.
33. *Id.* at 200, 204, 214–15.
34. *Id.* at 203–04.
35. *See* Renan, What Is a Nation?, *supra* note 5, at 251 ("The act of forgetting, I would even say, historical error, is an essential factor in the creation of a nation."); *id.* ("[T]he essence of a nation is that all individuals have many things in common, and also that they have forgotten many things.").
36. Scott A. Small, Forgetting: The Benefits of Not Remembering 43–44 (2021) (explaining that forgetting is necessary to forming the generalizations necessary for accumulating knowledge); Jorge Luis Borges, Collected Fictions 137 (Andrew Hurley trans., 1999) ("To think is to ignore (or forget) differences, to generalize, to abstract.").
37. Zelizer, *Reading the Past against the Grain, supra* note 15, at 220.
38. *Cf.* George Orwell, 1984, at 37 (Everyman's Library ed. 1987) ("'Who controls the past,' ran the Party slogan, 'controls the future: who controls the present controls the past.'").
39. *See* Robyn Autry, Desegregating the Past: The Public Life of Memory in the United States and South Africa 27 (2017); Elizabeth Jelin, State Repression and the Labors of Memory 33–34 (2003); Francesca Lessa, Memory and Transitional Justice in Argentina and Uruguay: Against Impunity 19 (2013) (summarizing Jelin's concept of memory entrepreneurs); *see also* Gary Alan Fine, Difficult Reputations: Collective Memories of the Evil, Inept, and Controversial 63 (2001) (offering the related concept of "reputational entrepreneurs").
40. Jelin, State Repression and the Labors of Memory, *supra* note 39, at 33.
41. *Id.* at 33–35; Autry, Desegregating the Past, *supra* note 39, at 27–29.
42. R. B. Bernstein, The Founding Fathers Reconsidered 116 (2009) (noting that Jefferson's and Hamilton's reputations "have risen and fallen almost in complementary historical cycles, suggesting that their struggles with one another when alive continue by proxy long after their deaths.").
43. Philip J. Cohen, Serbia's Secret War: Propaganda and the Deceit of History 134 (1996).
44. Schudson, *Dynamics of Distortion in Collective Memory, supra* note 24, at 351–55 (noting the many ways that memory is instrumentalized for present-day purposes).
45. *Cf.* Carl N. Degler, *Why Historians Change Their Minds*, 45 Pac. Hist. Rev. 167, 184 (1976) ("[I]f historians did not change their minds about the past as the values of the society shifted, their history would cease to be part of the culture and therefore incapable of illuminating the present with the light of the past.").
46. Jan Assmann, Moses the Egyptian: The Memory of Egypt in Western

Monotheism 9–10 (1997) ("Events tend to be forgotten unless they live on in collective memory. . . . The reason for this living on lies in the continuous relevance of these events. This relevance comes not from their historical past, but from an ever-changing present in which these events are remembered as facts of importance.") (internal quotations omitted).

47. *See, e.g.,* John Fabian Witt, American Contagions: Epidemics and the Law from Smallpox to COVID-19 (2022).

48. Jelin, State Repression and the Labors of Memory, *supra* note 39, at 33–37.

49. Timothy Kubal & Rene Becerra, *Social Movements and Collective Memory,* 8 Soc. Compass 865, 868 (2014); *cf.* Jelin, State Repression and the Labors of Memory, *supra* note 39, at 36 ("The role of memory entrepreneurs is central to the dynamics of the conflicts that surround public memory.").

50. *See* chapters 14 and 15, *infra.*

51. Nikolay Koposov, Memory Laws, Memory Wars: The Politics of the Past in Europe and Russia (2018).

52. *Id.* at 1–8.

53. Timothy Snyder, *The War on History Is a War on Democracy,* N.Y. Times (June 26, 2021), https://www.nytimes.com/2021/06/29/magazine/memory-laws.html [https://perma.cc/UXU4-TCS6].

54. Reva B. Siegel, *2005–06 Brennan Center Symposium Lecture, Constitutional Culture, Social Movement Conflict and Constitutional Change: The Case of the De Facto ERA,* 94 Calif. L. Rev. 1323, 1350 (2006).

55. *See* Sharon K. Hom & Eric K. Yamamoto, *Collective Memory, History, and Social Justice,* 47 UCLA L. Rev. 1747, 1756–58 (2000) ("[F]raming injustice is about social memory.").

56. Siegel, *Constitutional Culture, supra* note 54, at 1357 ("[A]dvocates must defend their interpretation of the Constitution as vindicating principles and memories of a shared tradition"); *id.* at 1358 ("[I]n attempting to persuade men outside its ranks to enfranchise women, the [suffrage] movement emphasized the principles and memories that united citizens into a community rather than the values and interests that divided citizens in the community.").

57. Simon J. Gilhooley, The Antebellum Origins of the Modern Constitution: Slavery and the Spirit of the American Founding 73 (2020).

58. Lisa Tetrault, The Myth of Seneca Falls: Memory and the Women's Suffrage Movement, 1848–1898, at 12 (2014).

59. Kermit Roosevelt III, The Nation That Never Was: Reconstructing America's Story 35–38 (2022).

60. *See* Jack M. Balkin, *The Constitution of Status,* 106 Yale L.J. 2313, 2326–32 (1997).

61. *Id.* at 2328–29.

62. Ryan Best, *Confederate Statues Were Never Really about Preserving History*, FiveThirtyEight (July 8, 2020, 7:00 AM), https://projects.fivethirtyeight .com/confederate-statues/ [https://perma.cc/AU4P-NDKY]; *Whose Heritage? Public Symbols of the Confederacy*, S. Poverty L. Ctr. (Feb. 1, 2019), https://www.splcenter.org/20190201/whose-heritage-public-symbols -confederacy [https://perma.cc/4FKU-7DAT]; Becky Little, *How the US Got So Many Confederate Monuments*, History.com (Sept. 8, 2021), https:// www.history.com/news/how-the-u-s-got-so-many-confederate -monuments [https://perma.cc/5X2T-YB85].

63. Ruth Terry, *Teaching about Racism*, 32 CQ Researcher 1 (2022), https:// library.cqpress.com/cqresearcher/document.php?id=cqresrre2022 012100 [https://perma.cc/YF2M-EFCS]; Snyder, *The War on History Is a War on Democracy*, *supra* note 53.

64. Terry, *Teaching about Racism*, *supra* note 63, Snyder, *The War on History*, *supra* note 63.

65. Balkin, *The Constitution of Status*, *supra* note 60, at 2333–35 (noting the "paradox of status hierarchy," in which status conflicts become increasingly bitter as subordinate groups gain any degree of status or recognition).

66. *See, e.g.*, Terry, *Teaching about Racism*, *supra* note 63.

67. Balkin, *The Constitution of Status*, *supra* note 60.

68. Jake Silverstein, *The 1619 Project and the Long Battle over U.S. History*, N.Y. Times Mag. (Nov. 12, 2021), https://www.nytimes.com/2021/11 /09/magazine/1619-project-us-history.html? [https://perma.cc/6NWM -V5VC]; *The 1619 Project*, N.Y. Times (Aug. 14, 2019), https://www.ny times.com/interactive/2019/08/14/magazine/1619-america-slavery.html [https://perma.cc/4758-87BH].

69. Michael Tesler, Post-Racial or Most-Racial: Race and Politics in the Obama Era 146–49, 163–64 (2016); German Lopez, *Donald Trump's Long History of Racism, from the 1970s to 2020*, Vox (Aug. 13, 2020, 7:00 PM), https://www.vox.com/2016/7/25/12270880/donald-trump-racist-racism -history [https://perma.cc/H3EE-SJK8]; Peter Baker, Michael M. Grynbaum, Maggie Haberman, Annie Karni & Russ Buettner, *Trump Employs an Old Tactic: Using Race for Gain*, N.Y. Times (July 20, 2019), https:// www.nytimes.com/2019/07/20/us/politics/trump-race-record.html [https://perma.cc/F6G9-NB43]; Thomas B. Edsall, *The Deepening "Racialization" of American Politics*, N.Y. Times (Feb. 27, 2019), https://www .nytimes.com/2019/02/27/opinion/trump-obama-race.html [https:// perma.cc/Q9BV-5JJ2].

70. *See* 1776 Commission Takes Historic and Scholarly Step to Restore Understanding of the Greatness of the American Founding, Whitehouse.gov (Jan. 18, 2021), https://trumpwhitehouse.archives.gov/briefings-statements

/1776-commission-takes-historic-scholarly-step-restore-understanding
-greatnessamerican-founding/ [https://perma.cc/8JNX-PQDA].

71. *Id.*

Chapter Twelve. Constitutional Memory
and Constitutional Interpretation

1. Reva B. Siegel, *The Politics of Constitutional Memory*, 20 Geo. J.L. & Pub. Pol'y 19, 21 (2022); *see also* Reva B. Siegel, *She the People: The Nineteenth Amendment, Sex Equality, Federalism, and the Family*, 115 Harv. L. Rev. 947, 1032 (2002) ("We invoke the aspirations, values, choices, commitments, obligations, struggles, errors, injuries, wrongs, and wisdom of past generations of Americans as we make claims about the Constitution. . . . Collective memory thus plays a central role in constitutional reason.").

2. *See* Jack M. Balkin, Constitutional Redemption: Political Faith in an Unjust World 3–4 (2011) ("[B]ehind every constitutional interpretation there lies a narrative, sometimes hidden and sometimes overt, a story about how things came to be, injustices fought or still to be rectified, things 'we' (the People) did before, things we still have to do, things that we learned from past experience, things that we will never let happen again."); *cf.* Robert M. Cover, *The Supreme Court, 1982 Term—Foreword: Nomos and Narrative*, 97 Harv. L. Rev. 4, 4 (1983) ("No set of legal institutions or prescriptions exists apart from the narratives that locate it and give it meaning. For every constitution there is an epic, for each decalogue a scripture.").

3. *See, e.g.,* Justin Collings, *The Supreme Court and the Memory of Evil*, 71 Stan. L. Rev. 265, 269–70 (2019) (arguing that the Supreme Court often engages in "parenthetical" uses of memory, which treat past evils "as exceptional—a baleful aberration from an otherwise noble tradition"); Aziz Rana, *Colonialism and Constitutional Memory*, 5 U.C. Irvine L. Rev. 263, 267 (2015) ("[W]hat is especially remarkable about the contemporary framing of the United States as a civic polity is how it erases, almost entirely, the colonial structure of the American past.").

4. *See* Balkin, Constitutional Redemption, *supra* note 2, at 3 ("Often constitutional principles and doctrines are justified by stories about decisions and actions taken (or not taken) in the past. We do this now because we did that then.").

5. *See generally* Jack M. Balkin & Sanford Levinson, *The Canons of Constitutional Law*, 111 Harv. L. Rev. 963, 975 (1998) (describing the differences between pedagogical, cultural literacy, and academic theory canons).

6. Richard A. Primus, *Judicial Power and Mobilizable History*, 65 Md. L. Rev. 171, 173 (2006) ("Courts play an important role in developing and transmitting narratives and images of constitutional history.").

7. Another key intersection of law and cultural memory, beyond the scope of this chapter, is the role of criminal trials and tribunals in constructing and propagating memory. *See, e.g.*, Martha Minow, Breaking the Cycles of Hatred: Memory, Law, and Repair (2009); Carlos Nino, Radical Evil on Trial (1996); Mark J. Osiel, *Ever Again: Legal Remembrance of Administrative Massacre*, 144 U. Pa. L. Rev. 463 (1997).

8. Balkin & Levinson, *The Canons of Constitutional Law*, *supra* note 5, at 970, 986–91 (describing the role of canonical narratives as a form of "deep canonicity").

9. 198 U.S. 45 (1905).

10. Balkin, Constitutional Redemption, *supra* note 2, at 185–98; Jamal Greene, *The Anticanon*, 125 Harv. L. Rev. 379, 417 (2011); Richard A. Primus, *Canon, Anti-Canon, and Judicial Dissent*, 48 Duke L.J. 243, 244–45 (1998); Balkin & Levinson, *The Canons of Constitutional Law*, *supra* note 5, at 1018.

11. Balkin, Constitutional Redemption, *supra* note 2, at 189–91.

12. *Id.* at 193–95.

13. Thomas B. Colby & Peter J. Smith, *The Return of Lochner*, 100 Cornell L. Rev. 527, 531 (2015).

14. *E.g.*, Randy E. Barnett, Our Republican Constitution: Securing the Liberty and Sovereignty of We the People (2016); Amity Shlaes, The Forgotten Man: A New History of the Great Depression (2007).

15. Jack M. Balkin, The Cycles of Constitutional Time 81 (2020).

16. *Id.*

17. *Id.* at 97 ("[C]onstitutional theories are shaped by the living memory of the theorists who create them.").

18. *Id.* at 99–100.

19. Hammer v. Dagenhart, 241 U.S. 251 (1918); Pollock v. Farmers' Loan & Trust Co., 157 U.S. 429 (1895), *aff'd on reh'g*, 158 U.S. 601 (1895); Felix Frankfurter & Nathan Greene, The Labor Injunction (1930) (describing and criticizing judges' use of injunctions against organized labor).

20. Balkin, The Cycles of Constitutional Time, *supra* note 15, at 101–02.

21. *Id.* at 110–11; Citizens United v. FEC, 558 U.S. 310 (2010); Shelby County v. Holder, 570 U.S. 529 (2013).

22. *Cf.* Norman W. Spaulding, *Constitution as Countermonument: Federalism, Reconstruction, and the Problem of Collective Memory*, 103 Colum. L. Rev. 1992 (2003) (arguing that the Rehnquist Court justified its federalism revolution by elevating the memory of the founding and forgetting the memory of Reconstruction); *Cf.* Akhil Reed Amar, *The Lawfulness of Section 5—and Thus of Section 5*, 126 Harv. L. Rev. F. 109, 110 (2013) (arguing that in hobbling the Voting Rights Act, the Roberts Court failed to understand the meaning of Reconstruction).

23. Siegel, *The Politics of Constitutional Memory*, *supra* note 1, at 24; *see also* Rana, *Colonialism and Constitutional Memory*, *supra* note 3, at 269 (de-

scribing the forgotten critique of American colonialism by Black radical activists in the 1960s).

24. *See* Abrams v. United States, 250 U.S. 616 (1919) (Holmes, J., dissenting); Gitlow v. New York, 268 U.S. 652 (1925) (Holmes, J., dissenting); *cf.* Whitney v. California, 274 U.S. 357, 372 (1927) (Brandeis, J., concurring).

25. *See, e.g.,* An Indispensable Liberty: The Fight for Free Speech in Nineteenth-Century America (Mary M. Cronin ed., 2016); Stephen M. Feldman, Free Expression and Democracy in America: A History (2008); Michael Kent Curtis, Free Speech, "The People's Darling Privilege": Struggles for Freedom of Expression in American History (2000); David M. Rabban, Free Speech in Its Forgotten Years, 1870–1920 (1997); Mark A. Graber, Transforming Free Speech: The Ambiguous Legacy of Civil Libertarianism (1991).

26. Feldman, Free Expression and Democracy in America, *supra* note 25, at 5 ("women, indigents, African Americans, and Native Americans"); Linda J. Lumsden, Rampant Women: Suffragists and the Right of Assembly (1997) (suffragists); Rabban, Free Speech in Its Forgotten Years, *supra* note 25, at 68–71 (advocates of contraception and labor advocates); Patrick Rael, Black Identity and Black Protest in the Antebellum North 45–46 (2002) (free Black people).

27. David M. Rabban, *The IWW Free Speech Fights and Popular Conceptions of Free Expression before World War I*, 80 Va. L. Rev. 1055, 1062 (1994).

28. *E.g.,* Rabban, Free Speech in Its Forgotten Years, *supra* note 25, at 23 (describing "[t]he lost tradition of libertarian radicalism obscured by post-war civil libertarians"); Rabban, *The IWW Free Speech Fights, supra* note 27, at 1157 (noting that the IWW argued that governments had an "obligation . . . to provide forums for effective speech to those who lack them" and that "the First Amendment [applied] to private action").

29. *See* Janus v. Am. Fed'n of States, Cty., and Mun. Emps., Council 31, 138 S. Ct. 2448 (2018) (holding unconstitutional state laws that allowed public-sector unions to collect fees from nonmembers).

30. The meaning of the text to the general public would presumably also include the meaning of the text to those shut out of formal constitution-making. But conservative original public meaning originalism focuses on the meaning to the hypothetical reasonable speaker of the English language, and does not differentiate between the views of different social groups. Moreover, most conservative originalists tend to focus on the generally understood legal effect of the Constitution's words and phrases at the time of adoption. So although women, free Black people, and enslaved people spoke English, their distinctive views about the interpretation of the Constitution before they gained the right to vote and hold office would not ordinarily matter to conservative public meaning originalism unless their activism influenced the words or the generally accepted legal understandings of the Constitution or its amendments.

31. *See* Reva B. Siegel, *Memory Games:* Dobbs's *Originalism as Anti-Democratic Living Constitutionalism—and Some Pathways for Resistance*, 101 Tex. L. Rev. 1127, 1133 (2023) ("Originalism turns to the past in search for authority whose claim on the collective imagination is powerful enough to displace—and ultimately to kill off—rival claims on the collective imagination.").

32. Jack M. Balkin, *Constitutional Interpretation and the Problem of History*, 63 NYU L. Rev. 911, 915 n.19, 938–42, 953 (1988).

33. *Cf.* Primus, *Judicial Power and Mobilizable History*, *supra* note 6, at 192 ("Checking the judiciary's power to shape the resources of argument in constitutional history therefore calls on constitutional interpreters who are not judges to make affirmative efforts to foreground aspects of constitutional history different from those that are familiar from judicial opinions.").

34. Dobbs v. Jackson Women's Health Org., 142 S. Ct. 2228 (2022); Roe v. Wade, 410 U.S. 113 (1973); Planned Parenthood of Se. Pa. v. Casey, 505 U.S. 833 (1992).

35. New York State Rifle & Pistol Assn., Inc. v. Bruen, 142 S. Ct. 2111 (2022); District of Columbia v. Heller, 554 U.S. 570 (2008); McDonald v. City of Chicago, 561 U.S. 742 (2010).

36. *Bruen*, 142 S. Ct. at 2122.

37. Washington v. Glucksberg, 521 U.S. 702 (1997); *Dobbs*, 142 S. Ct. at 2242.

38. *Glucksberg*, 521 U.S. at 721.

39. *Dobbs*, 142 S. Ct. at 2236, 2249; Cleveland Clinic, *Quickening in Pregnancy*, https://my.clevelandclinic.org/health/symptoms/22829-quickening-in-pregnancy#:~:text=Quickening%20is%20when%20a%20pregnant ,feel%20it%20sooner%20or%20later [https://perma.cc/R7PD-9HJ2].

40. *Dobbs*, 142 S. Ct. at 2324; *id.* at 2324 n.2 (Breyer, Sotomayor, and Kagan, JJ., dissenting) (citing 1 W. Blackstone, Commentaries on the Laws of England 129–30 (7th ed. 1775); E. Coke, Institutes of the Laws of England 50 (1644) (stating the common-law rule); James Mohr, Abortion in America: The Origins and Evolution of National Policy, 1800–1900, at 3–4 (1978) (noting that the common-law rule was adopted in the United States); Brief for Am. Hist. Ass'n et al. as Amici Curiae at 5–11, *in* Dobbs v. Jackson Women's Health Org., 142 S. Ct. 2228 (No. 19-1392).

41. *Dobbs*, 142 S. Ct. at 2250–52.

42. *Id.* at 2252–53.

43. *Id.* at 2253–56.

44. *Id.* at 2254 ("Not only are respondents and their amici unable to show that a constitutional right to abortion was established when the Fourteenth Amendment was adopted, but they have found no support for the existence of an abortion right that predates the latter part of the 20th century—no state constitutional provision, no statute, no judicial deci-

sion, no learned treatise. The earliest sources called to our attention are a few district court and state court decisions decided shortly before *Roe* and a small number of law review articles from the same time period.").

45. This paragraph and the next are adapted from Jack M. Balkin, *More on Text, History, and Tradition—Discussion Questions for* Dobbs, *Part One*, Balkinization (July 8, 2022), https://balkin.blogspot.com/2022/07/more-on-text-history-and-tradition.html [https://perma.cc/CWM8-AETA].

46. Brief for Am. Hist. Ass'n, *supra* note 40, at 14–18; Mohr, Abortion in America, *supra* note 40, at 30–85, 147–59.

47. Brief for Am. Hist. Ass'n, *supra* note 40, at 15–16; Mohr, Abortion in America, *supra* note 40, at 46–85.

48. Mohr, Abortion in America, *supra* note 40, at 30–39; Reva Siegel, *Reasoning from the Body: A Historical Perspective on Abortion Regulation and Questions of Equal Protection*, 44 Stan. L. Rev. 261, 283–84 (1992).

49. Brief for Am. Hist. Ass'n, *supra* note 40, at 20 (quoting Horatio Robinson Storer, Why Not? A Book for Every Woman 64, 75–76 (2d ed. 1868)); Siegel, *Reasoning from the Body*, *supra* note 48, at 293–97 (describing arguments based on women's moral and biological duties to reproduce). On the mid-nineteenth-century campaign to criminalize abortion, *see* Mohr, Abortion in America, *supra* note 40, at 147–59; Frederick N. Dyer, The Physicians' Crusade against Abortion (2005); Siegel, *Reasoning from the Body*, *supra* note 48, at 282–86. In contrast, some suffragists opposed abortion because they saw it as the almost inevitable result of women's complete lack of freedom in marriage. Their reasons were almost the opposite of the reasons given by the dominant forces in the movement to criminalize abortion; *see* Siegel, *Reasoning from the Body*, *supra* note 48, at 307–14.

50. *Dobbs*, 142 S. Ct. at 2255.

51. *Id.*; *id.* at 2256.

52. *Id.*

53. 140 S. Ct. 2246, 2267–70 (2022) (Alito, J. concurring).

54. This paragraph is adapted from Balkin, *More on Text, History, and Tradition, supra* note 45.

55. Nancy F. Cott, Public Vows: A History of Marriage and the Nation 11–12 (2000); Hendrik Hartog, Man and Wife in America: A History 99–100 (2000).

56. Jill Elaine Hasday, *Contest and Consent: A Legal History of Marital Rape*, 88 Calif. L. Rev. 1373, 1389–95 (2000).

57. *See* Siegel, *She the People, supra* note 1, at 981–84 (describing theory of virtual representation).

58. *See* Siegel, *Memory Games, supra* note 30, at 1187 (explaining that abortion opponents in the nineteenth century "often embedded arguments about protecting unborn life in arguments that criminal bans were needed to enforce women's maternal and marital duties, and to protect the ethno-

religious character of the nation. Arguments for protecting unborn life
were not free-standing, as Justice Alito claimed, but instead were deeply
entangled in arguments that today we would clearly judge unconstitutional, as documents from the period make clear.") (footnote omitted).

59. Jane J. Mansbridge, Why We Lost the ERA 99–100 (1986) (describing
women's movement demands); Robert C. Post & Reva B. Siegel, *Legislative Constitutionalism and Section Five Power: Policentric Interpretation
of the Family and Medical Leave Act*, 112 Yale L.J. 1943, 1988–90 (2003)
(same).

60. New York State Rifle & Pistol Ass'n, Inc. v. Bruen, 142 S. Ct. 2111, 2135
(2022); *id.* at 2126.

61. *Id.* at 2137–38.

62. *Id.*

63. *Id.* at 2138.

64. *Id.*

65. *See, e.g.*, Saul Cornell, *History, Text, Tradition, and the Future of Second
Amendment Jurisprudence: Limits on Armed Travel under Anglo-American
Law, 1688–1868*, 83 Law & Contemp. Probs. 73 (2020); Saul Cornell, *The
Right to Keep and Carry Arms in Anglo-American Law: Preserving Liberty
and Keeping the Peace*, 80 Law & Contemp. Probs. 11 (2017); Patrick J.
Charles, *The Faces of the Second Amendment outside the Home: History Ver-
sus Ahistorical Standards of Review*, 60 Clev. St. L. Rev. 1 (2012).

66. *See Bruen*, 142 S. Ct. at 2140–42 (emphasizing the importance of Sir
John Knight's Case, 3 Mod. 117, 87 Eng. Rep. 75, 76 (K. B. 1686) in
order to negate the importance of the Statute of Northampton, which
regulated the right to carry weapons); *id.* at 2143 (discounting evidence
of colonial regulations); *id.* at 2146–48 (discounting and distinguishing
early antebellum statutes and decisions); *id.* at 2148–50 (discounting the
relevance of surety statutes); *id.* at 2153 (discounting Texas's statute); *id.*
at 2154 (discounting laws in western territories); *id.* at 2155–56 (discounting regulations in Kansas and Arkansas).

67. *Id.* at 2133.

68. *Id.*

69. *Id.* at 2177 (Breyer, J., dissenting).

70. *Id.* at 2130 n.6.

71. *Id.* The case Thomas cites for this proposition, *United States v. Sineneng-
Smith*, has nothing to do with historical fact-finding. Rather, it concerns
a different point—that, in general, judges should allow the parties to
develop the issues and arguments that they will present before the court
rather than assigning amici to develop the best arguments. United States
v. Sineneng-Smith, 140 S. Ct. 1575, 1579 (2020).

72. *Bruen*, 142 S. Ct. at 2130.

73. *See id.* at 2132 ("[W]e find no such tradition [of gun regulation] in the
historical materials that respondents and their amici have brought to

bear on that question."); *id.* at 2143 ("Respondents, their amici, and the dissent all misunderstand these statutes.").

74. Amanda Hollis-Brusky, Ideas with Consequences: The Federalist Society and the Conservative Counterrevolution 25–26 (2015) (describing the multiple pathways—including amicus briefs, professional relationships, and clerkships—through which the conservative legal movement and conservative legal networks influence conservative judges); *id.* at 45–57 (describing the role of amicus curiae briefs by Federalist Society members in *Heller v. District of Columbia* and *McDonald v. City of Chicago*).

75. *See* Neal Devins & Lawrence Baum, The Company They Keep: How Partisan Divisions Came to the Supreme Court 148 (2019) ("[T]he strongest sources of influence on the Justices from outside the Court are the various elites with which Justices are connected. Justices are drawn toward the values of those elites, and they are likely to see the world from the perspective of the elites that are most important to them.").

76. The American Historical Association and the Organization of American Historians emphasized this problem in the context of *Dobbs*. *See* History, the Supreme Court, and *Dobbs v. Jackson*: Joint Statement from the AHA and the OAH (July 2022), https://www.historians.org/news-and-advocacy /aha-advocacy/history-the-supreme-court-and-dobbs-v-jackson-joint -statement-from-the-aha-and-the-oah-(july-2022) [https://perma.cc/ M7FC-WHHW] ("These misrepresentations are now enshrined in a text that becomes authoritative for legal reference and citation in the future.").

77. *Bruen*, 142 S. Ct. at 2130.

Chapter Thirteen. Expanding Constitutional Memory

1. Reva B. Siegel, *The Politics of Constitutional Memory*, 20 Geo. J.L. & Pub. Pol'y 19, 27 (2022) ("This silence reflects understandings that continue to shape women's authority in politics, law, the academy, the household, and other social spheres. Constitutional memory depicts a world in which men speak for women; women lack political voice and have yet to exercise authority to lead.").

2. *Id.* at 26.

3. *Id.*

4. *Id.* at 25–26.

5. *Id.* at 27.

6. *Id.* at 26.

7. Reva B. Siegel, *The Nineteenth Amendment and the Democratization of the Family*, 129 Yale L.J. F. 450, 452–53 (2020); Siegel, *The Politics of Constitutional Memory, supra* note 1, at 32–33, 45.

8. Siegel, *The Politics of Constitutional Memory, supra* note 1, at 45.

9. *Id.* at 32–33.

10. *Id.*; Siegel, *The Nineteenth Amendment and the Democratization of the Family*, *supra* note 7, at 457.

11. Siegel, *The Politics of Constitutional Memory*, *supra* note 1, at 32–33; Siegel, *The Nineteenth Amendment and the Democratization of the Family*, *supra* note 7, at 457.

12. Siegel, *The Nineteenth Amendment and the Democratization of the Family*, *supra* note 7, at 456–57; Siegel, *The Politics of Constitutional Memory*, *supra* note 1, at 36–38, 45.

13. Siegel, *The Politics of Constitutional Memory*, *supra* note 1, at 26–27.

14. *Id.*

15. Women were not completely shut out of the amendment process before the adoption of the Nineteenth Amendment, but their opportunities to participate were quite limited. Several states allowed women to vote in local or state elections before 1920. *See 19th Amendment by State*, NPR.org, https://www.nps.gov/subjects/womenshistory/19th-amendment-by-state.htm [https://perma.cc/7E4J-K4UF]. Some states, particularly in the West, had granted women both the right to vote and the right to hold public office. *See* Noah Johnson, *Sylvia Thompson: Oregon's Third Female State Legislator, 1916–1922*, Oregon Women's History Consortium, http://www.oregonwomenshistory.org/sylvia-thompson-oregons-third-female-state-legislator-1916-1922-by-noah-johnson/ [https://perma.cc/V89F-ZB6D] (noting state Senator Sylvia Johnson's role in Oregon's ratification of the Nineteenth Amendment). One woman, Jeannette Rankin, served in the U.S. Congress as a representative from Montana before the ratification of the Nineteenth Amendment. *Jeannette Rankin's Historic Election: A Century of Women in Congress*, History, Art, and Archives, United States House of Representatives, https://history.house.gov/Exhibitions-and-Publications/WIC/Century-of-Women-Jeannette-Rankin/ [https://perma.cc/E5K9-AFG9].

16. Siegel, *The Politics of Constitutional Memory*, *supra* note 1, at 45, 53–58.

17. For a recent bill of particulars, *see* Erwin Chemerinsky, Worse than Nothing: The Dangerous Fallacy of Originalism 139–65 (2022); Eric J. Segall, Originalism as Faith 4 (2018).

18. Siegel, *The Politics of Constitutional Memory*, *supra* note 1, at 23, 47–50.

19. *Id.*

20. *Id.* at 50 ("[W]hen the Court's originalists debate the meaning of the Constitution's liberty and equality guarantees, they make no pretense of employing originalist methods. Instead, they offer all manner of reasons and draw on all manner of resources, including post-ratification history, dissenting opinions, and social-movement arguments.").

21. Trump v. Hawaii, 138 S. Ct. 2392, 2423 (2018) (denouncing Korematsu v. United States, 323 U.S. 214 (1944), as "gravely wrong the day it was decided" and "overruled in the court of history"); *id.* at 2435, 2447–48 (Sotomayor, J., dissenting) (comparing the majority decision to *Korematsu*).

22. *E.g.*, Parents Involved in Cmty. Schs. v. Seattle Sch. Dist. No. 1, 551 U.S. 701, 705, 746–48 (2007) (plurality opinion of Roberts, C.J.); *id.* at 748–50, 763, 770, 772–82 (Thomas, J., concurring); *id.* at 788, 793 (Kennedy, J., concurring in part and concurring in the judgment); *id.* at 799–803 (Stevens, J., dissenting); *id.* at 803–04, 842, 866–68 (Breyer, J., dissenting). *E.g.*, United States v. Husayn, 142 S. Ct. 959, 992–93 (2022) (Gorsuch, J., dissenting); *Trump*, 138 S. Ct. at 2423; *Trump*, 138 S. Ct. at 2435, 2447–48 (Sotomayor, J., dissenting).

23. *E.g.*, Espinoza v. Mont. Dep't of Revenue, 140 S. Ct. 2246, 2268–73 (2020) (Alito, J., concurring); Everson v. Board of Educ. of Ewing Twp., 330 U.S. 1, 8–11 (1947).

24. *E.g.*, United States v. Alvarez, 567 U.S. 709, 727–28 (2012); Holder v. Humanitarian L. Project, 561 U.S. 1, 38 (2010); *id.* at 45, 52, 54 (Breyer, J., dissenting); Morse v. Frederick, 551 U.S. 393, 438, 448 (2007) (Stevens, J., dissenting).

25. Dred Scott v. Sandford, 60 U.S. (19 How.) 393 (1857); Lochner v. New York, 198 U.S. 45 (1905). *E.g.*, Gamble v. United States, 139 S. Ct. 1960, 2006 (2019) (Gorsuch, J., dissenting) (invoking the memory of *Lochner*, *Dred Scott*, and *Korematsu*); Obergefell v. Hodges, 576 U.S. 644, 694–98 (2015) (Roberts, C.J., dissenting) (invoking the memory of *Dred Scott* and *Lochner*).

26. *E.g.*, *Obergefell*, 576 U.S. at 687 (Roberts, C.J., dissenting) ("[T]he Court invalidates the marriage laws of more than half the States and orders the transformation of a social institution that has formed the basis of human society for millennia, for the Kalahari Bushmen and the Han Chinese, the Carthaginians and the Aztecs. Just who do we think we are?").

27. McDonald v. City of Chicago, 561 U.S. 742, 849–50 (2010) (Thomas, J., concurring in part); Grutter v. Bollinger, 539 U.S. 306, 349–50 (2003) (Thomas, J., concurring in part and dissenting in part); Zelman v. Simmons-Harris, 536 U.S. 639, 676 (2002) (Thomas, J., concurring). Justice Elena Kagan has also cited to Douglass. Brnovich v. Democratic Nat'l Comm., 141 S. Ct. 2321, 2352 (2021) (Kagan, J., dissenting). The only previous citation to Frederick Douglass before 2000 is in Justice William O. Douglas's concurrence in Jones v. Alfred H. Mayer Co., 392 U.S. 409, 446 (1968) (Douglas, J., concurring).

28. Shelby Cty. v. Holder, 570 U.S. 529, 581–82 (2013) (Ginsburg, J., dissenting) (invoking Bloody Sunday in Selma and King's march from Selma to Montgomery to call for passage of the Voting Rights Act); Parents Involved in Cmty. Schs. v. Seattle Sch. Dist. No. 1, 551 U.S. 701, 747 (2007) (plurality opinion of Roberts, C.J.) (citing oral argument of Robert Carter of NAACP in Brown v. Bd. of Educ., 347 U.S. 483 (1954)).

29. *See* Van Wyck Brooks, *On Creating a Usable Past*, 64 Dial 337, 339 (1918), http://www.archive.org/stream/dialjournallitcrit64chicrich#page/337/mode/1up [https://perma.cc/D9ZB-5P8J]. ("The past is an inexhaust-

ible storehouse of . . . adaptable ideals. . . . [I]t yields up, now this treasure, now that, to anyone who comes to it armed with a capacity for personal choices.").

30. *See* Serena Mayeri, *"A Common Fate of Discrimination": Race-Gender Analogies in Legal and Historical Perspective*, 110 Yale L.J. 1045, 1053 (2001); *see also* Paula Giddings, When and Where I Enter: The Impact of Black Women on Race and Sex in America 123–29 (1984); Ellen Carol DuBois, Feminism and Suffrage: The Emergence of an Independent Women's Movement in America, 1848–1869, at 54–55, 94–98 (1978) (describing Elizabeth Cady Stanton's and Susan B. Anthony's alliance with racist politicians to promote woman suffrage); *id.* at 174 (describing Stanton's and Anthony's objections to the Fifteenth Amendment as "simultaneously feminist and racist").

31. Van Wyck Brooks, *On Creating a Usable Past*, *supra* note 29, at 340–41.

32. *Id.* at 340.

33. *Id.* at 340–41.

34. Akhil Reed Amar, The Words That Made Us: America's Constitutional Conversation, 1760–1840 (2021).

35. Daniel Carpenter, Democracy by Petition: Popular Politics in Transformation, 1790–1870 (2021) (describing how women, Black people, and others excluded from formal participation in politics made their voices heard through petitions stating political grievances); Kate Masur, Until Justice Be Done: America's First Civil Rights Movement, from the Revolution to Reconstruction (2021) (describing the work of free Black people in pushing for civil and political rights through petitions and conventions).

36. Carpenter, Democracy by Petition, *supra* note 35.

37. *See, e.g., id.*; Masur, Until Justice Be Done, *supra* note 35; James Fox, *Fourteenth Amendment Citizenship and the Reconstruction-Era Black Public Sphere*, 42 Akron L. Rev. 1245 (2009) (describing the role of Black conventions in advocating for rights).

38. Ellen Carol DuBois, Suffrage: Women's Long Battle for the Vote (2021); Masur, Until Justice Be Done, *supra* note 35; Fox, *Reconstruction-Era Black Public Sphere*, *supra* note 37.

39. Jack M. Balkin, Living Originalism 14–16 (2011).

40. *Id.* at 4–5.

41. Siegel, *The Politics of Constitutional Memory*, *supra* note 1, at 54.

42. *See* Christina Mulligan, *Diverse Originalism*, 21 U. Pa. J. Const. L. 379, 413 (2018) ("[D]istorted interpretations can also occur if a present-day interpreter primarily looks at how the Constitution was understood by a subset of the public and mistakenly concludes that the views of the subset accurately represent the views of the majority or even the whole.").

43. *See id.* at 412–28 (arguing for identifying historical speakers who offered interpretations of the Constitution but who were excluded from formal

participation, and giving multiple examples). In a series of articles, James Fox has argued for a "counterpublic" originalism that looks to the constitutional views of excluded groups. *See* James W. Fox Jr., *The Constitution of Black Abolitionism: Reframing the Second Founding*, 23 U. Pa. J. Const. L. 267 (2021) (arguing for the inclusion of the work of Black conventions in interpreting the Reconstruction Amendments); James W. Fox Jr., *Counterpublic Originalism and the Exclusionary Critique*, 67 Ala. L. Rev. 675 (2016) (arguing for the importance of including counterpublics). *See also* Gregory Ablavsky & W. Tanner Allread, *We the (Native) People? How Indigenous Peoples Debated the U.S. Constitution*, 123 Colum. L. Rev. 243 (2023) (arguing for inclusion of interpretive claims by Native American peoples); *see* Hendrik Hartog, *The Constitution of Aspiration and "The Rights That Belong to Us All,"* 74 J. Am. Hist. 1013, 1032–33 (1987) (arguing for a "vision of constitutional history [with a] perspective wide enough to incorporate the relations between official producers of constitutional law, and those who at particular times and in particular circumstances resisted or reinterpreted constitutional law").

44. Siegel, *The Politics of Constitutional Memory, supra* note 1, at 54; *see also* Kim Lane Scheppele, *Constitutional Interpretation after Regimes of Horror, in* Legal Institutions and Collective Memories 233, 255 (Susanne Karstedt ed., 2009) (describing how new constitutions are written and interpreted to ensure that past injustices do not occur again); Kim Lane Scheppele, *Aspirational and Aversive Constitutionalism: The Case for Studying Cross-Constitutional Influence through Negative Models*, 1 I-CON (International Journal of Constitutional Law) 296, 300 (2003) ("Aversive constitutionalism . . . calls attention to the negative models that are prominent in constitution builders' minds.").

45. Siegel, *The Politics of Constitutional Memory, supra* note 1, at 54, 55–57 (explaining how the history of the suffrage movement can guide judicial scrutiny with respect to a wide range of issues including pregnancy discrimination and sexual violence); *see also* Elizabeth Jelin, State Repression and the Labors of Memory 35 (2003) ("A human group can remember an event . . . in an exemplary way. . . . [W]orking through analogy and generalization, the recollection turns into an example that leads to the possibility of learning something from it, and the past develops into a guide for action in the present and in the future.").

46. Siegel, *The Politics of Constitutional Memory, supra* note 1, at 54.

47. *See, e.g.*, Brief of ACLU as Amicus Curiae at 15–17, Frontiero v. Richardson, 411 U.S. 677 (1973) (No. 71-1694) (brief authored by Ruth Bader Ginsburg quoting a speech by Sojourner Truth and excerpts from the Seneca Falls Declaration of Sentiments).

48. U.S. Const. amend. XIII; The Civil Rights Cases, 109 U.S. 3, 20–21 (1883).

49. *Cf.* Jack M. Balkin & Sanford Levinson, *The Dangerous Thirteenth Amend-*

ment, 112 Colum. L. Rev. 1459, 1470 (2012) ("Perhaps the most basic reason for the Thirteenth Amendment's neglect . . . is that . . . it is so potentially far-reaching that it might justify a truly radical transformation of the American social and political order.").

50. Masur, Until Justice Be Done, *supra* note 35.

51. *Id.* at 33–37.

52. Dorothy Roberts, Killing the Black Body: Race, Reproduction and the Meaning of Liberty 23 (1998) ("Black women bore children who belonged to the slaveowner from the moment of their conception. This feature of slavery made control of reproduction a central aspect of whites' subjugation of African people in America."); Andrew Koppelman, *Originalism, Abortion, and the Thirteenth Amendment*, 112 Colum. L. Rev. 1917, 1941–42 (2012) (arguing that sexual domination of Black women was a paradigmatic feature of chattel slavery).

53. Roberts, Killing the Black Body, *supra* note 52, at 24–33; *see* Koppelman, *Originalism, Abortion, and the Thirteenth Amendment, supra* note 52, at 1938–39 ("Slave women's capacity to bear children was integral to their value and status from the earliest beginnings of the New World slave system, but it became crucial after the slave trade was abolished in 1808. . . . Slave women faced constant, coercive inducements to bear children.").

54. Roberts, Killing the Black Body, *supra* note 52, at 24, 27, 30–31; *see* Pamela D. Bridgewater, *Reproductive Freedom as Civil Freedom: The Thirteenth Amendment's Role in the Struggle for Reproductive Rights*, 3 J. Gender Race & Just. 401, 401–02 (2000) (recounting slave owners' practices of breeding enslaved women for profit and offering a Thirteenth Amendment argument for equal reproductive autonomy for women and men and for Black women and white women); Andrew Koppelman, *Forced Labor: A Thirteenth Amendment Defense of Abortion*, 84 Nw. U. L. Rev. 480, 508 (1990) ("[M]andatory motherhood and loss of control over one's reproductive capacities were partially constitutive of slavery for most black women of childbearing age, whose principal utility to the slaveholding class lay in their ability to reproduce the labor force. Unlike (unmarried) white women, they had no right even in theory to avoid pregnancy through abstinence; they were often raped with impunity, by their masters and others.").

55. Roberts, Killing the Black Body, *supra* note 52, at 24, 27, 30–31; Rachel A. Feinstein, When Rape Was Legal: The Untold History of Sexual Violence during Slavery 16–28 (2018); *see* Koppelman, *Originalism, Abortion, and the Thirteenth Amendment, supra* note 52, at 1942 (arguing that compulsory pregnancy is a paradigmatic example of chattel slavery—"a badge of slavery, a practice that signifies the inferiority of the victim, and an incident, a legal consequence of the status of being a slave"); Jill Elaine Hasday, *Federalism and the Family Reconstructed*, 45 UCLA L. Rev.

1297, 1332–33 (1998) ("Slaves had no legal protection against rape, and slave women were sold into concubinage or prostitution at 'fancy girl' markets devoted specifically to that purpose.").

56. Peggy Cooper Davis, Neglected Stories: The Constitution and Family Values 31–35 (1997).

57. *Id.* at 38–39; Peggy Cooper Davis, *Neglected Stories and the Sweet Mystery of Liberty*, 13 Temple Pol. & Civ. Rts. L. Rev. 769, 783 (2004) ("Enslaved people were precluded not only from claiming the protection of laws governing marriage and parenting, but also from arguing the applicability or inapplicability of the laws to their situations, and from challenging the laws' terms in formal exercises of civil freedom."); Hasday, *Federalism and the Family Reconstructed, supra* note 55, at 1329–30 ("American slaves had no right to marry and no legal claim to their children. Every slave state permitted the forced separation of slave families, and the best evidence suggests that approximately one in six slave marriages ended in involuntary separation.").

58. Davis, Neglected Stories, *supra* note 56, at 90–93.

59. *Id.* at 31–35; Frederick Douglass, Life and Times of Frederick Douglass 118 (1892 rev. ed.) ("One word of the appraisers, against all preferences and prayers, could sunder all the ties of friendship and affection, even to separating husbands and wives, parents and children.").

60. Peggy Cooper Davis, *Neglected Stories and the Lawfulness of* Roe v. Wade, 28 Harv. C.R.-C.L. L. Rev 299, 318 (1993) ("The human claim to family independence and integrity and the devastating effect of slavery upon the African-American family were paramount concerns of the anti-slavery movement."); Harriet Beecher Stowe, A Key to Uncle Tom's Cabin 133 (1853) ("[T]he worst abuse of the system of slavery is its outrage upon the family; and . . . it is one which is more notorious and undeniable than any other.").

61. Davis, Neglected Stories, *supra* note 56, at 113.

62. *Id.* at 379 (quoting extensively from congressional debates); *see also* David Gans, *Reproductive Originalism: Why the Fourteenth Amendment's Original Meaning Protects the Right to Abortion*, 75 S.M.U. L. Rev. 191, 203 (2022) ("The through line in the debates over the Freedman's Bureau Act, the Civil Rights Act of 1866, and the Fourteenth Amendment was the idea that true freedom would be impossible without securing those freed from enslavement the right 'to be protected in their homes and families.'").

63. *E.g.*, Harriet Jacobs, Incidents in the Life of a Slave Girl 64 (Nellie Y. McKay & Frances Smith Foster eds., 2001) (1861) ("Slavery is terrible for men, but it is far more terrible for women."); *e.g.*, Roberts, Killing the Black Body, *supra* note 52, at 23; Davis, Neglected Stories, *supra* note 56; Feinstein, When Rape Was Legal, *supra* note 55.

64. Jed Rubenfeld, Freedom and Time: A Theory of Constitutional Self-

Government 182 (2001) (arguing that the Black Codes, which denied economic rights to Black people, are the paradigmatic case underlying the Fourteenth Amendment); *Cf.* Koppelman, *Originalism, Abortion, and the Thirteenth Amendment, supra* note 52, at 1924–25, 1942 (arguing that in addition to the Black Codes, denial of reproductive rights should also be counted as a paradigmatic case).

65. This concern is explicitly stated in the Civil Rights Act of 1866, Act of Apr. 9, 1866, ch. 31, § 1, 14 Stat. 27 (protecting the rights "to make and enforce contracts, to sue, be parties, and give evidence, to inherit, purchase, lease, sell, hold, and convey real and personal property, and to [the] full and equal benefit of all laws and proceedings for the security of person and property, as is enjoyed by white citizens").

66. Hasday, *Federalism and the Family Reconstructed, supra* note 55, at 1341.

67. *Id; id.* at 1341 n.159 ("All sides of the abolitionist debate saw the right to marry as a contractual right.").

68. *Cf.* Hasday, *Federalism and the Family Reconstructed, supra* note 55, at 1333–34 ("In an era in which marital rape remained wholly legal, many abolitionists assumed without question, and argued without hesitation, that male slaves, like free men, should control sexual access to their female relatives.").

69. *Id.* at 1328.

70. As reflected in the title of Peggy Cooper Davis's 1997 book, Neglected Stories. Davis, Neglected Stories, *supra* note 56.

71. *E.g.*, John Hart Ely, *The Wages of Crying Wolf: A Comment on* Roe v. Wade, 82 Yale L.J. 920, 935–36 (1973) (arguing that the right of privacy recognized in *Roe v. Wade* "is not inferable from the language of the Constitution, the framers' thinking respecting the specific problem in issue, any general value derivable from the provisions they included, or the nation's governmental structure").

72. *Id.* at 939–40 ("The Court continues to disavow the philosophy of *Lochner.* Yet as Justice Stewart's concurrence admits, it is impossible candidly to regard *Roe* as the product of anything else. That alone should be enough to damn it.").

73. Davis, *Neglected Stories and the Lawfulness of* Roe v. Wade, *supra* note 60, at 309 ("The idea that family rights are aspects of national citizenship was, however, unambiguously asserted in the aftermath of the Civil War; anti-slavery advocates were explicit in their determination that all Americans would be protected against the family violations that characterized slavery."); *cf.* Davis, *Neglected Stories and the Sweet Mystery of Liberty, supra* note 57, at 784 (arguing that constitutional protection of the rights of gays and lesbians to marry and form families makes sense "[w]hen the Fourteenth Amendment is understood in light of the history and traditions of anti-slavery").

74. Siegel, *The Politics of Constitutional Memory, supra* note 1, at 32.

75. *See* Siegel, *The Nineteenth Amendment and the Democratization of the Family, supra* note 7, at 452, 458 (2020).

76. *Id.* at 452–53, 458–65; Reva B. Siegel, *She the People: The Nineteenth Amendment, Sex Equality, Federalism, and the Family*, 115 Harv. L. Rev. 947, 991–92 (2002).

77. *See* Siegel, *She the People, supra* note 76, at 949 ("Today, women's struggle for enfranchisement plays no role in the ways we understand or interpret the Constitution.").

78. Siegel, *The Politics of Constitutional Memory, supra* note 1, at 35–39.

79. Balkin, Living Originalism, *supra* note 39, at 60.

80. Jack M. Balkin, *The American Constitution as "Our Law,"* 25 Yale J.L & Human. 113, 113 (2013).

81. *Id.*

82. Balkin, Living Originalism, *supra* note 39, at 60.

83. *Id.* at 61.

84. *Id.*

85. *Id.*

86. *Id.*

87. *Id.*

88. *See* Jamal Greene, *Originalism's Race Problem*, 88 Denver U. L. Rev. 517, 520–21 (2011) ("[T]he authority of the ratifying generation derives from its normative continuity with our own. . . . On this account, originalism is best defended as a persuasive form of ethical argument; it is a normative account of national identity.").

89. U.S. Const. pmbl.

90. *See* Greene, *Originalism's Race Problem, supra* note 88; Mulligan, *Diverse Originalism, supra* note 42, at 380 ("Originalism has a difficult relationship with race and gender."); Mary Anne Case, *The Ladies? Forget about Them: A Feminist Perspective on the Limits of Originalism*, 29 Const. Comment. 431, 445 (2014) ("[N]o version of original meaning . . . holds much promise for yielding what Abigail Adams demanded of John—a constitutionally mandated code of laws more 'generous and favorable to women' than the one the Framers inherited.").

91. Annette Gordon-Reed, *Writing about the Past That Made Us: Scholars, Civic Culture, and the American Present and Future*, 131 Yale L.J. 948, 959–60 (2022) (reviewing Akhil Reed Amar, The Words That Made Us: America's Constitutional Conversation, 1760–1840 (2021)).

92. *See* John O. McGinnis & Michael B. Rappaport, Originalism and the Good Constitution 111 (2013) ("[L]ike the exclusion of African Americans, the exclusion of women has been substantially corrected."). For a critique, *see* Fox, *Counterpublic Originalism and the Exclusionary Critique, supra* note 43, at 689–96.

93. Plessy v. Ferguson, 163 U.S. 537, 544 (1896) ("The object of the amendment was undoubtedly to enforce the absolute equality of the two races before the law, but, in the nature of things, it could not have been intended to abolish distinctions based upon color, or to enforce social, as distinguished from political, equality, or a commingling of the two races upon terms unsatisfactory to either."); The Civil Rights Cases, 109 U.S. 3, 25 (1883) (arguing that if the Constitution gave Congress the power to prevent private discrimination, it would make Black people "the special favorite of the laws"); Bradwell v. Illinois, 83 U.S. 130, 141 (1873) (Bradley, J., concurring) (explaining that states could prevent women from becoming lawyers because "[t]he paramount destiny and mission of woman are to fulfil the noble and benign offices of wife and mother. This is the law of the Creator.").

94. Indian Citizenship Act of 1924, Pub. L. No. 68-175, 43 Stat. 253 (1924) (codified at 8 U.S.C. § 1401(b) (2012)); *see also* Elk v. Wilkins, 112 U.S. 94, 102 (1884) (holding that the Fourteenth Amendment's guarantee of birthright citizenship did not apply to Native Americans who at the time of their birth were subject to tribal jurisdiction).

95. Carol Nackenoff & Julie Novkov, American by Birth: Wong Kim Ark and the Battle for Citizenship 3 (2021); Balzac v. Puerto Rico, 258 U.S. 298, 313 (1922) (holding that Sixth Amendment right of trial by jury in criminal cases did not apply in unincorporated territories).

96. Jerome McCristal Culp Jr., *Toward a Black Legal Scholarship: Race and Original Understandings*, 1991 Duke L.J. 39, 75 ("Almost all notions of originalism are subject to the criticism that they ask black concerns to defer to white concerns. . . . 'Defer to the past' is the implicit message. Listen to the wiser and greater (and whiter) founders.").

97. Greene, *Originalism's Race Problem, supra* note 88, at 517–18.

98. Mike Rappaport, *Originalism, Minorities, and Women*, L. & Liberty (Feb. 23, 2018), https://lawliberty.org/originalism-minorities-and-women/ [https://perma.cc/CQ99-RYV5].

99. Gordon-Reed, *Writing about the Past That Made Us, supra* note 91, at 959–60.

100. *Id.* at 960.

101. *Cf.* Jack M. Balkin, Constitutional Redemption: Political Faith in an Unjust World 135 (2011) (arguing that the Constitution's legitimacy depends on a political faith that its promises can be redeemed in history); Paul Gowder, *Reconstituting We the People: Frederick Douglass and Jürgen Habermas in Conversation*, 114 Nw. U. L. Rev. 335 (2019) (arguing that constitutional legitimacy for excluded people depends on a provisional attachment to the constitutional project in the hope that political activity can realize promises latent in the Constitution that actually produce a political system worthy of identification and allegiance).

102. The attempt to deny the constitutional tradition's dialectical character and proclaim a unitary tradition of constitutional commands is what Robert Cover once called "jurispathic." Robert M. Cover, *The Supreme Court, 1982 Term—Foreword: Nomos and Narrative*, 97 Harv. L. Rev. 53 (1983). "Confronting the luxuriant growth of a hundred legal traditions," jurispathy is the attempt to "assert that this one is law and destroy or try to destroy the rest." *Id.* If the limitation of memory is jurispathic, asserting authority by sending competitors down the memory hole, the expansion of constitutional memory can be what Cover called "jurisgenerative," because it recognizes the possibility of multiple legal worlds. *Cf. id.* at 11 (defining "jurisgenesis" as "the creation of legal meaning").

Chapter Fourteen. Historians Meet the Modalities

1. Alfred H. Kelly, *Clio and the Court: An Illicit Love Affair*, 1965 Sup. Ct. Rev. 119, 122, 122 n.13 ("By 'law-office' history, I mean the selection of data favorable to the position being advanced without regard to or concern for contradictory data or proper evaluation of the relevance of the data proffered."). Kelly was no stranger to the use of history in constitutional argument; he had helped the NAACP Legal Defense Fund in preparing its historical arguments in *Brown v. Board of Education*. But he worried that in doing so he had become less of a historian and more of an advocate. Richard Kluger, Simple Justice: The History of *Brown v. Board of Education* and Black America's Struggle for Equality 638–40 (1977). Although the expression "law office history" is often associated with Kelly, he was not the first to use it. *See* Paul L. Murphy, *Time to Reclaim: The Current Challenge of American Constitutional History*, 69 Am. Hist. Rev. 64, 77 (1963) (associating the phrase with Howard J. Graham).
2. Kelly, *Clio and the Court*, *supra* note 1, at 125–26.
3. *Id.* at 130–32.
4. *Id.* at 125.
5. *See, e.g.*, Martin S. Flaherty, *Can the Quill Be Mightier than the Uzi? History "Lite," "Law Office," and Worse Meets the Second Amendment*, 37 Cardozo L. Rev. 663, 665 (2015) (reviewing Michael Waldman, The Second Amendment: A Biography (2014)) (denouncing "the sorry tale of misuse and manipulations" of the history of the Second Amendment by legal scholars); William G. Merkel, Heller *as Hubris, and How* McDonald v. City of Chicago *May Well Change the Constitutional World as We Know It*, 50 Santa Clara L. Rev. 1221, 1225 (2010) ("My own objections to Justice Scalia's work product in *Heller* focus on the fact that his allegedly history-driven method depends fundamentally on numerous false historical claims.").
6. *See, e.g.*, Flaherty, Can the Quill Be Mightier than the Uzi?, *supra* note 5; Paul Finkelman, *The Living Constitution and the Second Amendment: Poor*

History, False Originalism, and a Very Confused Court, 37 Cardozo L. Rev. 623, 624 (2015) ("In both *Heller* and *McDonald* the Court bases its conclusions on a false history that is, for the most part, a fantasy of the majority of the Court and opponents of reasonable firearms regulation."); Nelson Lund, *The Second Amendment, Heller, and Originalist Jurisprudence*, 56 UCLA L. Rev. 1343, 1356 (2009) (arguing that Justice Scalia pronounced a wide range of gun control regulations constitutional with no historical evidence or grounding in original meaning).

7. *See* Matthew J. Festa, *Applying a Usable Past: The Use of History in Law*, 38 Seton Hall L. Rev. 479, 513–14 (2008) (noting the advantages of the distinctively adversarial culture of lawyers); Larry D. Kramer, *When Lawyers Do History*, 72 Geo. Wash. L. Rev. 387, 395, 402–05 (2003) (noting that law is an adversarial system that uses history to claim authority); John Phillip Reid, *Law and History*, 27 Loy. L.A. L. Rev. 193, 195 (1993) (arguing that law is governed by the "logic of authority" rather than the "logic of evidence") (quoting Frederic W. Maitland, *Why the History of English Law Is Not Written, in* 1 The Collected Papers of Frederic William Maitland 480, 491 (H. A. L. Fisher ed., 1911)); *id.* at 195–96 ("In discovering the past, the historian weighs every bit of evidence that comes to hand. The lawyer, by contrast, is after the single authority that will settle the case at bar.").

8. *See* Laura Kalman, *Border Patrol: Reflections on the Turn to History in Legal Scholarship*, 66 Fordham L. Rev. 87, 114–15 (1997) (distinguishing "lawyers' legal history" and "historians' legal history") (quoting Richard B. Bernstein, *Charting the Bicentennial*, 87 Colum. L. Rev. 1565, 1578 (1987), and William E. Nelson & John Phillip Reid, The Literature of American Legal History 185, 235–37, 261–87 (1985)).

9. Bernard Bailyn, Sometimes an Art: Nine Essays on History 22 (2015) ("[T]he past is a different world."); Jonathan Gienapp, *Historicism and Holism: Failures of Originalist Translation*, 84 Fordham L. Rev. 935, 942–43 (2015) (arguing that the founders' world was different in its assumptions, in its conceptual structures, and in how it used language, so that one cannot assume "that Founding-era utterances are fairly easy to understand because they were spoken and written in English").

10. *See, e.g.*, Adam Serwer, *The Fight over the 1619 Project Is Not about the Facts*, The Atlantic (Dec. 23, 2019), https://www.theatlantic.com/ideas /archive/2019/12/historians-clash-1619-project/604093/ [https://perma .cc/5DEJ-NU5Q].

11. Reid, *Law and History, supra* note 7, at 196 ("The search for authority, the need to find 'the law' or 'the right law' is the main reason lawyers speak of the legal past in terms quite different from the historian's.").

12. *See* Kelly, *Clio and the Court, supra* note 1, at 144 (noting that the NAACP's brief in *Brown v. Board of Education* presented "a great deal of perfectly valid constitutional history" but that "it also manipulated history in the

best tradition of American advocacy, carefully marshaling every possible scrap of evidence in favor of the desired interpretation and just as carefully doctoring all the evidence to the contrary, either by suppressing it when that seemed plausible, or by distorting it when suppression was not possible").

13. *See* Joshua Stein, *Historians before the Bench: Friends of the Court, Foes of Originalism*, 25 Yale J.L. & Human. 359, 362–80 (2013) (describing how historians had to alter their practices in writing Supreme Court amicus briefs involving the Second Amendment, gay rights, and detainees at Guantánamo Bay). A famous example is the historians' brief in Webster v. Reproductive Health Services, 492 U.S. 490 (1989), which spawned considerable reflection among legal historians. Brief of 281 American Historians as Amici Curiae Supporting Appellees, reprinted in 12 Pub. Historian 37 (1990); *see* Wendy Chavkin, Webster, *Health, and History*, 12 Pub. Historian 53 (1990); Estelle B. Freedman, *Historical Interpretation and Legal Advocacy: Rethinking the* Webster *Amicus Brief*, 12 Pub. Historian 27 (1990); Michael Grossberg, *The* Webster *Brief: History as Advocacy, or Would You Sign It?*, 12 Pub. Historian 45 (1990); Jane E. Larson & Clyde Spillenger, *"That's Not History": The Boundaries of Advocacy and Scholarship*, 12 Pub. Historian 33 (1990); Sylvia A. Law, *Conversations between Historians and the Constitution*, 12 Pub. Historian 11 (1990); James C. Mohr, *Historically Based Legal Briefs: Observations of a Participant in the* Webster *Process*, 12 Pub. Historian 19 (1990).

14. *See* Gary Lawson, *Dead Document Walking*, 92 B.U. L. Rev. 1225, 1231 (2012) (distinguishing between the task of ascertaining original meaning, theories of political legitimacy, and theories of adjudication).

15. *See also* Kramer, *When Lawyers Do History*, *supra* note 7, at 402–08 (noting that lawyers have distinctive ways of making arguments, using evidence, imposing burdens of proof, and resolving uncertainties that are not shared in other disciplines). As Larry Kramer puts it, "[I]nsofar as the originalist interpretive method unavoidably involves a creative act by the modern interpreter—that of completing an argument that may have been unfinished when the Constitution was adopted—this link [between the founders and the present] is just as unavoidably broken. At that point, there is literally no difference between what an originalist does and what is done by the most anti-historicist non-originalist—except, of course, for the results (each approach producing its share of outcomes that adherents of the other approach view as bizarre, made up, and unjustifiable)." *Id.* at 407; *see also id.* at 412–13 ("Taking sides in an unresolved historical debate is no different from taking sides in an unresolved contemporary one, and doing so severs the link to what supposedly gives [an originalist] (or any) historical argument its normative legal significance.").

16. Mike Rappaport, *An Important Difference between Historians and Originalist Law Professors*, Law & Liberty (Oct. 11, 2018), https://old.lawliberty

.org/2018/10/11/an-important-difference-between-historians-and
-originalist-law-professors/ [https://perma.cc/M8UR-42T3].

17.   Randy E. Barnett, *Challenging the Priesthood of Professional Historians*, The
      Volokh Conspiracy (Mar. 28, 2017, 11:51 AM), https://www.washington
      post.com/news/volokh-conspiracy/wp/2017/03/28/challenging-the
      -priesthood-of-professional-historians/ [https://perma.cc/YDN3-VNAV].
      Barnett responded to a critique of originalism by Stanford historian Jon-
      athan Gienapp. Jonathan Gienapp, *Constitutional Originalism and History*,
      Process: A Blog for Am. Hist. (Mar. 20, 2017), http://www.processhistory
      .org/originalism-history/ [https://perma.cc/Y3V9-7772] ("By understand-
      ing how [originalism] has changed, we can appreciate the unique, little
      understood, and urgent threat it now poses to the practice of history.").

18.   Jack N. Rakove, Original Meanings: Politics and Ideas in the Making of
      the Constitution (1996); Saikrishna B. Prakash, *Unoriginalism's Law with-
      out Meaning*, 15 Const. Comment. 529, 539 (1998).

19.   *See, e.g.*, Prakash, *Unoriginalism's Law without Meaning, supra* note 18, at
      539–40 (arguing that historians do not understand what originalist law-
      yers are doing); Barnett, *Challenging the Priesthood of Professional Histo-
      rians, supra* note 17; Mike Rappaport, *Historians and Originalists*, The
      Originalism Blog (Aug. 21, 2013), http://originalismblog.typepad.com
      /the-originalism-blog/2013/08/historians-and-originalistsmike-rappaport
      .html [https://perma.cc/6A8Y-3LNP] (same).

20.   Barnett, *Challenging the Priesthood of Professional Historians, supra* note 17;
      see also Rappaport, *Historians and Originalists, supra* note 19 (arguing that
      "[h]istorians often do not understand or apply [originalism] correctly,"
      because "historians often lack legal training" and are "trained to be skep-
      tical of reaching conclusions that suggest a single (or dominant) view at
      a time" and because "if one has the skills to be a historian, he or she may
      not have other skills."); *cf.* Mark Tushnet, *Interdisciplinary Legal Scholar-
      ship: The Case of History-in-Law*, 71 Chi.-Kent L. Rev. 909, 917 (1996)
      (explaining, with some degree of irony, that "the criteria for determining
      whether someone has done well at the practice of history-in-law may be
      different from those for determining whether someone has done well at
      the practice of history, and they may be developed and applied by law-
      yers and legal academics rather than historians").

21.   *See, e.g.*, Robert W. Gordon, *Historicism in Legal Scholarship*, 90 Yale L.J.
      1017, 1055 (1981) ("Many of the criticisms that historians make of law-
      yers' history are indeed irrelevant to the lawyer's task. . . . [Sometimes]
      they want . . . to make new, mythic, traditions out of it to use in current
      argument."); Paul Horwitz, *The Past, Tense: The History of Crisis—and the
      Crisis of History—in Constitutional Theory*, 61 Alb. L. Rev. 459, 504–07
      (1997) (reviewing Laura Kalman, The Strange Career of Legal Liber-
      alism (1996)) (noting the argument that lawyers are more interested in
      myth and heritage than in historical niceties); Cass R. Sunstein, *The Idea*

of a Useable Past, 95 Colum. L. Rev. 601, 604 (1995) (arguing for "identify[ing] those features of the constitutional past" that a lawyer views as "especially suitable for present constitutional use"); Tushnet, *Interdisciplinary Legal Scholarship*, *supra* note 20, at 924–28 (noting, without specifically endorsing, this feature of history-in-law).

22. Sunstein, *The Idea of a Useable Past*, *supra* note 21, at 603.

23. Alexander M. Bickel, The Least Dangerous Branch: The Supreme Court at the Bar of Politics 109–10 (2d ed. 1986).

24. *See* Stuart Banner, *Legal History and Legal Scholarship*, 76 Wash. U. L. Rev. 37, 37 (1998) ("History, or at least history written according to the conventions of late twentieth century professional historians, with an emphasis on the ways in which the past differed from the present—history as an account of the pastness of the past, as the standard expression goes—enormously complicates the task of legal argument."); Gordon, *Historicism in Legal Scholarship*, *supra* note 21, at 1055 ("[T]he immediate interest of historians is always in 'historicizing' the past as much as possible, tamping it down firmly into departed times and places."); Helen Irving, *Outsourcing the Law: History and the Disciplinary Limits of Constitutional Reasoning*, 84 Fordham L. Rev. 957, 961 (2015) ("The instrumental use of history is entirely at odds with the skeptical discipline required of historians."); Tushnet, *Interdisciplinary Legal Scholarship*, *supra* note 20, at 915 (noting the familiar historical tropes of showing the complexity, contradiction, foreignness, and strangeness of the past).

25. *See*, Stein, *Historians before the Bench*, *supra* note 13, at 362–70 (describing how historians had to alter their practices in writing Supreme Court amicus briefs involving the Second Amendment); Tomiko Brown-Nagin, Linda Gordon, Kenneth Mack, *Historians in Court: A Roundtable*, OAH. org (November 2017), https://www.oah.org/tah/issues/2017/november /historians-in-court-a-roundtable/ [https://perma.cc/Z4SN-HEY3] (discussing the differences between legal advocacy and historical inquiry); *see also* sources cited *supra* note 13 (discussing the choices historians had to make in the *Webster* amicus brief to explain to courts why *Roe v. Wade* was correctly decided).

26. *See, e.g.*, Nell Gluckman, *Why More Historians Are Embracing the Amicus Brief*, The Chron. of Higher Educ. (May 3, 2017), https://www.chronicle .com/article/why-more-historians-are-embracing-the-amicus-brief/ [https://perma.cc/T4XD-4SBP] ("Historians say they feel that they are being asked to write or sign amicus briefs in Supreme Court cases more frequently."); Michael Grossberg, *Friends of the Court: A New Role for Historians*, Persps. on Hist. (Nov. 1, 2010), https://www.historians.org /publications-and-directories/perspectives-on-history/november-2010 /friends-of-the-court-a-new-role-for-historians [https://perma.cc/E4NX -CN5R] ("[H]istorians are carving out a crucial new role for themselves as direct contributors to debates about contested legal issues such as

same-sex marriage."); *See, e.g.,* Jonathan D. Martin, *Historians at the Gate: Accommodating Expert Historical Testimony in Federal Courts,* 78 N.Y.U. L. Rev. 1518, 1519 (2003) ("Historians are increasingly being called to testify as expert witnesses. They appear in cases adjudicating a vast array of matters."); Kritika Agarwal, *Historians as Expert Witnesses,* Persps. on Hist. (Feb. 1, 2017), https://www.historians.org/publications-and-directories /perspectives-on-history/february-2017/historians-as-expert-witnesses -can-scholars-help-save-the-voting-rights-act [https://perma.cc/J8LS -LQUD] ("Historians' testimony has had significant impact in voting rights cases.").

27. Philip C. Bobbitt, Constitutional Interpretation 28–30 (1991).

28. *See* Annette Gordon-Reed, *Uncovering the Past: Lessons from Doing Legal History,* 51 N.Y. L. Sch. L. Rev. 855, 858–59 (2006–07) (arguing that lawyers are often better equipped than non-legally-trained historians to think imaginatively about how historical figures would handle hypothetical problems given the legal materials of their day).

29. *See* Stein, *Historians before the Bench, supra* note 13, at 380 (2013) ("Historians can make their advocacy more effective—and more in line with their professional methodology—by using alternative (rather than definitive) versions of the past to destabilize originalist argumentation.").

30. *See, e.g.,* Saul Cornell, *Meaning and Understanding in the History of Constitutional Ideas: The Intellectual History Alternative to Originalism,* 82 Fordham L. Rev. 721, 724, 734–38 (2013) (criticizing original public meaning originalism for abstracting away from the complexities of language during the founding era and projecting contemporary understandings onto the past in the form of an imagined reasonable person); Jack Rakove, *Tone Deaf to the Past: More Qualms about Public Meaning Originalism,* 84 Fordham L. Rev. 969, 975 (2015) (criticizing original public meaning originalism for neglecting "the linguistic ideas that were dominant in eighteenth-century America").

31. *See, e.g.,* Kelly, *Clio and the Court, supra* note 1, at 156–57 (arguing that the Supreme Court's inquiry into history in the Establishment Clause "asks questions of the past that the past cannot answer"); Reid, *Law and History, supra* note 7, at 202 (noting that "judges often read the records of the past as if they were prepared similarly to the legislative history of today's congresses, by professional staffs anticipating issues likely to arise in litigation, . . . [and] ask the past to answer questions about matters that were not thought of at the time").

32. *See, e.g.,* Mary Sarah Bilder, Madison's Hand: Revising the Constitutional Convention (2015) (showing how James Madison revised his notes of the Constitutional Convention over many years, often for political reasons); Saul Cornell, *Originalism on Trial: The Use and Abuse of History in* District of Columbia v. Heller, 69 Ohio St. L.J. 625, 632–36 (2008) (arguing that Justice Scalia's opinion in *Heller* misunderstood how pre-

ambles were used at the founding and failed to cite any founding-era sources for his claims).

33. Kramer, *When Lawyers Do History, supra* note 7, at 389–94 (pointing out the effort required to become even minimally competent in understanding the thought of a given historical period).

34. For example, in litigation over the Foreign Emoluments Clause, Seth Barrett Tillman was able to show that a key document listing the officers under the United States (but not including the president) had been prepared and signed by Alexander Hamilton in 1793. He also showed that another document said to contradict this account was not signed by Hamilton and was actually a copy prepared many years later. *See* Adam Liptak, *"Lonely Scholar with Unusual Ideas" Defends Trump, Igniting Legal Storm*, N.Y. Times (Sept. 25, 2017), https://www.nytimes.com/2017/09 /25/us/politics/trump-emoluments-clause-alexander-hamilton.html [https://perma.cc/4VJV-6YTD]. The legal historians who accused Tillman of failing to cite the second document subsequently agreed with him and apologized. *Id.*

Perhaps the most famous example of lawyers correcting the work of legal historians is James Lindgren's efforts in exposing the errors and unsupported claims in the work of historian Michael Bellesiles. *See* James Lindgren, *Fall from Grace: Arming America and the Bellesiles Scandal*, 111 Yale L.J. 2195 (2002) (book review). Bellesiles had won the prestigious Bancroft Prize for his 2000 book *Arming America: The Origins of a National Gun Culture* (2000), which argued that, at the time of the founding, most Americans did not own guns. Following the work of Lindgren, amateur historian Clayton Cramer, and other scholars and historians, Columbia University revoked the prize. Robert F. Worth, *Prize for Book Is Taken Back from Historian*, N.Y. Times (Dec. 14, 2002), https://www .nytimes.com/2002/12/14/business/prize-for-book-is-taken-back-from -historian.html [https://perma.cc/6HU2-8SVS].

Chapter Fifteen. The Special Skill and Knowledge of Lawyers

1. Mike Rappaport, *Historians and Originalists*, The Originalism Blog (Aug. 21, 2013), http://originalismblog.typepad.com/the-originalism-blog/2013 /08/historians-and-originalistsmike-rappaport.html [https://perma.cc /6A8Y-3LNP].

2. *Id.*; *see also* Saikrishna B. Prakash, *Unoriginalism's Law without Meaning*, 15 Const. Comment. 529, 539–40 (1998) ("Rakove's primary problem is that he approaches the law as a historian. Although Rakove appears to understand that what matters is the original meaning of legal text, his historian's bent predominates. Rakove recounts events in the time-

honored tradition of the historian less concerned about the meaning of legal text and more concerned with ideas.").

3. Rappaport, *Historians and Originalists, supra* note 1; *see* Prakash, *Unoriginalism's Law without Meaning, supra* note 2, at 535 ("Originalism simply does not rest on a theory of definite meanings; it only requires an ability to determine which of several possible meanings better reflects the most natural reading of the word or phrase when the text was ratified.").

4. Rappaport, *Historians and Originalists, supra* note 1; *see* Gary Lawson, *No History, No Certainty, No Legitimacy . . . No Problem: Originalism and the Limits of Legal Theory,* 64 Fla. L. Rev. 1551, 1559 (2012) ("'[H]istory department law' is a much greater threat to sound constitutional interpretation than is 'law office history.'"); Prakash, *Unoriginalism's Law without Meaning, supra* note 2, at 534, 541 (criticizing "history department law").

5. *See, e.g.,* Larry D. Kramer, *When Lawyers Do History,* 72 Geo. Wash. L. Rev. 387, 395, 405 (2003) ("Legal interpretation is fundamentally about resolving ambiguities and uncertainties in language: about determining and bringing to closure that which is undetermined and open."); H. Jefferson Powell, *Rules for Originalists,* 73 Va. L. Rev. 659, 669 (1987) ("The originalist's use of history is goal-directed: he wants to understand past thought and action in order to address present concerns."); Prakash, *Unoriginalism's Law without Meaning, supra* note 2, at 535 (arguing that the point of originalist methodology is to do the best we can in order to solve current legal problems).

6. *See, e.g.,* Lawson, *No History, No Certainty, No Legitimacy . . . No Problem, supra* note 4, at 1554 (arguing that an originalism "in which meaning is determined by the hypothetical understandings of a fictitious reasonable observer, rather than those of any concrete historical figures," can solve practical problems of adjudication).

7. For a forthright defense of the practice, *see* Gary Lawson & Guy Seidman, *Originalism as a Legal Enterprise,* 23 Const. Comment. 47, 80 (2006) ("Lawyers create the object of interpretation, so it is not surprising that lawyers might play a key role in understanding it."); *see also* Kramer, *When Lawyers Do History, supra* note 5, at 407 (pointing out that both originalists and nonoriginalists are engaged in creative extensions of historical materials).

8. For examples of criticisms of Rappaport's theory from nonoriginalists, *see* Frederic Bloom & Nelson Tebbe, *Countersupermajoritarianism,* 113 Mich. L. Rev. 809 (2015); John W. Compton, *What Is Originalism Good For?,* 50 Tulsa L. Rev. 427 (2015); Stephen M. Feldman, *Constitutional Interpretation and History: New Originalism or Eclecticism?,* 28 BYU J. Pub. L. 283 (2014); James E. Fleming, *Fidelity, Change, and the Good Constitution,* 62 Am. J. Compar. L. 515 (2014); Heidi Kitrosser, *Interpretive Modesty,* 104 Geo. L.J. 459 (2016). For examples of criticisms from originalists,

  see Kurt T. Lash, *Originalism All the Way Down?*, 30 Const. Comment. 149 (2015); Lawrence B. Solum, *Originalism and Constitutional Construction*, 82 Fordham L. Rev. 453, 503–11 (2013).

9. The number of critiques of originalism by lawyers and law professors is seemingly endless. For two recent examples of the genre, *see* Erwin Chemerinsky, Worse than Nothing: The Dangerous Fallacy of Originalism (2022); Eric J. Segall, Originalism as Faith (2018).

10. *See* Paul Horwitz, *The Past, Tense: The History of Crisis—and the Crisis of History—in Constitutional Theory*, 61 Alb. L. Rev. 459, 503 (1997) ("The use of history in law, after all, is at bottom a question of legal theory, and just as this method of constitutional interpretation [originalism] is demonstrably flawed as a matter of practice, so it may also be a weak candidate as a matter of theory.").

11. Consider, for an example, the argument that we cannot ground originalism on original legal methods because there was no agreement about how to interpret the Constitution at the time of the founding. This argument has been made both by a historian, Saul Cornell, and by law professors Larry Kramer and Caleb Nelson. *See* Saul Cornell, *Reading the Constitution, 1787–91: History, Originalism, and Constitutional Meaning*, 37 Law & Hist. Rev. 821, 835–40 (2019); Larry Kramer, *Two (More) Problems with Originalism*, 31 Harv. J.L. & Pub. Pol'y 907, 912–13 (2008); Caleb Nelson, *Originalism and Interpretive Conventions*, 70 U. Chi. L. Rev. 519, 555–56, 561, 571–73 (2003).

12. Jack N. Rakove, *Joe the Ploughman Reads the Constitution, or, the Poverty of Public Meaning Originalism*, 48 San Diego L. Rev. 575, 585–88 (2011).

13. *Id.* at 586.

14. Not surprisingly, nonoriginalist law professors have also attacked this approach to originalism. *See, e.g.*, Feldman, *Constitutional Interpretation and History, supra* note 8; Kitrosser, *Interpretive Modesty, supra* note 8; John T. Valauri, *Originalism and the Necessary and Proper Clause*, 39 Ohio N.U. L. Rev. 773 (2013).

15. Randy Barnett, *Can Lawyers Ascertain the Original Meaning of the Constitution?*, The Volokh Conspiracy (Aug. 19, 2013, 4:22 PM), http://volokh.com/2013/08/19/can-lawyers-ascertain-the-original-meaning-of-the-constitution/ [https://perma.cc/RN6F-PQTE].

16. *Id.*

17. *Id.*

18. *See also* Lawrence B. Solum, *Originalist Methodology*, 84 U. Chi. L. Rev. 269, 292–93 (2017) (noting that historians are interested in questions of motive, purpose, and causation, the development of ideas over time, and the discovery of archival material, which may not be relevant to the discovery of original public meaning).

19. *E.g.*, Saul Cornell, *Originalism as Thin Description: An Interdisciplinary Critique*, 84 Fordham L. Rev. Res Gestae 1 (2015); Cornell, *Reading the*

Constitution, 1787–91, supra note 11; Jonathan Gienapp, *Historicism and Holism: Failures of Originalist Translation*, 84 Fordham L. Rev. 935 (2015); Jack Rakove, *Tone Deaf to the Past: More Qualms about Public Meaning Originalism*, 84 Fordham L. Rev. 969 (2015); Rakove, *Joe the Ploughman Reads the Constitution, supra* note 12.

20. *See* Lawrence B. Solum, *Intellectual History as Constitutional Theory*, 101 Va. L. Rev. 1111, 1162 (2015).

21. William Baude & Stephen E. Sachs, *Originalism and the Law of the Past*, 37 Law & Hist. Rev. 809, 812 (2019).

22. *Id.* at 810.

23. *Id.*

24. *Id.* at 810–11.

25. *Id.* at 811.

26. *Id.*

27. *Id.*

28. *Id.* at 818.

29. *Id.*

30. *Id.* at 818–19.

31. *Id.* at 819 (emphasis in original).

32. *See, e.g.,* Josh Blackman & James C. Phillips, *Corpus Linguistics and the Second Amendment*, Harv. L. Rev. Blog (Aug. 7, 2018), https://blog.harvard lawreview.org/corpus-linguistics-and-the-second-amendment/ [https://perma.cc/VL8J-DTAJ] ("Applying corpus linguistics to the Second Amendment leads to potentially uncomfortable criticisms for both the majority and dissenting opinions in *Heller*.").

33. William Baude & Stephen E. Sachs, *Grounding Originalism*, 113 Nw. L. Rev. 1455, 1457 (2019) ("[W]hatever law [enacting the Constitution] made back then remains the law, subject to de jure alterations or amendments made since.").

34. Baude & Sachs, *Originalism and the Law of the Past, supra* note 21, at 810.

35. Bowen v. Gilliard, 483 U.S. 587, 602 (1987); Washington v. Glucksberg, 521 U.S. 702, 719 (1997); Lynch v. Donnelly, 465 U.S. 668, 688 (1984) (O'Connor, J., concurring).

36. Baude & Sachs, *Originalism and the Law of the Past, supra* note 21, at 811.

37. *Id.*

38. Lawrence Lessig, Fidelity & Constraint: How the Supreme Court Has Read the American Constitution (2019).

39. Ollman v. Evans, 750 F.2d 970, 995 (D.C. Cir. 1984) (*en banc*) (Bork, J., concurring), *cert. denied*, 471 U.S. 1127 (1984).

40. Parents Involved in Cmty. Schs. v. Seattle Sch. Dist. No. 1, 551 U.S. 701, 705 (2007) (plurality opinion) (arguing that it was important to remember that the point of Brown v. Bd. of Educ., 347 U.S. 483 (1954), was to outlaw "using race to assign children to schools").

41. Baude & Sachs, *Originalism and the Law of the Past, supra* note 21, at 818.

Chapter Sixteen. Lawyers' Need for a Usable Past

1. Van Wyck Brooks, *On Creating a Usable Past*, 64 Dial 337 (1918), http://www.archive.org/stream/dialjournallitcrit64chicrich#page/337/mode/1up [https://perma.cc/D9ZB-5P8J]. Many people now associate the phrase with the work of Henry Steele Commager and Herbert Muller. *See* Henry Steele Commager, The Search for a Usable Past and Other Essays in Historiography 3–27 (1967); Herbert J. Muller, The Uses of the Past: Profiles of Former Societies (1967).

2. On the Young Americans, *see* Casey Nelson Blake, Beloved Community: The Cultural Criticism of Randolph Bourne, Van Wyck Brooks, Waldo Frank, and Lewis Mumford (1990).

3. Friedrich Nietzsche, *On the Use and Abuse of History for the Present, in* Untimely Meditations (Daniel Breazeale ed., R. J. Hollingdale trans., 1997).

4. Brooks, *On Creating a Usable Past, supra* note 1, at 339.

5. *Id.* at 337–38.

6. *Id.* at 339 ("[T]he American writer floats in [a] void because the past that survives in the common mind of the present is a past without living value. But is this the only possible past? If we need another past so badly, is it inconceivable that we might discover one, that we might even invent one? Discover, invent a usable past we certainly can, and that is what a vital criticism always does.").

7. *Id.*; *see also id.* at 340 ("*What is important for us?* What, out of all the multifarious achievements and impulses and desires of the American literary mind, ought we elect to remember?").

8. Blake, Beloved Community, *supra* note 2, at 296–97 (quoting Lewis Mumford, *The Emergence of a Past*, 45 New Republic 19 (1925)).

9. Brooks, *On Creating a Usable Past, supra* note 1, at 339–40.

10. *Id.* at 341.

11. *Id.* at 340.

12. Cass R. Sunstein, *The Idea of a Useable Past*, 95 Colum. L. Rev. 601 (1995).

13. Cass R. Sunstein, *Beyond the Republican Revival*, 97 Yale L.J. 1539 (1988); Frank I. Michelman, *Law's Republic*, 97 Yale L.J. 1493 (1988); Frank I. Michelman, *The Supreme Court, 1985 Term—Foreword: Traces of Self-Government*, 100 Harv. L. Rev. 4 (1986); Cass R. Sunstein, *Interest Groups in American Public Law*, 38 Stan. L. Rev. 29 (1985). Civic republican themes were also combined with feminism and critical legal studies. *See, e.g.*, Mark Tushnet, Red, White, and Blue: A Critical Analysis of Constitutional Law (1988); Suzanna Sherry, *Civic Virtue and the Feminine Voice in Constitutional Adjudication*, 72 Va. L. Rev. 543 (1986).

14. *See* Joyce Appleby, Capitalism and a New Social Order: The Republican Vision of the 1790s (1984); J. G. A. Pocock, The Machiavellian Moment: Florentine Political Thought and the Atlantic Republican Tra-

dition (1975); Gordon S. Wood, The Creation of the American Republic 1776–87 (1969); Bernard Bailyn, The Ideological Origins of the American Revolution (1967).

15. Laura Kalman, The Strange Career of Legal Liberalism 175 (1996).

16. Matthew J. Festa, *Applying a Usable Past: The Use of History in Law*, 38 Seton Hall L. Rev. 479, 495–96 (2008).

17. *Id.*

18. Kalman, The Strange Career of Legal Liberalism, *supra* note 15, at 175–76 (quoting Wood, The Creation of the American Republic, *supra* note 14, at viii).

19. Linda K. Kerber, *Making Republicanism Useful*, 97 Yale L.J. 1663, 1667–69 (1988).

20. Mark Tushnet, *The Concept of Tradition in Constitutional Historiography*, 29 Wm. & Mary L. Rev. 93, 96 (1987); *see also* Hendrik Hartog, *Imposing Constitutional Traditions*, 29 Wm. & Mary L. Rev. 81–82 (1987).

21. H. Jefferson Powell, *Reviving Republicanism*, 97 Yale L.J. 1703, 1706, 1711 (1988).

22. Barry Friedman, *The Turn to History*, 72 NYU L. Rev. 928, 945 (1997) (reviewing Kalman, The Strange Career of Legal Liberalism, *supra* note 15).

23. Martin S. Flaherty, *History "Lite" in Modern American Constitutionalism*, 95 Colum. L. Rev. 523 (1995).

24. Sunstein, *The Idea of a Useable Past*, *supra* note 12, at 603; *cf.* Brooks, *On Creating a Usable Past*, *supra* note 1, at 340 ("Only by the exercise of a little pragmatism . . . can the past experience of our people be placed at the service of the future.").

25. Sunstein, *The Idea of a Useable Past*, *supra* note 12, at 603.

26. Ronald Dworkin, Law's Empire vii, 52–55, 62, 77, 229 (1986); Sunstein, *The Idea of a Useable Past*, *supra* note 12, at 602 (emphasis in original).

27. Sunstein, *The Idea of a Useable Past*, *supra* note 12, at 602.

28. *Id.* at 603.

29. *Id.* at 604.

30. *Id.*

31. *Id.*

32. *Id.*

33. *Id.* at 605.

34. *Id.* at 604–05.

35. *Id.* at 605.

36. *Id.*

37. *Id.*

38. *Id.* at 604.

39. *Id.*

40. *Id.* at 603.

41. *Id.* at 606.

42. *Id.*
43. *Id.*
44. Blake, Beloved Community, *supra* note 2, at 297 (quoting Lewis Mumford, *The Emergence of a Past*, 45 New Republic 19 (1925)).
45. Sunstein, *The Idea of a Useable Past, supra* note 12, at 603.
46. *Id.* at. 605.
47. *See* Cass R. Sunstein, Democracy and the Problem of Free Speech xvi–xviii, 132–33, 241–44 (1993).
48. J. M. Balkin, *Populism and Progressivism as Constitutional Categories*, 104 Yale L.J. 1935, 1955 (1995) (reviewing Sunstein, Democracy and the Problem of Free Speech, *supra* note 47).
49. See the discussion in chapter 11, *supra.*
50. Sunstein, Democracy and the Problem of Free Speech, *supra* note 47, at 132.
51. Whitney v. California, 274 U.S. 357, 373–74 (Brandeis, J., concurring) (1927) ("Those who won our independence believed that the final end of the State was to make men free to develop their faculties, and that in its government the deliberative forces should prevail over the arbitrary.") See the discussion in chapter 4, *supra.*
52. Sunstein, *The Idea of a Useable Past, supra* note 12, at 605.
53. For example, Alexander Bickel anticipates many of Sunstein's arguments. *See, e.g.,* Alexander M. Bickel, The Least Dangerous Branch: The Supreme Court at the Bar of Politics 109 (2d ed. 1986) (quoting Herbert Muller for the view that "[o]ur task is to create a 'usable past,' for our own living purposes"); *id.* (quoting Jacob Burckhardt for the view that history "is on every occasion the record of what one age finds worthy of note in another"); *id.* ("We are guided in our search of the past by our own aspirations and evolving principles, which were in part formed by that very past."); *id.* at 109–10 (arguing that "[w]hen we find in history, . . . principles that we can adopt or adapt, or ideals and aspirations that speak with contemporary relevance," we should focus on "the rhetorical tradition and its implications, not the inconsistent commitment"). Like me, Howard Vogel connects the idea of a usable past in constitutional law to the forms of argument. *See* Howard J. Vogel, The "Ordered Liberty" of Substantive Due Process and the Future of Constitutional Law as a Rhetorical Art: Variations on a Theme from Justice Cardozo in the United States Supreme Court, 70 Alb. L. Rev. 1473, 1545–52 (2007) ("[L]egal argument is always, in various ways, a search for a 'usable past' in light of the need to resolve disputes in the present.").
54. Reva B. Siegel, *The Politics of Constitutional Memory*, 20 Geo. J.L. & Pub. Pol'y 19, 19 (2022).
55. *See* Stephen M. Griffin, *Constitutional Theory Transformed*, 108 Yale L.J. 2115, 2153 (1999) ("Sunstein does not come to grips with the reality that *all* of American history is potentially relevant to his project.").

56. Sunstein, *The Idea of a Useable Past, supra* note 12, at 606.
57. *See, e.g.,* Nomi Maya Stolzenberg, *A Book of Laughter and Forgetting: Kalman's "Strange Career" and the Marketing of Civic Republicanism,* 111 Harv. L. Rev. 1025, 1084 (1998) (reviewing Kalman, The Strange Career of Legal Liberalism, *supra* note 15) (arguing for employing the civic republican tradition in all its interpretive complexity and normative ambiguity).

Index

abolitionism, 41, 47, 197, 220, 264
abortion, 38, 42–43, 62, 91, 167, 202–6
Ackerman, Bruce, 273n2, 292n5
actual malice, 52
Adams, John, 79, 83, 155
administrative state, 112, 131
admirable ancestors, model of, 263–64, 267
adoption history, 15–17, 34, 35, 48–49, 65, 118, 163, 214, 263; in constitutional construction, 11–12, 117; in counterarguments, 154; forms of argument and, 149–54; liberals' and nonoriginalists' use of, 90, 119, 152, 160, 172–73; and original expected applications, 107; selective use of, 113, 116–17, 127; sources of, 164, 166; Thomas's focus on, 31, 33; usable past and, 259
adversarial systems, 24
advertising, 109–10
Aeneas, 83
affirmative action, 91, 114, 215
Affordable Care Act (2010), 310n57
Alexander the Great, 83
Alien and Sedition Acts (1798), 40, 125, 142
Alito, Samuel, 57, 58; and abortion rights, 38, 42–44, 52, 202–3; on

Second Amendment incorporation, 31–33; selective uses of history, 204–5
Amar, Akhil, 46, 217, 281n22, 315n7, 317–18n16
ambiguity, 101–2, 123, 125
amendments to Constitution, 16, 104, 119
American Revolution, 39–40, 78–85, 93, 188–89
Americans with Disabilities Act (1990), 161
amicus briefs, 208–9, 234, 237
anachronism, 5, 9, 24, 26, 110–11, 135–40
Anthony, Susan B., 20, 84, 211
anticanonical cases, 48, 160, 194
Anti-Federalists, 47, 264
Antioriginalist argument, 65
Appleby, Joyce, 258
Aquinas, Thomas, Saint, 159
Aristotle, 159, 276n14
Arming America (Bellisles), 352n34
Arthur, King, 83
Articles of Confederation, 79–80, 81, 82
Assmann, Jan, 272n8, 325n9–11, 19, 327n46
Australia, 75
Avins, Alfred, 147